ISSUES IN INTERNATIONAL COMMERCIAL LAW

Issues in International Commercial Law

Edited by
IWAN DAVIES
University of Wales Swansea

Routledge
Taylor & Francis Group
LONDON AND NEW YORK

First published 2005 by Ashgate Publishing

Reissued 2019 by Routledge
2 Park Square, Milton Park, Abingdon, Oxon, OX14 4RN
52 Vanderbilt Avenue, New York, NY 10017

Routledge is an imprint of the Taylor & Francis Group, an informa business

A Library of Congress record exists under LC control number:

ISBN 13: 978-0-8153-8988-0 (hbk)
ISBN 13: 978-1-351-15524-3 (ebk)

Contents

PART III: INTERNATIONAL REGULATION

List of Contributors

Professor Anu Arora is Dean of Law at the University of Liverpool

Dr Indira Carr is a Reader in Commercial Law at the Kent Law School, University of Canterbury

Professor Aldo Chircop is Professor of Marine Environment Protection at the World Maritime University, Sweden

Dr Tony Ciro and **Dr Vivien Goldwasser** are Lecturers in Law at La Trobe University, Australia

Professor Iwan Davies is the Hodge Chair in Law and Head of the Swansea University Law School

Dr Louise Gullifer is a Fellow in Law at Harris Manchester College of the University of Oxford

Professor Elizabeth Macdonald is a Professor of Law at Swansea University Law School

Dr Héctor José Miguens is a Professor of Law at Austral University, Buenos Aires, Argentina

Mr David Poyton is a Lecturer in Law at the University of Wales, Aberystwyth

Dr Nicholas Ryder is a Lecturer in Law at the University of the West of England

Dr Andrius Smaliukas is a Lecturer in Law at Vilniaus University, Lithuania

Introduction

The twentieth century has witnessed the growth of international commercial law. Indeed, it is now possible to identify a distinct corpus of transnational commercial law which has emerged from the increasing regulation of international commercial transactions. At the same time, the influence of the codification movement seen in national commercial law, as well as established trade usages cannot be underestimated as providing a rich source in the interchange between domestic and international commercial law.

The merits or otherwise of harmonization of law are still subject to considerable debate. As such, the various types of harmonization fall into four broad categories, namely, legislation, judicial parallelism and judicial corporation, business practice codes and model forms and, lastly, international restatements. The trend towards the harmonization of commercial laws has been concerned either with the creation of a regime dealing with international transactions while preserving the identity of national laws or, alternatively, the emergence of supranational entities where the focus has been upon progressing a common market or political or economic grouping. The legal instruments that have promoted harmonization have mainly revolved around a model law, such as the UNCITRAL Model Law on International Commercial Arbitration (1985) or those instruments that deal with international commercial contracts and depend for their application on incorporation into contracts. Clearly, there are limits on the effectiveness of international proposals for contractual incorporation. By definition, they are not mandatory and for them to have any realistic effect there must exist a considerable degree of homogeneity in commercial practice, as seen, for example, with documentary letters of credit. In addition, contractual mechanisms have mainly an *inter-partes* dimension and are not therefore apt to deal with third party rights.

This volume includes some papers submitted to the *Journal of International Commercial Law* and as such, is simply a selection of essays. A wide range of specialist contributors can be seen. This demonstrates the breadth and scope of the subject matter, which is international commercial law, and many of the themes are cross-cutting between national and international commercial law. There are three parts to this volume: Credit and Security; Contractual Issues; International Commercial Regulation. It can be seen that international commercial law is concerned with public and private law within which there are particular disciplines ranging from banking law, e-commerce, intellectual property, insolvency and increasingly international regulation through criminal law extending beyond frontiers.

In the first part of the volume, the focus is upon credit and security. During the course of the twentieth century, several attempts were made to achieve some degree of uniformity within the international community with respect to security interests. These initiatives failed, mainly because of the difficulty and complexity of the law and the refusal of receiving states to recognize security interests attached to mobile property before it entered the receiving state. At the close of the twentieth century, a significant shift can be seen in the attitude of legal policy makers to the challenge posed of recognizing international security interests, largely due to the following factors: first, increasing globalization of the world economy and the privatization of state monopolies with the consequent conversion of sovereign risk to enterprise risk has brought into focus the need for an international framework of security interests; secondly, there has been a growing international recognition of the standing of Article 9 of the American Uniform Commercial Code (UCC) as an appropriate model for reform; thirdly, the collapse of the Soviet Bloc has resulted in the re-writing of the commercial law of these emerging states so as to facilitate the growth of a market economy; fourthly, the European Bank for Reconstruction and Development Model Law on Security Transactions (1994) clearly draws its inspiration from Article 9 and this has been evident in various world bank initiatives; lastly, the work of UNCITRAL in respect of the convention on assignments of accounts receivable and also that of UNIDROIT in respect of security interests in mobile equipment, are highly significant. Both of these initiatives deal with a specific type of secured transaction rather than secured transactions generally and also ensure that adoption of these rules does not at least, prima facie, require domestic law changes to secured credit.

Article 9 of the UCC is often portrayed as the most modernized, rational and comprehensive system of security interests in the developed world. Article 9 has now been revised and thereby represents an expanded restatement of the law of personal property security. Historically, Article 9 has influenced the debate over the reform of personal property security interests and there has been a renewed impetus provided by the revised Article 9 as a model for reform. This has had implications in discussions over the reform of English personal property security law and the development of bright line priority rules associated with Article 9 are at the heart of the recommendations made in the Law Commission Consultation Paper No 164, *Registration of Security Interests: Company Charges and Property other than Land* (2002) and the more recent Consultation Paper No 176, *Company Security Interests* (2004).

A central feature in Article 9 which has been adopted in the reform proposals for English law is the development of a generic unitary concept of the security interest and the specific rejection of formalism in security transactions. In effect, the list of financing arrangements to which the notice filing of Article 9 applies extends to all functionally equivalent security devices which are referred to as "quasi-security interests". This is the theme pursued in Louise Gullifer's chapter. The dilemma for the English Law Commission is whether all transactions within the reformed scheme should be re-classified as security interests and should the legislation provide for the incidence of security. These two questions are inter-related and depend largely on how functionalism is embraced which could cut across the parties' allocation of risks and rewards. Ultimately, this involves a question of policy, namely, that of balancing notice functional filing against freedom of contract.

In his chapter, Andrius Smaliukas describes the transformation of Lithuanian credit and security laws away from the Soviet model to one informed by the EBRD's Model Law on Secured Transactions. The European Bank for Reconstruction Model Law on Secured Transactions (1994) identifies the core principles of a model secured transaction regime as being: first, reducing the risk for creditors on default; second, simplicity in the creation of security interests; third, expeditious satisfaction on default; fourth, prompt enforcement to the market value of the charged assets; fifth, priority on insolvency; sixth, creation and maintenance of security should be at a low cost; seventh, security should be available over all types of assets to secure all types of debts and between all types of person and organizations; eighth, there should be an effective means of publicizing the existence of security rights; ninth, clear rules governing priority; and tenth, the parties should be able to adapt security to the needs of a particular transaction. As such, the approach of the EBRD is to present the Model Law as an illustration of the principal rules for secured transaction. It is deliberately "non-national" in terms of its approach, the emphasis being inspiration for reform rather than imposition. The issue of the treatment of formalism in Lithuanian credit and security law is discussed in this chapter.

The North American experience in respect of the reform of personal property security law reflects its antecedents in the mid-twentieth century and arguably addresses the needs of an historical economy, that is, one where the emphasis is upon manufacturing. Over the last thirty years, the value of intangible assets relative to the value of physical and financial assets has increased considerably. It is curious therefore that the North American approach to the treatment of intellectual property rights is only partly dealt with in this legislation, although a probable explanation for this is the overlap between state and federal laws. In Chapter 3, Iwan Davies considers the extent to which, especially technology-driven, small and medium sized enterprises can use patents as collateral. This has implications for the reform of English personal property security law and the development of priority rules associated with Article 9 of the UCC. In addition, this chapter considers the function and effect of patents and, in particular, whether the legal process associated with the grant of patents promotes economic activity. This is significant because patenting is an output of a creative process and the intensity of patenting activity is often used as a proxy for technological dynamism in a firm, industry or economy.

An effective security interest regime is often linked to the development of a market economy. The more advanced the economy becomes, the greater the demand for credit. Nic Ryder, in his Chapter, examines the influence of a flexible legal framework upon the development of credit unions in Great Britain and this is important as it goes to the access of credit for disadvantaged sections of society. The focus of this chapter is upon the more flexible approach to the development of credit unions seen in the US and Ireland. The legislature in the US has been concerned to promote the credit union movement and reverse adverse judicial decisions from the Supreme Court which would have seen credit unions fragmenting into smaller institutions. In particular, the Credit Union Membership Access Act 1998 has enabled the credit union membership base to expand by expressly allowing for multiple common-bond credit unions. In Ireland, the credit union movement has enjoyed great success. The modernization of credit union law was brought into effect by the Credit Union Act 1997 which provided an up-dated framework for the development and supervision of a credit union movement. This can be illustrated by the range of additional services that credit unions are permitted to offer their members in Ireland. Such an approach is in stark contrast to the position seen in Great Britain, which it is argued lacks an adequate legislative framework to develop credit unions and thereby restricts their ability to meet their members' financial needs.

In the revision process of Article 9, the question of whether secured credit is, in effect, efficient had little impact on the debate for reform. In large measure, this was because the whole efficiency debate is presented as a puzzle, as distinct from a demonstration of inefficiency. In any event, there are limitations in the efficiency debate, not least because it fails to address considerations of fairness and distribution on insolvency. Whilst at first sight the recognition of security interests appears to be inconsistent with the *pari passu* principle of distribution, in practice, all it means is that creditors within a particular class must be treated equally within the particular distribution regime. Distributional consequences of a secured credit regime are the major determinant in the setting of sound insolvency policy.

An issue that has troubled banking lawyers is the liability of parent companies in respect of insolvent subsidiaries. In some cases, the subsidiaries are part of a corporate grouping. Indeed, in recent years, there has been a change in the structure and conduct of large business corporations which brings into question the validity of those legal concepts derived from a world of much smaller and more simply organized corporate structures. In his Chapter, Héctor Miguens considers the American and Argentine law in respect of the liability of the parent company on the insolvency of its subsidiary. There is a clash in legal doctrine between "Entity Law", which for almost all purposes treats each corporation as a separate legal entity with its own legal responsibilities, and "Enterprise Law", which recognizes that companies in a modern commercial environment are a constituent part of a corporate group conducting an integrated enterprise. The approach of the American courts is to act as courts of equity in bankruptcy with the overriding objective of achieving equality of distribution and fairness for creditors. US case law is examined where it is seen that, increasingly, "Enterprise Law" has been applied to transactions involving "insiders" and "Entity Law" has been abandoned in order to achieve the goals of equality of distribution and fairness to creditors. Liability of a parent for obligations of an insolvent subsidiary strikes directly at limited liability. It is argued, on the basis of an examination of US and Argentine case law and statutes, that equitable subordination provides an appropriate legal response for the application of "Enterprise Law", as distinct from the direct imposition of liability, since the latter approach would entail an attack on the principle of limited liability which would involve piercing the corporate veil.

In Part 2 of this volume, contractual issues are highlighted. In their Chapter, Tony Ciro and Vivien Goldwasser argue that commercial expectations are playing an increasingly prominent role in the development of law within Australia and the United Kingdom. The law of privity and compound interest, although unrelated, are selected for examination because they are both controversial and problematic: the established legal principles are shown to be out of synchronization with commercial reality. The increasing willingness of the courts in Australia and the United Kingdom, as well as the legislatures and reform bodies to overcome the gap created between commercial expectations and commercial reality on the one hand and the application of strict doctrine on the other, is discussed.

In Chapter 7, Elizabeth Macdonald and David Poyton consider the applicability of traditional English contract rules to e-commerce in the international regulatory context, notably the jurisdiction and recognition and enforcement of judgments in civil and commercial matters. A broad range of legal challenges and opportunities are identified in terms of the development of new concepts suitable to the distinctive electronic environment.

Part 3 of this volume deals with the increasing global regulation in commercial law. Anu Arora evaluates the global legislative and regulatory framework in respect of money laundering. The impact of money laundering upon national economies is discussed. The inflow of large amounts of funds from laundering can create artificial demand in certain sectors of economies and in some cases can undermine the stability of an economy. The significance of the Vienna Convention (1988) in this regard is considered because this has informed the approach adopted in the 1991 European Directive on Money Laundering. More recently, the Second Money Laundering Directive 2001 requires member states to criminalize money laundering, whilst the draft Third Money Laundering Directive is intended to repeal the 1991 Directive and give effect to the recommendations of the Financial Action Task Force established by the Group of Seven Nations in 1989. The impact of these initiatives on the development of English Law is also considered in this chapter.

In Chapter 9, Indira Carr examines the development of international instruments seeking to regulate corrupt practices in international trade, as well as the various schemes adopted in combating corruption in the international business environment. The chapter identifies other anti-corruption mechanisms besides regulation, with a view to assessing their usefulness in dealing with corruption. In many respects, corruption is a multi-faceted phenomenon and in this regard Indira Carr argues that a variety, and perhaps a combination, of means is necessary for combating it, ranging from the legal, cultural, political and the administrative to the economic.

In Chapter 10, Aldo Chircop considers international regulation in the context of the protection of the marine environment from vessel-source pollution. The emphasis of this chapter is upon particularly sensitive sea areas and analyses trends, controversies and issues in the protection of the marine environment from the risk of vessel-source pollution.

I am grateful to those who have helped in producing this volume. In particular, I wish to thank the publishers for their efficient editorial work and their efforts to produce this book promptly.

Iwan Davies

PART I
CREDIT AND SECURITY ISSUES

Chapter 1

Quasi-security Interests: Functionalism and the Incidents of Security

Louise Gullifer

Introduction

In 2002 the Law Commission of England and Wales published a Consultation Paper which considered the reform of the law of the registration of personal property security interests.[1] Recently, it published a further Consultative Report[2] including Draft Regulations, which clarifies and expands many of the provisional recommendations in the Consultation Paper. This is not the first time such reform has been considered in this country,[3] and the Consultation Paper and Consultative Report builds on the earlier work. There is, however, one important impetus to the current work which has never been realistic before: the system now under consideration would be completely online. Not only does this mean that there will be considerable savings in cost and improvements in efficiency were such a system to be adopted, but also that there is a considerable imperative towards at least some reform of the English system: it is surely totally unsatisfactory for a developed economy such as the UK not to have an online registration system. Given, therefore, that some reform is inevitable, the Law Commission have the task of determining the best possible system for England and Wales.

There is no shortage of comparisons. The law of personal property security has been comprehensively reformed in a large number of countries and states over the past 70 years, ranging from the introduction of Article 9 of the Uniform Commercial Code in the United States of America in 1952 to the reform of the law of security in the Slovak Republic which became effective on 1 January 2003.[4] It

---

1 *Registration of Security Interests: Company Charges and Property other than Land* (2002) Law Commission Consultation Paper No 164 hereafter "LCCP". The references to the Law Commission's views are to this Consultation Paper: it should be noted, however, that this does not necessarily represent the Law Commission's current thinking on all issues.

2 "Company security Interests: A Consultative Report" (Consultation Paper No 176, 2004) hereafter "LCCR" including draft regulations hereafter "DR".

3 *Report of the Committee on Consumer Credit* (1971) Cmnd 4596 (the Crowther report), *Report by the Working Party on Security over Moveable Property* (1986) (the Halliday report), Diamond, *A Review of Security Interests in Property* (1989) (the Diamond report).

4 Acts No 526/2002 and 527/2002.

is tempting to consider copying wholesale a system from a country similar in legal tradition to our own, such as the recently introduced and fully online personal property security regime in New Zealand.[5] However, while the Law Commission are very sensibly considering adopting wholesale the computer system that seems to be working very well in New Zealand, they are consulting widely and with an open mind on the legal details of the system for England and Wales.[6]

In this chapter I wish to consider the most controversial part of the proposed reforms: the inclusion of quasi-security interests in the scheme, focussing particularly on whether they should be treated for all purposes as security interests. The options, I will argue, are reasonably open in relation to this area, and it is important to consider the whole spectrum of possibilities that are to be found exemplified in other legal systems. The policy considerations in the UK are not necessarily the same as those found in other common law countries, and it is important to consider the ramifications of adopting a particular system both in the light of our domestic concerns, and in the light of the UK's position in the international trading community.

The Scheme in General

It is necessary to refer very briefly to the various components of the Law Commission's scheme. First, it is proposed that there should be a registration system based on notice filing, so that only brief details of a security transaction need be filed: this can be done before the interest is created, so that notice of intention to create can be filed, and one filing will suffice for a series of transactions between the same parties. Secondly, priorities will be determined largely on the basis that the first to file wins, with some exceptions (notably a super-priority for purchase money security interests). Thirdly, the scheme may extend to quasi-security interests. Fourthly, there will be a restatement of the law relating to security interests: the incidents of security such as the mode of enforcement. Fifthly, the scheme is initially proposed to cover interests created by companies, but can be extended to cover interests created by non-corporate debtors. In this chapter, I will refer solely to interests created by companies, although much of the argument can also apply to non-corporate debtors.

---

5 New Zealand Personal Property Securities Act 1999. See also the regimes in Canada, typified by the Saskatchewan Personal Property Security Act 1993 (which is very similar to the Model Personal Property Security Act adopted by the Canadian Conference on Personal Property Security Law) and the Ontario Personal Property Security Act 1990, which has some significant differences to the Model PPSA.

6 See a similar view taken by the Australian Law Reform Commission, Goldring, *A Commentary on Chapters by Professor Ralph Simmonds and Tony Duggan*, in *Securities over Personalty* (1994) Gillooly (Ed) at pp 298-9.

Quasi-security Interests: The Problem

The orthodox definition of a security interest[7] under English law has been that it is a grant of an interest less than absolute ownership by a person who already has or will obtain an interest[8] in property. A security interest cannot be created by reservation.[9] Thus transactions where a party giving credit (the 'creditor') seeks to protect itself by reservation of title are not classified as security and are not registrable under the current system.[10] Further, even where an interest is granted by the debtor, this can either be a security interest or an absolute interest by way of sale.[11] The difference between these two has been the subject of a considerable body of case law and refinement,[12] with the English courts taking an approach that attempts to find the "substance of the transaction", while allowing the parties to define that substance by reference to the form of the obligations between them, rather than the purpose of the transaction. Thus the indicia of a security interest are said[13] to be the following:

- The ability of the debtor to redeem its interest in the property by repaying the debt;
- The obligation of the creditor to account to the debtor for any surplus value in the property over and above the outstanding amount of the debt;
- The survival of the obligation of the debtor to pay any outstanding amount over and above the value of the property, once the creditor had appropriated the property to the satisfaction of the debt.

---

7 Security interests which fulfil this definition will be referred to as security interests in the strict sense.

8 Usually proprietary but sometimes possessory, for example, grant of a sub-pledge.

9 Goode, *Commercial Law*, 2nd ed (1995) 642, *Clough Mill Ltd v Martin* [1985] 1 WLR 111 at 123, *Armour v Thyssen Edelstahlwerke AG* [1991] 2 AC 339 at 353. This view has not been uncontroversial, see for example, Oditah, *Legal Aspects of Receivables Financing* (1991) at p 92.

10 Only some, not all charges and mortgages (included in the definition of charges in the Act) are registrable under s 385 Companies Act 1985.

11 The situation is further complicated by the fact that a non-possessory security interest can either be granted by way of mortgage, where absolute title is transferred but with an obligation to reconvey on fulfilment of the secured obligation, or by charge, which is an encumbrance and does not transfer title. The distinction between the two is often blurred, particularly in cases considering receivables financing.

12 *Lloyds & Scottish Finance Ltd v Cyril Lord Carpets Sales Ltd* (1979) [1992] BCLC 609, *Re Curtain Dream plc* [1990] BCLC 925, *Welsh Development Agency v Export Finance Co Ltd* [1992] BCLC 148, *Orion Finance Ltd v Crown Financial Management Ltd* [1996] 2 BCLC 78. See also Berg, "Recharacterization after Enron" [2003] *JBL* 205.

13 *In re George Inglefield Ltd.* [1933] Ch 1 at 23, *per* Romer LJ. However, Millett LJ's view in *Orion Finance Ltd v Crown Financial Management Ltd* [1996] 2 BCLC 78 at 84 was that the presence or absence of any one of these requirements was not conclusive.

Parties frequently enter into transactions involving reservation of title, or granting of an absolute interest, or a combination of both, in order to fulfil similar purposes to transactions involving the creation of security interests as defined above,[14] that is, from the debtor's point of view, the obtaining of credit or the raising of finance, and from the creditor's point of view, protection against default and insolvency of the debtor. This similarity in function has led many to argue that all transactions with the purpose of security to be treated equally under a personal property security regime, and has led to the functionalist approach of UCC Article 9 and the Personal Property Security Act regimes in Canada and New Zealand ("PPSA regimes").

Functionalism has had its critics[15] and I will explore some of its drawbacks shortly. First, it is important to examine some of the arguments in favour of similar treatment of security interests and quasi-security interests. In doing so, it is necessary to touch on a related argument, which has inspired much of the Article 9 type thinking. This is that unreformed systems suffer from legal complexity even with regard to security interests in the strict sense, in that different rules apply to different types of interests in relation to perfection, priorities and the incidents of security. Thus a reformed scheme which only has one kind of security interest, with one set of applicable rules is very attractive.[16] It is possible to react to this argument merely by unifying the rules applicable to security interests in the strict sense. In England this would have the effect of abolishing the distinction between a mortgage and a charge, so that the same registration and priority rules would apply to both, and that the method of enforcement would be the same.[17] The registration requirements for possessory interests (pledge and lien) would be likely to be different, but they would also fall within the priority and enforcement rules. However, it would also be possible merely to specify the rules relating to perfection and priority, and leave the question of enforcement up to the specific provisions of the security agreement.

What arguments are made in favour of treating quasi-security interests in the same way as security interests?

---

14 The interests created by such transactions are often referred to collectively as "quasi-security" interests.

15 Bridge, Macdonald, Simmons, Walsh, "Formalism, Functionalism and Understanding the Law of Secured Transactions" (1999) 44 *McGill LJ* 567 ("Bridge *et al*"), Boodman & Macdonald, "How far is Article 9 of the Uniform Commercial Code Exportable? A Return to Sources" (1996) 27 *Can Bus Law Journal* 249.

16 See Ziegel, "Canadian Perspectives on 'How Far is Article 9 Exportable?'" (1996) 27 *Can Bus Law Journal* 226 at 232 (Canadian reforms); Allen, "Personal Property Security – Rip Van Winkle awakes in the Antipodes" [1998] *JIBL* 1 at 2 (commenting on Article 9 and possible reform in Australia).

17 As regards priorities, this would have the effect of removing the distinction between legal and equitable mortgages, and would to some extent alter the distinction between fixed and floating charges. See Gullifer, "Will the Law Commission sink the floating charge?" [2003] *LMCLQ* 125. As regards enforcement, both mortgages and charges usually give the creditor powers of sale and the appointment of a receiver, but only a mortgagee can foreclose or take possession.

1. *The transactions have the same function and so should be treated alike.*[18] This is partly at least an extension of the simplification argument referred to earlier; rather than have a number of different rules applying to similar agreements and interests, there should be one set of universal rules. However, this begs the question of what interests and agreements are similar. It is no more logically necessary to draw the line at the difference between quasi-security interests and absolute transfers, than it is to draw it between security interests in the strict sense and quasi-security interests. The choice is a policy one, and as such needs to be justified on coherent policy grounds. Points 2 to 5 below examine arguments based on perceived similarities in various areas of personal property security law.

2. *The transactions all share a common need for publicity.* If is accepted that a public registration system is necessary,[19] then arguably all non-possessory interests should be registered, since all carry the same danger of giving the impression of "false wealth". This argument based on ostensible ownership, while popular among the supporters of Article 9 style regimes,[20] is not necessarily enough by itself to justify registration requirements.[21] It has been criticised on the grounds that non-possessory security and title retention devices (including leases) are so common that possession is no longer indicative of ownership, nor is there any evidence that potential creditors are misled.[22] Justification of a filing requirement for quasi-security interests needs to be on the basis that the benefits outweigh the costs: it is certainly arguable that this is the case.[23] It should also be pointed out that there are transactions other than quasi-security in

---

[18] See Ziegel, "The New Provincial Chattel Security Law Regimes" (1990) 70 *Can Bar Rev* 681 at 685-6, and the critical analysis in Bridge *et al.*

[19] Although this is a given for nearly all personal property security regimes, it is instructive to see that under the 1992 Dutch Civil Code there is no public register for security interests at all, and in relation to non-possessory or undisclosed rights of pledge, the pledgor is obliged to make third parties aware of the secured creditor's rights in the charged assets. See Kellermann & Versteeg, "Netherlands, International Bar Association Secured Transaction Survey" [2001] *BJIBFL* 186 at 188 (point 7).

[20] Goode, "The Modernisation of Personal Property Security Law" [1984] 100 *MLR* 234, Diamond Report chapter 17; Baird & Jackson, "Possession and Ownership: An Examination of the Scope of Article 9" (1983) 35 *Stanford Law Review* 175.

[21] See, for example, the debate concerning registration of non-security leases, Mooney, "The Mystery and Myth of 'Ostensible Ownership' and Article 9 filing: a critique of the proposals to extend filing requirements to leases" (1988) 39 *Ala L Rev* 683; Ziegel, "Should Canada adopt an Article 2A type law?" (1990) 16 *Can Bus Law Journal* 369; Mooney, "Filing requirements for personal property leases" (1990) 16 *Can Bus Law Journal* 419.

[22] Mooney, "The Mystery and Myth of 'Ostensible Ownership' and Article 9 filing: a critique of the proposals to extend filing requirements to leases" (1988) 39 *Ala L Rev* 683 at 739-40.

[23] Gullifer, *The Law Commission's Proposals: a Critique,* (2004) 15 EBLR 811 at 824-825. LCCR paras 2.123-134.

relation to which public notice is also desirable, for example, operating leases and absolute assignment of receivables.[24]

3. *The form of the transaction should not affect the creditor's priority position vis-à-vis other creditors.* This argument is clearly far too general without qualification. There are certain cases in all regimes which permit security where the form of the transaction affects priority. Secured creditors can improve their position *vis-à-vis* unsecured creditors by making an agreement for security.[25] Further, a seller who sells and delivers goods outright with no reservation of title will usually lose any priority rights over other creditors.[26] Furthermore, it is central to Article 9 style regimes that purchase money security interests have priority over other security interests registered earlier. However, a comprehensive notice-filing does enable there to be a universal default rule of priority (first to file). This has the benefit of simplicity, although it still begs the basic questions of why the transactions should have the same priority rule, and why the creditor should not be allowed to bargain his way into a superior position if he and the debtor agree.[27]

4. *If the basic purpose of the transaction is security the transaction should bear the incidents of security.* This argument is based partly on the simplicity idea: there should only be one enforcement regime, so that all creditors and debtors know where they stand, and straightforward rules can be worked out and administered. It is also partly a matter of

---

[24] Bridge *et al*, *op cit* fn 15 at p 585. Outright sales before delivery could also be added to this list, although the temporary nature of this situation means that registration is not particularly appropriate, cf Baird & Jackson, "Possession and Ownership: An Examination of the Scope of Article 9" (1983) 35 *Stanford Law Review* 175, 189-94.

[25] This particular point is the subject of a protracted debate that will not be addressed here. See, for example, Jackson & Kronman, "Secured Financing and Priorities among Creditors" (1979) 88 *Yale LJ* 1143; A Schwartz, "Security interests and Bankruptcy Priorities: a review of current theories" (1981) 10 *J Legal Stud* 1; LoPucki, "The Unsecured Creditor's Bargain" (1994) 80 *Virginia L Rev* 1887; Harris & Mooney, "A Property-Based Theory of Security Interests" (1994) 80 *Virginia L Rev* 2021; Bebchuck & Fried, "The Uneasy Case for the Priority of Secured Claims in Bankruptcy" (1996) 105 *Yale LJ* 857.

[26] Compare the unpaid seller's resolution remedy under the Civil Code of Quebec, article 1741.

[27] For example, by means of an all monies clause in a reservation of title sale agreement. Under English law at present this gives the seller priority over all other creditors in respect of the goods sold until not only the payment is made for those particular goods, but of all debts outstanding to the creditor from the debtor (*Armour v Thyssen Edelstahlwerke AG* [1991] 2 AC 339). Under some PPSA regimes the creditor's interest would only have purchase money security interest status as regards the purchase price of the collateral in question (s 16 and 73 NZPPSA, Gedye, Cuming, Wood: *Personal Property Securities in New Zealand* (2002) at pp 285-7, s 2(1)(jj) and s 34(10) SPPSA, but cf UCC (revised) 9-103(a)(2) which covers "cross-collateralization") and DR 4(2) which follows the US model (LCCR para 3.220).

protecting other creditors and debtors (particularly non-corporate debtors): they should not be subjected to unregulated enforcement regimes and loss of surplus value when these are not expected or desired results of the transaction. It is this area, and the overlap with freedom of contract, that I will examine in detail below.

5. *The location of title in a transaction with the function of security should be irrelevant.* Article 9 type regimes classify transactions as security regardless of the location of title.[28] This has the effect that the security interest under those regimes is not necessarily the interest created by the agreement itself, but is redefined by the statute. The nature of that interest is not always clear, but it generally agreed to be a security interest similar to an English charge.[29]

The Options[30]

In deciding how to deal with quasi-security interests there are a number of options:

a) *Limit the new regime to security interests in the strict sense.* The regime could just extend to the existing consensual security interests: mortgage, charge, pledge and lien. It would be perfectly possible for a notice filing system to be created in this way: it could be online, cheap and efficient, simplify priorities and could even, if desired, provide for universal rules as to enforcement of the interests included within the regime. The Consultative Report explains that the Draft Regulations have been drawn up on the basis that quasi-securities are included, but the changes which would be needed to the Regulations were quasi-securities to be omitted are set out.[31] Within this option there are two further possibilities:

   (i) Make specific provision for the enforcement of all security interests.

   (ii) Leave questions of enforcement to be dealt with by the contract between the parties. However, there might need in any event to be some default positions specified in the regime for where no agreement is made. These could either flow from the nature of the

---

[28] UCC (revised) 9-202, NZPPSA s 17, SSPPSA, s 3(1).

[29] See Cuming, "The Internationalization of Secured Financing Law" in chapter 22 in *Making Commercial Law: Essays in Honour of Roy Goode* (1997) Cranston (Ed), also Gedye, Cuming, Wood: *Personal Property Securities in New Zealand* (2002) at p 73 and *Royal Bank of Canada v Sparrow Electric Corp* [1997] 1 SCR 411.

[30] For discussion of similar options from a civil law perspective, see Boodman & Macdonald, "How Far is Article 9 Exportable? A Return to Sources" (1996) 27 *Can Bus Law Journal* 249 at 256-260, and Bridge *et al op cit* fn 15 at pp 568–570.

[31] LCCR Appendix B.

transaction (pledge, mortgage, charge etc), which would be a truly formalist approach, or they could be the same for all security interests[32], a limited functionalist approach.

b) *Follow the approach of Article 9 and the Personal Property Security Acts.* This would entail a fully functional approach: transactions would be reclassified as creating security interests if they had the (objective) purpose of security[33] and the same regime of registration, priorities and incidents of security would apply to all. [34]

c) *Make all quasi-security interests registrable and apply the first to file priority rule to them, but leave their contractual and proprietary nature to be determined by the agreement between the parties.* This compromise position acknowledges the good policy reasons for making all quasi-security transactions registrable, defined by a criteria based on the objective function of the transaction. Other transactions, such as assignments of receivables and leases over one year could also be made registrable. It would also include a unified approach to priorities based on comprehensive registration (first to file). However, it would be left up to the parties to determine the location of title and whether any other incidents of security applied to these transactions. This split between rules relating to registration/perfection and rules relating to other matters can be seen even under Article 9 in relation to absolute assignments of receivables, and even more clearly in relation to non-security leases for over one year under the New Zealand PPSA and the Canadian PPSAs (except Ontario).[35] Option c) was also the position recommended by the Australian Law Reform Commission[36] and the New Zealand Law Commission,[37] although the New Zealand Law Commission did recommend a single security interest which would appear to have resulted in a change in the location of title, and did in fact make provision in the legislation for the incidents of security.

d) *As c), but make only some quasi-security interests registrable.* This is, broadly speaking, the regime that applies in some reformed civil law

---

[32] Little distinction is made under Article 9 as to whether the security interest is possessory or non-possessory (9-207(b): the same rules apply even if the secured party has taken possession after default).

[33] See footnote 39 below.

[34] This is the approach provisionally recommended by the Law Commission (part 5 LCCR) and included in the draft regulations, although views on whether option (c) should be adopted are welcomed and the Law Commission expresses the view that the provisions could be altered without affecting the structure as a whole (para 5.9).

[35] See footnote 45 below and LCCR paras 2.87-88 and 2.96-98.

[36] ALRC Report no 64, *Personal Property Securities*, para 10.18.

[37] NZLC Report no 8, *A Personal Property Securities Act for New Zealand* (1989) at 11.

jurisdictions.[38] The main difference from c) would be that the interests that are registrable are identified by form (for example, reservation of title, conditional sale, sale and leaseback etc) rather than by any general functional criteria.[39] It would, of course, be possible to widen the list so that the effect was nearly the same as c), but the possibilities for parties to construct complex transactional structures that did not fit within the list of registrable interests would be greater. This approach is inconsistent with the idea of recharacterization of all registrable interests as a single security interest, whereas (possibly) approach c) is not.

Acceptance of option a) would entail rejection of the arguments in favour of registration of any quasi-security interests. This is a very real debate, but I have addressed the arguments elsewhere[40] and will not discuss them here. On the basis, then, that there is a good reason to register quasi-security interests, should options c) or d) be considered as real alternatives to the fully functional approach?

An Assessment of Functionalism

If one accepts that quasi-security interests should be registered and that priority should be determined by the first to file rule, what potentially results from the recharacterization of the transaction as creating a security interest? There appear to be two kinds of consequences. The first is that the proprietary structure of the transaction is changed, so that title resides in the debtor subject to the security interest of the creditor. This can potentially affect the situation both on the insolvency of the debtor and the creditor, as well as the tax and accounting position. The second is that the incidents of security apply to the transaction. These are covered by specific provision in Article 9 and the PPSAs.

It must be borne in mind that there are three types of interests which come under the classification of "security interest" in Article 9 and the PPSAs. The first

[38] For example, under the Civil Code of Québec (see Boodman and Macdonald, *op* cit fn 14 and the Civil Code of Lithuania (Smaliukas, "Reform of Laws on Security Interests in Lithuania" chapter 2).

[39] As is found in UCC (revised) 1-201. It should, perhaps, be pointed out that even under Article 9 the criteria for defining a security interest is objective, so that it is based on the substance of the transactions created rather than whether the parties actually intended the transaction to be used as security, Simmonds, "Some Notes on the Reform of Personal Property Law in Australia" in *Securities over Personalty* (1994) Gillooly (Ed) p 210, Bridge *et al, op* cit fn 15 at p 579. For example, UCC (revised) 2-401 provides that "Any retention or reservation by the seller of the title (property) in goods shipped or delivered to the buyer is limited in effect to a reservation of a security interest". This is irrespective of the parties' true purpose in deciding on reservation of title. NZPPSA s 17 provides both for a general functional definition of a security interest, and then in s 17(3) a non-exhaustive list of included transactions.

[40] Gullifer, *The Law Commission's Proposals: a Critique,* (2004) 15 EBLR 811.

are security interests in the strict sense.[41] The second are quasi-security interests. The third are absolute interests which are included within the regime because there are good reasons for making them registrable and for applying the priority rules to them. They may also be included because of the difficulties in telling the difference between security transfers and others. The obvious examples are outright assignments of receivables,[42] leases for more than one year[43] and commercial consignments.[44] These third type are often called "deemed" security interests and the provisions on the incidents of security do not apply to them.[45] It is interesting to consider the case of the deemed security interests, since they raise the question very starkly as to what happens to title when such interests are brought within the regime, and whether it is possible to bring transactions within the regime without changing the location of title.

There are two fundamental policy questions raised. The first is whether it is desirable (or perhaps necessary) to change the location of title in transactions in order to bring them within the perfection and priority provisions of a personal property security regime. The second is whether it is desirable (or necessary) to provide that the incidents of security apply to some or all transactions within the regime, and if only some, to which ones. The two questions are closely inter-related, in that the incidents of security flow from an interest being characterized as security, but also the nature of the single security interest under an Article 9/PPSA regime comes largely from the incidents of security which are said to apply to all such interests.

Title is Deemed to Reside in the Debtor, Subject to the Security Interest of the Creditor

Since quasi-security transactions achieve their effect either by reservation of title, or by the grant of an absolute title to the creditor, the form of the transaction involves the title residing in the creditor until the debt is paid. In many transactions, title is transferred to the debtor on payment of the debt, although there are transactions, such as a finance lease,[46] where the debtor never gains the title. The location of title potentially affects many of the matters discussed below.

Under an Article 9 type regime, the location of title is not expressly mentioned within the regime itself. The question of priorities is stipulated by the regime, so is the procedure on enforcement, and so the location of title is not often relevant.

---

[41] Charges, mortgages, pledges, liens.

[42] UCC (revised) 1-201(37), OPPSA s 1(1), SPPSA s 2(1)(qq), NZPPSA s 17(1)(b), DR 3(3).

[43] SSPPSA s 2(1)(qq), NZPPSA s 17(b), DR 3(3)(c) and 8.

[44] UCC (revised) 1-201(37), SPPSA s 2(1)(qq), NZPPSA s 17(1)(b), DR 3(3)(d).

[45] UCC (revised) 9-601(g), NZPPSA s 105, SPPSA s 55(2)(b) and 3(2). There does not appear to be a direct equivalent in the OPPSA. The Law Commission also provisionally recommend this approach DR 56(1).

[46] For a detailed description of a typical finance lease see *On Demand Information plc v Michael Gerson (Finance) plc* (at first instance) [1999] 1 All ER (Comm) 512 at 514-5.

However, one can extrapolate from the provisions of the regime where title would be, if it were necessary to know: the debtor has title subject to the security interest of the creditor.[47] First, it is clear from the concept of a single security interest that the property analysis (if it were needed) must be the same for quasi-security interests as it is for true security interests, for example, charges. Since title to the charged property is in the debtor, the same must be true for quasi-security interests such as sales with reservation of title. Secondly, any surplus value in the security over and above realization of the debt goes to the debtor,[48] thus indicating that the security interest is limited to the amount of the debt, and that residual title must be in the debtor. Thirdly, the debtor is liable for any deficiency.[49] Fourthly, an unregistered interest is (usually)[50] void against a trustee in bankruptcy so that the whole value goes to other secured creditors or the unsecured creditors. If the unregistered "security interest" were the grant of absolute title, then on a void grant title would revert anyway to the debtor.[51] But if the void "security interest" were a reservation of title, title cannot revert to the debtor as the debtor never had title: if the debtor is to have title (so that the trustee can distribute to other creditors) it must be because that is the result of the statutory regime.[52]

The change in the location potentially affects some matters other than the application of the incidents of security, for example:

(i) The position if the creditor becomes insolvent This is not an area covered by the Article 9 and PPSA regimes: it is a matter for the bankruptcy law of the relevant jurisdiction. It could be, however, affected by the nature of the interest of the insolvent creditor. If a secured creditor becomes insolvent, its liquidator would not be able merely to disclaim the security agreement under the power to disclaim onerous property[53] because of the debtor's proprietary interest in the asset. Where the creditor reserves title, the position is much less clear. It is possible to argue that the debtor's interest is merely contractual, and so the contract can be

---

47 See above, fn 29, *James Talcott Inc v Franklin National Bank* 292 Minn 277, 194 NW 2d 775, 10 UCC Rep 11.

48 UCC (revised) 9-615(d)(1), NZPPSA s 117, 119, SPPSA s 60(2), OPPSA s 64(1), DR 65(1)-(3).

49 UCC (revised) 9-615(d)(2), 9-608(4), OPPSA s 64(3), SPPSA s 60(5), DR 66.

50 This is not the case in New Zealand where an unregistered interest is not void against a trustee in bankruptcy (Gedye, Cuming, Wood: *Personal Property Securities in New Zealand* (2002) at p 8).

51 *Agent's Equity Inc v Hope (Trustee of)* (1996) 29 DLR (2d) 287.

52 That this is true in Canada can be seen from a combination of two cases: *Marcel Equipment Ltd v Equipements Benoit D'Amours et Fils Inc* (1995) PPSAC (2d) 31 (noted at Bridge *et al op* cit fn 15 at p 603, fn 129): here the interest of a mortgagee in a piece of equipment which was bought by the debtor under a conditional sale agreement, which was not registered in time to gain PMSI status, was held to attach to the collateral as a whole and not just the buyer's possessory interest in the equipment and *Re Giffen* [1998] 1 SCR 91, see text to footnotes 72-80 below.

53 Section 178 Insolvency Act 1986.

disclaimed,[54] although under English law the debtor's possessory interest may be protected.[55] From a policy point of view, however, it is hard to see why the debtor should not be protected in the insolvency of the creditor.

(ii) Accounting and tax treatment In the past, parties chose the form of quasi-security transactions for accounting and tax reasons: so as to achieve "off balance sheet" financing. However, in the UK both accounting practice and tax assessments have, over the years, moved away from depending on the legal form of transactions and has adopted an approach based on the substance of the transaction. The location of legal title has long been seen as irrelevant, so that, for example, goods the subject of hire purchase and conditional sale agreements are treated as assets in the hirer's balance sheet from the time of the agreement, with the outstanding balance of the instalments being treated as a loan[56] and the agreements are treated as disposals of the goods so that the hirer is treated as the owner of the goods from the beginning of the transaction.[57] Thus the recharacterization as security interests of quasi-security transactions is unlikely to make much difference to their accounting treatment.

Even with leases, the stark distinction between finance and operating leases seems soon set to disappear. At present, finance leases are recorded on the balance sheet as an asset and an obligation to pay future rentals,[58] while under an operating lease the leased property is treated as an asset of the lessor and the payments as an expense of the lessee.[59] Distinguishing between the two types of leases depends upon whether substantially all the risks and rewards of ownership are transferred to the lessee, which in practice almost invariably means whether the minimum lease payments amount to 90% or more of the value of the asset.[60] It is proposed[61] that finance and operating leases be treated the same way, so that the lessee should record in its accounts the fair value of the rights and obligations transferred by the

---

[54] See the argument of Dalhuisen, "Security and Ownership Based Funding Techniques" [1998] *European Business Law Review* 43 at p 54 regarding the position regarding finance leases under Dutch law.

[55] Dalhuisen, *supra* at fn 179, although for the contrary view see Swadling, "The Proprietary Effect of a Hire of Goods", Chap 1 of Palmer & McKendrick (Eds) *Interests in Goods (*1993) 3.

[56] Sander, Reisbach, Thomas, *Equipment Leasing* para 1.18 (Ed Fitzpatrick).

[57] *Equipment Leasing* para 1.9.

[58] So that the accounting treatment of a finance lease is indistinguishable from that of a secured loan, see Inland Revenue Finance Leasing Manual - FLM5.20, at http://www.ir.gov.uk/manuals/flmmanual/flmch05/06_0008_flm520.htm.

[59] SSAP 21.

[60] *Equipment Leasing op cit* fn 53 para 1.5

[61] Discussion paper, "*Leases: Implementation of a New Approach*" (Accounting Standards Board, Dec 1999) presenting a Position Paper developed by the G4+1 (a standard setting body of Australia, New Zealand, Canada, the US and the UK). The Accounting Standard Board is now undertaking a research project to inform the International Accounting Standards Board's development of a new leasing standard. (ASB website, http://www.asb.org.uk/asb/technical/projects/project0025.html.)

lease, which would be large in relation to a "finance lease" and small in relation to an "operating lease". If this proposal were adopted, any vestige of having to determine the function of the transaction would vanish.

Further, unlike hire purchase and conditional sale agreements, finance leases have considerable tax benefits, based largely on the timing of tax profits and losses.[62] Many other specific benefits of finance leasing[63] have, however, been eroded by a number of recent provisions.[64] However, despite such measures, the tax system looks to the form of the transaction, so that neither finance leases nor sales and leasebacks are treated as secured loans.[65]

Thus it can be seen that although there seems to be a gradual move towards basing tax as well as accounting rules on substance rather than form, at present the form of the transaction still does have some tax significance and any reclassification from personal property security law could have serious implications for the tax position of transactions.

(iii) Transactional advantages of the location of title One of the main justifications of a system based on the form rather than the function of a transaction is that it respects the parties' freedom of contract to structure a transaction as they wish. The possible reasons for agreeing a particular structure are many, and may or may not be connected with the function of transaction as security. Examples of reasons are accounting, tax, a perception that ownership is a "stronger" interest than a

---

62 So that the lessor could claim a 25% writing down capital allowance on the cost of acquiring the equipment. This gave the lessor essentially a tax benefit based on timing, so that it made tax losses in the first part of the lease and tax profits later, whereas with a loan the profits would be larger in the earlier part of the lease. This is advantageous because of the time value of money (money now is worth more than money later), see Inland Revenue Finance Leasing Manual at FLM6.14.

63 Deferral of income or conversion of income into capital, acceleration of capital allowances, acceleration of capital allowances through group relief, use of sales and leasebacks.

64 Finance Act 1997 Schedule 12.

65 Inland Revenue, *Finance Leasing Manual,* FLM5.01. This approach is perhaps supported by the decision of the Court of Appeal in *Barclays Mercantile Business Finance Ltd v Mawson,* [2002] EWCA Civ 1853, which upheld the right of the tax payer to capital allowances under a complicated lease structure set up to gain those particular tax advantages. The case is now being considered by the House of Lords. It should be noted that the scheme was set up before the 1997 reforms and would not have succeeded had those reforms been in force. Further, the Government have put forward ideas in a Consultation Paper (HM Treasury, *Corporation Tax Reform: a Consultation Document (August 2003*) which includes radical changes to the capital allowance system, which could spell the end of tax advantages for equipment leasing. The Law Commission's views are set out in para 2.111-2.199 of the LCCR. Rather strangely, it is denied that the scheme will result in any transfer of ownership to the lessee (para 2.116) although this is the logical conclusion from the reforms (see above). The Law Commission are still consulting with the Inland Revenue, but take the view that the scheme will not necessarily lead to the recharacterization of finance leases for tax purposes.

security interest,[66] the creditor's entitlement to the surplus value in the asset,[67] avoidance of negative pledge provisions in a previously created charge,[68] priority over other secured creditors, priority over *bona fide* purchasers of the asset[69] and the avoidance of registration.[70]

At present, the parties use the form of the agreement to fix the risk pattern between them.[71] Under English law they currently have the contractual freedom to do this, subject to certain restraints as to unfairness. If a personal property security regime is to alter that balance, there has to be good policy reasons for doing so. The fact that the parties' agreement as to the location of title may affect third parties may well constitute such a reason. However, those third parties may be able to be protected by methods which do not involve a change in the location of title: by giving notice to third parties of the transactions and, perhaps, of relevant terms, by compulsory registration, and by providing for a priority regime to apply to such transactions.

At present, parties can use the location of title to gain priority over other secured creditors, for example, by the use of a retention of title clause. Under an Article 9/PPSA regime, the priority rules to some extent replicate the priority structure of a title based system, so that, for example, many retention of title clauses will still have super priority as purchase money security interests. To the extent that there is no such replication, the questions arise whether the parties should be allowed to contract out of the regime's priority rules, and also how technically the desired result is to be achieved. Take, for example, an "all monies" clause, whereby title is retained until all monies owing from the debtor to the creditor are paid. Under some PPSA systems, an interest created by such a transaction only has super priority to the extent of the debt due in relation to that

---

66 Inland Revenue, *Finance Leasing Manual,* FLM 5.05. Thus, it is said, lessors are more prepared to lend to less solid businesses, to lend cheaper than ordinary lenders and to lend 100% of the asset's value (see Dalhuisen, "Security and Ownership Based Funding Techniques" [1998] *European Business Law Review* 43 at p 45).

67 Dalhuisen at p 45 and p 139. See further the practice of some finance lessors to take part of their return in the form of a share of the sale proceeds of the asset at the end of the lease, Inland Revenue, *Finance Leasing Manual,* FLM 6.44. The creditor's entitlement to residual value is a crucial element in operating leases (see the Financial Leasing Association, *Definitions and Acromyns,* at http://www.fla.org.uk/fla_home/Definitions_and_Acronyms.asp).

68 For example, as in *Welsh Development Agency v Exfinco* [1999] BCLC 148.

69 Still the case in relation to assets covered by hire purchase agreements, except for private purchasers of motor vehicles to which the Hire Purchase Act 1964 Part III applies. In relation to other assets section 25 of the Sale of Goods Act 1979, which enables a buyer who buys from a buyer in possession to obtain good title, does not apply to hire purchase agreements (*Helby v Matthews* [1895] AC 471). This distinction between conditional sales and hire purchase agreements would not survive if both such transactions were brought within a personal property priority regime.

70 *Re George Inglefield* [1933] Ch 1.

71 For a detailed discussion of this, see Dalhuisen, "Security and Ownership Based Funding Techniques" [1998] *European Business Law Review* 43, especially at pp 137-142.

asset.[72] Once the price for the asset has been paid the super priority is lost, and other security interest registered first have priority. This conclusion may not be objectionable from a policy point of view, but unless the retention of title is recharacterized as a security interest, the debtor has no proprietary interest in the collateral to which the other security interest (which now has priority) can attach. If the problem is not dealt with by a change in the location of title[73] it would have to be specifically addressed in any statute, and any such provision would be open to criticism of conceptual inconsistency.[74]

(iv) The position of unregistered but registrable interests A similar problem arises in relation to unregistered but registrable interests. If the sanction for this is invalidity against other secured creditors, or against a liquidator, a change in the location of title means that the debtor has a residual title to which the interest of the other creditors can attach, and to which the liquidator can be entitled. If the location of title does not change, again specific provisions would be required.

A good example of this is the British Columbian case of *Re Giffen*.[75] This is a case of a deemed security interest, but the issue would be the same in relation to a quasi-security interest. Here the lessor had failed to register the lease, which was for more than one year and therefore registrable as a security interest.[76] An unregistered security interest was not effective against a debtor's trustee in bankruptcy.[77] The British Columbian Court of Appeal held that, despite this, the lessor was entitled to the proceeds of sale of the car since the trustee in bankruptcy could not be entitled to a greater interest than the debtor had, and since title remained with the lessor, the lessee debtor had no title. The Supreme Court of Canada reversed the decision on the grounds that location of title was irrelevant to the personal property security regime,[78] that under that regime the lessor had only an unperfected security interest[79] which, being unperfected, was ineffective against the lessee's trustee in bankruptcy and that the lessee had possessory rights in the car, which the operation of the PPSA turned into a full proprietary right enjoyed by the trustee.[80]

The case concerned a deemed security interest, which even under the PPSA regime is not treated as a security interest for all purposes. The result does not just come from the drafting technique of deeming all interests to be covered by the

---

72 See fn 27 above.

73 The solution adopted in the *Marcel Equipment* case mentioned in fn 49 above.

74 This particular problem will not arise under the Law Commission's provisional recommendations in LCCR, which favour cross-collateralisation (para 3.220).

75 [1998] 1 SCR 91.

76 British Columbia PPSA ss 2 and 3.

77 BCPPSA s 20(1)(b).

78 [1998] 1 SCR 91 para 28.

79 Para 32.

80 Para 44. The PPSA therefore modified the principle that a trustee in bankruptcy cannot obtain greater rights to the asset than the bankrupt had (para 56).

regime as security interests.[81] It comes from the policy choice that the perfection requirements of the regime should apply to all leases over one year, and that the sanction for non-registration is that the lease is not only ineffective against other secured creditors, but also against the unsecured creditors of the lessee (who, arguably, are less likely to be affected by the failure to register).[82] But the issue would also arise if a personal property regime were to introduce perfection and priority requirements for quasi-security interests without providing for a change in the location of title.

This case also points up the fact that under a PPSA regime where invalidity is the penalty for non-registration, the penalty is harsher where the creditor is entitled to surplus value (usually where the location of title did not shift) than where it is not (where the creditor's interest is a security interest), since the effect of invalidity is that the creditor loses its entire (ownership) interest in the asset. The creditor does, of course, have an unsecured claim for outstanding rentals and damages, but it has to prove for this together with all other unsecured creditors.[83]

(v) Harmonization While in many ways it can be argued that England and Wales should adopt the system that appears the best possible for this country, without regard to how closely it harmonizes with those of other countries, there is a growing interest in the internationalization of personal property security law, stemming partly from a perceived harmonization of domestic law in this area.[84] While adopting the full concept of a single security interest would harmonize English law with US, Canadian and New Zealand law, retaining ownership based financing techniques would, arguably, enable more harmonization with the civil law countries of Europe, including some of those with new security regimes based on the European Bank for Research and Development's Model Law. Views on this subject can be diametrically opposed. While functionalists argue that adopting a unified approach in all respects is essential to the further harmonization of personal property security law,[85] some formalists see the development of ownership based financing techniques as the way towards internationalism, and see the Article 9 regime as somewhat out of line and lacking in nuance.[86]

---

[81] Though this itself has the potential to cause confusion, see Bridge *et al op cit* fn 15 at p 585 in relation to the assignment of receivables.
[82] Bridge *et al* p 604. This result is not the case in New Zealand.
[83] See Ziegel, "Should Canada Adopt an Article 2A Type Law on Personal Property Leasing?" (1990) 16 *Can Bus Law Journal*, 369 at pp 391-395.
[84] Cuming, "The Internationalization of Secured Financing Law" chapter 22 in *Making Commercial Law: Essays in Honour of Roy Goode* (1997) Cranston (Ed).
[85] Cuming, "The Internationalization of Secured Financing Law" chapter 22 in *Making Commercial Law: Essays in Honour of Roy Goode* (1997) Cranston (Ed) at p 523.
[86] Dalhuisen, "Security and Ownership Based Funding Techniques" [1998] *European Business Law Review* 43.

The Incidents of Security Apply to the Transaction

This area is considered in some detail in the Law Commission's Consultative Report, which follows most of the provisions of Article 9 and the PPSA regimes.

(i) The security interest at any time only extends to the value of the outstanding debt. This is most obvious when the security is enforced, when the creditor has to give any surplus value to the debtor, or its liquidator or to the creditor next in line. Under Article 9 and PPSA regimes, it is assumed that because the transaction has the function of security, the parties intend (or should intend) the surplus to be available to the debtor and its creditors. The regimes specifically provide for this,[87] and this, together with all the other enforcement provisions, is seen largely as a matter of protecting the interests of the debtor and its other creditors. The regimes vary as to the extent to which the debtor can contract out of its rights to receive the surplus.[88]

The question of the right of the debtor to the surplus in quasi-security transactions has largely been viewed in English law as a matter of contract, and is dependant on the express or implied intentions of the parties. To take, for example, cases of simple retention of title clauses. In *Armour v Thyssen Edelstahlwerke AG*[89] (a Scottish case decided by the House of Lords), the relevant clause retained title until all monies due from the buyer to the seller were paid. Lord Keith considered that the effect of such a clause was that if the seller repossessed the goods, he was entitled to retain any excess value over and above the contract price.[90] However, in the later Scottish case of *Kinloch Damph Ltd v Nordvik Salmon Farms Ltd*[91] the parties had clearly felt that Lord Keith's analysis did not reflect their true intentions, and had included a clause limiting the sellers' rights to repossession or recovery in value "to an amount equivalent to any principal outstanding plus interest as allowed in the contract plus reasonable costs of recovery". Lord MacFayden, in the Outer House, commented that:

> The restriction mitigates the potential unfairness of the rule mentioned by Lord Keith in *Armour v Thyssen* that any increase in value belongs to the unpaid seller who has retained title to the goods. By restricting the pursuers' right to repossess the goods to an amount equivalent in value to the outstanding debt, Clause 13 ensures that the retention of title cannot be operated oppressively.

Further, in the English case of *Clough Mill Ltd v Martin*[92] at least two members of the Court of Appeal (Goff LJ and Sir John Donaldson) assumed that the parties intended that the seller should only be entitled to the amount outstanding and

---

[87] Fn 48 above.

[88] See below page 20.

[89] [1991] 2 AC 339.

[90] At 353D.

[91] (1999) Outer House Cases 30 June 1999.

[92] [1985] 1 WLR 111.

should account for any surplus. They differed as to how this was to be achieved: Goff LJ thought it could be only by means of an implied term in the contract, which would not apply to the situation where the seller had accepted the buyer's repudiation unless the contract specifically provided that it should. Thus, when the contract no longer subsisted, the seller had the right to retain the entire value of the repossessed goods.[93] Sir John Donaldson, however, appeared to interpret the contractual phrase "until the price of that material has been paid in full" as applying even after the contract had come to an end, and limiting the seller's right of recovery to the amount outstanding.[94]

From this it can be seen that it is generally assumed that the parties to a sale with retention of title do not intend the seller to retain any surplus value, and that if that is the result of the applicable legal principle then it is potentially oppressive to the buyer. It should be recognized that there are two potential sources of surplus value in a conditional sale or hire purchase transaction:[95] that resulting from part of the outstanding debt already paid by the debtor before default, and that resulting from an increase in the value of the asset. In many spheres the latter is rare,[96] and is generally ignored by the parties. The problem of part-payment, however, is a very real one. The more instalments that are paid by the buyer, the more it loses on a repossession of the asset. It is, of course, perfectly possible for the contract to provide expressly for the return of payments in the event of termination of the contract, even if the buyer defaults. If this is not done, it may be that the buyer can claim back payment already made on the grounds of failure of consideration: this was the solution suggested by Goff LJ in *Clough Mill Ltd v Martin*.[97] However, it is not clear under English law that money can be recovered on the grounds of partial, as opposed to total, failure of consideration, and where the contract is structured as a hire purchase agreement, or a finance lease, some of the consideration is the use of the goods, which has not failed.[98] English law does allow relief in the part payment situation in two ways, both falling under the equitable doctrine of relief against forfeiture. The first is relief against forfeiture of payments made. Here the majority of the Court of Appeal in *Stockloser v Johnson*[99] specified two criteria: (a) that the forfeiture was penal and (b) that it would be unconscionable for the performing party to retain the money. However, the doctrine is not without controversy and its application has been

---

93 At pp 117-8. This was subject to an obligation to pay back part payments already made, based on failure of consideration.

94 At p 126. Oliver LJ thought that, at least once the contract had come to an end, the seller was under no obligation to account for the surplus.

95 And also with a finance lease, in that the lessee is eventually to be put in the economic position as if it acquired the asset.

96 The property is more likely to depreciate in value, and it is this which is provided for in the contract.

97 At pp 117-8.

98 See Smith, "Relief against forfeiture: a restatement" (2001) 60 *CLJ* 178 at pp 183-4, *Chitty on Contracts* para 38-304, *Kelly v Lombard Banking Co* [1959] 1 WLR 41.

99 [1954] 1 QB 476.

rejected in the two hire purchase cases in which it has been considered.[100] The alternative way of protecting a buyer in such circumstances is by allowing the agreement to continue if the buyer makes good its default.[101] The English law of relief has been limited to forfeiture of proprietary and possessory interests, and thus has been held to include loss of possessory rights under a finance lease,[102] a hire purchase agreement[103] and even an operating lease.[104] This development can be seen as a move towards treating such agreements as creating security interests.[105] However, one can also view the equitable controls as part of a general control of unconscionable terms in contracts, which can be seen as appropriate in consumer and, possibly, standard term contracts, but less so for large scale commercial contracts.[106]

Clearly the question of entitlement to surplus potentially affects three constituencies: other secured creditors ranking below the first,[107] unsecured creditors and the debtor itself. If the debtor is not insolvent, the only party affected by the entitlement to the surplus is the debtor itself. Thus, provisions providing for the debtor's entitlement are there to protect the debtor from an unconscionably harsh bargain. However, on insolvency it is secured and unsecured creditors who will receive any surplus due to the debtor.

The question therefore is whether the law should prescribe that the debtor and other creditors should be entitled to the surplus in all transactions within the

---

[100] *Campbell Discount Co Ltd v Bridge* (CA) [1961] 1 QB 445, *Galbraith v Mitchenall Estates Ltd* [1965] 2 QB 473.

[101] A similar procedure applied in Canada before the PPSA legislation see Bridge *et al*, p 591, fn 76 and 77. PPSA regimes vary in whether they give the debtor a right to claim reinstatement. The New Zealand and Saskatchewan regimes give all debtors (business and consumer) such a right (s 133 NZPPSA, s 62(1) SSPSA, while the right in Ontario is limited to consumer debtors, (s 66(2) OPPSA), and in British Columbia only consumer debtors have a right to demand reinstatement, but it can be ordered by the court in other cases (s 62(2) and (3) BCPPSA). The Law Commission are not recommending the inclusion of such a right: the view is taken that, at least in non-consumer transactions, this should be left to be agreed between the parties (para 5.111-113).

[102] *Transag Haulage Ltd v Leyland DAF Finance plc* [1994] 2 BCLC 88, *On Demand Information plc v Michael Gerson (Finance) plc* [2002] 2 WLR 919 (HL).

[103] *Goker v NWS Bank plc*, 1 August 1990, CA.

[104] *Barton Thompson & Co v Stapling Machines Co* [1966] Ch 499, where the point was considered arguable.

[105] Smith, "Relief against forfeiture: a restatement" (2001) 60 *CLJ* 178; Gullifer, "Agreed remedies" in *Commercial Remedies* (2003) 191.

[106] See Law Commission Consultation Paper 166 (2002), and cases on the rule against penalties cited at footnote 118.

[107] This assumes that the quasi-security transaction has priority over all other security interests in the asset. This is likely to be the case, because it is likely to be a PMSI, which has such priority irrespective of the time when it was created. This would come from the application of the regime's priority rules, and not because of the location of title. The location of title would not prevent other security interests having priority over the quasi-security interest if that is the result of the application of the regime's priority rules, but see discussion above (text to fns 73–84).

regime, or whether that entitlement should be a matter for agreement between the parties. Freedom of contract would suggest that it should be up to the parties, with perhaps some safeguards against unconscionable bargains as currently apply in England. This would have the advantage that the controls could be fine-tuned to take into account the commercial bargaining position of the parties. However, on the insolvency of the debtor, it is the junior secured creditors and the unsecured creditors who lose out if the creditor with a quasi-security interest is allowed to keep the surplus. Since many debtors either do not anticipate insolvency, or are indifferent to its effects as between their creditors, they may happily bargain away their entitlement to the surplus in return for, for example, a lower price. Should the law prevent this in order to protect other creditors?

The regimes vary as to the extent to which the debtor can contract out of its rights to receive the surplus. Under the UCC and the Ontario and Saskatchewan PPSAs, there is no general contracting out provision, but the debtor may waive rights to the extent that this is not prohibited: however, the right to receive the surplus is in the list of unwaivable rights.[108] In New Zealand the debtor may contract out of the right to receive surplus itself but the parties may not affect the rights of subordinate secured creditors to be paid out of any surplus.[109] This provision has been criticised[110] as inconsistent with the functionalist nature of the regime: if one views the creditor's interest as a security interest, then allowing the debtor to contract out of the right to receive the surplus is allowing it to contract out of a fundamental right. It is also said that the courts might be more willing to allow contracting out where the transaction is one of quasi-security than a true security transaction: this offends the principle underlying the regime that all security interests are treated in the same way. The New Zealand compromise has also been criticised for inconsistency in that it protects third party secured creditors, but not unsecured creditors of the debtor. Further, it can be avoided by an unscrupulous debtor who creates a subordinate secured interest in favour of a friendly creditor who can recover the surplus and then pay it back to the debtor. Arguably there is no reason to adopt the New Zealand approach to protect third party secured creditors: another way is to give future creditors notice (on the register) of the contractual provisions concerning the surplus.[111]

To what extent, then, is it necessary to protect other secured creditors? Debtors are free to dispose of their assets outright, which has the effect of taking them outside the availability to all other creditors, providing that such dispositions

---

[108] UCC (revised) 9-602, SPSA s 56(3), OPPSA 59(5).

[109] NZPPSA, s 107(1). This is a specific application of a wider policy that the debtor cannot contract out of any enforcement provisions that affect third parties, although any thing that affects the debtor potentially affects its unsecured creditors. See fn 151 for a description of the drafting difficulties raised by this approach.

[110] Gedye, Cuming, Wood, *Personal Property Securities in New Zealand* (2002) at pp 389, 414.

[111] This possibility is suggested in the LCCP at para 11.36.

are not within the run-up to insolvency.[112] If assets the value of the surplus had been disposed of in the ordinary course of business, a prior chargee, for example, could not complain of such a disposition of the charged property. However, such dispositions are usually for value, which may not have a net effect on the position of the secured creditor, whereas bargaining away the right to the surplus would.

In its Consultative Report, the Law Commission provisionally recommends that the right to receive the surplus cannot be waived, on the grounds that in practice lenders using title retention devices are not interested in recovering more than capital and interest due to them, and also that a mandatory rule is simpler and more effective to protect third parties than merely a default provision.[113]

(ii) The debtor remains obliged to pay the balance of the debt if the security does not realize enough to cover the amount due. This comes from the view that the security interest is separate from the debt which it secures, so that the debt remains even after part of it has been fulfilled by recovery of the asset by the creditor. It is the corollary of the debtor having an interest in the surplus: the debtor must take the burden as well as the benefits of the transaction being recharacterized as security.[114] It is expressly provided for in Article 9 and the PPSAs.[115] In situations where the "secured" asset depreciates in value, the survival of the debt is a real issue, even when part payment has been made. However, in very many cases the parties will have provided for the survival of the debt in the contract anyway. This time the bargain between the parties only affects the debtor and, if it is insolvent, its unsecured creditors to a small extent in that the personal claim for the deficiency is also an unsecured claim. In England, a provision for the survival of the debt in the context of hire purchase and conditional sale agreements has been subject to the rule against penalties, so that it is only enforceable if it is a genuine pre-estimate of loss: if it is not, then the creditor only is entitled to damages assessed under normal principles.[116] Again, this rule can be seen as part of the general jurisdiction against unconscionable terms, so that courts should be slow to apply it in negotiated contracts between businesses.[117]

Where the quasi-security transaction takes the form of an absolute sale rather than a reservation of title, for example, in the factoring of receivables, a purchaser

---

[112] When transactions at an undervalue (Insolvency Act 1986 s 238) and preferences (Insolvency Act 1986 s 239) can be set aside.
[113] Paras 5.160-162.
[114] Bridge *et al, op* cit fn 15 at p 592.
[115] UCC (revised) 9-608(4), OPPSA s 64(3), SPPSA s 60(5). These provisions can be contracted out of by the parties. There does not appear to be an express provision in the NZPPSA, but would appear to be the case, see Gedye, Cuming, Wood, *Personal Property Securities in New Zealand* (2002) at p 398.
[116] *Bridge v Campbell Discount Co Ltd* [1962] AC 600, *Cooden Engineering Co Ltd v Stanford* [1953] 1 QB 86, *Financings Ltd v Baldock* [1963] 2 QB 104, *Lombank Ltd v Excell* [1964] 1 QB 415, *Lombard North Central v Butterworth* [1987] QB 527.
[117] *Phillips Hong Kong Ltd v The Attorney General of Hong Kong* (1993) 61 Building Law Reports 49, *Lordsvale Finance plc v Bank of Zambia* [1996] 3 All ER 156, *Cenargo Ltd v Izar Construcciones Navales SA* [2002] EWCA Civ 524.

may well want to protect itself against the receivables yielding less than it paid for them (that is a deficiency). Often this is done by a recourse provision,[118] and/or by a guarantee given by the buyer. The presence of such recourse provisions have been a very significant factor in the difficulties found by the courts in classifying assignments of receivables as charges or sales.[119] Such difficulties in classification have been one of the reasons why Article 9 and the PPSA regimes have included all assignments of receivables in the regime,[120] although only the perfection and priority provisions apply, leaving the problem of classification still applicable when deciding whether the enforcement provisions apply. The presence of a recourse provision gives the transaction the same effect as if the debtor were liable for a deficiency, even though the enforcement provisions do not apply.[121]

(iii) The creditor is obliged to follow the procedure for enforcement on default laid down by the relevant statute. The Article 9 and PPSA regimes[122] prescribe rights of taking possession, sale and retention of collateral.[123] The Saskatchewan regime also provides for the appointment of a receiver.[124] The secured party is obliged to act commercially reasonably in disposing of the asset[125] and to give notice to other registered creditors before the sale.[126] The order and manner of distribution of proceeds is prescribed.[127] The provisions are unremarkable in relation to security interests in the strict sense: many of them are echoed in the English common

---

[118] An obligation on the seller to buy back unpaid receivables.

[119] *Lloyds & Scottish Finance Ltd v Cyril Lord Carpet Sales Ltd* [1992] BCLC 609, *Orion Finance Ltd v Crown Financial Management Ltd* [1996] 2 BCLC 78, where Millett LJ said "the presence of a right of recourse by the transferee against the transferor to recover a shortfall may be inconsistent with a sale, but it is not necessarily so and its absence is not conclusive".

[120] UCC (revised) 9-109 (and see official comment: "This approach generally has been successful in avoiding difficult problems of distinguishing between transactions in which a receivable secures an obligation and those in which the receivable has been sold outright. In many commercial financing transactions the distinction is blurred"). NZPPSA s 17(1)(b), SSPPSA s 2(1)(qq), OPPSA S 1(1), DR 3(3).

[121] LCCR para 5.29 fn 39.

[122] UCC (revised) Article 9 part 6, NZPPSA Part 9, OPPSA Part V, SPPSA Part V, DR Part 5.

[123] Including provisions for notice to affected third parties.

[124] SSPSA s 64, DR 58 (LCCR para 5.99 – 5.101). The NZPPSA Part 9 expressly does not apply if a receiver is appointed (s 106): that is governed by the Receivers Act 1993.

[125] UCC (revised) 9-610, OPPSA s 63(2), NZPPSA s 110 imposes an arguably more onerous obligation to obtain the best price reasonably obtainable at the time of the sale. There is a general good faith obligation in SSPSA s 65(3). The Law Commission have not included a general requirement of good faith, but have provisionally recommended that a specific requirement of commercial reasonableness be included in relation to certain provisions including the disposal of collateral (DR 62(6), para 5.135).

[126] UCC (revised) 9-611, SSPPSA s 59(6), OPPSA s 63(4), NZPPSA s 114, DR 63.

[127] UCC (revised) 9-615, SSPPSA s 60, OPPSA s 64, NZPPSA s 116-118, DR 65.

law.[128] However, their application to quasi-security interests has to be justified. Within an Article 9 regime this justification is that the interest is a security interest, which only extends to the outstanding debt. Therefore, the creditor who holds the asset has an obligation to distribute the excess value to other creditors who have interests in the asset, and to the debtor or its liquidator. This, however, begs the question as to the nature of the creditor's interest. If the parties are allowed to agree that it is not a security interest limited to the extent of the outstanding debt, the justification for subjecting the creditor to enforcement obligations could be said to fail.

(iv) The debtor can redeem the security by payment of the outstanding sum. The Article 9 and PPSA regimes also provide that the debtor has a right to redeem the collateral on fulfilment of the secured obligations and payment of costs[129] until the creditor has exercised its enforcement rights.[130] The main thrust of the provisions relate to redemption after the creditor has seized the collateral, although the terms of the sections are general.

Under English law, the right to redeem is implied into a security agreement in the strict sense[131] and a contractual entitlement to redeem is seen as indicative that the agreement is one of security.[132] Such a right is not, however, seen as conclusive where title is retained rather than an interest granted.[133] The same is true of an outright assignment of receivables.[134]

Should the Regime Provide that the Incidents of Security Apply to All Transactions Within the Regime?

The provisions about the incidents of security usually come both at the end of a Personal Property Security statute and also the end of a legislature's deliberations about them. Thus one reason for leaving them out is lack of time to consider them

[128] For example, the duty to exercise reasonable care to obtain a proper price on sale (*Cuckmere Brick Co Ltd v Mutual Finance Ltd* [1971] Ch 949) and the duty on the secured party to use his powers "for the sole purpose of securing repayment of the moneys owing under his mortgage and a duty to act in good faith" (*Downsview Nominees Ltd v City Corporation Ltd* [1993] AC 295).

[129] UCC (revised) 9-623, SSPPSA s 62, OPPSA s 66, NZPPSA s 132, DR 68.

[130] The exact criteria vary between the jurisdictions.

[131] *Durham Bros v Robertson* [1898] 1 QB 765.

[132] *Re George Inglefield Ltd* [1933] Ch 1 at 27, *Re Bond Worth Ltd* [1980] Ch 228 at 248, *Re Curtain Dream* [1990] BCLC 925, where Knox J said that the redemption requirement was the most important of the three tests enumerated in *Re George Inglefield, E Pfeiffer Weinkellerei-Wewineinkauf GmbH v Arbuthnot Factors Ltd* [1987] BCLC 522 at 532, *Compaq Computer Ltd v Abercorn Group Ltd* [1991] BCC 484 at 495.

[133] *Clough Mill Ltd v Martin* [1985] 1 WLR 111 at 119, *Armour v Thyssen Edelstahlwerke AG* [1991] 2 AC 339.

[134] *Lloyds & Scottish Finance Ltd v Cyril Lord Carpets Sales Ltd* [1992] BCLC 609.

properly.[135] It is true that the detail of such provisions can be complex, and has given rise to a great deal of litigation in jurisdictions where in force. Another is that on one level they are regulatory rules, and they may be either otherwise provided for in other legislation[136] or that the regime might be seen as unduly regulatory.[137] The main concern, however, is interference with freedom of contract: that parties should be free to make whatever contractual arrangements they wished subject to other (regulatory) laws.[138] Yet another argument is that it raises difficult characterization issues since deemed security interests would not be subject to such provisions, while quasi-security interests would be. So one of the main reasons for including deemed security interests in the regime[139] fails to be overcome in this area. The same problem arises, though less acutely, if it is decided to codify the incidents of security merely for security interests in the strict sense: the old law on whether a quasi-security transaction was to be classified as a charge would remain for this purpose.

There are five main arguments in favour of including such provisions in a regime. First, it is a natural corollary from the concept of a single security interest, and it is frequently argued that without such provisions the true goal of treating like transactions alike is not fully realized.[140] If, of course, this goal is not accepted in that quasi-security transactions are not recharacterized as security interests, then this argument loses a good deal of its force. Secondly, a unified enforcement regime promotes certainty, both for the parties and for the courts, and efficiency: such a system should result in lower transaction costs.[141] Thirdly, if parties have

---

[135] See New Zealand Law Commission Report No 8, *A Personal Property Securities Act for New Zealand* (1989) at 11. Compare LCCP para 11.11, where the Law Commission thought that it was not sensible to do the work without knowing whether it was thought desirable to include such provisions within the scheme. There is also concern about legislative time (LCCP para 11.43). It has now had time to consider such provisions and takes the view that a statement of rights and remedies would have significant benefits in terms of clarity and simplicity (paras 2.188-2.191).

[136] The New Zealand Law Commission were concerned that consumer protection legislation covering this area was under consideration by the Minister for Consumer Affairs (Report No 8 p 11).

[137] According to Professor J Goldring in "A comment on chapters by Professor Ralph Simmonds and Professor Tony Duggan", Chapter 10 in *Security over Personalty* (1994) Gillooly (Ed), the concern of the Australian Law Reform Commission, who recommended that no provisions about rights and duties upon default should in included in their proposed scheme (ALRC Report No 64, *Personal Property Securities*).

[138] ALRC Report No 64, *Personal Property Securities* paragraph 5.50.

[139] Difficulty of distinguishing such interests from quasi-security interests, see above footnote 123.

[140] Gedye, Cuming, Wood: *Personal Property Securities in New Zealand* (2002) at p 380.

[141] See, for example, discussion in Simmonds, Some Notes on the Reform of Personal Property Security Law in Australia, Chapter 8 in *Security over Personalty* (1994) Gillooly (Ed) at p 205. It is pointed out, however, that there is little empirical evidence that the cost of secured financing is lowered by the introduction of an Article 9 type regime, although see LCCR para 2.129, referring to Ziegel and Denomme "How Ontario Lawyers view the PPSA: an Empircial Survey" (1992) 20 CBLJ 90.

not included terms in their agreement dealing with enforcement, legislative default provisions mean that the parties' rights and obligations are not only easy to determine, but are also not dependent upon classifying the form of the agreement. Fourthly, the rights of subordinate creditors in the collateral should be protected.[142] Of course, this too begs the question of the nature of the interest of the creditor: if it is that of an absolute owner then there is no scope for subordinate security interests. Fifthly, such provisions impose minimum standards of fairness on creditors, who often have superior bargaining power.[143] It is hard to argue against this protection against unconscionability, but it can be done in legislation other than personal property security law, and can then be more finely tuned so as to take into account the fairness between the parties. This argument is less strong where the personal property security regime applies only to business to business transactions, as is likely to be the case in the first stage of the reforms in England and Wales.

One compromise approach is for the legislation to prescribe a regime but allow the parties to opt out of it. This would preserve freedom of contract, while providing a unified regime for security interests in the strict sense[144] and providing a default regime where the parties had not specifically provided for this. Article 9 does allow limited waiver,[145] but debtor's rights and secured parties' duties arising in specified sections[146] may not be waived. The limits come from concern about

---

[142] See argument above at text to footnotes 109–115.

[143] Gedye, Cuming, Wood, *Personal Property Securities in New Zealand* (2002) at p 380.

[144] Eliminating the distinctions between mortgages and charges, for example.

[145] UCC (revised) 9-602.

[146] These are: (1) Section 9-207(b)(4)(C), which deals with use and operation of the collateral by the secured party;

(2) Section 9-210, which deals with requests for an accounting and requests concerning a list of collateral and statement of account;

(3) Section 9-607(c), which deals with collection and enforcement of collateral;

(4) Sections 9-608(a) and 9-615(c) to the extent that they deal with application or payment of noncash proceeds of collection, enforcement, or disposition;

(5) Sections 9-608(a) and 9-615(d) to the extent that they require accounting for or payment of surplus proceeds of collateral;

(6) Section 9-609 to the extent that it imposes upon a secured party that takes possession of collateral without judicial process the duty to do so without breach of the peace;

(7) Sections 9-610(b), 9-611, 9-613, and 9-614, which deal with disposition of collateral;

(8) Section 9-615(f), which deals with calculation of a deficiency or surplus when a disposition is made to the secured party, a person related to the secured party, or a secondary obligor;

(9) Section 9-616, which deals with explanation of the calculation of a surplus or deficiency;

(10) Sections 9-620, 9-621, and 9-622, which deal with acceptance of collateral in satisfaction of obligation;

(11) Section 9-623, which deals with redemption of collateral;

(12) Section 9-624, which deals with permissible waivers; and

(13) Sections 9-625 and 9-626, which deal with the secured party's liability for failure to comply with this article.

the dangers of overreaching, and that no agreement can clog the equity of redemption:[147] a mixture of debtor protection and protection of other secured creditors. The Canadian PPSAs have similar provisions.[148] The New Zealand Act allows more extensive contracting out, reflecting the more protracted debate about whether there should be enforcement provisions in the Act at all.[149] Limits on contacting out were set merely to protect third party creditors,[150] which in practice meant other secured creditors, leaving freedom of contract between the parties. This may have been because consumer interests were already protected by the Credit (Repossession) Act 1997, and freedom of contract should prevail in business to business contracts.[151] In its Consultative Report, the Law Commission provisionally recommends the UCC model, and the Draft Regulations set out the provisions which cannot be waived.[152]

Conclusion

There are thus two choices: should all transactions within the scheme be reclassified as security interests, and should the legislation provide for the incidents of security. These two questions are closely interrelated, and depend largely on how far functionalism, as exemplified by Article 9 and the PPSAs, is embraced. The conceptual neatness of functionalism cannot be denied,[153] and the resulting unified prescriptive regime[154] can lead to efficiency and reduction in transaction costs. However, this is at the cost of cutting across the parties' allocation of risks and rewards, which can be given effect to in a more nuanced way by a system

---

[147] Official comment to UCC (revised) 9-602.

[148] OPSSA s 59(5), SPPSA s 56(3).

[149] Gedye, Cuming, Wood, *Personal Property Securities in New Zealand* (2002) at p 388.

[150] This proved difficult from a drafting point of view. Originally the legislation provided that "[t]he parties to a security agreement may make their own terms in respect of provisions in this Part to the extent that those provisions do not relate to the rights of third parties" (s 107 NZPPSA 1999). This was then amended, on the grounds that there would be uncertainty as to when a section related to the rights of third parties and the Act now provides that the parties can only contract out of certain listed provisions (The new s 107 was added as from 1 May 2002 by s 9 Personal Property Securities Amendment Act 2001).

[151] Gedye, Cuming, Wood, *Personal Property Securities in New Zealand* (2002) at p 388.

[152] DR 59(3). The list of provisions that cannot be waived is almost identical to that in UCC 9-602.

[153] Although it could be argued that the resulting regime is in fact complex, for example, the revised UCC Article 9.

[154] How far the Article 9/PPSA regime is prescriptive is a matter of some debate. UCC (revised) 9-201 (a) provides that "Except as otherwise provided in [the Uniform Commercial Code], a security agreement is effective according to its terms between the parties, against purchasers of the collateral, and against creditors". This is called the "flexibility principle" by some (Simmonds, Some Notes on the Reform of Personal Property Security Law in Australia, Chapter 8 in *Security over Personalty* (1994) Gillooly (Ed). However, since the parties are not free to agree on the location of title, or on whether the incidents of security apply to their transaction, flexibility as to form could be said to be somewhat illusory.

which preserves the location of title decided upon by the parties.[155] Such a system will necessarily be more complex. Technically, it should be possible to devise a regime which stipulated which transactions were registrable without recharacterising all such interests, although it would be necessary to decide on a definition of a registrable interest, or to draw up a list which left room for drafting innovations to be included. It would also be possible to provide for a first to file priority scheme to apply to those registrable interests, including priorities in relation to *bona fide* purchasers of the absolute title.[156] Certain problems might well have to be dealt with expressly: for example, the *Re Giffen* situation where an unregistered registrable interest was void against a liquidator, the liquidator's interest in the asset may have to be specifically provided for. Protection of other secured creditors could be achieved by notice provisions, and debtor protection by provisions regulating unconscionable transactions.[157] The choice, however, of whether a fully functional approach should be adopted is ultimately one of policy, balancing simplicity and efficiency against freedom of contract.

[155] See the argument in Dalhuisen, "Security and Ownership Based Funding Techniques" [1998] *European Business Law Review* 43.

[156] The Law Commission provisionally recommends that buyers and lessees of goods sold in the ordinary course of business take free of security interests (DR 31).

[157] The Law Commission is also currently considering the regulation of unfair terms in contracts, see Law Commission Consultation Paper 166 (2002).

Chapter 2

Reform of Laws on Security Interests in Lithuania: Convergence of Legal Concepts

Andrius Smaliukas

Introduction

Lithuania is one of the jurisdictions of Central and Eastern Europe that has recently reformed its law of secured transactions. Reform was urgently needed, because after the restoration of independence in 1990, Lithuania inherited the Soviet model of security law. This system was unsuitable for the needs of market economy. An entire legislation on security interests was contained in several short articles of a Civil Code.[1] The code was silent on the possibility of using ownership for security purposes and the only security interests that it expressly recognized were the close equivalents of the Roman *pignus* and *hypotheca*, yet classified as *ius in personam*.[2] Thus, the pre-reform security law was extremely unsophisticated and rarely employed in practice.

However, the Soviet model was an ideal starting point for comprehensive security law reform. First, it was not hostile towards non-possessory security interests. The Civil Code allowed a non-possessory security without any specific limitations on the scope of collateral being imposed, although it was not required to record this form of security right in a public registry.[3] Secondly, prior to the

1 Compare Ioffe, *Soviet Civil Law* (1988) 198-201.

2 Compare Oda, *Russian Commercial Law* (2002) 174; Dovgert, "Das ukrainische Recht der Mobiliarsicherheiten" in *Mobiliarsicherheiten in Osteuropa*, Drobnig, Roth, Trunk (Eds) (2002) 229.

3 This was not only different from the absolute majority of the Civil Law jurisdictions, but also from other former socialist states of Central and Eastern Europe, which were not part of the USSR. Soviet civil law ignored the so-called problem of the "false wealth", which is deemed to be created by the undisclosed non-possessory security rights. See Wood, "Comparative Financial Law: A Classification of the World's Jurisdictions", in *Making Commercial Law. Essays in Honour of Roy Goode*, Cranston (Ed) (1997) 38-41; Kaufhold, *Internationales und europäisches Mobiliarsicherungsrecht. Eine Analyse des gegenwärtigen Rechtszustands und der Möglichkeiten internationaler Koordinierung* (1999) 34. The main reason for such a fundamental difference in the treatment of security interests in socialist law is that the drafters of the socialist legislation on secured transactions did not intend it to

reform Lithuania did not have a working system of real security, hence there was no one, who could influence the lawmaking process, with an interest in preserving the *status quo*. Consequently, the process of reform was impeded neither by the desire of practitioners to save the system, which, though not ideal, still often functions well enough, nor the negative influence of many traditional legal concepts: factors which undermined security law reform in numerous economically advanced jurisdictions.[4]

Security law reform in Lithuania was structured in two stages. The aim of the first stage was to provide for a general framework of secured transactions law and, most importantly, to create a modern registry system for publication of security over movable property.[5] The legislation package was introduced in 1997, and the newly created registration system began to operate from 1 April 1998. The EBRD's Model Law on Secured Transactions inspired the substantive provisions of the Law on Charges over Movable Property[6] (*lit Kilnojamojo turto įkeitimo įstatymas*), which was the major legal enactment of the first stage of reform.[7] This stage of Lithuanian reform was internationally acclaimed – in the EBRD's Regional Survey of Secured Transactions Laws Lithuania was allocated to a small group of "advanced reform" countries.[8] The second stage of reform was mostly meant to crystallize the scope and the core concepts of the reform: namely, to what extent functionalism should influence the newly developed security legislation.[9] Although the new Civil Code brought into practice the major changes of

be widely used in practice. Compare Oda, "Law and Practice of Real Security Rights in Russia", 42 (2001) *JOR* 305; Drobnig, "Mobiliarsicherheiten in Osteuropa – Materielles Recht" in *Mobiliarsicherheiten in Osteuropa*, *op cit* fn 2.

4 See Dahan, "Secured Transactions Law in Western Advanced Economies: Exposing Myths" (2001) 16 *BJIBFL* 60, 66.

5 In this chapter the terms "security over movable property" and "chattel security" are used interchangeably unless from the context clearly stems otherwise.

6 The title of this act is sometimes translated into English using the umbrella term "pledge" instead of "charge".

7 On the EBRD Model Law and its impact on security law reform in the region see, for example, Simpson & Menze, "Ten Years of Secured Transactions Law Reform" [2000] (Autumn) *Law in Transition* 20; Mistelis, "The EBRD Model Law on Secured Transactions and its Impact on Collateral Law Reform in Central and Eastern Europe and the Former Soviet Union" (1998) 5 *JEEL* 455, 460; Dageförde, "Das besitzlose Mobiliarpfandrecht nach dem Modellgesetz für Sicherungsgeschäfte der Europäishen Bank für Wiederaufbau und Entwicklung" (1998) *ZEuP* 686. Lithuanian Law on Charges over Movable Property was discussed in Bartkus & Petrauskaite, "Lithuania's Law on Pledge over Movable Property" [2000] (Autumn), *Law in Transition* 50; Petrauskaitė, "Secured Transactions in Lithuania" in *Mobiliarsicherheiten in Osteuropa*, *op cit* fn 2 at pp 87-90.

8 Fairgrieve & Andenas, "Securing Progress in Collateral Law Reform: the EDRD's Regional Survey of Secured Transaction Laws" [2000] (Autumn) *Law in Transition* 28.

9 See generally Bridge *et al*, "Formalism, Functionalism, and Understanding the Law of Secured Transactions" (1999) 44 *McGill LJ* 567-664. Another major reason for the second stage of reform was the need to remedy a number of particular inadequacies of the legislation.

substantive law from 1 July 2001, this stage of reform was only finalized on 1 January 2003 when the new Code of Civil Procedure came into force.[10]

The purpose of this chapter is to provide an overview of the recently reformed Lithuanian secured transactions law, focusing exclusively on creation, perfection and priority of a real security over movable property, as well as the remedies of a secured creditor. It is also sought to reveal the concepts which explain the enactment of national legal provisions and will frequently represent the aim of the parliament to converge differing legal philosophies, underpinning a modern security law reform.[11]

The System of the New Lithuanian Law of Security over Movables

Form v Substance Approach

The Law on Charges over Movable Property, which laid the background for the future sophisticated reform of secured transactions law, was founded on the principles of functionalism. The uniform concept of registered charge embraced retention of title devices and leases for security purposes.[12] However, eventually Lithuania did not opt for the functional approach towards the security law. The new Civil Code, which, *inter alia*, repealed and replaced the Law on Charges over Movable Property, reveals a different philosophy of comprehensive secured transactions law reform, largely reflecting the theories that substantiated the modern security law reform in Quebec.[13] Thus, a wholesale formalistic reform was pursued: secured transactions remain classified according to their form rather than substance but, unless they are possessory, they must be recorded in a single public registry. Consequently, the Lithuanian Civil Code covers not only charges *stricto sensu*, but also their functional equivalents – the so-called quasi-security interests, which might bear some incidents of a charge.

---

[10] On the reform of Lithuanian private law in general see Mikelėnas, "Unification and Harmonization of Law at the Turn of the Millennium: the Lithuanian Experience" (2000-2) *Unif L Rev* 243-261; Mizaras & Nekrošius, "Das neue Zivil – und Zivilprozessrecht in Litauen" (2002) *ZEuP* 466-488.

[11] Compare Goode, "The Unidroit Draft Mobile Equipment Convention: Confluence of Legal Concepts and Philosophies" in *Mélanges en l'Honneur de Denis Tallon. D'ici, d'Ailleurs: Harmonisation et Dynamique du Droit* (1999) 69, 72-74; Dahan & McCormack, "International Influences and the Polish Law on Secured Transactions: Harmonization, Unification or What?" (2002-3) *Unif L Rev* 713, 718-722.

[12] See Article 19 of the Law on Charges over Movable Property.

[13] See Boodman & Macdonald, "How Far is Article 9 of the Uniform Commercial Code Exportable? A Return to Sources?" (1966) 27 *CBLJ* 250-277; Ciotola, "La Réforme des Sûretés sous la Code Civil du Québec" (1993) in *La Réforme du Code Civil*, Vol III, 303-443.

Charges Stricto Sensu

Charges *stricto sensu*, both possessory and non-possessory, are regulated by Book 4 of the new Civil Code, which is devoted to the rights *in rem.*[14] The Civil Code defines a charge as a real right belonging to the creditor and encumbering the ownership of the security provider, be it a debtor or a third party, created to secure the performance of an obligation.[15] Thus, a charge is an absolute right that can be enforced against everyone, entitling its holder to rights of pursuit and preference. Moreover, the fact the charge is held to be a real but not a personal right determines its enforceability in the debtor's insolvency. Nevertheless, the Civil Code upholds the accessory nature of the charge, expressly stating that the charge extinguishes when the secured obligation ceases to exist.[16] Apart from consensual charges the code also covers charges imposed by law. A charge over movable property is legally distinguished from a non-possessory security over immovables, which is called a hypothec[17] and is regulated in a separate section of Book 4 of the Civil Code.[18]

The charge itself is a uniform security right in the sense that, despite being non-possessory, it can cover all types of movable assets, both present and future. Moreover, it can secure all sorts of debts, including future debts, between all types of persons. Although the general principles of security law that are vested in the Civil Code can be construed as fully compatible with the concept of a universal charge,[19] which covers a fluctuating pool of movable assets, the Civil Code also retains a special charge over stock in trade, thus restating the provisions of the Law on Charges over Movable Property.[20] Only goods and raw materials owned by an enterprise can be charged pursuant to the rules on this charge over stock in trade, but in keeping with the notion of a universal business charge, the collateral can be described in broad terms instead of *in specie* and the debtor is entitled to dispose of the property free of charge in the ordinary course of his business.[21] The rationale

---

[14] Articles 4.198-4.228 of the Civil Code.

[15] Article 4.198 of the Civil Code. See also *dictum* of the decision of the Lithuanian Supreme Court delivered on 15 May 2000 in *AB Lietuvos žemės ūkio bankas v AB Šėtos sūrinė* (Case No 3K-3-545/2000).

[16] Article 4.200 of the Civil Code.

[17] In many of the official translations from Lithuanian into English "hypothec" is translated as "mortgage". This, however, is not precise. Under hypothec, unlike the mortgage, there is no conveyance of title, since the creditor *de jure* only receives limited proprietary rights and the ownership of collateral is vested in the debtor.

[18] Articles 4.170-4.197 of the Civil Code.

[19] See Wood, *Comparative Law of Security and Guaranties* 10-11 (1995). The best example of the universal security interest is English floating charge.

[20] See Article 4.202 of the Civil Code and compare Drobnig, "Mobiliarsicherheiten in Osteuropa - Materielles Recht", in *Mobiliarsicherheiten in Osteuropa*, *op cit* fn 2 at pp 7-9.

[21] This form of charge is somewhat similar to French *nantissement du fonds de commerce* and Russian *залог товаров в обороте*. See Malaurie & Aynès, *Les Sûretés. La Publicité Foncière*, 10th ed, (2000) 210-234; Zevrev, "Security issues under Russian Law" in

of the need to have such a special regime can be questioned. Apparently, it was included in the new Civil Code for practical reasons, as the charge of stock in trade, in spite of its limited scope, has been widely used since it was introduced by the first stage of reform.[22]

Aside for the charge over stock in trade, which is the only legal exception from the concept of a charge as a uniform security right, some macro tangible movables are by law presumed to be immovable property and, therefore, subject to the regime of hypothecs. These are seagoing vessels[23] and civil aircrafts, including the aircraft engines that, once installed on the airframe, are deemed to be part of an aircraft.[24]

A possessory charge is deemed to be created and perfected after the conclusion of a written contract. The time when actual or constructive transfer of collateral to the creditor occurs does not determine the date of creation of this form of a charge: this is the moment when consensus is expressed and reduced to writing. In the case of a non-possessory charge, a written contract will not suffice for its creation even as between the parties. The parties must draw up an official standard form document,[25] called a Charge deed (*lit įkeitimo lakštas*),[26] which must be approved by the notary public. A Charge deed enshrines all the major clauses of the transaction creating a charge. If the security agreement has been concluded in a foreign language, it must be translated into Lithuanian using the form of a Charge deed. Once the Charge deed has been approved by the notary public, it must be registered with the Hypothecary Register (*lit Hipotekos registras*). The requirement of registration applies to all non-possessory charges of movable property. Under Lithuanian law, registration is not merely a precondition for a perfection of a charge, because unregistered non-possessory charges are absolutely void.[27] Therefore, the act of registration creates a non-possessory charge, and simultaneously makes it enforceable against the third parties. This seems strange

---

Emerging Financial Markets and Secured Transactions, Norton, Andenas (Eds) (1998) at pp 298-299.

22 See Central Hypothecary Office, *Report on Hypothecary Register 3 years activity*, published at <http://www.lhr.lt/LimoE/statistics3.htm>.

23 Hypothecs over the seagoing ships also fall under the *sui generis* regime of the Law on the mercantile shipping, enacted on 24 September 1996.

24 Compare Arundell & Wilson, "The Need for International Secured Transactions and Leasing Rules for Aircraft Engines Through the Proposed Unidroit Convention" (1998) 23 *Air & Space Law* 283-286.

25 The form of a Charge deed was approved by the Decree of the Minister of Justice of 26 February 1998, as amended on 20 February 2002. The detailed instructions on filing the form of a Charge deed were approved by the Decree of the Minister of Justice of 22 April 2004, which amended the Decree of 20 February 2002.

26 This term is sometimes translated into English as "Collateral bond" - see Bartkus & Petrauskaite, "Lithuania's Law on Pledge over Movable Property" [2000] (Autumn), *Law in Transition* 52.

27 However, validity of an underlying obligation is not affected.

in the context of the new Civil Code,[28] as the rationale for the requirement of registration is that charges can be enforced against third parties rather than their creation *per se*.[29]

Quasi-security Interests

The new Lithuanian Civil Code extends registration requirements to a number of quasi-security interests. It was decided to cover only ownership-based structures that, from the non-functionalistic perspective, vest in the creditor the real rights of an owner. Such transactions include transfer of ownership for security purposes and retention of title devices. Since quasi-security interests were not recharacterized as charges, each type of transaction is regulated separately following the usual pandect system of the private law codifications, based on a Civilian tradition. Therefore, every transaction that under the Civil Code can give rise to quasi-security interests is regulated in Book 6, which is devoted to the different aspects of the law of obligations. These transactions are: sales with the right of redemption,[30] financial leases, installment sales with reservation of title,[31] general assignments of receivables and, finally, factoring.[32]

Transfers of ownership for security purposes All transfers of ownership in movables other than receivables from the debtor to the creditor, if contracted for security purposes, fall under the regime of sale with the right of redemption.[33] The provisions of the Civil Code regulating this contract can cover, for example, a sale and leaseback as well as other structures, based on the retransfer of ownership in

[28] The general rationale of a registration, stemming from the Article 1.75 of the Civil Code, is the enforceability of rights against the third parties and settlement of priorities, but not the constitutive effect *inter partes*. This notion was comprehensively developed by the civil law reform in Quebec. See Charron, "De la publicité des droits" in *La Réforme du Code Civil* (1993) Vol III, 589-669.

[29] Recent case law of the Lithuanian Supreme Court indicates the possibility of a fundamental shift towards this position, since the Court ruled that a charge must not be deemed void *inter partes* if the registration had not been completed due to a fault of the Hypothecary Register. See *ratio decidendi* of the decision of the Lithuanian Supreme Court delivered on 8 October 2001 in *A.Siškuvienė v Litimeks bank (in liquidation) and UAB Adolta* (Case No 3K-3-916/2001).

[30] Articles 6.417-6.418 of the new Civil Code.

[31] Articles 6.567-6.574 of the Civil Code govern leasing or finance lease, whereas instalment sales with the reservation of title or conditional sales are regulated by Articles 6.411-6.416 of the Code.

[32] Articles 6.101-6.110 and 6.903-6.912 of the new Civil Code.

[33] Repurchase agreements of securities entered into between the central bank - Bank of Lithuania - and any commercial bank, operating in Lithuania, are not recharacterized as a sale with the right to redeem and remain regulated pursuant to special rules adopted by the Bank of Lithuania. They must not be registered with the Hypothecary Register.

collateral. Although such a transaction generally remains regulated as a sale, there are two main legal aspects that distinguish it from the so-called true sales.[34]

Firstly, unless it is a consumer credit transaction, a sale with the right to redeem must be recorded in the Hypothecary Register.[35] Otherwise it cannot be enforced against third parties. It is noteworthy that even if the sale with the right to redeem does not fulfill the function of security, it must still be filed in the Hypothecary Register. This requirement solves two problems. First, it eliminates the potential difficulties of characterization of sales for security purposes. Second, the "false wealth" problem can be created not only by non-possessory quasi-security interests, but also by a number of other undisclosed rights, including true leases and all sales with the right to redeem. Therefore, all these transactions, subject to some further conditions, must be publicly disclosed in order to be enforceable *erga omnes*. The sale with the right of redemption is registered with the Hypothecary Register pursuant to its formal legal classification. The Hypothecary Register keeps separate registers for charges *stricto sensu* and notifiable transactions that usually give rise to quasi-security interests. Although there is only one register for all such transactions, any interested person will acquire the information about the exact form of the quasi-security interest.

Secondly, a sale with the right to redeem, when used as quasi-security, bears some incidents of a charge. The creditor can only satisfy his claim pursuant to the fundamental equitable principles of security law. That means the Civil Code does not allow the creditor to retain unconditionally the ownership in the collateral on the default of the debtor, as the creditor is required to account for any surplus if the value of the property exceeds the amount of the debt. This shift from the freedom of contract is justified on the basis of public policy, because it is perceived that the principle of equity requires any surplus to be available to the general body of creditors.

Retention of title All retention of title devices are regulated by the Civil Code as installment sales with reservation of title.[36] The retention of title bears no incidents of a charge, yet it must be registered with the Hypothecary Register in order to be enforceable against the third parties. However, the requirement of registration does not apply to the retention of title devices used in consumer credit transactions. Further, the Civil Code tries to impose indirectly equitable principles of security

---

[34] Compare Cuming, "The Internationalization of Secured Financing Law: the Spreading Influence of the Concepts UCC, Article 9 and its Progeny" in *Making Commercial Law. Essays in Honour of Roy Goode*, *op cit* fn 3 at p 518.

[35] However, any registration will not be relevant to the sales with the right to redeem that fall within the meaning of "title transfer financial collateral arrangements", as it is understood in the Directive 2002/47/EC of the European Parliament and of the Council of 6 June 2002 on financial collateral arrangements (OJ L168, 2002), provided such a transaction also satisfies other requirements of scope laid down by the Lithuanian legislation that implements the Directive.

[36] The term "instalment sale" in this context is somewhat misleading, as Articles 6.411-6.416 of the Civil Code can also be applied when the purchase price is not paid in instalments.

law, and limit the creditor's right to foreclose, if the debtor defaults after more than half of a purchase price has already been paid. The provisions of the code that limit foreclosure are not mandatory and, therefore, it is possible for the parties to contract out of them. The Civil Code does not expressly regulate any other retention of title clauses but simple ones.[37] However, the requirement of registration should undoubtedly be construed as also embracing more sophisticated retention of title structures, for instance all monies clauses or retention of title in proceeds or goods used in manufacturing other goods. Rules governing the drafting of formal applications, which are filed to the Hypothecary Register in order to register the creditors interests under sales with the reservation of title, allow the parties to elaborate the scope of creditor's interest. Therefore, the exact nature of creditors rights – be it a simple retention of title or a more complex structure – is available to those who might search the register.

Financial leases The substantive provisions of the new Civil Code that regulate the tripartite financial leasing are in line with the 1988 Unidroit Convention on International Financial Leasing, although Lithuania is not a party to this international instrument.[38] They are also applicable to bipartite financial as well as operating leases. Unlike some Civil Law jurisdictions, the lessee's option to purchase the leased equipment is not regarded as *conditio sine qua non* for the rules on financial leasing to be applicable. On the other hand, a clause providing that the lessee has an unconditional right to eventually become an owner of the property leased does not requalify the transaction as a conditional sale. It was perceived by the drafters of the Civil Code that leasing is too specific and versatile for any attributes of a charge to be imposed.[39] For example, the lessor is deemed to retain a full ownership[40] and hence upon substantial default of the lessee he is entitled to both exercise all the rights of an owner and enforce any liquidated damages clause. The lessee, however, is granted the rights of quiet possession. Thus, the only link that connects leasing with other quasi-security devices is the requirement of registration in the Hypothecary Register. Yet even this rule is not all-inclusive and bears a significant exception made for the interests of the leasing industry. Only leases of unregistered movable property must be recorded in the Hypothecary Register. If the title in leased movables is registered in some other state register, as is the case with the cars, trucks and other vehicles, it is sufficient for the lessor to publish his title in that register. This registration, despite its

[37] Compare Davies, "Retention of Title Clauses and Non-Possessory Security Interests: A Secured Credit Regime within the European Union?" in *Security Interests in Mobile Equipment*, Davies (Ed) (2002) at pp 358-361.

[38] On the 1988 Ottawa Convention see Stanford, "From Ottawa to Cape Town: Unidroit's Role in the Modernisation of the Law Governing Leasing and the Taking of Security" in *Security Interests in Mobile Equipment*, Davies (Ed) (2002) at pp 436, 448-464.

[39] Compare Goode, *Commercial Law*, 2nd ed (1995) 776.

[40] If a lessor is not an owner, as the case may be eg in a sub-leasing arrangement, his rights can nevertheless be protected in bankruptcy of a lessee. The lessor's right to claim liquidated damages does not depend on ownership of the leased property.

different purpose and limited search ability, will have the same legal effect as publication of quasi-security rights in the Hypothecary Register – that is, the lessor's rights will become enforceable *erga omnes*. Finally, even though it was decided not to extend the registration requirements to ordinary leases of movable property, since the practicality arguments once again prevailed over the "false wealth" problem, all leases of immovables with tenure for more than a year must be registered with the Register of land and other real property.[41] The failure to comply with this requirement also renders the rights of the lessor unenforceable against the third parties.

Assignments of receivables Under the new Lithuanian Civil Code receivables can be assigned for security purposes either pursuant to general rules on the assignment of claims or to special provisions dealing with factoring. The rules of factoring are more elaborate, yet this structure can only be employed provided a bank or other profit-making legal person[42] acts as a factor. The Civil Code does not impose any direct restrictions on the use of bulk assignments or the transfers of future receivables. Further, in the case of factoring an anti-assignment clause does not invalidate the assignment as between the assignee and the debtor under the assigned receivable. There are no specific requirements as to the form of the factoring contract stipulated in the code, although generally an assignment of claims must correspond to the form of the original contract that gives rise to the assigned receivables. Therefore, the safest, yet not always necessary, option is for a notary to approve bulk transfers of receivables, contracted pursuant to the general rules of assignments.

One of the most difficult issues faced in the course of the second stage of security law reform was the choice of perfection rule for assignments of receivables for security purposes. It seems to be a good argument that the assignments of receivables used as quasi-security should be perfected pursuant to the same rules as absolute assignments; and these rules should be based on the public notice.[43] This would allow to avoid tricky questions of classification and, moreover, would solve the "false wealth" problem, because there is no external sign of any assignment of receivables. However, it was decided that the requirement to register all assignments of receivables would be impractical and too burdensome for the interested parties to comply with. Instead of providing for more sophisticated rules, which, for instance, require to register only bulk assignments,[44] the new Civil Code dropped the entire idea of public registration of assignment and pursued the principle of notification of the debtor. The failure to

---

[41] The register of immovable property is kept by the state enterprise Centre of Registers. This enterprise also maintains the central register of legal persons.

[42] As it stems from Article 6.904 of the Civil Code, the profit-making legal persons can engage in factoring activities subject to special restrictions, imposed by law. None of them currently exist.

[43] See Schwarcz, "A perfection system for cross-border receivables financing" (1999) 20 *UPA J Int'l Econ L* 455-456.

[44] Compare Article 1642 of the Civil Code of Quebec.

give notice to the debtor makes assignment unperfected, since the assignee cannot enforce its rights *erga omnes*. Thus, the sanction for not giving notice is even stricter than the traditional English rule, stemming from *Dearle v Hall*, where it merely results in lack of priority to an assignee who notifies the debtor first.[45] The rule that is enshrined in the Lithuanian Civil Code is not fully satisfactory not only because its application might lead to fraud and injustice, but also since it creates a potential problem of classification of charges of receivables that are absolutely void unless registered and assignments of receivables for security purposes, which must not be registered *in toto*. The problem of characterization is not so serious when receivables are assigned for security purposes under a contract of factoring, since the Civil Code here uses precise language and the courts are unlikely to reclassify this transaction as a charge. The situation is less clear where receivables are assigned under the general rules for transfer of claims. If Lithuania joins the United Nations Convention on the Assignment of Receivables in International Trade, which is very likely, it would be sensible to adopt the principles proposed in the Articles 4 and 5,[46] thus subjecting the perfection of assignments to public notice requirements, achieved by their registration in the Hypothecary Register. Finally, although under the new Civil Code assignments of receivables that are used as security are not publicly registered, they bear the same incidents of a charge as are imposed on sales with the right to redeem. Therefore, a creditor must account to an assignor for any surplus received from the collection of assigned receivables.

Registration of Charges and Quasi-security Interests

General Observations

All non-possessory charges over movable property and the quasi-security interests mentioned above are registered with a single institution – the Hypothecary Register, which is operated by the state. Apart from registering security over movables, the Hypothecary Register also records hypothecs over immovables, grants execution orders to secured creditors and provides for the official or unofficial information on the data stored to all interested persons.[47] Security interests have only to be registered in this single registry – double registration in property or companies registers is not required, because the Hypothecary Register

---

[45] *Dearle v Hall* (1828) 3 Russ 1.

[46] See Bazinas, "UNCITRAL's Contribution to the Unification of Receivables Financing Law: the United Nations Convention on the Assignment of Receivables in International Trade" (2002) *Unif L Rev* 62-64.

[47] The detailed coverage of Hypothecary Register's functions, as well as other relevant information, is published in English at its official web site <http://www.lhr.lt/LimoE/e_main.htm>.

itself electronically transfers the data on the registrations made to other relevant state registers.[48]

The Hypothecary Register consists of the Central Hypothecary Office and Hypothecary divisions that are the part of the general competence courts of first instance (*lit apylinkės teismas*). The Central Hypothecary Office is primarily responsible for the maintenance of a central database that accumulates all relevant information about registrations made, and also provides information on the registered data to the public. Instant registration of chattel security interests is conducted by Hypothecary judges, who sit in one of the fifteen territorial Hypothecary divisions.[49]

Differences Between the Systems of Registration of Charges and Quasi-security Interests

Although charges and quasi-security interests are registered by the same institution, there are some conceptual differences between the systems of their registration.

First, charges over movable property are registered under the document-registration system, which requires filing of the Charge deed that must have already been certified by the notary public. Thus, the inputting data can be only presented in a hardcopy form. On the other hand, a notice-registration procedure is used for the publication of quasi-security interests.[50] However, the content of the application to the Hypothecary Register is quite extensive. The data that identifies the parties and indicates the debtor's consent to file a quasi-security interest must be provided and also a description of the property subject to the security and of the contracts that create the creditor's rights.[51] Since the Hypothecary Register is fully computerized and even the Charge deeds in the process of their registration are transformed into electronic format in order to enable interested persons to conduct the on-line searches of the register,[52] it would be consistent to suppose that notice-

---

[48] Except charges of certain types of industrial property, such as trademarks or patents, that must also be recorded in the State Patent Bureau.

[49] See Articles 542-553 of the new Code of Civil Procedure.

[50] On the differences between notice-registration and document-registration see the Law Commission Consultation Paper No 164, *Registration of Security Interests: Company Charges and Property other than Land*, para 4.2-4.14. This document can be accessed at <www.lawcom.gov.uk/library/lccp164/cp164.pdf>; Cuming, "Considerations in the design of an International Registry for interests in mobile equipment" (1999-2) *Unif L Rev* 275, 281.

[51] On this problem, for example, see Dolan, Vegter, "A voluntary filing system for secured financing transactions in the European Union" (1988) 6 *European Review of Private Law* 219-221; Cuming, "The Internationalization of Secured Financing Law: the Spreading Influence of the Concepts UCC, Article 9 and its Progeny" in *Making Commercial Law. Essays in Honour of Roy Goode, op cit* fn 3 at p 50.

[52] If the Hypothecary judge decides to register a charge, the relevant data is instantly put in the local database, which is kept in the computer terminal of the Hypothecary division in question. The data must be sent to the central computer terminal maintained by the Central

registration of quasi-security interests could be processed electronically. Nevertheless, the recent Decree of the Lithuanian Ministry of Justice that regulates the procedure of registration of quasi-security interests and other registrable transactions surprisingly provides for extremely undeveloped rules, which, if interpreted literally, could raise serious doubts whether it will be possible to effectively register on-line.

Secondly, whilst filing of a non-possessory charge effects its creation, registration of quasi-security interests merely perfects creditor's rights by making them enforceable *erga omnes* and sets their priority. However, the priority status of charges is determined not by the time of their actual registration, but by the moment a Charge deed is presented before the Hypothecary Register, provided an application is successful and eventually results in the registration of a charge.

Finally, unlike registration of quasi-security interests, the role that the Hypothecary judge performs in the filing of charges is not simply a managerial one, where only a compliance with formalities is being screened. Here the judge must ensure that the entire transaction is contracted in accordance with the relevant legal provisions.[53] Since a Hypothecary judge must proceed promptly and usually deliver the decision on the issue of registration in one working day without having heard any of the parties,[54] the essence of prior notarization of a Charge deed is to guarantee that the security provider has expressed a genuine consent to create a charge. Such role of a Hypothecary judge can be explained on two grounds. First, if the registration is a precondition of a creation of a charge, then the judge cannot authorize any illegal transactions. Secondly and most importantly, the data contained in the register is by law presumed to be materially correct and the Hypothecary Register can be held liable for any damage caused by errors attributable to it.

In fact the whole registration system of charges was developed on the premise that the registry data must be deemed formally accurate, that is, corresponding to a hard copy of a Charge deed, and materially correct. This was thought to be a condition *sine qua non* for a fast and non-contentious procedure for the satisfaction of creditors' claims.[55] It is on default of the debtor, especially if the debtor becomes insolvent, when security matters most and a modern security law should provide the creditor for the quick and effective means of redress. If the Charge deed had not been screened by the judge upon the creation of the charge and, consequently, the particulars it contains would not have been deemed correct, redress without the interference of the court or even without the need for the creditor to obtain a judgment through the ordinary civil proceedings might be incompatible with the otherwise applicable legal principles that limit self-help and

---

Hypothecary Office within twenty-four hours. The charge is deemed to be created after the data has entered the central database.

[53] See *dictum* of the decision of the Lithuanian Supreme Court delivered on 30 May 2000 in *Re AB Dumbla* (Case No 3K-3-643/2001).

[54] Article 549 of the new Code of Civil Procedure.

[55] See Nekrošius, "Vorschriften über die Verpfändung von Mobilien sowie über das Prinzip der Prozeßkonzentration" in *Mobiliarsicherheiten in Osteuropa op cit* fn 2 at p 99.

require every dispute to be settled in court. This problem is faced by many Civil Law dominated jurisdictions. On the one hand, it would be desirable to ensure the speedy and very cheap registration of security interests, which, as the practice of the USA, Canadian Common Law jurisdictions and, more recently, New Zealand indicates, can be achieved with electronically conducted notice-registration that serves merely as a warning to the interested parties, enabling them to make further enquiries.[56] On the other hand, such notice-registration based system would not be fully compatible with fast execution from the collateral, because the civil procedure laws would require a creditor to prove his case – registration like this only presumes the debt and, hence, a security might still exist. In case of quasi-security interests, which are ownership-based structures, the latter problem is less compelling, as upon the debtor's material default a creditor can usually unilaterally terminate the secured contract out of court and exercise his ownership rights. Therefore, the notice-registration system with its warning provision philosophy can be perfectly employed. However, if a debtor refuses to transfer the property to a creditor then, despite of being an owner, the creditor would still be forced to bring a case before a court.

Registration of Charges: Practical Assessment

Even though theoretically a notice-registration system, which merely perfects security interests and puts the searcher "on notice" that the secured party might claim a security interests in the collateral, is more modern than document-filing based mechanisms, where the input of data can not practically be conducted on-line,[57] the primary question applied to a registration system should be whether it adequately serves the needs of the parties to financing transactions.[58] In this regard, the Lithuanian system of registration of charges so far has been functioning fairly soundly. Despite the fact that registration can not be obtained immediately after the parties have agreed upon the terms of a secured transaction and prospective registration is impossible, the Lithuanian business community currently finds the period of five working days, which is usually sufficient to carry out the process from the notarization of a Charge deed till its actual registration by the Hypothecary judge, quite satisfactory. Indeed, a creditor can secure priority over the competing claimants in a couple of hours, as to this end a Charge deed must only be submitted to the Hypothecary judge, whereas the initial notarization

[56] See Ziegel, "The New Provincial Chattel Security Law Regimes" (1991) 70 *Can B Rev* 683; McCormack, "Personal Property Security Law Reform in England and Canada" [2002] *JBL* 113, at pp 122-123.

[57] Compare Wohlers, "The registry: essential element in secured lending" (2001) 18 *Ariz J Int'l & Comp Law* 711-719; Cuming, "Considerations in the design of an International Registry for interests in mobile equipment" (1999) *Unif L Rev* 275, at p 281.

[58] Mooney, Jr, "Relationship between the prospective UNIDROIT International Registry, Revised Uniform Commercial Code Article 9 and national civil aviation registries" (1999) *Unif L Rev* 335 at pp 337-339.

in general[59] can be promptly conducted. Moreover, registration fees, which cover both the stamp duty for the registration in the Hypothecary Register and the notarization costs, are also relatively low, since they cannot exceed seven hundred Lithuanian litas.[60] Though in absolute figures registration of a charge, apart from the representation and other legal costs, is a moderately cheap process, the notice filing of quasi-security interests is less expensive, because in this case a registration fee is only twenty litas. Further, the registration system is centralized, fully computerized and easily accessible at modest cost using the Internet. All interested persons can search and receive the registered data, including the particulars of a charge, electronically. In addition, every person can rely on the registered information, as it is by law deemed materially correct, and it is not necessary to contact the parties of the transaction in order to find out whether the charge still exists and what its terms are. Finally, registration provides constructive notice both of the fact of the creation of the charge and on its content. While such a rule might be criticized as potentially hindering the rights of bona fide purchasers,[61] it has two significant legal effects. First, every subsequent secured creditor, purchaser or other acquirer, who acquires a legal interest in the collateral subject to the duly registered prior charge, would obtain rights in the collateral subordinated to that charge, unless they succeeded in proving that they did not have notice of the charge and, due to some special circumstances, could not have reasonably been expected to search the registry. This rule is not fully applicable to charges over stock in trade and, despite some uncertainty in the law, to the universal charge in relation to collateral that a chargor can dispose of in the ordinary course of business, as bona fide purchasers are not bound by these forms of a charge. Secondly, negative pledge clauses are enforceable against everyone except *bona fide* purchases.[62] This outcome stems from the fact that such a clause can be registered as a part of the content of the Charge deed, so that the doctrine of constructive notice is extended to negative pledge clauses.

Major Trends for Improvement of the Current System

Nevertheless, the legal provisions that regulate registration of non-possessory charges do have some important shortcomings. First, the registration process is unreasonably burdensome, as there are too many formalities to comply with. Most importantly, the mandatory requirement to certify the Charge deed by the notary

---

[59] Exceptions to this general practice are not uncommon.

[60] From 2 February 2002 the official litas-EURO exchange rate has been fixed by the Bank of Lithuania at 0.29 EURO for 1 litas. Thus, the maximum fee, including the notary costs, payable for the registration of a charge is 203 EURO. The fees, which depend on the value of collateral and the amount of the secured debt, are set by Resolution of Lithuanian Government No 184, enacted 17 February 1998 and Decree of Lithuanian Minister of Justice No 203, passed 27 September 2001.

[61] See Calnan, "Registration of company charges: proposals for reform" (2001) 16 *BJIBFL* 54-56.

[62] On this concept see Goode, *Legal problems of Credit and Security*, 2nd ed (1988) at p 5.

public can hardly be justified, because the Hypothecary judge subsequently conducts the similar legal screening of the entirety of its terms and conditions. The argument that a notary is better placed to check the presence of a debtor's genuine consent for creation of a charge cannot be upheld. The judge has wide procedural powers, which could be applied to solve the matter, if in certain and, as a practice indicates, exceptional cases doubts arise that the attempted registration might be fraudulent or speculative. Thus, the elimination of the need to notarize the Charge deed would make the existing document-filing system half as expensive and avoid situations where delay in registration occurs due to long notarization process. Secondly, the effect of the registration, which is deemed a condition *sine qua non* for a charge to exist even *inter partes*, is too restrictive. Though it is true that such concept of the effects of the registration was inspired by the equivalent provisions of the Civil Code of Quebec, it is inconsistent with the purpose and effect of the registration of quasi-security interests. This might create problems of characterization, since the form of unregistered security interest determines its validity as between the parties. Moreover, it might be reasonably questioned whether the sanction of absolute nullity resulting from the failure to comply with the current requirements for the registration of charges constitutes a disproportionate "deprivation" of a person's possessions in contravention of Article 1 of Protocol 1 of the European Convention on Human Rights.[63] The existing document-registration system would become more flexible and consistent if the registration is merely set as a condition for the enforceability of a charge *erga omnes* but not its creation. As it has already been mentioned, the recent practice of the Lithuanian Supreme Court demonstrates the partial shift to this direction.[64] Finally, since the legally binding instruction of the Ministry of Justice that sets the requirements for the drafting of the Charge deeds is extremely unsophisticated and the Civil Code is silent on the matter, practical problems arise whether it is possible when registering a charge to identify the collateral using a generic description. This is essential for the proper functioning of universal charges, yet the instruction, apart from charge over stock in trade, only provides for the possibility of charging separate items but not universality of assets, described in general terms. Such regulation must be amended for it is incompatible with the overall philosophy of the security law reform, as enshrined in the new Civil Code, which supports the prevailing view in contemporary legal doctrine that a universal security interest should be recognized as important feature of modern security law.[65] At least this problem can as well be solved by the creative jurisprudence of

---

[63] See The Law Commission, *Registration of Security Interests: Company Charges and Property other than Land* Consultation Paper No 164, para 4.41-4.42.

[64] See the text in fn 30 above.

[65] Goode, "The Protection of Interests in Movables in Transnational Commercial Law" (1998) *Unif L Rev* 458-459; *Possible future work in the security interests*, UNCITRAL (A/CN.9/496) 8-9 (2001). For the position to the contrary see Dalhuisen, "The Conditional Sale is Alive and Well!" in *Emerging Financial Markets and Secured Transactions*, Norton, Andenas (Eds) (1988) at pp 86-87; Drobnig, "A Comparative Introduction to Security over

the Lithuanian Supreme Court, as the Lithuanian legal system upholds the doctrine of *stare decisis* so that judicial precedent becomes a legally binding source of law.[66]

Issues of Enforcement and Priority

The Rules of Priority

The priority rules of secured creditors' claims are clear and systematically coherent. A creditor, who holds a duly registered charge over movable property, can enjoy absolute priority in relation to all other unsecured creditors, both preferential and ordinary, and all subsequent secured creditors, unless a subordination agreement has been made.[67] It should be noted that the new Civil Code does not allow subsequent charging of collateral with a non-possessory charge if it has been already subject to possessory security.[68] This is necessary for consistency of the priority rules, as priority between concurrent non-possessory charges over the same collateral is determined by the date of application for registration with the Hypothecary Register, while priority of possessory charges is fixed at the moment the relevant contract has been concluded. As it had already been pointed out, a non-possessory charge obtains priority not from the date it is registered but from the moment a Charge deed has been delivered to the Hypothecary judge.[69] However, the priority from the date of application is only secured if an application is not denied and the Charge deed is subsequently registered with the Hypothecary Register. Furthermore, the insolvency legislation also upholds absolute priority of secured creditors' rights. The new Lithuanian insolvency laws, namely the Law on the Enterprise Bankruptcy and the Law on the Enterprise Restructuring, that were enacted on 20 March 2001 and replaced the Lithuanian bankruptcy legislation of 1997 can generally be described as exceptionally creditor-oriented, where the implications of the rescue culture are only rudimentary.[70] This makes a position of secured creditors particularly solid. Those creditors who are protected by duly disclosed ownership-based quasi-security interests are not subject to the priority rules described above, as they enjoy super priority status. However, the position of the creditors under transfer of

---

Movables and Intangibles" in *Emerging Financial Markets and Secured Transactions*, Norton, Andenas, (Eds) (1998) at pp 11-12.

[66] This stems from Article 23 of the Lithuanian Law on Courts. See Mikelėnas, "Unification and Harmonization of Law at the Turn of the Millennium: the Lithuanian Experience" *Unif L Rev* 245 (2000-2).

[67] See Article 4.198 of the Civil Code together with Article 754 of the Code of Civil Procedure.

[68] Article 4.211 of the Civil Code.

[69] Article 4.212 of the Civil Code.

[70] Compare Omar, "International Insolvency, Security Interests and Creditor Protection" in *Security Interests in Mobile Equipment op cit* fn 37 at p 298.

ownership for security purposes arrangements, retention of title devices and financial leases might be subordinated to contractual or legal rights *in rem*, which were established prior in time. Finally, the priority between the competing assignees of receivables is determined by the "first to notify the debtor" principle.

Justification of an Absolute Priority Rule

Although the absolute priority rule has been extensively criticized for unjustifiably overprotecting the interests of secured creditors at the expense of all others, in particular nonadjusting creditors of a debtor,[71] the decision of the Lithuanian government to opt for the principle of absolute priority should be considered as the right one at the right time. There are two major reasons to support this submission. First, this rule increased the practical application of charges over movable property and thus promoted the development of the Lithuanian economy.[72] The official data provided by the Hypothecary Register indicates that on 1 April 2001, that is, three years after the reformed chattel security system began to function, charges over movable property secured a larger amount of corporate debts than hypothecs over immovables. Secondly, prior to the reform of security law, Lithuanian legal system was obviously too much debtor-oriented. Security interests, though rarely used, were subordinated to a number of preferential claims, including taxes and customs duties. Creditors lacked reliable official information on the legal status of the debtors and their property. Therefore, it was quite easy for a bad faith debtor to undermine the legitimate interests of his creditors. The atmosphere of legal uncertainty made the country's credit market less attractive for lenders, particularly foreign ones. At present the law generally allows the creditor to take security which would adequately protect his rights upon the default of a debtor.

Enforcement of Secured Creditor's Rights

In the event of a debtor's default the law provides for quick, effective and relatively cheap enforcement of chargee's rights.[73] This is true both within and outside the debtor's insolvency, as insolvency of a debtor does not materially hinder the enforcement of the creditor's rights. Even though execution from the

---

[71] See *inter alia* Bebchuk & Fried, "The Uneasy Case for the Priority of Secured Claims in Bankruptcy: Further Thoughts and a Reply to Critics" (1997) 82 *Cornell L Rev* 1281-1349; Drukarczyk, "Secured Debt, Bankruptcy, and the Creditors' Bargain Model" (1991) 14 *International Review of Law and Economics* 204-205; Kanda & Levmore, "Explaining Creditor Priorities" (1994) 80 *Va L Rev* 2103-2154; LoPucki, "The Unsecured Creditor's Bargain" (1994) 80 *Va L Rev* 1892-1915.

[72] On a theoretical discussion whether security is really efficient and contributes to the country's economic growth see Ali, *The Law of Secured Finance. An International Survey of Security Interests over Personal Property* (2002) 33-46; Fleisig, "Economic Functions of Security in a Market Economy" in *Emerging Financial Markets and Secured Transactions*, Norton, Andenas, (Eds) (1998) 15-36.

[73] See Nekrošius, "Vorschriften über die Verpfändung von Mobilien sowie über das Prinzip der Prozeßkonzentration" in *Mobiliarsicherheiten in Osteuropa op cit* fn 2 at pp 95-99.

collateral provided by the insolvent debtor[74] is subject to a provisional stay imposed by insolvency legislation, this usually does not preclude a secured creditor from obtaining a satisfaction of his claims in a commercially reasonable manner. Legal provisions on the enforcement of charges are not generally applicable to quasi-security interests. However, when a quasi-security interest bears the incident of a charge, such as the requirement that a creditor accounts for any surplus, the rules on enforcement of charges are applied *mutatis mutandis*. Otherwise the rights of a quasi-security holder are those of an owner.

In order to start enforcement a chargee does not need to obtain a judgment of the court. Instead, in the event of a default of a debtor, a secured creditor has to serve a debtor with a written notice of enforcement, requiring discharge of the debt immediately after the notice has been received. The notice of enforcement must be sent via the Hypothecary judge.[75] This rule is not applicable to possessory charges, as a chargee in possession is entitled to exercise his security rights without the intervention of the Hypothecary judge or any other official. Once the notice has been served on the debtor certain legal restrictions are imposed on him. First, after having received the execution notice, the debtor is precluded from selling, leasing or otherwise disposing of the collateral. Secondly, the debtor is obliged to return the collateral to the creditor immediately. If the debtor fails to return the collateral, the creditor is entitled to apply to a Hypothecary judge with a request to seize the collateral. The Hypothecary judge has to take a decision within three working days of the creditor's request. The procedure is purely documentary, since the sitting of the court is conducted *in camera* without the parties or their legal representatives being heard.[76] The decision of a Hypothecary judge becomes immediately enforceable and is usually sent to a bailiff to be executed under the rules of the Code of Civil Procedure. Furthermore, if the debtor fails to settle the creditor's claims in the statutory twenty days period of grace,[77] the creditor is entitled to sell the collateral and satisfy his claims out of the proceeds of sale. The new Civil Code gives the parties the right to agree that this period should be reduced by up to ten days. Moreover, the Charge deed can provide expressly for the private sale of collateral. The speed and overall effectiveness of execution proceedings are considerably enhanced by the rule that a Hypothecary judge is not entitled to solve any disputes on law or on fact, which arise between the parties to the secured transaction.[78] This is because of the legal presumption that all the information

[74] Which means there must be judicial or extrajudicial insolvency proceedings launched.

[75] See, for example, the *dictum* of the decision of the Lithuanian Supreme Court delivered on 26 February 2001 in *Volvo Truck Corporation v UAB Motor Servis* (Case No 3K-3-22/2001).

[76] See the decision of the Lithuanian Supreme Court delivered on 23 April 2001 in *AB Lietuvos taupomasis bankas v UAB Elix and UAB Spec drabužiai* (Case No 3K-3-458/2001).

[77] This means the time that the creditor must await a voluntary discharge of the obligation after the debtor defaults which is counted from the day the notice has been served to the debtor.

[78] See the decision of the Lithuanian Supreme Court delivered on 23 January 2001 in *Re UAB Lukoil Baltija* (Case No 3K-7-178/2001).

contained in the Charge deed and its supplements is deemed materially correct unless there is a court's judgment ruling to the contrary.[79] Such a rule diminishes the debtor's opportunities to delay enforcement by raising speculative defences, which used to be normal practice before the reform. Under the reformed system a debtor can only raise defences to execution by launching a separate lawsuit before the courts of general competence under the rules of contentious civil procedure. Even in such a case enforcement can only be suspended if the debtor obtains an injunction from the court. Moreover, the new Civil Code expanded the remedies that are available to a chargee by introducing the limited possibility of foreclosure.[80] Foreclosure is now the standard method of enforcement of charges over receivables and can be used for charges over other property subject to the chargor's consent.

Conclusion

Lithuania pursued wholesale reform of its secured transactions law. This jurisdiction has created a workable framework of relevant legislation based on the fundamental principles of modern security law. Eventually it was decided not to adopt a fully functional concept of security. Therefore, the chattel security system consists of charges *stricto sensu* and quasi-security interests. A charge is defined as a uniform concept: a possessory or non-possessory real right that secures the performance of an obligation by vesting in the creditor priority to satisfy his claim out of the value of the collateral. All non-possessory charges must be registered in the Hypothecary Register. Major functional equivalents to a charge, such as retention of title devices, financial leases and arrangements that transfer ownership for security purposes, despite having retained their traditional legal identity, should, with a few exceptions, be also registered with the Hypothecary Register.

However, Lithuanian experience of the security law reform demonstrates that to create and implement the coherent legislative framework of the modern security law is extremely difficult even in a jurisdiction where reform is not hindered by the desire to retain the *status quo* and where prior to the reform the theoretical attitude towards non-possessory security interests was highly liberal. Existing philosophies differ significantly on key issues of the modern security law reform, and the path of their convergence that Lithuania has tried to pursue is very challenging. Apart from some conceptual inconsistencies, such as the absence of registration for assignments of receivables, major problems emerge at the level of detailed drafting. Thus, the process of registration of charges is too burdensome and the unsophisticated requirements for the description of collateral might preclude the application of universal security. Hopefully, a number of the existing

---

79 See the decision of the Lithuanian Supreme Court delivered on 4 April 2001 in *UAB Lukoil Baltija v AB Lietuvos kuras* (Case No 3K-3-425/2001).

80 Article 4.219 of the Civil Code. On this concept see Wood, *Comparative Law of Security and Guaranties* (1995) at pp 137-138.

shortcomings will be promptly solved by the creative jurisprudence of the Lithuanian Supreme Court.

Chapter 3

Patent Grants, Signals and Commodification: A Legal Dilemma?

Iwan Davies

The twentieth century witnessed the metamorphosis of British industry and the British labour market. In particular, the past three decades have seen a decline in traditional heavy industry with increased activity in the technological and service sector industries. These developments have ultimately led to the emergence of a "knowledge-based"[1] society where considerable emphasis is placed upon the creation and safeguarding of intellectual property (IP) rights[2] in copyrights, patents, trade marks, design rights, as well as "intangible rights" such as goodwill and confidentiality.

Patents are registrable intellectual property rights which provide a legal framework to encourage and protect innovation in return for transferring information. By maintaining a protected monopoly on a new product or process for a fixed period patents are considered to provide an incentive to innovation and invention.[3] Much of the literature in this respect has focused upon whether the

---

1 The value of intangible assets relative to the value of physical and financial assets have increased considerably since the 1980s. Thus, for example, in 2000 the market-to-book value in the USA for the S&P 500 companies showed that approximately 83.3% of the companies' market value stemmed from intangible assets. The importance of these assets can be demonstrated in many contexts, including intellectual property management, acquisitions, sales, joint ventures and licensing. See Hagelin, "Valuation of Intellectual Property Assets" (2002) 30 *AIPLA QJ* 353. At the same time, it is important to differentiate between IP assets, that is, where the owner/originator has the right to enforce the benefits derived from the assets from intellectual advantage, for example, management skill, as this cannot be transferred independently of the company.

2 In England and Wales, the principal statutes are the Patents Act 1977 (as amended) Trade Marks Act 1994, Registered Designs Act 1949, the Copyright Designs and Patents Act 1988. A careful distinction should be drawn here with rights such as passing off or breach of confidential information are essentially procedural in nature and are, as such, "weaker rights" than IP rights which arise under intellectual property statutes.

3 The right is for a period of 20 years so long as the relevant renewal fees are paid after the first 5 year period has elapsed. The definition of patentability is included in s 1(1) of the Patents Act 1977 (as amended) and the core concepts are novelty (s 2) and invention (s 3) and also industrial application (s 4). In return for full disclosure of the technical basis of the patent, it gives a limited monopoly to the inventor or his employer or other applicant. Not only must the patent be capable of industrial application, the application must be explored

legal rules grant the optimal amount of exclusivity so as to maximise the exchange of information in return for legal protection. There has been little consideration of the function and effect of patents and, in particular, whether the legal process associated with the grant of patents promotes economic activity. This is significant because patenting is an output of a creative process and the intensity of patenting activity is often used as a proxy for technological dynamism in a firm, industry or economy.[4] The legal process of patenting is not, however, confined to protecting the output of a creative activity because it also represents a mechanism for publicising information concerning the knowledge capital of a firm.

This chapter will consider whether there is a correlation between patent grants and an increase in economic activity and the extent to which the law facilitates the effective use of patents by owners/originators as economic assets to secure loans made by third party financiers. Here the signal function of patenting activity is important and the patent grant will be discussed in terms of providing a mechanism for imparting *credible* information about a firm, especially to third party financiers. The extent to which especially technology-driven small and medium sized enterprises (SMEs) can use patents as security will be examined. This has implications for the reform of English personal property security law and the development of bright line priority rules associated with Article 9 of the Uniform Commercial Code, which is at the heart of the recommendations made in the Law Commission Consultation Paper No 164, Registration of Security Interests: *Company Charges and Property other than 'Land* (2002) and the more recent Consultation Paper No 176, *Company Security Interests* (2004).

Patent Grants and Economic Activity

---

and this is ensured through the licenses of right legal mechanism. Thus, the invention becomes part of the knowledge bank available to competitors (that is, part of the state-of-the-art) and it must be tested on the market. The Patents Act 2004 seeks to improve the patent legal framework, especially in respect of enforcement of patent rights.

4 The impact of patenting activity on research and development (R&D) in a region was considered by the Danish Ministry of Trade and Industry in its Report, *Economic Consequences of Legal Expense Insurance for Patents* (2003). Using data for 46,000 Danish patents applied for between 1967-1995, the authors of this report attempted to estimate a combined value for Danish patents. The method adopted to achieve this used the annual renewal fee paid to the Patent Office by patent holders to maintain the patent. The theory is that if the patent holder considers that it was not worth paying the renewal fee, the patent would be allowed to lapse. By observing the rate at which patents are not renewed, it was possible to develop a model that retrospectively valued an entire cohort of patents. The values they found from their model would place at today's prices an average Danish patent at a value of 20,000 euros. Only 1% of patents they found had a value of over 134,000 euros and 50% had a value of less than 8,000 euros. The total value of patents owned by Danish firms in Europe in 1997 was extrapolated to be 256 million euros. This compared with R&D expenditure of 2,060 million euros in Denmark, so that, in theory, patents represent an implicit subsidy to R&D of 12%. The implicit subsidy comes from the ability of patents to exclude others from the benefits of R&D. The majority of the benefits of R&D it was concluded must take other forms such as the ability to be first in the market with a product, or the ability to develop a product that can be trade marked.

Patents are dichotomous because their static and dynamic effects are very different. In a static context a patent appears to be an anti-competitive device that prevents the free competition which economists often consider to be the best way to organise a market. However, in a dynamic context the legal monopoly aspect of a patent gives a firm the incentive to be innovative. If any firm could immediately copy any invention or process, then firms would have little incentive to innovate because they would face immediate competition. Nevertheless, the patent allows some exemption from competition, which gives the patent holder the incentive to produce new goods. It is often argued[5] that this is good for the economy because it allows new and better products to be brought to consumers and also adds to the stock of knowledge in the economy in that the published patents assist other firms trying to innovate. The optimal patent balances these conflicting considerations.[6] The best outcome occurs when the static losses at the margin due to a lack of competition are exactly balanced by the marginal gains from innovation due to existence of a patent. In general, if innovation is not protected well enough, no-one will innovate: protect it too well and second generation benefits of research will be lost and the monopoly power will adversely impact upon consumers.[7]

The impact of patent grants on R&D, or more generally on economic growth has been considered at both the macro and micro economic levels. Looking at the impact of economic growth, Gould and Gruben[8] offered evidence that countries with stronger patent protection experienced higher long-run growth. The theory behind this is that by offering more incentive for firms to innovate, the economy becomes more dynamic.[9] However, this result appears to be conditional on the country being active in international trade, as there is very little incentive to innovate if a firm already has a domestic monopoly in a closed economy. Indeed,

---

5 See Schotchmer, "Standing on the Shoulders of Giants: Cumulative Research and the Patent Law" (1991) 5 *Journal of Economic Perspectives* 29.

6 See Nordhaus, "The Optimum Life of a Patent: Reply" (1972) 62 *American Economic Review* 428.

7 Ordover, "A Patent System for Both Diffusion and Exclusion" (1991) 5 *Journal of Economic Perspectives* 43.

8 Gould and Gruben, "The Role of Intellectual Property Rights in Economic Growth" (1996) 48, *Journal of Development Economics* 323.

9 Using data for large production firms in the UK between 1987 and 1994, Greenhalgh and Longland have found evidence that new patents were associated with a rise in value added within those firms. From their results it would appear that new patents are associated with more efficient production techniques. Similarly, using 1986-1994 data they discovered that new patents were associated with a future rise in employment within firms. One extra patent taken out per year was found to have increased employment in an average firm by around 20 jobs. From this, it may be inferred that not only does productivity appear to benefit from patenting activity but employees also benefit through the job creation effects. See Greenhalgh and Longland, "Running to Stand Still? Intellectual Property and Value Added in Innovating Firms" (2002), *Oxford Intellectual Property Research Centre Working Paper* 01/02 and Greenhalgh and Longland, "Intellectual Property in UK Firms: Creating Intangible Assets and Distributing the Benefits via Wages and Jobs" (2002) forthcoming in *Oxford Bulletin of Economics and Statistics*.

Lee and Mansfield[10] found that US foreign direct investment went to countries that were perceived by firms as having strong IP protection from which it could be inferred that, for poorer countries, a stronger protection of IP may attract foreign investment.

An interesting insight into the effects of changing patent laws occurred in the 1980s, in that during this period, two of the world's leading economies changed their IP legal framework. The US courts became much more protective in the 1980s[11] and Japan also strengthened the protection provided by its patent laws in 1988.[12] The evidence for the effects this strengthening has had is mixed. Kortum and Lerner[13] reported a surge in patenting activity from 1985 onwards that they found that R&D activity was unaffected. It would appear that the same level of R&D was generating more patents. Their explanation for this was that management strategies had improved innovation application, that is, the R&D had been focused much more towards outcomes that could be patented, with the driving force being the rise of venture capitalism.[14] Typically, venture capitalists require firms to have significant assets before they are prepared to invest in them and it was the need to provide these assets that drove the increase in patenting activity.[15]

In another survey, Jaffe[16] identified the rise in patenting activity without a matching rise in R&D activity. He considered that the changes in US intellectual property protection might have moved firms away from innovation towards strategic behaviour. Hall and Ziedonis[17] presented evidence for this in the US semiconductor industry. In this industry the important factor in the profitability of a firm is time to market, that is, if a firm can get their product in the market place before their rivals they are able to reap economic advantage. However, the evidence from the 1980s was that semiconductor firms were patenting more heavily. The authors attributed this to the firms using patents for strategic purposes.[18] The patents helped their holders to negotiate with other firms, and also prevented other patent holders from being able to out-bargain them.

---

[10] Lee and Mansfield, "Intellectual Property Protection and US Foreign Direct Investment" (1996) 78 *Review of Economics and Statistics* 181.

[11] Jaffe, "The US Patent System in Transition: Policy Innovation and the Innovation Process" (2000) 29 *Research Policy* 531.

[12] Sakakibara and Branstetter, "Do Stronger Patents Induce More Innovation? Evidence from the 1988 Japanese Patent Law Reforms" (2001) 32 *RAND Journal of Economics* 77.

[13] Kortum and Lerner, "What is Behind the Recent Surge in Patenting?" (1999) 28 *Research Policy* 1.

[14] Kortum and Lerner, "Assessing the Contribution of Venture Capital to Innovation" (2000) 31 *RAND Journal of Economics* 674.

[15] See below.

[16] Jaffe, "The US Patent System in Transition, Policy Innovation and the Innovation Process" (2000) 29 *Research Policy* 531.

[17] Hall and Ziedonis, "The Patent Paradox Revisited: An Empirical Study of Patenting in the US Semiconductor Industry, 1979-1995" (2001) 32 *RAND Journal of Economics* 101.

[18] *Ibid* at p 125.

It would appear therefore that stronger patent protection does not necessarily promote economic activity. Indeed, a rise in patenting activity can be for strategic commercial motives rather than for innovative reasons. In this respect, Sakakibara and Branstetter[19] found little evidence that stronger IP protection had led to more innovation in the Japanese economy although they did note a rise in the number of patent litigation cases.[20] Of course, it may be that patent laws are too blunt an instrument for providing protections in all cases involving ideas and creations.[21] Patents create a stronger form of protection, which give the innovator a more powerful monopoly over their ideas by excluding close, as well as, direct copies. On the other hand, copyright offers weaker protection in that much closer copying and development of the ideas contained within the copyright are allowed. In this respect, a distinction can be drawn between patents and copyrights.[22] In industries where only a small number of firms are involved in innovation, where R&D costs are high and where innovation brings little potential for further innovation, a persuasive case for strong protection can be made. For example, it is often contended that new pharmaceutical products should receive strong protection because firms sink large amounts of money into their development, and formulas for new drugs very rarely can be built upon to create further new products.[23] Strong protection gives the incentive to innovate while not denying further innovation opportunities. In contrast, in the case of computer software, the weaker protection of copyright may be more appropriate.[24] This is because a large number of innovating firms are not spending vast amounts of money, but each development gives the opportunity for further advancement. Thus, it is argued,[25] a firm needs less incentive to innovate because their costs are lower, and the potential spill-overs imply that one firm should be allowed to build on the work of others.

When patent protection became stronger in the USA in the 1980s,[26] the computer software industry probably became less innovative as a result of this.[27] The reasoning here is that since the creation of software in a sequentially innovative industry where one innovation is built upon another, patent protection actually slowed this process down. In this context, looser patent protection would benefit all the firms in the industry because it would allow it to be more innovative and profitable[28] which would help create a dynamic industry where all firms learn from all other firms.[29]

---

19 *Op cit* fn 12.

20 *Ibid* at p 86.

21 Waterson and Ireland, "An Auction Model of Intellectual Property Protection: Patents Versus Copyright" (1998) 49 *Annales D'Economie et de Statistique* 247.

22 *Ibid.*

23 *Ibid* at pp 259-260.

24 *Ibid* at p 260.

25 *Ibid.*

26 Besen and Maskin, "Sequential Innovation, Patents and Imitation" (2000) *MIT Economics Working Paper* 00-01.

27 *Ibid* at p 2.

28 *Ibid* at p 20.

29 *Ibid.*

The protection provided by patents to originators may actually hinder innovation. As we have discussed, there are conflicting objectives: the stronger the protection afforded to innovators, the less society is likely to benefit from innovation. However, if protection is too weak, then individuals and firms will not have the incentive to create new ideas because they will not benefit sufficiently from the process. The balancing of these objectives raise interesting policy questions, not least because the *fact* of patenting activity itself provides an important mechanism for conveying information about a firm's knowledge capital. In this sense, patents can reduce the "informational asymmetries" between patentees and observers.[30] It may be that this informational function may be at least as valuable to the rights holder as the substance of those rights. We shall now consider this in greater detail.

Patent Grants and Signals

The conventional approach is to justify the patent legal monopoly on the basis of an exchange of information in return for protection. Rational investors on this view will only seek patent rights when the expected rents[31] from a patent outweighs the expected costs of disclosing the information as distinct from keeping it as a trade secret.[32] As Ayres and Klemperer have pointed out:[33]

> The current patent system – which grants the patentee a monopoly for a limited number of years – . . . allows the patentee to capture a rough and limited proxy of consumer value and then lets the potential innovator decide whether the benefits of innovation justify the costs.

The proxy of consumer value is the economic rent received by the patentee and this is "measured by the difference between the patentee's per-unit costs and competitors' per-unit costs (to the extent attributable to the patented innovation) multiplied by the patentee's volume".[34] This model of patent rights represents the

---

30 See Long, "Patent Signals" (2002) 69 *University of Chicago LR* 625.

31 The literature dealing with IP in terms of rents and products markets is enormous. See, for example, Merges, "Intellectual Property Rights and the New Institutional Economics" (2000) 52 *Vand LR* 1857; Lemley, "The Economics of Improvement in Intellectual Property Law" (1997) 75 *Texas LR* 989.

32 For a discussion as to whether or not trade secrets and confidential information can amount to property in a legal sense, see Wheeldon, "Reflections on the Concept of 'Property' with Particular Reference to Breach of Confidence", (1997) *Auckland Univ LR* 353; Beckerman-Rodan, "Are Ideas Within the Traditional Definition of Property?: A Jurisprudential Analysis", (1994) 47 *Ark LJ* 603. See also Lipton, *Security Over Intangibles* (2000).

33 "Limiting Patentees' Market Power Without Reducing Innovation Incentives: The Perverse Benefits of Uncertainty and Non-Injunctive Remedies" (1999) 97 *Mich LR* 985 at p 1008.

34 See Dam, "The Economic Underpinnings of Patent Law" (1994) 23 *J Legal Studies* 247.

orthodox position, and even the so-called "defensive patenting" models, which consider that companies take out patents in order to raise costs for competitors, still treat the value of a patent as stemming from exclusive rights and rents to be captured in product markets.[35]

Whilst patents are often portrayed in terms of exclusivity and rents, it is still the case that worthless patents abound. Thus, Kitch has argued that most patented technologies will not be economically viable or have little or no market value.[36] This suggests that inventors may find IP protection valuable for reasons other than capturing rents and maximising control over the subject matter of the rights.[37] For example, a portfolio of IP rights is a readily measurable attribute of a company which can provide a clear signal of otherwise a less measurable attribution of a company, namely, its *knowledge* capital. On this view, possession of a patent can provide a cost-effective signal the quality of a firm and provides information to the market regarding the financial prospects of the firm.[38] This is important when information otherwise about a firm is ambiguous or that the costs of obtaining such information is too costly relative to the benefit of doing so. Under such conditions, investors may undervalue some companies and overvalue others.

There is no doubt that capital markets believe that patent activity can be correlated with certain characteristics, for example, venture capitalists correlate patent applications with good company management.[39] Also, if investors consider that the future value of a firm is linked with its R&D output, then the quantity and quality of patents is an easily measurable indicator of R&D output in that time period, whilst patent portfolios may also indicate how quickly research is proceeding. In this respect, it is important to appreciate that a patent has two parts – the specification and the claims. In the specification, the patentee describes the

---

[35] See Ayres and Klemperer *op cit* fn 33 at pp 1008-1012. Strategic or defensive patenting is where patents are filed in order to block product development. The purpose of such a patent filing is not to commercialise the product or process but simply to derail competitors or to force them to cross license or pay royalties. They are sometimes referred to as paper patents.

[36] See "Property Rights in Inventions, Writings and Marks" (1990) 13 *Harv JL* and *Pub Policy* 199 at pp 122-123. At the same time, a study of global IP practices has shown that US companies ignore in excess of 35% of their own patented technologies which represents more than $115 billion in R&D because these inventions do not fit into their core business operations. These are sometimes referred to as "orphan patents" because they are outside a company's core technology. Many valuable patents are under-utilised because the present owners do not appreciate their potential utility and/or cannot afford to commercialise them or to enforce them. See Berman (Ed), *Hidden Vale: Profiting from the Intellectual Property Economy* (1999) at p 17.

[37] See Long, "Patent Signals" (2002) 69 *University of Chicago LR* 625 at p 627.

[38] Long, *ibid*, takes insights from finance and corporate literature to demonstrate how patents can reduce informational asymmetries in capital markets, thereby reducing information costs. It should be noted that over 80% of the patents granted in the US are assigned to companies. See Allison and Lemley, "Who: Patenting What? An Empirical Exploration of Patent Prosecutions" (2000) 53 *Vand LR* 2099.

[39] See Lemley, "National Ignorance at the Patent Office" (2001) 95 *Nw U L Rev* 1495 at pp 1505-6.

invention in great detail, for example, how it is different from prior art which gives the patentee an opportunity to criticise competing products. Furthermore, patent portfolios indicate what lines of research a firm is employing and this provides a research trajectory for a firm. In this sense, patent activity discloses how fast the firm is proceeding within a particular area of research. At the same time, the nature of the patent process itself is such that from an investor's perspective there can be confidence in the claims made because investors have a legal obligation in making patent applications to make honest claims.[40]

Many observers correlate patents with desirable firm attributes so that, for example, in academic literature, patent counts have been used as a measure of a firm's productivity and innovative activity.[41] Capital markets are influenced by patent counts which are used to measure knowledge capital or the productivity of R&D spending. It is also used to benchmark firms relative to each other. Nevertheless, the heterogeneous nature of patents and the fact that, by definition, they will contain information in varying amounts and quality means that patent signals are essentially ambiguous, not least because patents do not represent all of the output of R&D, despite often being used as a measure.[42] Even so, it should be recognised that patent portfolios themselves bring their own information costs, for example, while it may be easily verified that a firm has a numerical quantity of patents, it is a different matter to qualitatively assess them in terms of their true innovation and this will require considerable investment in information processing.

Patents play a particularly important role in the start-up phase of a technologically-based small firm.[43] This is because start-ups have short histories and often have no market reputation and there is often a lack of tangible assets which may be used as collateral.[44] The capacity for such businesses to fulfil their potential depends on the availability of finance and markets for small firm finance are notoriously problematical.[45] Finance gaps can arise because of information and transaction costs.[46] The problems associated with information relate to the asymmetries of information which preclude investors from evaluating the quality

---

40 *Op cit* fn 37 at p 650.

41 See Griliches, "Patent Statistics as Economic Indicators: A Survey" (1990) 28 *J Econ Lit* 1661.

42 See European Commission Report, *Enforcing Small Firms' Patent Rights* (2001) Directorate-General for Enterprise, EUR 17032.

43 See *Financing of Technology-Based Small Firms*, Bank of England Report (2001). This report identified the key characteristics of technology-based small firms to be: 1. Their value is linked to longer-term growth potential derived from scientific knowledge and intellectual property; 2. Lack of tangible assets which may be used as collateral; 3. Their products have little track record and are largely untested and may be subject to high rates of obsolescence. In view of these characteristics, the risk of traditional finance is high and in this respect equity finance is more appropriate than debt.

44 See Drobnig, "Secured Credit in International Insolvency Proceedings" (1998) 33 *Texas International Law Journal* 47.

45 See generally Whincop (Ed), *Bridging the Entrepreneurial Financing Gap* (2001).

46 Transactional costs arise in respect of expenditure on due diligence inquiries, legal documentation and the cost of advertising for investors.

of the investment proposal. These costs will vary according to the nature of the financier.[47] Family and friends may demand little contract protection and may not require due diligence investigation, whilst at the same time the originator may be able to service debt through personal wealth. The dilemma increases when the informal sources of finance are exhausted and, in this context, the benefit of a credible means of conveying information in respect of such a patenting activity will be very high for a firm that has no market reputation, especially where value is linked to longer-term growth potential derived from intellectual property.

The quantity and quality of patents are taken into account by venture capitalists in deciding whether to invest and there is evidence that as a consequence start-up firms are more eager to obtain patents than established firms.[48] Public equity is not an option because of cost.[49] This is why private equity through venture capital is important, although the complexities of due diligence for high technology projects[50] requires experienced venture capital teams,[51] and business angels[52] who

---

[47] The identity of investors changes as the amount financed rises. Close to origin the finance comes from the originator of the intellectual property, family and friends. At the other end of the market investment will be sourced from public capital markets when the firm is able to go public. Prior to this, finance will be sourced from formal and informal venture capitalists who are sometimes referred to as "business angels". See below at fn 52.

[48] See Hall and Ziedonis, "The Patent Paradox Revisited: An Empirical Study of Patenting in the US Semiconductor Industry 1979-1995" (2001) 32 *RAND J Econ* 101.

[49] The substantial fixed costs associated with flotation often make this an uneconomic option. The UK has a three-tier capital market structure – an Official List, the Alternative Investment Market (AIM) with less onerous admission and trading requirements and also an off-market trading facility, OFEX. For a discussion, see *Financing for Small Firms*, Bank of England Report (8th Report) 2001 at 4.35-4.49.

[50] Various public sector initiatives and fiscal incentives in respect of investments in technology-based small firms have been made available in recent years, including a tax credit for investment in R&D. See Bank of England Report (No 8) *ibid* at pp 71-72.

[51] The proportion of funds invested through formal private equity in start-up and early stage companies which may be regarded as a proxy of finance available for small firms fluctuates greatly. Thus, in 2001, £400m was made available by venture capitalists, that is, banks, special investment schemes and venture capital firms. However, in 2002 this sum decreased to £40m. See *Financing of Small Firms*, Bank of England Report (10th Report) 2003 at para 8.3.

[52] Angel financiers are high net worth, non-institutional private equity investors that have the desire and have sufficient net worth to enable them to invest part of their wealth into risk high return entrepreneurial ventures in return for a share of voting control, income and capital gain. They are able to provide capital and also expertise. It is estimated that the UK has around 18,000 actual and potential business angels investing annually £500m. See Mason and Harrison, "Public Policy in the Development of the Informal Venture Capital Market" in Cowling (Ed), *Individual Policy in Europe* (1999). Angels vary in the way they have an involvement in the investment. Active angels closely monitor the firm they invest in, sit on the board and advise the firm on various matters. Passive angels provide money but rarely monitor as they are usually part of an informal network led by active angels who perform the due diligence, syndicate the deal and manage the investments. See Acs and Prowse, "Angel Investors and the Angel Capital Electronic Networth" Chapter 3 in Whincop (Ed) *op cit* fn 45.

provide informal venture capital are renowned for high information costs associated with the assessment of patents as commercial investors. In this respect, venture capitalists are reluctant to invest in companies that do not have an adequate IP strategy dealing with the promotion, protection and enforcement of IP rights.[53] The ability to enforce[54] a patent is crucial to its inherent value as an asset and the originator's ability or otherwise to use the patent as collateral in order to obtain debt finance.

Historically, patents have rarely been used as security for debt financing[55] and where they have been used this has been in addition to security taken over tangible assets almost as a catch-all security provision with little acknowledgement of the

---

[53] The survey, commissioned by the London office of US law firm Howrey Simon Arnold & White, canvassed the views of 100 fund managers, analysts, private equity firms and venture capitalists. See "IP Under Greater Scrutiny from Investors", *Managing Intellectual Property* (December 2001/January 2002).

[54] For a patent, as a clearly defined property right, this implies that it must not be subject to challenge and that it is clear to all parties what behaviour would imply infringement of the patent. The perfect enforcement of the patent anticipates that any infringement will be noticed and punished. However, it is now acknowledged that there are significant difficulties in practice, especially for small and medium sized enterprises (SMEs), in the enforcement of their patents which relate to the costs of litigation. The Patents Act 2004 which amended the Patents Act 1977 seeks to provide a more supportive framework, particularly for small businesses to enforce patent rights, in particular the provision of the Patent Office to provide an independent non-binding opinion on patent validity or infringements to settle disputes over patent rights. There has been considerable interest in Europe in the use of legal expenses insurance as a mechanism to assist in the enforcement of IP rights. In the past, the provision of IP insurance, of which patent litigation insurance is a part, has not been successful in Europe. See *Patent Litigation Insurance: A Study for the European Commission on possible insurance schemes against patent litigation rights*, Final Report, January 2003. The reasons are set out as follows in 5.2.1:

- High level of premium (for example, averaging 20-50,000 euros annually)
- Low level of indemnity, perhaps 200,000 euros in large countries where costs are highly variable
- Lack of awareness of the insurance
- Low level of appreciation of the importance of patents
- Inadequate understanding of the limitation of a patent grant and the need to be able to litigate to enforce
- Poor experiences in the past with conflict between insured and insurer
- Bad press reports from professional bodies such as CIPA.

Restricted scope of policies including:

- Low indemnity
- Territorial restrictions frequently exclude the USA and Canada
- Need for complex and expensive evaluation of risk for insurers
- Burdensome restrictions and exclusions
- Poor definition of the IP covered leading to disputes with insurers.

[55] See especially Bezant, "The Use of IP as Security for Debt Finance" (1998), *Journal of Knowledge Management* 237.

value of the patent.[56] Financing is traditionally provided by way of a combination of fixed charges over a business's tangible assets, such as land, and a floating charge over all of the business's assets. Evaluation of patents as specific collateral has not generally occurred, which may be significant because as the Bank of England Report, *Financing of Small Firms*[57] pointed out, "the availability of collateral does not impact on the birth of new firms but on [their] survival rates".[58] In turn, this invites scrutiny of the extent to which the law facilitates the effective use of patents by originators as financial assets capable of raising secured finance with an extractable value.

The Commodification of Patents

As a matter of legal principle, all registered IP rights are assets in the sense that they are fully transferable to third parties and are property rights, that is, they are owned, exclusive and are binding against third parties.[59] This is the effect of registration. The *nature* of the property right though is problematical, for example, under s 30(1) of the Patent Act 1977, the patent is referred to as personal property and not as a chose in action.[60] However, a careful analysis of the nature and effect of a patent is that it is a chose in action since the essential function of registration and the certificate of registration is to promote the exclusive rights to exploit the invention evidenced therein.

IP rights are hybrid rights developed from principles of property law and equity as well as drawing upon the wider commercial, company, insolvency and banking law contexts. The approach of the law is not systematic in respect of IP when the issues do not relate to the main function of IP law which is to encourage and protect marketable ideas. This is especially the case when IP is used as security. Thus, in the context of patents, priority is determined by the date of registration of the security interest created by a charge over a patent or a mortgage over a patent created in writing or some other form of notice.[61] Section 33(1) of the Patents Act 1977 provides that any person acquiring property in a patent through a "transaction instrument or event"[62] will take free of an unregistered right if the prior right was unregistered "and he had no knowledge of the prior right". Similarly, s 33(2)

---

56 A distinction should be drawn between intangible assets and intangible value. This goes to the nature of the analytical method of valuation of IP assets. See below. Cowper Reilly, "Valuation of Intangible Assets in Dot.Com and Intellectual Property Intensive Companies" (2001) 15, *American Journal of Family Law* 36.

57 Bank of England, Sixth Report, *Financing of Small Firms* (1999) at p 25.

58 *Ibid* at p 6.

59 Patents Act 1977 (as amended), s 30; Registered Designs Act 1949, s 19; Trade Marks Act 1994, s 25.

60 The Trade Marks Act 1994 refers to trade marks as "personal property" whilst the Registered Designs Act 1949 is silent as to the nature of the property.

61 Patents Act 1977 (as amended), s 33(1).

62 This is defined in s 33(3) of the Patents Act 1977 (as amended) to include an assignment and also a mortgage.

provides that the acquisition of any right in or under the patent will take free of an unregistered right or interest where the prior right is "incompatible with any such right acquired under the earlier transaction, instrument or event" again subject to actual knowledge. As a result, until the interest is registered it will be vulnerable to relegation behind subsequent charges or mortgages which includes licenses made under such charges or mortgages. In the light of this, it is appropriate to consider the issue of constructive notice, particularly of a charge registered in the companies register and not in the patents register.[63]

Failure to register a charge under the companies charges register will make it void as against third parties. If a charge is registered on the companies charges register and not on the patent register then it will appear that the patent is unencumbered. Whilst the onus is upon the financier to search all the registers, if this is not achieved then apparently binding charges could be void for failure to register in either register. The issue of constructive notice may be relevant here as this imputes knowledge to a party who should have made inquiries in respect of the interest that would have been disclosed pursuant to proper and usual inquiries. However, it is unlikely that the registration in the companies register will be notice for the purposes of the Patents Act 1977 because actual notice is the mischief of the legislation as the burden is upon the prior rights holder to protect his position by registering under the 1977 legislation.[64] In a sense, the current position bears a resemblance to the pre-1925 unregistered land schemes.[65] Thus, actual knowledge gleaned outside of the registration process binds a potential lender and this leads to significant evidential problems.

It is absurd to refer to the need to protect unregistered equitable and legal interests by reference to an actual notice doctrine since registration under the Patents Act does not offer complete protection for potential creditors. The problem is that the IP statutes set up both a compulsory and non-compulsory registration scheme at the same time. The Acts do not refer to actual or constructive

---

[63] Under present law, any charges created over IP owned by a company are subject to a registration requirement under s 395(1) Companies Act 1985. For the purposes of that Act, a charge is construed widely to include mortgages (see s 396(4)). Non-registration of a registrable interest is fatal in respect of establishing prior rights in insolvency and liquidation in that a charge is void against third parties but not as between the parties themselves. There is 21 days to register a charge or mortgage from the date of creation. A problem is that there is no grace period linked to a certification of search of the registry so that an invisible interest can emerge thereby "trumping" a chargee by a supervening registration between the creation of the charge and its appearance on the register.

[64] The Patents Act 1977 (as amended) refers to actual notice as being sufficient unless the interest is registered. Does this mean that unless the subsequent interest holder can be shown to have known about the previous interest he will not be bound by it? If so, constructive notice may be relevant in the sense that he should be deemed to have notice of a charge on the companies register, that is, it must be registered under the 1985 Act as distinct, for example, from negative pledge clauses. See Law Commission Consultation Paper No 164, *Registration of Security: Company Charges and Property other than Land* (2002) at para 2.42 and 3.18; Law Commission Consultation Paper No 176, *Company Security Interests*.

[65] See Townend, *Using Intellectual Property As Security* (1996) at p 23.

knowledge *per se*, they simply refer to the fact that unless the interest is registered, only actual notice is sufficient. There is a conceptual problem here in terms of the treatment of legal interests. Normally, such interests "bind the world" but because registration is not compulsory, the effect of such interests are only binding as equitable interests against a subsequent interest holder who has no notice of its existence. In effect, the legal interest must be protected by notice either on the register or in another form. It is disappointing that the Law Commission did not deal with this issue in either of its recent Consultation Papers,[66] even though there was a general recommendation that notice filing should be implemented within the company charges regime and perhaps even extended beyond this.[67] In the context of IP, the recommendation was simply that the priority scheme should be determined by the specialist IP register, for example, in the case of patent rights whilst, on the other hand, copyright and some design rights have no registration provisions and with respect to these categories of IP rights, the proposal is that the notice filing mechanism should apply.[68]

There are real problems under the present system associated with the proliferation of the systems involved. This can be illustrated further in the context of insolvency. If a financier failed to register under the companies registration procedure but did register earlier in point of time under the relevant IP statute, whilst another financier did not register under the IP statute but registered later with the company registration procedure, the latter financier would prevail upon the insolvency of the company debtor. The result would be otherwise outside of the insolvency context.[69]

In the discussion on the reform of English personal property security law,[70] there has been little consideration of the impact of security interests upon IP law or the need for reform in this context. The logic of the establishment of a notice filing mechanism and the restatement of the security law in England and Wales would dictate the removal of the security requirements from the registrable intellectual property right regimes and also the removal of the same provisions under the

---

[66] *Op cit* fn 64.

[67] *Ibid.* For a discussion here see Davies, "Functionalism and the Reform of English Personal Property Security Law" (2004) 24 *Legal Studies* 295.

[68] Law Commission Consultation Paper No 176 *op cit* fn 64 at paras 3.292 and 3.339.

[69] Compare Townend *op cit* fn 65 at p 42: "the outcome is that the law appears to be confused and without clear expression of the duties and schemes that it seeks to effect".

[70] In 1971, the proposed Lending and Security Act, suggested by the Crowther Committee Report on *Consumer Credit* Cmnd 4596 (1971) leaned very heavily on Article 9. In addition, the Scottish Law Commission's Working Party on *Security over Moveable Property* (1986), the Halliday Report, as well as the DTI Paper prepared by Professor Diamond, *A Review of Security Interests in Property* (1989) drew on the Crowther Report. The Diamond report recommended that the law should be reformed by the introduction of a new law of security and the creation of a notice-filing system. The Halliday report, whilst recommending the establishment of a register of security interests with notice filing, was more selective in its drawing on the Crowther report and, in particular, avoided recommendations that would introduce alien concepts into Scots law. None of these reports specifically considered security interests in respect of intellectual property rights.

Companies Act 1985, and the replacement of these elements with a single security register such as that seen under Article 9 of the Uniform Commercial Code (UCC). There is a conceptual gulf between the current patent register and an Article 9 regime. This can be conveniently illustrated in their respective treatment of filing and priority issues.

As we have discussed, s 33 of the Patents Act requires that certain types of transaction are registered, namely, an assignment of the patent or application for a patent; a mortgage of the patent or application or the grant of a security over it; the grant or assignment of a licence or sub-licence. Registration is necessary for two reasons: First, registration defeats earlier transactions that have not been registered (that is, it is proof of title); second, the subsequent proprietor of the patent or an exclusive licensee may be compromised in terms of a claim for damages or an account of profits for any infringement of an unregistered patent.[71] Essentially, the current registration process is a form of transaction filing and contemplates individual and discrete filings as additional patent assignments are made. The Patents Act 1977 (as amended) does not authorise the filing of a broad "umbrella" document that would give notice of possible future patent assignments in addition to the current one.[72] The underlying rationale for the present English position is that what is made public is the actual transaction in which the parties transferred an interest in IP. This is in stark contrast to an Article 9 type system[73] where a single financing statement is sufficient to perfect multiple security interests between the same debtor and creditor.[74]

[71] Patents Act 1977 (as amended), s 68.

[72] An agreement to assign future inventions may be upheld where the agreement relates to improvements of named inventions. Under s 33(3)(b) of the Patents Act 1977 (as amended) there is set down a procedure by which a notice of mortgage transactions can be recorded. This creates the possibility of a legal mortgage automatically arising upon the grant of a patent. Under current legislation there is no mechanism to take security over after-acquired property – pure future patents over which no registration application has been made. Such future rights only find expression as floating charges under the companies regime and are not registrable under the Patents Act 1977 (as amended).

[73] Under the pre-reformed Article 9 of the UCC, it was unclear whether US patent and trademark legislation came within the scope of the regime. The confusion arose out of apparently conflicting state and federal schemes for perfection of security interests in and the recording of transfers and assignments of IP. Under revised Article 9 it is now clear (UCC 9:106) that copyrights, trademarks and patents all fall within the definition of "general intangibles" to which Article 9 provides the means for perfecting security interests. Even so, this does not resolve the position and there have been several proposals to change the law in the USA to seek to resolve the federal versus state issue in IP security law matters. See Driza, "Perfecting Security Interests in Intellectual Property" (2000) 98 *Illinois Bar Journal* 162.

[74] The significance of the filing scheme is that a secured creditor is provided the means of determining the issue of priority. The Article 9 notice filing provides for this through a first to perfect mechanism linked to filing – this is not necessarily first in time. The effect of filing is that it provides information to third parties about potential claims to the property of a debtor. For a discussion here see Davies, "The Reform of Personal Property Security

The case for a notice-filing mechanism that embraces IP rights and patents in particular,[75] is that financing tends to be ongoing and fluid, particularly in the case of small and medium sized enterprises. In the situation of ongoing finance, a transactional approach involves more expense than notice-filing because this will involve multiple registration at the specialist patent register. This expense falls on the borrower and decreases the value of patents for financing purposes. A direct advantage of moving to an Article 9 regime is that this will reduce transactional costs and searching and filing of security interests would become simpler and cheaper and less numerous because of the shift from transaction to notice filing.

The underlying assumption in the above discussion is that patents are economic assets in the sense that they have a market value and can be transferred. The issue of valuation is especially difficult. As Nimmer has pointed out:[76]

> How we should approach the question of value and the definition of property rights in an age where information systems dominate differs from the approach appropriate in the receding era where control over goods and real estate was the defining element of wealth, power and the ability to engage in commerce? Intangibles cannot be bent, folded, kicked or burned. The old axiom that possession is nine-tenths of the law makes little sense when discussing a form of property and value that can be simultaneously possessed (known) by hundreds, thousands and even millions of people.

Of course, at one level, the concept of value is easy to state as it is the worth of the asset to the buyer and seller with price being the expression of the perceived value of an asset.[77] Value in this sense is subjective[78] and even sophisticated valuation

---

Law: Can Article 9 of the US Uniform Commercial Code be a Precedent?" [1988] *ICLQ* 465.

75 The Patents Act (2004) is silent in respect of the creation of security interests in patents.

76 See Nimmer, "Information Age in Law: New Frontiers in Property and Contract" [1996] *New York State Bar Journal* 28 at p 29.

77 See Posner, *Economic Analysis of Law* 5th ed (1998) at pp 14-15. There are significant problems associated with the valuation of IP assets in general arising out of the fact that: (1) The public trading markets that exist for financial and physical assets do not exist for IP assets; (2) The terms and conditions of IP transfers vary widely; (3) Patents are by definition dissimilar; (4) The details of IP transfers are rarely made available to the public as they are crafted by lawyers to suit the special needs of their clients. For a discussion see Neifeld, "A Macro-Economic Model Providing Patent Valuation and Patent Based Company Indicators" (2001) 83 *Journal of the Patent and Trademark Office Society* 211.

78 Because of the undeveloped nature of a market in patents, the lender will often apply a conservative capitalisation value and actually depress the estimated value of the patent. The advance offered to the originator may not therefore be an attractive one. Licences of patents given by originators to third parties are more attractive because the subjective element is reduced because the cash flows generated from third parties can be estimated. In addition, they conform to the traditional view of a security instrument in that: (i) the licence separates the IP asset from the underlying business; (ii) valuation is based on cash flows representing the royalty income of the licence; (iii) the licence establishes a market credibility in that an established market is identified; (iv) on default, the licensee is at least a potential purchaser of the IP asset. See generally Bezant, "The Use of IP as Security for Debt Finance" (1998) 1 *Journal of Knowledge Management* 237.

methods adopted for patents ultimately reflect this fact. What is anticipated is an analysis of the claims made in respect of the patent; the identification of what are the products covered by the patent; a determination of the size of the market covered by the patent; the determination of the cost advantage of the patented technology compared to alternative technologies for the market. Such an analysis is very labour intensive[79] and costly[80] and some of the data may not be available and, even where it is, much of the information will be regarded as being commercially sensitive.

The ability to define the economic benefits generated by a specific patent is important to a financier from the point of view of realising the secured asset on default. This goes to the nature of the analytical method of valuation of patents. Under the discrete method, it is necessary to identify which patent creates what amount of intangible value. In the collective method, it is sufficient to identify that intangible value exists and what the total amount of this value is. Traditionally in the UK, the collective method has been the one employed in respect of taking security in the aggregate intangible value or goodwill, usually by way of a floating charge, that is, the aggregate intangible value is taken which alleviates the problem of identifying the value of each element. Such an approach reflects the fact that a robust valuation method should be taken into account, not merely the patent itself but also the "know how" surrounding it, that is, the innovation necessary to translate and transform the patent into a viable product.[81] This collective process is sometimes referred to as the "intellectual assets" of a firm.[82] The main difficulty here is that there exists no standardised market for intellectual assets unlike other forms of tangible assets which have an established market and tradition of valuation. At the same time, patents are uniquely vulnerable to attack on the basis that the invention was not new or was obvious or that there was "prior art"[83] and the difficulties are compounded by the threat of infringement, obsolescence and the costs associated with maintaining the registration of patents which are necessary to protect legal monopoly associated with a valid patent grant.[84]

---

[79] This might require combining the skills of bankers, venture capitalists, economists, accountants, financial analysts, patent attorneys and lawyers. See above.

[80] See Neifeld, "A Macro-Economic Model Providing Patent Valuation and Patent Based Company Financial Indicators" (2001) 83 *Journal of the Patent and Trademark Office Society* 211.

[81] Know how could include manuals and instructions in respect of a product, in addition to source codes and formulas. Where know how is sourced in employees, it will be necessary for the financier to obtain an express right to solicit and hire the debtor's personnel in the event of foreclosure. Of course, there is the risk that highly skilled employees will move to another business if they sense that the borrower's business is in financial difficulty.

[82] See Hagelin, "Valuation of Intellectual Property Assets" (2002) 30 *AIPLA QJ* 353.

[83] The search for "prior art" as a mechanism for undermining a competitor's patent has become a business with on-line offering of rewards for those who can help an adversary's patent. See http://www.bountyquest.com.

[84] The problem is that financiers are not generally concerned with the maintenance of property securing the loan. Policing renewals of patents is potentially time-consuming, whilst the patent registrar will send reminder notices and a grace period is given within

There is therefore no neat or comprehensive method for valuation and taking security over patents, despite the fact that there has been a shift in the valuable asset bases of many businesses from tangible assets to intellectual assets.[85] What is required is a re-evaluation of property theory as the basis of secured financing law which is often conceived of as a series of rights and obligations between individuals in a particular jurisdiction and time in respect of an object.[86] Intellectual assets, on the other hand, incorporate different types and levels of rights[87] and obligations over time[88] which often entail contractual services.[89] Ultimately, this may lead to the emergence of a new body of commercial finance law to support the development and exploitation of intellectual assets.

Conclusion

The legal process involved in the grant of patents involves a balance between the conflicting objectives of protecting the knowledge capital of a firm and providing an incentive to innovate whilst at the same time facilitating innovation by others. The balancing of these objectives raise interesting policy questions, not least because the legal profession provided by patents to originators may in some cases actually hinder innovation and some firms may patent for strategic or defensive reasons. However, the fact of patenting activity provides an important mechanism for conveying information about a firm's knowledge capital. The quantity and quality of patents are taken into account by financiers in deciding whether to invest

---

which time a lapsed patent right can be restored on the payment of a fee (s 25(4) Patents Act 1977). Nevertheless, where the patent grant is allowed to lapse, this will obviously undermine the security. It is to avoid over-reliance on one patent that lenders take a security interest over a portfolio of IP assets.

85 See Clarkson, "Avoiding Suboptimal Behaviour In Intellectual Asset Transactions: Economic and Organizational Perspectives on the Sale of Knowledge" (2001) 14 *Harvard Journal of Law and Technology* 712.

86 See, for example, Eleftheriadis, "The Analysis of Property Rights" (1996) 16 *Oxford Journal of Legal Studies* 31.

87 The commerciality of an intellectual asset is dynamic and this is problematical in terms of its suitability for security as an asset. It can be transferred many times to multiple entities in different places, for example, rights can be licensed or sold outright. The nature of licensing is multifarious – it can be exclusive (to one licensee) or non-exclusive (a multiple of licensees), it may be limited to a geographical region and/or to a specific time period and/or for a specific purpose or field of use. Additionally, some licensees are permitted to sub-licence the right to a technology.

88 It may be that the borrower will inadvertently reduce the value of the security in a patent by a licensing agreement which may be substantially equivalent to an ownership right, for example, an exclusive licence.

89 Compare Nimmer and Krauthaus, "Information as a Commodity: New Imperatives of Commercial Law" (1992) 55(3) *Law and Contemporary Problems* 103 at p 107: "In intellectual property law, the relationship between information and creative services provides a fulcrum on which the law balances proprietary rights and public use."

in a firm and patents can provide a cost-effective signal of the quality of a firm and can provide information to the financial markets of the prospects of a firm.

Historically, financiers have not focused upon the use of intangibles as security and the evaluation of patents as specific collateral has not generally occurred. In many cases, patents simply feature as part of the general assets of a company for the purpose of a floating charge or perhaps identified as a fixed charge within a portfolio of company assets generally. The security potential of patents as assets for the purpose of raising debt finance is compromised by this approach which may deprive industry of an important source of capital.

The commercial context is which a patent operates requires careful evaluation not least because the full exploitation of the patent may not be separable from the know how surrounding it. The proper goals for an effective credit and security regime in respect of such intellectual assets include the need to provide clear rules which facilitate finance planning as well as the establishment of a system that minimises the costs and risks involved in taking a security interest in such assets. The current IP registries in England and Wales are concerned only with documenting the conferral of rights, the identity of the original owner and also assignees and licensees. Crucially, each IP registry is designed for transaction filing rather than notice filing so that actual knowledge gleaned outside of the registration will bind third parties. In this sense, the current position bears a striking resemblance to the pre-1925 unregistered land schemes.[90] In contrast, the emphasis of a modern credit and security law regime is upon notice filing which fixes a priority point and is concerned to expand the pool of assets available to creditors by extending to after-acquired property. This is especially important in the context of the financing of on-going technology, perhaps involving the development of a series of patents. Under the current law there is difficulty in taking a security interest in future IP rights. It is a pity that recent Law Commission Consultation Papers which considered radical reform of security interests in England and Wales did not satisfactorily deal with these issues. The Law Commission's approach to maintain the specialist IP registers and that the determination of the validity of registered charges should be governed by the rules of that register effectively undermines the benefits of an Article 9-type of regime in the context of IP assets.[91]

An essential aspect of taking security in a patent or cluster of patents is the need to identify the benefit generated by the patent activity because this goes to the vibrancy of the patent as an economic asset. However, patents are vulnerable to challenge on the basis of lack of novelty and are also susceptible to infringement, whilst the behaviour of the borrower needs careful monitoring: a failure to pay patent renewal fees can be catastrophic and render the security interest unenforceable. At the same time, the borrower may grant licences that transfer valuable rights, thereby undermining the value of the patent.

---

[90] *Op cit* fn 65.

[91] Law Commission Consultation Paper No 176 *op cit* fn 64 at paras 3.337-342.

The current legal position reflects a clash of legal cultures[92] between an intellectual property law on the one hand, which is concerned to reward endeavour by protecting through monopolistic rights the owner of a patent and, on the other hand, that of credit finance law which is concerned to provide a framework for conducting transactions that establishes an effective security regime for creditors with clear priority and enforcement rules following default. It may be that the dissonance of the two legal regimes can only be resolved through the emergence of a new body of commercial finance law to support the development and exploitation of patents as assets.

[92] Compare Nimmer and Krauthaus, "Secured Financing and Information Property Rights" (1988) 2 *High Technology Law Journal* 195; Lipton, *Security Over Intangible Property* (2000).

Chapter 4

The Influence of a Flexible Legal Framework upon the Development of Credit Unions in Great Britain: The US and Irish Experience

Nicholas Ryder

Introduction

A credit union is a unique financial institution that is democratically controlled by its members for the benefit of its members. Donnelly and Haggett took the view that a credit union is a financial co-operative that encourages its members to save regularly and facilitates the borrowing of money at lower interest rates than those normally charged by other financial institutions.[1] Similarly, Masset defines a credit union as a non-profit, member owned, and democratically controlled institution chartered with the purpose of making loans available to people of small means.[2]

There are nearly seven hundred registered credit unions in Great Britain. Despite a significant increase in the number of credit unions, their overall impact in Great Britain is limited when compared to other jurisdictions, as their market share remains at just over one percent.[3] This leads to the question as to why credit unions have not developed in Great Britain? Some commentators have suggested that the main reason is that their legislative framework is extremely restrictive. The Association of British Credit Unions Limited (ABCUL) took the view that:

> Credit unions in Great Britain have been held back by an overly restrictive law that has limited their growth and services they offer . . . Indeed, a 1996 report from the World Council of Credit Unions stated "the current credit union legislation in Great Britain is amongst the most restrictive in the world".[4]

---

1 Donnelly & Haggett, *Credit Unions in Britain - A Decade of Growth* (1997).

2 Masset, "The Evolution of the Common Bond in Occupational Credit Unions: How Close Must the Tie that Binds Be?" *3 NC Banking Inst*, 387 (1999).

3 WOCCU (2002). The penetration rate is calculated by dividing the total number of reported credit union members by the economically active population.

4 ABCUL, *Why We Need a New Credit Union Law* (1977).

Other studies have also concluded that the Credit Unions Act 1979 is a major factor that has limited the development of credit unions in Great Britain.[5] This chapter aims to determine whether or not a flexible legal framework could assist the evolution of the movement, as will be demonstrated in other jurisdictions.

The Origins of the Credit Union Movement

According to MacPherson the development of credit unions can be divided into three stages.[6] During their formative stage, credit unions are heavily reliant upon the support of its members, other institutions, government departments and funding agencies.[7] Credit unions are rarely in a position to be self-sufficient during this stage of their development. Here, credit unions needed to utilize networks provided by such institutions as churches, other co-operatives, trade unions and professional associations.[8] Throughout this stage, credit unions have a limited set of needs, such as education and training, promotion, lobbying to secure legislation, the provision of insurance services and the procurement of inexpensive supplies, the need for which can be met by central organizations.[9]

The second stage in the development of credit unions is the national stage.[10] During this stage in their development, the national representative bodies are required to undertake more activities that relate to the expansion of the movement. On occasion, it can lead to serious fragmentation with the creation of rival groups of credit unions and credit unionists.[11] This stage of development is normally creative and it is at this time that credit unions reach out to larger constituencies, provide more services to their members, and begin to have a significant impact on the general economy. The third and final stage is the International Stage. In Great Britain, the credit union movement is at the second stage of development, thus illustrating that they have failed to develop when compared to those in other jurisdictions.

---

[5] For a more detailed discussion see Griffiths & Howells, "Slumbering Giant or White Elephant: Do Credit Unions Have a Role to Play in the Great Britain Credit Market" (1991) 42, *NILQ* 199-211; Griffiths & Howells, "Britain's Best Kept Secret? An Analysis of the Credit Union as an Alternative Source of Credit" (1990) 13, *Journal of Consumer Policy* 447-466; Ryder, "Credit Unions in the Great Britain: A Critical Analysis of their Legislative Framework and its Impact upon their Development" [2003] *JBL* 45-66.

[6] MacPherson, "Hands Around the Globe" (1999) 1.

[7] *Ibid.*

[8] See MacPherson *op cit* fn 6.

[9] *Ibid.*

[10] See MacPherson *op cit* fn 6.

[11] For a more detailed analysis of the disagreements between the representative bodies of the credit union movement in Great Britain see Donnelly and Haggett *op cit* fn 1 and Sibbald, Ferguson & McKillop, "An Examination of Key Factors of Influence in the Development Process of Credit Union Industries" (2002) 73 (2) Annals of Public and Co-operative Economics 399-428.

The Early Years in the UK

The origins of the co-operative movement, from which credit unions emerged, can be traced to the work of the Robert Owen New Lanark Mill and the Rochdale Society of Equitable Pioneers.[12] Moody and Fite described them as "two notable and widely publicised co-operative experiments".[13] The Rochdale Society of Equitable Pioneers developed a number of operating principles – open membership, the democratic control of the organization, a limited interest on share capital and the return on member's interests being in proportion to the member's patronage.[14]

The principles advocated by the Rochdale Society of Equitable Pioneers remain an important part of modern day movement. McCarthy stated it is important for all co-operatives, including credit unions to continue to reenergize their core values, particularly in the context of a rapidly changing environment.[15] The initial aims and success of the two co-operative experiments in England influenced the development of such institutions in Germany.

Europe

In 1846 and 1847 people in Germany faced a crop failure and one of their harshest winters, which resulted in the worst economic difficulties ever faced.[16] The only source of credit available at the time was via moneylenders who charged extortionate rates of interest.[17] In response to those problems, co-operatives of all kinds were formed including "bread unions" that distributed flour to the hungry and sold bread to the poor at very low prices. The development of credit co-operatives in Germany can be attributed to the efforts of two Germans, Herman Schulze-Delitzsch and Friedrich Wilhelm Raiffeisen.

Schulze-Delitzch pursued the passage of legislation for co-operative banking, a difficult struggle because of the opposition from other banking institutions and political foes. In 1867 he successfully introduced legislation on co-operative banking into the Prussian legislature, and it essentially became the basis for the German law that was passed in 1871.[18] It can therefore be argued that Schulze-Delitzch assisted the development of co-operative societies by encouraging

12 Moody & Fite, *The Credit Union Movement, Origins and Development - 1850-1970* (1970). Griffiths and Howells noted: "Credit unions have their origins in Europe and may be traced back to the middle of the nineteenth century". See Griffiths and Howells *op cit* fn 5 at p 205.

13 See Moody and Fite *ibid* at p 1.

14 *Ibid.*

15 McCarthy, "A Value Perspective of the Irish Credit Union Movement" (2002) 35 *Journal of Co-operative Studies*, 128.

16 See Moody and Fite *op cit* fn 12.

17 The problems of high interest rates from the then traditional suppliers of credit were apparent in the United States of America, Canada, the Great Britain and the Republic of Ireland.

18 See MacPherson *op cit* fn 6.

appropriate legislation for them. This view is supported by Griffiths and Howells who concluded that Schulze-Delitzch not only assisted the evolution of credit unions in Germany but also their law.[19]

Schulze-Delitzch and Raiffeisen influenced the development of credit unions in Germany and their efforts served both as an inspiration to and as a precedent for other jurisdictions. In 1864, Luigi Luzzatti, a 23-year old Italian scholar who visited Germany to study co-operation was "greatly" influenced by Schulze-Delitzch and Raiffeisen. Luzzatti established his first co-operative bank in Milan that later became known as the People's Bank of Milan. By 1909, the People's Bank of Milan was one of the largest banking institutions in Italy, with 70 unpaid staff and 100 salaried clerks. It numbered 25,000 members, had capital of nearly £2m and savings of over $32m. At the time, it served as a model for numerous other banks in Italy.[20]

Co-operative banking soon spread to other parts of Europe. Austrians organized their first Schulze-Delitzch society in 1858 and by 1913, there were 3,599 societies. The first Raiffeisen type society was established in 1866, and it numbered 8,000 by 1912. France also experimented with co-operative credit societies in the 1830s and 1840s. In south Eastern Europe, Serbia and Bulgarians created a strong co-operative movement.

North America

Mattson stated that credit unions arose in the United States of America in the early part of the nineteenth century to serve the financial needs of the working class, who were ignored by banks who only catered for corporations and successful individuals.[21] As a result of this "snub" the loan demands of the blue-collar workers went unsatisfied and such people were forced to either go without a loan or turn to loan sharks.

Pierre Jay, Commissioner of Banks in Massachusetts, became worried by the financial problems faced by small entrepreneurs and was especially concerned about the activities of pawnbrokers and moneylenders. He concluded that co-operative banking was a practical solution for credit problems. Pierre Jay discovered that there were about six associations who provided their members with the ability both to save and to obtain loans. This discovery led Pierre Jay to sponsor a legal project to authorise the organization of credit unions and Desjardins was invited to participate in the preparation of the legislation.[22] As a result of the

---

19 See Griffiths and Howells *op cit* fn 5 at p 205.

20 See MacPherson *op cit* fn 6 at p 6.

21 Mattson, "Banks Win The Battle – Credit Unions Win The War: An Examination Of NCUA v First National Bank & Trust Co's Effect on Occupational Credit Unions" [1999] *L Rev Mich St U Det CL*, 1021.

22 See Moody and Fite *op cit* fn 12. In 1909, Desjardins founded the first credit union in the United States of America, in Manchester, New Hampshire. His co-operative banks were not considered regular financial institutions, rather that they were an expression of high social ideal. By 1914, there were 150 such organizations.

work undertaken by Pierre Jay the Massachusetts Credit Union Act became law on the 15 April 1909. This legislation defined a credit union as a co-operative association formed for the purpose of promoting thrift among members.[23]

Massachusetts was the first state to pass a general statute for the incorporation of credit unions. It missed however the distinctions of having passed the first credit union law. On 6 April 1909, New Hampshire legislature enacted a special Act allowing the incorporation of the Saint Mary's Co-operative Credit Association. Bergengren took the view that it was essential to have legislation to make it possible to organize and develop credit unions everywhere.[24] Burger and Dacin stated that as a direct result of this law by 1933 thirty-eight states had enacted such laws that permitted establishment of credit unions and thereby illustrating the significance of the Massachusetts law.[25] Bergengren believed that for the continued expansion of credit unions it was necessary to have a federal credit union law to facilitate the organization and growth of credit unions in states where legislation had not been passed, the protection of credit unions against the possible repeal of state laws, and to bring some kind of general order to the rather fragmented state laws under which credit unions operated in the early 1930s.[26]

The Federal Credit Union Act 1934

In the United States of America, credit unions are organized under both state and federal laws. Credit unionists have placed great emphasis on the importance of a flexible legal framework for four reasons: firstly, it defines the governance and structure of credit unions; secondly, it stipulates many of the relationships between credit unions and government officials; thirdly, it establishes the fiduciary responsibilities of directors; finally, it often effects the taxation position that credit unions enjoy.[27]

By 1933, the situation had improved and credit union laws were in 38 states, covering 95% of the population. At this time a serious move began to pass a federal credit union law. Bergengren did not permit the Great Depression nor the banking crisis to deter him for what had become a major objective, the enactment of a federal credit union law, which would allow the incorporation of credit union law in any state or territory. He believed that such law would permit the organization of credit unions in states, which had refused to pass such legislation. Bergengren wrote: ". . . a federal credit union law would be a sort of blanket insurance policy for all out state laws, giving an alternative methods of

---

[23] MacPherson noted that the passage in 1909 of the Massachusetts Credit Union Enabling Act did not immediately usher in a Golden Age of credit union development. Not even in the United States, where the most extensive development would occur, was it a simple or easy matter to launch the movement. See MacPherson *op cit* fn 6.

[24] Bergengren, *CUNA Emerges, Madison, WI: Credit Union National Association* (1936) 23-25.

[25] Burger & Dacin, *Field of Membership: An Evolving Concept, Centre for Credit Union Research* (1991).

[26] See Bergengren *op cit* fn 24.

[27] See MacPherson *op cit* fn 6.

organization".[28] It is arguable that the critical event in the development of the credit union movement in the United States of America was the passing of the Federal Credit Union Act 1934 (FCUA 1934). The Act authorised the establishment of federally chartered credit unions in all states and made credit for provident purposes available to people of small means through a national system of co-operative credit. Burger and Dacin took the view that:

> The Federal Credit Union Act [1934] was primarily to be the piece of federal legislation that granted permission and established standards for nation-wide organization of credit unions. In addition, the Act would establish the economic role of credit unions in the reorganized US financial system.[29]

Prior to the enactment of the FCUA 1934, the financial crisis of the Great Depression prevented many Americans from obtaining credit at reasonable rates of interest because of the security demanded by banks.[30] This meant that in order to obtain credit; many Americans were forced to turn to loan sharks that charged extortionate rates of interest.[31] It is therefore unsurprising that Congress feared that the credit situation reduced the overall purchasing capacity of consumers, thus preventing the recovery of the economy.[32] In order to overcome this problem, Congress legislated and created the federal credit union system under the remit of the FCUA 1934. The Act was "seen as a way to provide the same credit opportunities to Americans living in states that were not currently served by credit unions due to a lack of state enabling legislation".[33]

The stated purpose of the FCUA 1934 was to promote credit "for provident and productive purposes".[34] Furthermore, the FCUA 1934 set out the basic structure for Federal credit unions with members purchasing shares to fund credit unions, membership of credit unions being limited to groups, each of which shared a common bond of occupation, association or location in well-defined neighbourhood, community or rural district, each member having only one vote regardless of the number of shares owned by the member, the management of the credit union being in the hands of volunteers and loans being made exclusively to members.[35] Bergengren stated that the FCUA 1934 was the greatest single step forward in the history of the credit union movement.[36]

---

[28] See Moody and Fite *op cit* fn 12 at p 151.

[29] See Burger and Dacin *op cit* fn 25.

[30] See Masset *op cit* fn 2.

[31] *Ibid.* For a more detailed discussion of how the Great Depression contributed towards the enactment of the Federal Credit Union Act 1934, see Hicks, "Common sense on the common bond: banks, federal credit unions, and field of membership rules" (1999) 66 *Tenn L Rev* 1201.

[32] See Masset *op cit* fn 2.

[33] *Ibid.*

[34] See Moody and Fite *op cit* fn 12 at p 166.

[35] See Burger and Dacin *op cit* fn 25.

[36] See Moody and Fite *op cit* fn 12 at p 166.

Legislative amendments The 1970s brought major changes in the products offered by financial institutions and credit unions found that they needed to expand their services. In 1977, legislation permitted credit unions to expand the services they offer to members, which included mortgage lending. Deregulation increased the flexibility in the merger of credit unions and the field of membership criteria, and expanded member services. The number of credit union members doubled and the assets of credit unions tripled to a $65 billion.

It can be argued that a flexible legal framework is an important factor in the development of credit unions. Burger and Dacin noted that these amendments assisted the development of the credit union movement in the United States of America in 1977 when its provisions were amended to liberalise the provisions of the common bond.[37] The key regulatory changes to the FCUA 1934 were the 1978 Financial Institutions Regulatory and Interest Rate Control Act; the 1980 Depository Institutions Deregulation and Monetary Control Act; the 1981 NCUA regulations, the 1982 Gart-St Germain Depository Institutions Act and the 1983 NCUA Regulations which extended the definition of family member in the common bond requirements.

By the end of the 1970s, the number of credit union members more than doubled and assets in credit unions tripled to over sixty five million dollars.[38] It has been argued that deregulation "had a profound effect on the kinds of products and services credit unions are entitled to provide, and on their financial and operational management. Deregulation . . . created new opportunities for growth and merger".[39] The legislative changes provided the "main stimulus for growth and consolidation in the US credit union movement".[40]

The total number of credit unions peaked in 1969 and then declined slightly through 1976. After 1976 this decline became more marked and ten years later the number of credit unions had fallen to about 17,000 compared to almost 24,000 in 1969. During most of the 1970s credit unions continued to expand their share of the market for consumer instalment credit. However, their share peaked at 16.7 percent in 1978, and then began declining in 1979.[41]

The common bond/field of membership Section 109 of the FCUA 1934 is an example of how a flexible legal framework has contributed towards the development of credit unions. This section provides that federal credit union membership shall be limited to groups having a common bond of occupation or association, or to groups within a well-defined neighbourhood, community, or rural district to permit federal credit unions to be composed of multiple, unrelated

---

37 *Ibid.*

38 See MacPherson *op cit* fn 6.

39 Goddard, McKillop & Wilson, " The Growth of US Credit Unions" (2002) 26 *Journal of Banking and Finance,* 2327-2356. Hereafter referred to as Goddard *et al.*

40 *Ibid.*

41 Goddard *et al, op cit* fn 39.

groups, each having its own distinct common bond.[42] The National Credit Union Administration's (NCUA) regulations establish three categories of common bond: occupational, associational, and community-based.

In the early 1980s the NCUA came under pressure from credit unions to expand the ambit of the common bond. This was due to the fact that a number of federal credit unions were failing; 222 in 1981.[43] These failures occurred because of a recession that was fuelling large-scale industrial downsizing and closures, resulting in dwindling memberships in some credit unions. This in turn caused a dangerous drain on the National Credit Union Share Insurance Fund.[44] As a response, in 1982, the NCUA interpreted this common bond provision to mean that members of each occupational federal credit union must be drawn from a single occupational group, however, later that year the NCUA further amended its interpretation to permit a federal credit union to comprise "multiple occupational groups" which only had to be within a "well defined area" according to an NCUA interpretative ruling. The term "well defined area" was interpreted by the NCUA as an area served by either an actual or planned office of the credit union. This is a very broad interpretation as there could be virtually any number of such offices. This broad interpretation of the common bond allowed the NCUA to merge and transfer assets and members of failed or failing credit unions into far healthier federally insured credit unions. The action seemed to have worked, as the number of credit union failures dropped to 112 in 1982 and 40 in 1983.[45]

The liberal interpretation of section 109 was beneficial because it provided credit unions with the flexibility needed to respond to changing social and economic conditions. Mattson stated "there is no doubt that the NCUA's liberal reading of section 109 was beneficial to the credit union industry".[46] Credit unions were able to offer their customers superior services, such as higher deposit rates and lower rates on consumer loans, thus assisting their development. Mattson postulated that this amendment combined with the NCUA's broad reading of section 109 resulted in "significant expansion" in the credit unions' membership base.[47] As a result of these legislative amendments, credit unions grew by four hundred percent, controlling more than $350 billion in assets from seventy million

[42] The common bond reflects the philosophy of the credit union movement in that it is something that unites its members. The sharing of the common bond is a type of principled or honourable influence that persuades borrowers to repay the money that other members have loaned them.

[43] Testimony of Norman E D'Amours, chairman NCUA to Committee of Banking and Financial Services, US House of Representatives, 11 March 1998.

[44] The National Credit Union Share Insurance Fund is a US Treasury fund that is managed by the NCUA and it protects the savings of members in the event of their credit union collapsing. Approximately 97% of all US credit unions are covered under this regime. For a more detailed assessment of how such a scheme could assist the development of credit unions in Great Britain see generally Ryder, "The Financial Services Authority and Credit Unions: The Final Piece of the Jigsaw?" (2002) 11 *Nott LJ* 17-32.

[45] *Ibid.*

[46] See Mattson *op cit* fn 21.

[47] *Ibid.*

members.[48] Goddard *et al* agreed with the view of Mattson and stated that the relaxation of the common bond has been important in permitting credit unions to sustain growth.[49]

Credit unions were eager to take advantage of the amendments. Communicator's Federal Credit Union of Houston expanded its membership to include "all retirees and citizens living within a 25 mile radius of Houston".[50] However, the activity of the AT&T Family Federal Credit Union (ATTF) brought the movement into direct conflict with the banks. The ATTF was formed in 1952, with its membership restricted to the occupational common bond of "Employees of the Radio Shops of Western Electric Company Inc, who work in Wintson-Salem, Greensboro, and Burlington, North Carolina; employees of this credit union; members of their immediate families; and organizations of such persons".[51] ATTF took great advantage of the wider NCUA interpretation of the common bond by applying for and being accepted to expand its field of membership to include a number of different companies including, *inter alia*, Coca-Cola Bottling Company, Black and Decker Corporation and American Tobacco Company.[52]

In December 1990, five North Carolina banks and the American Bankers Association sued the NCUA for permitting ATTF to serve employees at more than 150 different companies. It was argued that the NCUA interpretation violated the FCUA 1934 by allowing unaffiliated groups to join together in a credit union. On 30 July 1996, the US Court of Appeals for the District of Columbia Circuit issued an opinion that rejected the NCUA's new interpretation of the common bond language in the statute. The court held that the FCUA 1934 common bond provision requires all members of an occupational federal credit union to share a single common bond. NCUA had exceeded its statutory authority when it permitted the ATTF to expand its field of membership to include the employees of a variety of businesses that were unaffiliated with the credit union's original membership.

The US District Court for the District of Columbia issued an injunction declaring unlawful membership in a federal credit union by individuals or groups who do not share a "single common bond of occupation". The Court of Appeals issued a partial stay of this decision on 24 December 1996. Under this stay, federal credit unions were allowed to continue accepting members from existing groups that were not part of the credit union's original and core membership group. Credit unions were not, however, allowed to add new and unrelated groups that did not share a common bond with the credit union's original core membership group.

On 25 February 1998 the US Supreme Court issued a 5-4 decision concluding that the banks had standing to challenge the NCUA's interpretation of the FCUA

---

48 See Hicks *op cit* fn 31.

49 See Goddard *et al*, *op cit* fn 39.

50 Novajovsky, "From National Credit Union Administration v First National Bank & Trust to the revised Federal Credit Union Act: The debate over membership requirements in the credit union industry" (2000) 44 *NYL Sch L Rev* 221.

51 See Mattson *op cit* fn 21.

52 *Ibid.*

1934, and that the NCUA's interpretation was contrary to the intent of Congress,[53] and was therefore impermissible.[54] The court felt that the NCUA interpretation of the field of membership was so wide as to make the definition of the common bond "surplusage" in reference to federal credit unions made up of multiple unrelated employer groups.[55]

It has been noted that the Supreme Court decision would cause adverse effects for the credit union movement. In his testimony to the House of Representatives, Norman E D'Amours[56] noted that the ruling would put many credit unions in a difficult position. The very reason that NCUA made the interpretation, to combat recessionary pressures, would be overturned, once again making credit unions susceptible to economic downturn. Novajovsky noted that the decision would mean that credit unions would be unable to offer such diverse services such as ATM provision common among larger multiple group unions.[57]

D'Amours also commented that that credit union growth would be stifled as access to new members, particularly younger members at the borrowing stage of life,[58] was critical. To restrict the field of membership to a single occupational group would seriously restrict the possible membership numbers. He also stated that people employed by small businesses would lack access to credit unions,[59] and it was these employees of small businesses that were in greater need of access than those employed in larger enterprises.[60] In fact 94.2% of employee groups served by multiple group credit unions have fewer than 500 employees.[61] The result of the Court's interpretation of section 109 could have had an adverse impact upon the development of credit unions. One House Representative, Jim Leach, Chairman of the House Banking Committee commented that it was inconceivable that Congress will allow millions of Americans to be kicked out of the financial institution of their choice.[62]

Novajovsky argued that the decision of the Supreme Court could cause a high level of fragmentation within the credit union movement in the United States of

---

[53] The first part of the so-called Chevron Test from *Chevron USA Inc v Natural Resources Defence Council Inc* 467 US 837 (1984).

[54] The members of the court were split 5 – 4 on the issue of standing, however in the dissenting judgement no reference was made to the issue of the NCUA interpretation being impermissible.

[55] *NCUA v First National Bank & Trust* 118 US 927 (1998) *per* Justice Thomas.

[56] Chairman NCUA.

[57] See Novajovsky *op cit* fn 50.

[58] D'Amours pointed out that younger people borrow more and older people save more, it was therefore, important that credit unions have access to those at the borrowing stage to ensure continuity of revenue. See above at fn 43.

[59] Small business defined as one with 500 employees or fewer, while 500 persons is the minimum number of people required to set up a federally chartered credit union.

[60] Average salary of small business employee was $23,780, compared to $29,662 of large business employee. See above at fn 43.

[61] *Ibid.*

[62] Linda Greenhouse, Credit Unions Lose to Banks in High Court, *NY Times*, 26 Dec 1998.

America for four reasons:[63] firstly, this decision could result in smaller credit unions not being able to offer services or rates that would permit it to remain a viable competitor of commercial and savings banks; secondly, serious managerial and administrative problems pertaining to the structure and inter-relatedness of the "off-spring" credit unions would arise among affected institutions; thirdly, the prospective increase in the number of credit unions in existence would impose a hardship upon regulatory authorities that supervise and approve such activities; lastly, the inconvenience to credit union members and the negative impact on consumer protection would have a potentially adverse affect on the industry as a whole.

Credit Union Membership Access Act 1998

Having lost the battle in the Supreme Court, credit unions and the NCUA turned their efforts to Congress and were soon testifying before the House Banking Committee. The possible effects of the Supreme Courts decision were not lost on the US legislature, with the passing of a bill with a majority of 411 to 8 in the House of Representatives and 92 to 6 in the Senate; President Bill Clinton signed the Credit Union Membership Access Act[64] on the 7 August 1998. Within six months of the verdict, the Credit Union Membership Access Act negated the Supreme Court's decision.

This legislation amended and expanded in particular the FCUA's requirements regarding credit union membership. Paul Kanjorski, a House Representative stated that "it [the Act] stops the bleeding that would have killed the credit union industry".[65] Novajovsky took the view that:

> The revised Act . . . addressed the problems . . . faced by credit unions fragmenting into smaller institutions. The key distinction between Congress' approach and the Court's approach is that the process under Congress' amendment is suggested and subject to numerous qualifications, whereas the Court's decision would have arguably forced the fragmentation [of credit unions].[66]

Novajovsky added that the amendments by the Act are significant for three reasons: firstly, they are very protective of the industry itself as a whole, the individual credit unions, and the public they serve; secondly, the NCUA's broad authority to regulate and oversee the industry on all levels is reinforced; thirdly, the open-ended grant of authority indicates Congress' intent for the NCUA to be the guardian and keeper of the industry.[67] He concluded:

---

63 See Novajovsky *op cit* fn 50.

64 CUMAA 1998.

65 House votes to let credit unions expand their memberships, *NY Times*, 2 April 1998.

66 See Novajovsky *op cit* fn 50.

67 *Ibid*.

> . . . the credit union industry was rescued when Congress revised the Federal Credit Union Act, effectively overruling the Court's decision . . . its [the Act] net effect will likely be positive.[68]

Mattson pointed out:

> The Act's purpose was to ensure the safety and well being of the credit union industry and to protect members of modest means. The Act clearly marks a decided victory for the credit unions because it increases the industry's ability to expand its membership base by expressly allowing for multiple common-bond credit unions.[69]

The Act undoubtedly helps the credit union movement in the here and now, however, it is possible to envisage that at some point in the future credit unions will need to grow again, and this will only be achieved by further interpretative guidance from the NCUA and by legislative amendment. This could bring the movement into conflict, once again, with the mainstream financial service providers, and maybe next time the Congress will not be so accommodating. Nevertheless, the growth of credit unions in North America is extraordinary and this reflects a number of factors including the influence of "pioneers", economic conditions, a good organizational framework and a favourable legal framework.

Republic of Ireland

The success of the movement in the Republic of Ireland is illustrated by referring to statistical data. Since the establishment of the first credit union in 1958, the movement has grown and now numbers six hundred, with savings amounting to three billion pounds,[70] over 2,000 full-time employees and a market share of over 40%. Donnelly highlighted the success of the credit union movement in the Republic of Ireland and took the view that:

> Credit unions now provide a wider range of services, which in many cases rival those, provided by credit institutions. Furthermore, credit unions are now the most widely used financial institution with a membership of over 1,500,000 people. This modernisation of credit unions is now reflected in the law. The Credit Union Act 1997 allows credit unions to bring many of their services into line with those offered by credit institutions.[71]

This data provides an excellent indicator of the success of the movement in the Republic of Ireland.

---

68 See Novajovsky *op cit* fn 50.

69 See Mattson *op cit* fn 21.

70 For the purposes of this article pounds refers to the currency of the Republic of Ireland prior to the introduction of the Single European Currency, which came into effect on 1 January 2002.

71 Donnelly, *The Law of Banks and Credit Institutions* (2000).

The Credit Union Acts 1966 and 1997

A central factor that has assisted the development of the credit union movement in the Republic of Ireland is the statutory framework established by the Credit Union Act 1997. Until 1966, credit unions in the Republic of Ireland, like their counterparts in Great Britain, were regulated under Industrial and Provident Societies Acts. However, this legislation was deemed to be inappropriate for the regulation of credit unions.[72] The passing of the Credit Union Act 1966 was a landmark event in the development of the credit union movement in the Republic of Ireland. Under the Credit Union Act 1966, the membership of a credit union was based upon the basic concept of a common bond between the members of the credit union.[73] Each credit union under the Credit Union Act 1966, was a separate legal entity that was controlled by its members through a series of annual meetings.[74]

The implementation of the Credit Union Act 1966 was fundamental for the development and growth of the credit union movement. Quinn said:

> The [Credit Unions] Act was a landmark for the wider co-operative movement because of statutory recognition of co-operative concepts including the mutuality of members in ownership and organization of their societies.[75]

Donnelly concurred with the view of Quinn that the Credit Union Act 1966 had a major positive impact upon the development of the credit union movement in the Republic of Ireland and that the Act subsequently laid down the foundation for the Credit Union Act 1997.[76]

The purpose of the 1997 Act was to assist the continuing development of credit unions whilst ensuring that the principle ethos of the credit union movement was not lost.[77] A further aim of the Credit Union Act 1997 was to establish effective regulation of credit unions in the Republic of Ireland.[78] Quinn took the view that the purpose of the Act was to consolidate the existing legislation and to provide an updated framework for the development and supervision of the successful credit union movement.[79] The passage of the Credit Union Act 1997 was controversial as

---

[72] *Ibid.* For a similar comment regarding the appropriateness of the Industrial and Provident Societies Act 1965 towards the regulation of credit unions in the Great Britain see Griffiths and Howells *op cit* fn 5.

[73] Section 4.

[74] Sections 19-21.

[75] Quinn, *Credit Unions in Ireland* (1999).

[76] See Donnelly *op cit* fn 71.

[77] *Ibid.*

[78] See Quinn *op cit* fn 75.

[79] *Ibid.*

competing financial institutions complained that it gave too much power and freedom to credit unions.[80]

It has been argued that the 1997 legislation has attempted to maintain the mutual status of credit unions. Donnelly took the view that in order to do this, limits needed to be placed upon the amount of funds which could be raised per member through the issue of shares or the acceptance of deposits. Deposits can only be accepted from members who already hold a certain number of shares in the credit union. The legislation requires that the value of the member's shares at the time of the deposit must be at least £1,000. The Credit Union Act 1997 provides that a member shall not hold shares in the credit union, the value of which, when aggregated with the amount held by that member on deposit with the credit unions, exceeds £50,000 or one per cent of the total assets of the credit union, whichever is greater.[81]

There are statutory provisions that have assisted the development of the credit union movement in the Republic of Ireland. One such provision is that of the common bond.[82] Section 6(3) outlines the types of common bond that are permitted in the Republic of Ireland. These include occupation,[83] residing or being employed in a particular locality,[84] employed by an employer or having retired from employment with a particular employer,[85] being a members of a bonafide organization or being associated with other members of the society for a purpose other than that of forming a society to be registered as a credit union[86] or any other common bond approved by the Registrar.[87] These statutory requirements for the common bond in the Republic of Ireland provide credit unions with greater flexibility than under the corresponding provisions in Great Britain. Donnelly has taken the view that the common bond is the most important of the legislative requirements.[88]

The most frequently utilised common bond by credit unions in the Republic of Ireland is "residing or being employed in a particular locality".[89] The "being employed by a particular employer or having retired from employment with a particular employer" means that employees of large companies who are spread throughout the country still have a common bond of employment.[90]

---

80 McCarthy, Briscoe & Ward, *Redesigning the Credit Union for the New Millennium: A Case Study for Ireland*, (2000). This has subsequently led to banks and building societies taking the credit union movement in the Republic of Ireland to the European Court.

81 See Donnelly *op cit* fn 71.

82 *Ibid.*

83 Section 6(3)(a).

84 Section 6(3)(b).

85 Section 6(3)(c).

86 Section 6(3)(d).

87 Section 6(3)(e).

88 See Donnelly *op cit* fn 71.

89 See Quinn *op cit* fn 75.

90 Quinn noted that a number of companies have utilised this type of common bond, such as Telecom Eirann, ESB and Garda.

Section 6(5) of the Act demonstrates that flexible legislation is a key factor in determining the successful development of credit unions. Section 6(5) specifies that a member of a credit union whose "relative" or "family" member resides in the same household is entitled to become a member under the common bond. A member of the family is defined in section 2 of the Credit Union Act 1997 as including a father, mother, children, grand parents, uncles and aunts, nephews, nieces, in-laws and first cousins.[91] Such a broad definition has permitted more people to become members of a credit union, thus assisting their development. Another example of how the Credit Union Act 1997 has encouraged the development of the credit union movement in the Republic of Ireland is demonstrated by analysing its power to grant loans. Quinn maintains that: "One of the main advantages of joining a credit union is the facility to obtain loans at terms including interest rates that have traditionally been favourable compared with banks and building societies and other financial institutions".[92]

Section 35(1) of the Credit Union Act 1997 provides that a loan must be made for a provident or productive purpose with or without security and on such terms as the credit union's rules may provide. A loan to a member under the age of eighteen is not permitted unless an indemnity is given by the member's parent or guardian or by a person approved by the board of directors. Under section 35 it is possible for a large credit union to grant loans up to one million pounds to an individual member. The limits imposed upon credit unions illustrate that the legislation has assisted the development of the credit union movement in the Republic of Ireland.

Further evidence that suggests that the development of credit unions in the Republic of Ireland have been assisted by a flexible legislative framework is demonstrated by analysing the additional services that credit unions are permitted to offer their members.[93] As the level of competition within the financial services sector in the Republic of Ireland increases, it is essential that credit unions be permitted to offer additional services to enable them to continue developing.[94] McCarthy has added that credit unions must broaden the services they offer to members, as they compete with commercial banks which currently offer a far broader range of services such as credit card facilities, ATM networks and chequebooks.[95] Section 48 of the Credit Union Act 1997 permits a credit union, acting as a principal or agent, to provide additional services for its members. The Act does not define "additional services", but Quinn noted that it would include services that are not traditionally offered by a credit union. Quinn opined that the additional services would include chequebooks, foreign exchange, ATM facilities and mortgages.[96] Donnelly argued that one of the main aims of the Credit Union

---

[91] See Quinn *op cit* fn 75.

[92] See Quinn *ibid.*

[93] Section 48 Credit Union Act 1997.

[94] See McCarthy *op cit* fn 80.

[95] *Ibid.*

[96] See Quinn *op cit* fn 75.

Act 1997 was to enable credit unions to expand the services that they offer to their members.

One of the aims of the Credit Union Act 1997 was to enable credit unions to provide their member with a range of services beyond those traditionally offered. This object was fulfilled by section 48 of the legislation, which provides that a credit union may provide, as principal or agent, additional services of a description that appears to the Registrar to be of mutual benefit to its members. The Minister may also prescribe certain services as involving no risk to the assets of the credit union or the funds of its members. In this instance, the approval of the Registrar is not required. The services include ATM facilities and foreign exchange, both of which services are already provided by some credit unions.[97] In addition to the services as prescribed in section 48, credit unions are permitted to make, endorse or accept a Bill of Exchange,[98] have the power to vary, to enter into or discharge contracts,[99] and are allowed acquire and hold land in their own name.[100] Credit unions are permitted to make investments of their surplus funds, but only limited investments.[101]

Section 48 of the Credit Union Act 1997 enables credit unions to offer similar services to those offered by other financial institutions such as banks and building societies. This amounts to concrete evidence that a flexible legislative framework has enabled them to develop successfully in the Republic of Ireland. The impact of a flexible legal framework on the development of the credit unions in the Republic of Ireland cannot be under estimated. Credit unions are permitted to offer their members loans that might be classified as a mortgage and to provide additional services to meet both the demands of their members and in response to increasing competition.

Great Britain

Unlike credit unions in the United States of America and the Republic of Ireland, the movement in Great Britain is stagnant. The first credit union was not established in Great Britain until 1964, despite the early co-operative origins in 1844.[102] Credit unions in Great Britain were significantly restricted by the provisions of the Industrial Provident Societies Act 1965 and the Companies Act 1948, under which they were regulated. Many people who organized credit unions did not register them, thereby creating an image problem for credit unions, especially when one found itself in trouble.

---

97 *Ibid.*

98 Section 39 Credit Union Act 1997.

99 Section 40.

100 Section 41.

101 By virtue of section 43(1) of the Credit Union Act 1997 the power of a credit union is limited in that a credit union can only invest in authorised securities and shares or deposits in other credit unions and friendly societies.

102 Jones, *Towards Sustainable Credit Union Development - A Research Project* (1999).

It wasn't until the 1970s that credit unions began to expand within Great Britain. Donnelly and Hagett took the view that there are a number of reasons why they began to grow:

> First, prior to this time people in Britain were less used to the idea of using credit than some groups in other parts of the world. Second, around this period, banks also began to pull away from the retail sector and concentrate business on the wholesale markets. Third, immigrants from Ireland and the Caribbean had brought the idea of credit unions with them.[103]

The Crowther Committee on Consumer Credit provided the first formal recognition of credit unions by the Government in 1971.[104] The Committee stated that there was a case for encouraging the expansion of the credit union movement and for taking steps to make its existence, its aims and its methods widely known in the hope that it may take root here and more credit unions be formed.[105] John Roper MP embraced the cause of creating appropriate legislation and spearheaded the passage through parliament of legislation that would allow the specific incorporation of credit unions. The legislation however, was restrictive, limiting membership to employee groups or properly constituted associations. On 4 April 1979, the Credit Unions Act received Royal Assent.

Credit Unions Act 1979

The Credit Unions Act 1979 was intended to be simple in its form and content by limiting the size of membership, shareholding and loans to small amounts consistent with the formative years of credit unions.[106] The legislation has not been sufficiently amended to take into account the continued expansion of the movement, thereby limiting the impact of credit unions.

An example of how the provisions of the Credit Unions Act 1979 has affected the development of the credit union movement in Great Britain is illustrated by examining the statutory provisions that relate to the common bond. Section 1(2)(b) requires a credit union's membership to be restricted to people who fulfil a set qualification that is appropriate to the credit union and that a common bond exists between its members. The term "common bond" first appeared in credit union literature in 1914 and it refers to the association shared by members of a group served by a credit union.[107] Ferguson and McKillop have maintained that the common bond relates to the existence of a common identity "where the nature of

---

[103] See Donnelly and Haggett *op cit* fn 1.
[104] Cmnd, 4596 at para 9.2.12.
[105] *Ibid.*
[106] *Credit Unions in Great Britain - A Review of the Years 1979-1995* (1966) Registry of Friendly Societies.
[107] See Burger and Dacin *op cit* fn 25.

social relationships stems from reciprocal interdependence typical of traditional community relationships."[108]

There are a number of common bond criteria permitted by the Credit Unions Act 1979: following a particular occupation,[109] residing in a particular locality,[110] being employed in a particular locality,[111] being employed by a particular employer,[112] being a member of a bona fide organization[113] and live or association common bond.[114] By their very nature, the provisions have affected the development of the credit union movement. If a person wanted to become a member of a credit union but failed to meet the criteria laid down in section 1(4) that person would not be permitted to become a member and join. Lessons could be adopted from the legislative provisions in the Republic of Ireland and the USA.

A further way in which the Credit Unions Act 1979 has affected the development of credit unions is illustrated briefly by examining the provisions of section 6. This imposes restrictions on the number of people who are permitted to join a credit union. In particular, section 6(2) stipulates that the maximum number of members a credit union is entitled to is five thousand. Evidence from other jurisdictions indicates that if the ceiling imposed on the membership is lifted the credit union movement will expand. In their study, Burger and Dacin cited the policies adopted in the United States of America towards the membership ceiling:

> Numerical limits on the field of membership of credit unions were raised in the 1970s, although they were still determined in a somewhat arbitrary fashion. The original limit was approximately 5,000 population. The 1965 Manual provided that the population area should not be materially in excess of 7,5000. The 1972 Manual raised the population limit in the community to not greatly exceeding 25,000.[115]

Another example of how the Credit Unions Act 1979 has affected the development of credit unions can be seen by referring to section 9. This section provides that a credit union is permitted to take deposits of up to a total of £750 from a person who is "too young" to become a member.[116] This is one of the most restrictive sections of the Credit Unions Act 1979. If the credit union movement is to increase its market penetration it is essential that it attracts younger members.

---

[108] Ferguson & McKillop, *The Strategic Development of Credit Unions* (1997). For a more detailed discussion of the common bond see Ryder & Baker, "The Enemy Within? A Critical Analysis of the Credit Unions Act 1979 and the Common Bond" (2003) 36 (2) *Journal of Co-operative Studies* 117.

[109] Credit Unions Act 1979, S 1(4)(a).

[110] Section 1(4)(b).

[111] Section 1(4)(c).

[112] Section 1(4)(d).

[113] Section 1(4)(e).

[114] Deregulation (Credit Unions) Order 1996, SI 1996/1189, art 3.

[115] See Burger and Dacin *op cit* fn 25.

[116] Any deposit, which is held, will be held upon trust and shall be invested only in the manner which is permitted under Part I or Part II of Schedule 1 of the Trustee Investments Act 1961.

Banks and building societies offer more incentives to younger savers than credit unions currently offer and this gulf in potential membership needs to be addressed.

The Credit Union (Increase in Limits on Deposits by persons too young to be members and of Periods for the Repayment of Loans) Order increased the limits that were imposed by the 1979 legislation.[117] The limit upon which a credit union is permitted to take from youngsters who are "too young" to become members of the credit unions has been increased from £750 to £5,000. Although this amendment is beneficial, it will not entice young people to join a credit union.

The provisions of the Credit Unions Act 1979 limit the services that credit unions provide their members and has therefore affected their development in the Great Britain. This is a core issue that has affected their development and one that must be addressed. Ferguson and McKillop took the view that: " . . . credit unions are single product intermediaries providing basic savings and loan service pre-specified volume limits and interest rate ceilings. It is our contention that the time is approaching form credit unions to be permitted a broader role in retail financial services".[118] Credit unions must be permitted to offer members services as bill payments, the provision of ATMs, the ability to exchange foreign currency and to make limited investments to enable the movement to expand and develop.[119]

There have been a number of attempts to lessen the restrictions imposed by the Credit Unions Act 1979 upon credit unions in Great Britain. The first major attempt to reform the legislation occurred in 1996 via the Deregulation (Credit Unions) Order 1996. The purpose of the amendment was to make the growth of credit unions easier whilst continuing to ensure the safety of members' funds.[120] It was widely accepted that the movement welcomed the 1996 reforms, as they would increase the growth potential of credit unions. The amendments were the introduction of a new membership qualification, which means that all members must live or work within a defined geographical area, where the Registrar considers it proper to treat as sufficient evidence of the existence of a common bond a statutory declaration which is given by three members and the secretary of the society, and is to the effect that a common bond exists, to increase the limits on shareholding, to permit the use of shares as security, the relaxation of the restrictions on non-qualifying members and to increase limits on loans to members. The reforms could have gone further and argued that credit unions should not be subject to a membership ceiling and that the movement would benefit from a broader based common bond. Despite the merits of the measures many of the restrictions within the Credit Unions Act 1979 remain.

---

[117] Credit Union (Increase in Limits on Deposits by persons too Young to be members and of Periods for the Repayment of Loans) Order 2001, SI 2001/811. This statutory instrument increased the limits that were imposed under s 9 of the Credit Unions Act 1979.

[118] See Ferguson & McKillop *op cit* fn 117.

[119] A credit union is prevented from investing any part of its surplus funds except in a manner authorised by the Registry of Friendly Societies, Credit Unions Act 1979, s 13.

[120] *Op cit* fn 114.

In November 1998, the Treasury announced its intention to lift some of the legislative burdens imposed on credit unions by the Credit Unions Act 1979.[121] The measures included permitting credit unions to borrow from external sources,[122] to allow credit unions to offer interest bearing share accounts, to entitle credit unions to charge fees for providing services, to abolish the £750 maximum limit on youth accounts, to make the common bond requirement more flexible, to provide credit unions more flexibility to dispose of repossessed collateral, to remove the 5,000 maximum membership limit and to extend the repayment periods for secured and unsecured loans. A second Consultation Paper was published in October 2001 and contained proposals aimed at widening credit unions' ability to borrow from external sources; permit the payment of dividends more than once a year and at different rates and enable credit unions to charge for the provision of ancillary services.[123]

Conclusion

The Credit Unions Act 1979 has limited the development of the credit union movement in the Great Britain and, as such is flawed. Much can be learned from the experience in Ireland and the USA where a flexible legal framework has not only assisted the development of credit unions, but has ensured their future welfare and success. Credit unions in Great Britain lack an adequate legislative framework. Weak legislation and ineffective regulation imperil the safety and soundness of credit unions and restrict their ability to meet the members' financial needs. This has limited their development in Great Britain because credit unions are prevented from participating fully in the financial services sector.

---

[121] HM Treasury Consultation Document, *Proposed Amendments to the Credit Unions Act 1979* (1998).

[122] Other than authorised banks and other credit unions.

[123] HM Treasury Consultation Document, *Proposed Amendments to the Credit Unions Act 1979 – A Consultation Document* (2001). A majority of the proposals have been implemented by Schedule 18 Financial Services and Markets Act 2000. For a more detailed discussion as to how these amendments will assist the development of credit unions in Great Britain see Ryder, "Credit Unions in the United Kingdom: A Critical Analysis of their Legislative Framework and its Impact upon their Development" [2003] *JBL* 45-66.

Chapter 5

The Insolvent Subsidiary and Liability: The US and Argentine Experience

Héctor José Miguens

Introduction

Modern authors have stressed the increasing unacceptability of the concept of "Entity Law" and the emergence of the doctrine of "Enterprise Law" with respect to many aspects of the legal relationships of parent and subsidiary corporations. This change is very significant because it reflects a growing unwillingness on the part of the courts and legislatures to continue accepting the traditional view of corporate law when it no longer corresponds to the reality of the modern business enterprise in a complex industrialized international society.

The increase in the scale of business operations reflects a number of factors. First, the economic basis of all the industrialized nations has greatly expanded as evidenced by the fact that the national product has multiplied throughout the industrialized world. Moreover, most important businesses of a certain size tend to outgrow their original national limitations. The large corporation is now typically a multinational enterprise doing business in many countries throughout the world. Finally, aggregate concentration (the share of the nation's corporate assets, sales, and income represented by large corporations) has increased.[1]

To conduct economic undertakings of such magnitude, the large enterprise is inevitably driven to abandon the simple twentieth century form of corporate organization and must develop a complex corporate structure. For tax, accounting, political or administrative convenience, or to avoid qualification under foreign

---

[1] For example, by 1982, the 275 largest American manufacturing corporations represented 66.4% of the sales and 72.4% of the profits of all American manufacturing corporations. See *Statistical Abstract of the United States*, Table 921, at 546 (1984); Blumberg, *The Law of Corporate Groups, Problems in the Bankruptcy or Reorganization of Parent and Subsidiary Corporations, including the Law of Corporate Guaranties* (1985) [hereinafter Blumberg]. By 1993, the United Nations, Trans-national Corporations and Management Division estimated that there were 35,000 multi-national enterprises with 170,000 foreign affiliates. They were highly concentrated, with the largest 100 multinationals (excluding those in banking and finance) having assets of about $3.1 trillion, of which $1.2 trillion was outside their home countries. See UN Transnational Corp and Mgmt Div (1993) *World Inv Rep Studies*, cited in *Survey, Multinationals - Back in Fashion*, The Economist, 27 Mar 1993.

corporation statutes, the large corporation today almost universally conducts its business through many subsidiary corporations. The parent and the subsidiaries constitute a corporate group, which collectively conducts the business of the enterprise throughout the world.[2] In some cases, the subsidiaries conduct truly separate businesses and most often, the subsidiary is only a part or fragment of the larger business of its parent, which is collectively conducted by the various affiliates under common direction.

This change in the structure and conduct of the large business corporation is inevitably producing a decisive change in the way the law deals with the individual constituent companies of the corporate group. Older legal concepts derived from a world of much smaller and more simply organized businesses have become hopelessly inadequate. The older view, that for almost all purposes each corporation is a separate legal entity with its own legal responsibilities, is in the process of collapsing, particularly in situations where the corporation in question is a constituent part of a corporate group conducting an integrated enterprise. In many areas, a new concept, termed by Blumberg as "Enterprise Law", is winning increasing acceptance as the preferred method of analysis of the legal problems of parent and subsidiary corporations.

The new doctrine, suggested by Blumberg, seeks to trace the decline of "Entity Law" and the emergence of "Enterprise Law" as the standard for application to corporate groups and their constituent corporations. "Entity Law", the view that each corporation is a separate legal personality, originally arose from philosophical different roots. It was strongly reinforced by the acceptance of the doctrine of limited liability in the early nineteenth century in the United States and several decades later in England. With the development of limited liability for shareholders, "Entity Law" became firmly established as the legal framework that preserved a bright line of demarcation between the corporation conducting the enterprise and the shareholders who owned the enterprise.

When American corporations at the end of the nineteenth century were at last generally authorized to acquire the stock of other corporations, the operation through subsidiaries became possible for the first time, and a momentous change occurred in the structure of business. The major corporate undertaking soon ceased to be conducted by a single corporation owned by ultimate investors. The typical major enterprise increasingly developed a highly complex structure with various parts of the business allocated to numerous subsidiaries according to function (sales, manufacturing, finance, or the like) or geography. The distinction between the subsidiary corporation and its shareholder, the parent, no longer corresponded to the distinction between the enterprise and the ultimate investor, the concept on which "Entity Law" had been based. The parent and subsidiary together represented the enterprise. The older law of entity reflecting the older world of simple business organizations became anachronistic, particularly when the issue of substantive liability was not involved.

---

[2] For example, in 1982 the 1,000 largest American industrial corporations had an average of 48 subsidiaries each. Mobil Oil Corporation, as an extreme example, operated in 62 different countries through 525 subsidiaries. See Blumberg, *ibid* at pp 465-68.

In the area of bankruptcy law, as in procedure, the objectives and underlying policies of the law do not typically involve concerns of limited liability, although such concerns occur more frequently in the area of procedure. In bankruptcy, the American courts act as courts of equity with the overriding objective of achieving equality of distribution and fairness for creditors. Thus, it is to be expected that when the bankruptcy relates to one or more constituent corporations of a corporate group, the courts in many cases will not treat transactions between the bankrupt debtor or insolvent constituent of a group and its parent or controlling shareholder or affiliated corporation in the same manner as transactions between separate legal entities that are entirely unrelated. Increasingly, "Enterprise Law" has been applied to transactions involving "insiders," and "Entity Law" has been abandoned in order to achieve the goals of equality of distribution and fairness to creditors. This is particularly evident in the specialized areas of equitable subordination and substantive consolidation of proceedings. However, this approach is less evident in other areas of bankruptcy of corporate groups. The same trends can be seen in the Argentine bankruptcy law of corporate groups.[3]

This chapter studies the American Case Law and the Argentine Law[4] regarding this matter and provides new approaches and principles to the less developed European Continental Civil Law on a comparative law basis. The corporate fiction, the doctrine that a corporation represents a separate entity distinct from its shareholders with its own rights and obligations, is the very foundation of the doctrine of limited liability. When a subsidiary (or controlled corporation) is bankrupt, under what circumstances will a court impose liability on its parent (or controlling shareholder) for the obligations of the bankrupt? In a bankruptcy court applying equitable principles, will the court be more inclined to impose liability upon a parent or controlling shareholder for the debts of a subsidiary than in a contract or tort action in a court of general jurisdiction? If fairness is the guiding standard of the bankruptcy court, does it provide a greater impetus for the court to disregard the barriers of "Entity Law" in order to impose liability on affiliated companies in appropriate cases?[5]

---

3 See Blumberg, *ibid* at xxxiv-xxxvi.

4 This article contains citations to the Argentine Bankruptcy Act and other related Argentine Acts. The author has provided an unofficial translation for the cited provision of these Acts. "El Derecho", "La Ley" and "Jurisprudencia Argentina" are three different collections of case law, comments on judgements and law articles in Argentina. CNCom is the acronym of the Commercial Court of Appeals of Buenos Aires, the main Court of Commercial Law cases in Argentina. It is divided into five sections of three judges each, designated A, B, C, D and E. CSJN is the acronym for the (Federal) Supreme Court of Justice of Argentina. CNCiv is the acronym for the Civil Court of Appeals of Buenos Aires, the main Court of Civil cases of Argentina. It is divided into nine divisions of three judges each. RDCO is the acronym of "Revista del Derecho Comercial y de las Obligaciones", a Review of Commercial Law and the Law of Obligations edited in Buenos Aires, Argentina.

5 See Blumberg, *op* cit fn 1 at pp 589-90. See generally Cieri *et al*, "Braking up is Hard to Do: Avoiding the Solvency-Related Pitfalls in Spinoff Transactions" (1999) 54 *Bus Law* 533 (discussing impact of subsidiary's contingent liabilities on parent's solvency in context of spinoff transactions); Landers, "A Unified Approach to Parent, Subsidiary and Affiliate

Cases Imposing Liability

The review of the American cases discloses at least about two dozen cases, (not all of them in the bankruptcy field), that have upheld liability on a parent (or controlling shareholder) for the obligations of an insolvent subsidiary (or controlled corporation).[6] Most of these have relied on the "piercing the corporate veil" jurisprudence in a greater or lesser degree.

Questions in Bankruptcy" (1975) 42 *U Chi L Rev* 589 at pp 606-28; Note, "Creditors' Rights Upon Insolvency of a Parent Corporation or Its Instrumentality" (1933) 46 *Harv L Rev* 823 (1933); Bryant, Jr, Annotation, "Liability of Corporation for Contracts of Subsidiary" (1971) 38 *ALR* 3d 1102, 1146-54.

6 See generally *Consolidated Rock Prods Co v Du Bois*, 312 US 510, 523-24 (1941); *Federal Deposit of Insurance Company v Sea Pines Co*, 692 F 2d 973 (4th Cir 1982), *cert denied*, 461 US 928 (1983); *Baltimore & Ohio Tel Co v Interstate Tel Co*, 54 F 50 (4th Cir 1893); *Norfolk & WRR v Wasserstrom*, 1991 US Dist LEXIS 12969 (ED Pa 1991); *Federal Deposit of Insurance Company v Martinez Almodovar*, 671 F Supp 851 (DPR 1987); *Federal Deposit of Insurance Company v Allen*, 584 F Supp 386 (ED Tenn 1984); *Long v Mc Glon*, 263 F.Supp 96 (DSC 1967); *Palmer v Stokely*, 255 F Supp 674 (WD Okla 1966); *Henderson v Rounds & Porter Lumber Co*, 99 F Supp 376 (WD Ark 1951); *In re Plantation Realty Trust*, 232 BR 279 (Bankr D Mass 1999); *In re Mass*, 178 BR 626 (MD Pa 1995); *In re Keene Corp*, 164 BR 844 (Bankr SDNY 1994); *In re Hillsborough Holdings Corp*, 144 BR 920 (Bankr MD Fla 1992) (denying motion for summary judgment); *In re Farley, Inc*, 1992 Bankr LEXIS 1801 (Bankr ND Ill 1992) (denying motion for summary judgment); *In re Velis*, 123 BR 497 (DNJ 1991); *In re Major Funding Corp*, 126 BR 504 (Bankr SD Tex 1990); *In re Jarax Int'l, Inc* 122 BR 793 (Bankr SD Fla 1990); *In re Haugen Constr Serv, Inc*, 104 BR 1013 (Bankr ND 1989); *In re Charnock*, 97 BR 619 (Bankr MD Fla 1989); *In re Landbank Equity Corp*, 83 BR 362 (ED Va 1987); *In re BDW Assocs, Inc*, 75 BR 909 (Bankr WD Pa 1987) (noting sister controlled companies); *In re F & S Cent Mfg Corp*, 70 BR 569 (Bankr EDNY 1987); *In re B & L Labs, Inc*, 68 BR 264 (MD Tenn 1986); *In re Botten*, 54 BR 707 (Bankr WD Wis 1985); *In re Jones*, 50 BR 911 (Bankr ND Tex 1985); *In re Telemark Mgmt Co*, 47 BR 1013 (WD Wis 1985); *In re Ozark Rest Equip Co*, 41 BR 476 (Bankr WD Ark 1984), *rev'd*, 61 BR 750 (WD Ark 1986), *aff'd*, 816 F 2d 1222 (8th Cir 1986), *on demand*, 74 BR 139 (Bankr WD Ark 1987); *In re Tennessee Pools & Recreation, Inc*, 36 BR 602 (Bankr MD Tenn 1983); *In re D H Overmyer Telecasting Co*, 23 BR 823, 930 (Bankr ND Ohio 1982); *In re Typhoon Indus, Inc*, 6 BR 886 (Bankr EDNY 1980); *Ayr Composition, Inc v Rosenberg*, 619 A 2d 592 (NJ Super Ct App Div 1993); *Rounds & Porter Lumber Co v Burns*, 225 SW 2d 1 (Ark 1949). But compare *In re Mission of Care, Inc*, 164 BR 877 (Bankr D Del 1994) (stating sister corporation denied recovery of payments allegedly made on behalf of debtor). *In Haugen, supra*, the Court of Appeals for the Eighth Circuit subsequently held a final *alter ego* judgment against a controlling shareholder in bankruptcy rendered the shareholder liable for the amount of the claim on the date of the petition, as stated in the judgment. Since it was not appealed, the judgment creditor cannot subsequently contend that the shareholder is also liable for interest on the amount of the earlier judgment against the debtor corporation. *In re Haugen*, 998 F 2d 1442 (8th Cir 1993); *Kimberly Coal Co v Douglas*, 45 F 2d 25, 27 (6th Cir 1930); *First Huntington Nat'l Bank v Guyan Mach Co*, 5 SE 2d 532 (W Va 1939). Three additional cases have upheld objections to the discharge in bankruptcy of a controlling shareholder and imposed liability for the debts of the controlled corporation: *In re Long*, 35 BR 949 (Bankr SD Ohio 1983); *In re Harron*, 31 BR 466 (Bankr D Conn 1983); *In re Wade*, 26 BR 477

In *Baltimore & Ohio Tel Co v Interstate Tel Co*,[7] the oldest case, the Court of Appeals for the Fourth Circuit reached a comparable result. A creditor with an unsatisfied judgment against an insolvent subsidiary was successful in a suit on the judgment against the parent. The court relied in part on a "complete identity in action" of the two companies, with all the subsidiary's transactions under the direction of the parent. It also relied on the "trust fund" doctrine pointing to the subsidiary's distribution of all of its assets. In 1941, *Consolidated Rock Products Co v Du Bois*,[8] a case that involved the fairness of a reorganization plan under Section 77B of the Bankruptcy Act, the Supreme Court of the United States imposed liability on a parent in reorganization for the debts of a subsidiary also in the proceedings. It relied on "piercing the corporate veil" precedents and such factors as the lack of "meticulous regard to corporate forms", the commingling of the assets and operations, and the assumption by the parent of all management functions of the several components of the corporate group, resulting in the conduct of the enterprise as a single "unified operation".

In 1949, *Rounds & Porter Lumber Co v Burns*,[9] an action brought by a creditor, the Arkansas Supreme Court also imposed liability on the parent for lumber sold to the subsidiary. In this and the following case it should be noted that during the subsidiary's reorganization proceedings the parent emerged as the only secured creditor with a mortgage on the debtor's fixed assets, and that the proposed arrangement would have yielded unsecured creditors between fifteen and twenty percent on their claims. In the 1951 case of *Henderson v Rounds & Porter Lumber Co*,[10] the court imposed liability upon the bankrupt company's controlling shareholders where they had manipulated the company's affairs to their own advantage. The shareholders' interest in the corporation was not to maximize its profits but to operate it as a source of supply at below market prices. The bankrupt company had accordingly been compelled to sell lumber and flooring to the shareholders below cost. Under these circumstances, the court concluded that the general rule of respecting the corporate entity did not apply. In the familiar rhetoric of "piercing the corporate veil" jurisprudence, it termed the corporation a "mere agency or department for the advancement of the parent's own interest."

In the 1966 case of *Palmer v Stokely*,[11] the court held that the cancellation of intercompany indebtedness owed by a sister company that was a second-tier

---

(Bankr ND Ill 1983); see also *In re Alport*, 144 F 3d 1163 (8th Cir 1998); *In re Haakenson*, 159 BR 875 (Bankr DND 1993); *In re Fitzgerald, De Arman & Roberts, Inc*, 129 BR 652 (Bankr ND Okla 1991); *Fentress v Triple Mining, Inc*, 635 NE2d 102 (Ill App Ct 1994). But compare *In re Criswell*, 52 BR 184 (Bankr ED Va 1985); *In re Hillsborough Holdings Corp*, 176 BR 223 (Bankr MD Fla 1994); *In re Hillsborough Holdings Corp*, 166 BR 461 (Bankr MD Fla 1994); *In re Hillsborough Holdings Corp*, 150 BR 817 (Bankr MD Fla 1993) (granting a motion for additional discovery); *In re Hillsborough Holdings Corp*, 144 BR 920 (Bankr MD Fla 1992); *In re Emeral Oil Co*, 61 BR 656, 660 (Bankr WD La 1984).

7 54 F 50 (4th Cir 1893).

8 312 US 510, 523-24 (1941).

9 225 SW 2d 1 (Ark 1949).

10 99 F Supp 376, 378-81 (WD Ark 1951).

11 255 F Supp 674, 680 (WD Okla 1966).

subsidiary of the debtor's controlling shareholders was a fraudulent transfer by the debtor under Section 67(d)(2) of the Bankruptcy Act. The court then relied on the "instrumentality rule" of *Fish v East*[12] to find the controlling shareholders *alter ego* of the subsidiary and liable for the improperly cancelled indebtedness.

In 1967, the court in *In re Long v Mc.Glon*[13] denied a motion to dismiss a complaint by a Trustee in Bankruptcy of a (bankrupt) corporation to hold its two shareholders, who had also been officers and directors, personally liable. The complaint alleged intermingling of assets with corporate funds deposited in the shareholders' personal accounts and corporate debts paid out of their personal accounts. The court concluded that an *alter ego* relationship had been established and that the corporate form could be disregarded.

In the 1980 case of *In re Typhoon Industries, Inc*,[14] a bankruptcy court imposed liability on one affiliate for the tax liabilities of its three sister companies which had been dissolved. The corporations had functioned as "a single unit" under the common management of the sole shareholder and shared the same office with the same telephone. The debtor paid all major expenses and approved all contracts for its affiliates, deposited their sales proceeds in its bank account, appropriated all cash surpluses, and described the affiliates as its divisions on its letterhead. The court concluded that the affiliates were "mere instrumentalities and alter egos" and that it would be inequitable to allow the debtor to escape the affiliates' tax liability.

According to Blumberg,[15] the leading case is *Federal Deposit Insurance Corp v Sea Pines Co*,[16] decided in 1982. In this case, the court held a parent liable for the bank debt of its 90 percent-owned insolvent subsidiary where the parent had caused the insolvent subsidiary to mortgage an unencumbered property to secure the debts of the parent. It essentially relied on the conclusion that the acts of the parent were "fundamentally unfair," without referring to the Uniform Fraudulent Conveyance Act ("UFCA"), although the mortgage was obviously a fraudulent conveyance (we do not know why and this author do not express how he concludes that or what do the court says about that important conclusion). The court invoked the doctrine that when a corporation becomes insolvent, those in control have a fiduciary duty to creditors and may not divert corporate assets for their own benefit to the detriment of creditors.[17] The "piercing the corporate veil" doctrine was

---

[12] 114 F 2d 177, 191 (10th Cir 1940).

[13] 263 F Supp 96 (DSC 1967). See generally *Huntington Nat'l Bank v Parton* (*In re Parton*), 137 BR 902, 906-07 (Bankr SD Ohio 1991) (holding "piercing veil" of corporation controlled by debtor president and sole shareholder but not finding debt dischargeable).

[14] 6 BR 886, 890-92 (Bankr EDNY 1980); see *Kimberly Coal Co v Douglas*, 45 F 2d 25, 27 (6th Cir 1930) (relying on "instrumentality" rule); *In re Mushroom Transp Corp*, 90 Bankr 718, 722-23 (Bankr 718 ED Pa 1988) (finding parent liability based on ERISA rather than common law bankruptcy). See generally Blumberg, *op cit* fn 1 at Chap 16.

[15] See Blumberg, *ibid* at p 591.

[16] 692 F 2d 973, 975 (4th Cir 1982), *cert denied*, 461 US 928 (1983).

[17] See generally *Davis v Woolf*, 147 F 2d 629, 633 (4th Cir 1945) stating "[w]hen a corporation becomes insolvent, or in a failing condition, the officers and directors no longer represent the stockholders, but by the fact of insolvency, become trustees for the creditors, and that they then can not by transfer of its property or payment of cash, prefer themselves

otherwise applicable, based on intrusive management interference and inadequate capitalization.[18] In this case, the decision turned on the inherent "fundamental unfairness" to a creditor of a controlling shareholder's appropriation of its subsidiary's assets after the subsidiary had become insolvent. Liability was based on considerations virtually indistinguishable from the bankruptcy doctrine of fraudulent conveyance.

This case does not rest squarely on the conventional approach of "piercing the corporate veil" jurisprudence but rather, rests on concepts of fairness to creditors arising from the subsidiary's insolvency at the time of the challenged transactions. It recognizes a remedy from the common law that imposes liability on the parent due to the depletion of the insolvent's estate. Liability is imposed if assets are diverted to the parent (or for its benefit) and the transaction has the nature of a fraudulent conveyance, whether or not the technical requirements of the UFCA or the bankruptcy laws are satisfied. The common law fiduciary obligation of the controlling shareholder to creditors arising from the subsidiary's insolvency, not bankruptcy law, is the basis for the cause of action. The doctrine enunciated by *Sea Pines* thus significantly expands the remedies of a creditor or the Trustee in Bankruptcy to attack transactions of this nature that may not completely satisfy the provisions of the UFCA or the bankruptcy laws. Among other matters, an extended statute of limitations in place of the two-year limit under the bankruptcy laws will become available. Further, an individual creditor may pursue the remedy and obtain a judgment against the parent for its sole benefit without the recovery passing through the insolvent subsidiary's estate. Obviously, if the subsidiary was in bankruptcy, the cause of action would be the property of the estate, and if pursued by the Trustee in Bankruptcy, within the exclusive jurisdiction of the bankruptcy court. The result in this case can be understood only by assuming that the subsidiary was not in bankruptcy and that there were no other objecting creditors.[19]

In 1982, a bankruptcy court in *In re D H Overmyer Telecasting Co*[20] imposed liability on a controlling shareholder and on all affiliated corporations of an integrated group for all debts of the affiliated companies. Control in this case was so "pervasive" that a "unity of interest" existed, making it inequitable to treat the parties as separate entities. The court did not find it necessary to refer to "piercing the corporate veil". In *Ozark Restaurant Equip Co*,[21] a case involving closely held

---

or other creditors". This is one of the most important doctrines of the field of the liability within a corporate group and must be more developed and in the future must be technically defined in law terms by the usage of microeconomics principles applicable specifically to the managements of corporate groups.

[18] *Sea Pines Co*, 692 F 2d at 975.

[19] *See* Blumberg, *op cit* fn 1 at pp 596-97.

[20] 23 BR 823, 930 (Bankr ND Ohio 1982); see also *In re Plantation Realty Trust*, 232 BR 279, 282-283 (Bankr D Mass 1999) (approving proof of claim by creditor of debtor's affiliate based on blend of agency and "Enterprise Law", despite "substantial gaps in the record" concerning traditional veil-piercing factors).

[21] 41 BR 476 (Bankr WD Ark 1984), *rev'd*, 61 BR 750 (WD Ark 1986), *aff'd*, 816 F 2d 1222 (8th Cir 1986), *on remand*, 74 BR 139 (Bankr WD Ark 1987).

affiliated companies, the bankruptcy court imposed enterprise liability. After avoiding preferential payments to a bank on loans guaranteed by insiders within one year of the bankruptcy petition, the bankruptcy court held the insiders personally liable for the debts of the debtor company. The debtor had been grossly undercapitalized with only $1,000 in capital and debt of $109,000 and as a result was insolvent from the inception. Intragroup transactions had manipulated the debtor to its detriment with inside sales at low or no mark-ups and no interest payments on deferred receivables. Corporate formalities were not always respected. The court mentioned the insiders' fiduciary duties to creditors and characterized the debtor and the affiliates as "mere instrumentalities" of the controlling shareholders. On appeal, the district court reversed, holding that the Trustee in Bankruptcy lacked standing to bring a state law action resting on "piercing the veil jurisprudence" that did not involve a fraudulent transfer or a voidable preference. The Court of Appeals for the Eighth Circuit affirmed.[22] In the same year, the court in *In re FDIC v Allen*,[23] involving the Jake Butcher banking insolvency, found fraudulent transfers and imposed personal liability on the controlling shareholders relying on "piercing the corporate veil" jurisprudence.

As Blumberg points out, in five of these cases, the Trustee in Bankruptcy had instituted the action for the benefit of all creditors by reliance on the familiar jurisprudence of "piercing the corporate veil," just as if an individual creditor was proceeding at law.[24] There is no indication in these cases, with the exception of the *Sea Pines* case, that the equitable considerations governing bankruptcy provided any special incentive for the courts to disregard the barrier of the separate entity. As stated earlier in this article,[25] equitable subordination provides a much more acceptable avenue for the application of "Enterprise Law" than the direct imposition of liability. Although in form, equitable subordination of the parent's claim is not an imposition of liability, the result in the overwhelming number of cases will be the same. The subsidiary's assets will typically be inadequate to pay all claims. As a result of subordination, assets otherwise going to the parent will be paid to the public creditors.[26]

"Piercing the corporate veil" jurisprudence is the traditional safety valve in "Entity Law", under which in "exceptional" cases liability may be imposed on a parent or controlling shareholder for the debts of its subsidiary. The decisions in *Long v McGlon, Palmer v Stokey, FDIC v Allen* and *Henderson v Rounds & Porter Lumber Co* rest squarely on this conventional approach and are readily understood, with the exception of *Sea Pines*.

---

22 *In re Ozark Rest Equip Co*, 816 F 2d 1222, 1231 (8th Cir 1987) (affirming district court's order).

23 584 F Supp 386, 398 (ED Tenn 1984).

24 See Blumberg, *op cit* fn 1 at pp 595-96; see also Note, "Liability of a Corporation for Acts of a Subsidiary or Affiliate" (1958) 71 *Harv L Rev* 1122 at p 1133 n 87; Cataldo, "Limited Liability with One-Man Corporations and Subsidiary Corporations" (1950) 18 *Law & Contemp Probs* 473, 497; Note, "Parent Corporation's Claims in Bankruptcy of Subsidiary: Effect of Fiduciary Relationship" (1940) 54 *Harv L Rev* 1045 at pp 1045-46.

25 See above.

26 Compare Blumberg, *op cit* fn 1 at p 596.

In summary, these cases upheld the following doctrines and emphasized the following factors:

1. The fundamental unfairness of mortgaging an unencumbered property of an insolvent subsidiary to secure the debt of the parent.

2. When a corporation becomes insolvent, those in control (often called "insiders") have a fiduciary duty to creditors and may not divert corporate assets for their own benefit to the detriment of creditors. The common law fiduciary obligation of the controlling shareholder to creditors arising from the subsidiary's insolvency is the basis for the cause of action, not bankruptcy law itself.

3. Intrusive managerial interference exercised by the parent over the subsidiary.

4. Inadequate capitalization of the subsidiary by the parent.

5. The doctrine of "piercing the corporate veil," especially in these situations: the lack of "meticulous regard to corporate forms"; the commingling of assets and operations; the parent's assumption of all management functions of the several components of the corporate group, resulting in the conduct of the enterprise as a single unified operation; the *alter ego* doctrine: a relationship that has been established so that the corporate form could be disregarded; the labeling of the bankrupt corporation as a mere agency or department for the advancement of the parent's own interests.

6. Complete identity in action of the two companies, with all the subsidiary's transactions under the direction of the parent.

7. The trust fund doctrine pointing to the subsidiary's distribution of all of its assets.

8. The insolvency of the debtor from its inception, with a gross undercapitalization (a capital of $1,000 and debt of $109.000).

9. Intragroup transactions manipulated by the parent to the detriment of the debtor consisting of inside sales at low or no mark-ups and no interest payments on deferred receivables (money that is owed to a business and has not yet been received).

10. Corporate formalities not always respected.

11. The characterization of the debtor and the affiliated as mere instrumentalities of the controlling shareholder.

12. When the control was so pervasive that a unity of interest existed, it was inequitable to treat the parties as separate entities.

13. Intermingling or commingling of assets.

14. Corporate funds deposited in the shareholders' personal accounts and corporate debts paid out of other personal accounts.

15. The cancellation of intercompany indebtedness owed by a sister company that was a second-tier subsidiary of the debtor's controlling shareholders. This constitutes a fraudulent transfer by the debtor under Section 67d (2) of the Bankruptcy Act.

16. The instrumentality rule, finding the controlling shareholders "*alter egos*" of the subsidiary liable for the improperly cancelled indebtedness.

17. The manipulation of the bankrupt company's affairs to the advantage of its own controlling shareholders, consisting of the shareholders' interest in the corporation was not to maximize its profits but to operate it as a source of supply at below market prices and below costs.

18. The depletion of the insolvent's estate, when its assets are diverted to the parent or for its benefit.

19. The fact that in the subsidiary's reorganization proceedings the parent emerged as the only secured creditor with a mortgage on the debtor's fixed assets, and that the proposed arrangement would have yielded unsecured creditors between fifteen and twenty percent on their claims.

20. An affiliate of three dissolved sister companies was found liable for them because the corporations had functioned as a single unit under the common management of the sole shareholder and shared the same office with the same telephone. The affiliates were found to be mere instrumentalities and *alter egos*.

21. The inherent fundamental unfairness to a creditor of a controlling shareholder's appropriation of its subsidiary's assets after the subsidiary had become insolvent.

22. The bankruptcy doctrine of fraudulent conveyance of a transaction intragroup whether or not the technical requirements of the Uniform Fraudulent Conveyance Act or the bankruptcy laws are satisfied.

23. The existence of preferential transfers within the bankruptcy proceedings.

Cases Denying Liability

In contrast to the foregoing decisions imposing liability on the parent of the insolvent subsidiary, Trustees in Bankruptcy and creditors of an insolvent subsidiary (or controlled corporation) have been unsuccessful in their efforts to impose liability upon the parent corporation (or controlling shareholder) in the overwhelming majority of cases.[27] These decisions have typically analyzed the issue by referring to "piercing the corporate veil" jurisprudence and have inquired whether the subject case was an "exceptional case" calling for the remedy.

---

[27] See *In re Kreisler Group, Inc*, 648 F 2d 86, 87 (2d Cir 1981) (*per curiam*) (affirming decision of District Court expunging claim of creditor against parent based on debt of wholly-owed subsidiary; otherwise asserting reluctance to pierce corporate veil); *In re County Green Ltd P'ship*, 604 F 2d 289, 292 (4th Cir 1979) (*per curiam*) (affirming bankruptcy court's decision not to pierce the corporate veil of a corporation that was general partner in building project, considering such extensions of liability must be taken "reluctantly and cautiously"); *In re Bowen Transps, Inc*, 551 F 2d 171, 171 (7th Cir 1977) (affirming bankruptcy court's decision to sustain objection of debtor that adverse party was not its creditor and there was no basis for piercing the corporate veil; showing reluctance to pierce veil); see also *Duryee v Erie* RR, 175 F 2d 58, 58 (6th Cir 1949); *Beckley v Erie* RR 175 F 2d 64, 64 (6th Cir 1949) (*per curiam*); *Madden v Mac Sim Bar Paper Co* 103 F 2d 974 (9th Cir 1930); *Haskell v McClintic-Marshall Co*, 289 F 405, 405 (9th Cir 1923); *Martin v Dev Co of Am*, 240 F 42, 42 (9th Cir 1917); *In re Green Valley Seeds, Inc*, 27 BR 34, 34 (Bankr D Or 1982); *In re Mathes*, 23 BR 162, 162 (Bankr SD Tex 1982); *In re Nova Real Estate Inv Trust*, 23 BR 62, 62 (Bankr ED Va 1982); *In re Twin Lakes Village, Inc* 2 BR 532, 532 (Bankr D Nev 1980); *Jersey Boulevard Corp v Lerner Stores Corp*, 168 Md 532, 532 (1935); *Marsch v S New England R Corp*, 230 Mass 483, 483, (1918); *Bartle v Home Owners Coop, Inc*, 309 NY 103, 103 (1955); *Pagel, Horton & Co v Harmon Paper Co*, 258 NYS 168, 168 (4th Dep't 1932); *Ohio Edison Co v Warner Coal Corp*, 72 NE 2d 487, 487 (Ohio 1946). But compare *Gibraltar Sav v LD Brinkman Corp* 860 F 2d 1275, 1275 (5th Cir 1988); *Standard Dyeing & Finishing Co v Arma Textile Printers Corp*, 757 F Supp 230, 230 (SDNY 1991); *In re Hillsborough Holdings Corp*, 176 BR 223, 223 (M.D Fla 1994); *In re Parton*, 137 BR 902, 905-06 (Bankr SD Ohio 1991); *In re Moserbeth Assocs*, 128 BR 716, 716 (Bankr ED Pa 1991); *In re Moran*, 120 BR 379, 387-88 (Bankr WD Va 1990); *In re Woodstock Assocs I, Inc*, 120 BR 436, 449 (Bankr ND III 1990); *In re Denton*, 120 BR 310 (Bankr SD Tex 1990); *In re Murray*, 116 BR 473, 476 (Bankr ED Va 1990); *In re PR Hotel Corp*, 111 BR 22, 24-25 (Bankr DPR 1990); *In re McConnell*, 122 BR 41, 44-45 (Bankr SD Tex 1989); *In re Nielson*, 97 BR 269, 274 (Bankr WDNC 1989); *In re Cycle-Rama, Inc*, 91 BR 647, 649 (Bankr DNH 1988); *In re Simplified Info Sys, Inc* 89 BR 538, 544-46 (WD Pa 1988); *Butler v Collins*, 14 BR 546, 546 (ED La 1981); *In re* Tesmetges, 87 BR 263, 263 (Bankr EDNY 1988); *In re Lee*, 87 BR 697, 699-700 (Bankr MD Fla 1988); *In re Rosecrest Enters Inc*, 80 BR 354, 357 (Bankr WD Pa 1987); *in* re *Ipswich Bituminous Concrete Prods, Inc* 79 BR 511, 520 (Bankr D Mass 1987); *In re Burgess Mining and Constr Corp*, 68 BR 23, 25 (Bankr ND Ala 1986); *In re Gordon Car & Truck Rental, Inc*, 65 BR 371, 376-77 (Bankr NDNY 1986); *In re Am Cable Publ'ns, Inc*, 62 BR 536, 539 (D Colo 1986); *In re Chism*, 57 BR 23, 24 (Bankr MD.Ala 1985); *In re Alta Indus, Inc*. 53 BR 567, 569-70 (Bankr WD Tex 1985); *In re Int'l Horizons, Inc*, 51 BR 547 (ND Ga 1985); *In re Nash*, 49 BR 254, 260-61 (Bankr D Ariz 1985); *In re Baker Fence Inc*, 47 BR 273, 277 (Bankr D Mass 1985); *In re Carroll*, 11 BR 812, 816 (Bankr ED Va 1981); *Wolf v Walt*, 247 Neb 858, 865-70 (1995).

The English law is quite similar.[28] The same result has followed where creditors of a parent (or controlling shareholder) have attempted to impose liability on a subsidiary (or controlled corporation). This result is obviously sound where creditors have bargained for the credit of a particular component of a group without reliance on the credit of other components of the group. In the absence of such a showing, the decisions rest on a choice of "Entity Law" over "Enterprise Law". Common officers and directors, stock ownership, and the exercise of control are insufficient in themselves to uphold rejection of entity concepts or limited liability within the corporate group. The ultimate decision reflects consideration of numerous factors, including such matters as adequacy of capitalization; compliance with customary corporate formalities, including separate bank accounts, separate books and records, and separate meetings of directors and shareholders; the intrusive participation by the parent in the managerial decision-making of the subsidiary; the extent of economic integration of products; the subsidiary's administrative and financial dependence on group support; the use of group trademarks, logos, and warranties; presentation of the subsidiary to the public as an independent business or as an integral part of the group; and whether the subsidiary and the parent are engaged in the collective conduct of a single integrated economic enterprise.

In the tax law field, at least one court has refused to allow a Trustee in Bankruptcy to assert a claim of personal liability for debts of the debtor against its shareholder based on an *alter ego* theory, holding that this gave rise to a claim in favor of creditors, not a corporate claim which the Trustee in Bankruptcy could assert.[29]

The Position in Argentina

The Bankruptcy Act System

The liability of third parties In the Argentine Bankruptcy Act system[30] section 173 of the Bankruptcy Act deals with the liability of third parties.[31]

---

[28] See *In re Southard & Co Ltd* (1979) 1 WLR 1198, 1208 (refusing to "wind-up" insolvent company, wholly owned subsidiary, with its parent); the English law still rests on the decision of the House of Lords in *Salomon v A Salomon & Co* 75 LTR 426 (1897).

[29] *In re Green Valley Seeds, Inc*, 27 BR 34, 36 (Bankr D Or 1982); see *Ross Controls, Inc v United States Dep't of Treasury IRS*, 160 BR 527, 532-33 (ED Pa 1993) (finding company incorporated by debtor corporation's sole officer and shareholder after debtor's liquidation liable for liquidated company's tax indebtedness). But compare Blumberg & Fowler, *The Law of Corporate Groups, Problems in the Bankruptcy or Reorganization of Parent and Subsidiary Corporations, Including the Law of Corporate Guaranties* 384 (2000 Supplement) [hereinafter Blumberg & Fowler (2000 Supplement)].

[30] The history of the Argentine Bankruptcy Law system is as follows: In 1862 the Commercial Code was put into force for the whole nation as a federal law. It is similar to the French Commercial Code of 1807. A part of it dealt with bankruptcy provisions, at that time pertaining only to commercial individuals and corporations. The local Procedural Law

As a general rule under Section 173.2 of the Bankruptcy Act, the dominant party can be made liable in case of bankruptcy. Normally the law penalizes a person as a counterpart of the company for benefiting from the reduction of the assets. Thus, it is reasonable that it must penalize the worst case in which the third party not only takes part in that reduction but also in the decision-making process of the company creates the damage. The additional consequence is the loss of all rights in insolvency proceedings.[32]

By way of analogy (*a maiore ad minus* argument) the American case law described above is applicable to the Argentine legal system pertaining to the liability within a corporate group, in particular the first paragraph (liability of representatives and directors) and the second paragraph (liability of third parties) of Section 173 of the Bankruptcy Act 24.522.[33] The first time these provisions were enforced was in 1972, by the Bankruptcy Act No 19.551.[34]

---

of each of the Provinces dealt with the bankruptcy provisions for non-commercial persons. This Commercial Code was reformed in 1889. In 1902 Argentina issued a Bankruptcy Act (the first one) formally separated from the rest of the Commercial Code, with the number 4.156 (the numbering of all the National (Federal) Legal Acts of Argentina was established in 1853 when the first Federal Constitution was approved). It was completely replaced by another Bankruptcy Act in 1933 (with the number 11.719). It was again replaced in 1972 by a new Bankruptcy Act (number 19.551). It was partially reformed by Act number 22.917 in 1983. This last Act unified all bankruptcy procedures for every type of persons: commercial and non commercial. Finally it was replaced by Bankruptcy Act number 24.522 in 1995. In 2002, five sections were reformed in two occasions.

31 The text of Section 173.1 of the Argentine Bankruptcy Act of 1995 reads: "*Los representantes, administradores, mandatarios o gestores de negocios del fallido que dolosamente hubieren producido, facilitado, permitido o agravado la situación patrimonial del deudor o su insolvencia, deben indemnizar los perjuicios causados*". ["Representatives, managers or agents of the debtor who have willfully caused, facilitated, allowed or aggravated the debtor's economic condition or insolvency must pay damages arising therefrom."]

The text of Section 173.2 reads: "*Quienes de cualquier forma participen dolosamente en actos tendientes a la disminución del activo o exageración del pasivo, antes o después de la declaración de quiebra, deben reintegrar los bienes que aún tengan en su poder e indemnizar los daños causados, no pudiendo tampoco reclamar ningún derecho en el concurso*". ["Whoever willfully participates in any action intended to reduce the assets or increase the liabilities, before or after the entry of an order for relief in bankruptcy, shall return any property held in its possession, pay any damages arising there from and shall not be entitled to claim any rights in the bankruptcy proceeding."]

32 See Rafael Mariano Manóvil, *Grupos de Sociedades en el Derecho Comparado* 773, 779 (1998) [hereinafter Manóvil].

33 *See supra* text accompanying fn 31. In Italy, a Committee directed by Professor Giuseppe Ferri wrote the *Draft Enterprise Statute* in 1984, which is similar to the Argentine section, but specifically refers to the dominant corporation. It reads as follows: "*Cuando sea declarada la quiebra o el estado de insolvencia de la sociedad controlada, la sociedad controlante y sus administradores responden solidariamente por las obligaciones de la sociedad controlada, si el estado de insolvencia fue provocado o agravado por actos u omisiones perjudiciales a la sociedad, cumplidos por los administradores de la controlada a pedido o en interés de la sociedad controlante*". ["Whenever an order for relief in

Section 173.1 of the Bankruptcy Act of 1995 is applicable both in the case of *de facto* and *de jure* directors.[35] It is obligatory that the conduct of the dominant party would be fraudulent and not merely negligent in the corporate governance.[36] The parties with legal standing to claim the action are: a) the Trustee in Bankruptcy, and b) the creditors in the bankruptcy proceedings.[37] The goal of the provision is substantially to punish the violation of the duty of the debtor to maintain the solvency of his patrimony.[38]

The American case law identified above provides a strong lead to jurisdictions within the European Continental Traditions such as Argentina.

Extension of the Bankruptcy Proceedings

Another way of protecting the creditors within corporate groups in solvency cases in the Argentine Law is the Extension of the Bankruptcy Proceedings ("*Extensión de la quiebra*" in the Spanish words of the different Argentine Bankruptcy Acts since 1972). In 1969 there was a Bankruptcy Draft Act in Argentina (Section 168) that promoted the automatic extension of the bankruptcy proceedings in the case of

---

bankruptcy or a state of insolvency is entered against a controlled company, the controlling companies and the managers thereof shall be jointly and severally liable for the obligations of the controlled company, if the state of insolvency was provoked or aggravated by actions or omissions detrimental to the company, carried out by the managers of the controlled company at the request or in the interest of the controlling company."]; see also Manóvil, *op cit* fn 32, at p 669.

[34] Section 166 of the Bankruptcy Act of 1972 (repealed in 1995) was quite similar to the new Act introduced in 1995. It reads: "*Cuando con dolo o en infracción a normas inderogables de la ley se produjere, facilitare, permitire, agravare o prolongare la disminución de la responsabilidad patrimonial del deudor o su insolvencia, quienes han practicado tales actos por el deudor, ya sea como representantes, administradores, mandatarios o gestores de negocios, deben indemnizar los daños y perjuicios por los que se les declare responsables en virtud de tales actos*". ["Any person who willfully and in violation of mandatory legal provisions, caused, facilitated, allowed, aggravated or prolonged the reduction of the property of the debtor or its insolvency, acting on behalf of the debtor, as its representative, manager or agent, shall pay damages that may be attributed to such person".]

[35] See Manóvil, *op cit* fn 32, at pp 672, 775.

[36] See Rivera, Roitman & Vítolo, *Concursos y Quiebras* Ley 24.522, 283 (1995). This conduct is defined by Section 1072 of the Civil Code of Argentina, which states: "*El acto ilícito ejecutado a sabiendas y con intención de dañar la persona o los derechos de otro, se llama en este Código delito*". ["For the purposes of this Code, an intentional tort is any illegal action carried out willfully and with the intention of causing damage to the person or the rights of another person."]

[37] See Sections 174 and 175 of the Bankruptcy Act of 1995.

[38] See Bergel & Paolantonio, *Las Acciones de responsabilidad patrimonial contra terceros en la quiebra, La Reforma Concursal* Ley 24.522, *Derecho y Empresa,* 239 (1995). This is another "principle" or "standard" that has to be developed, explained and defined in the future (by the judges or by the scholars) as a fundamental principle of liability issues within bankruptcy situations.

bankruptcy of a subsidiary corporation versus the parent or dominant.[39] Because of its rigidity, it has been rejected by the authors of the draft and failed to be enacted as a Bankruptcy Act.[40]

Nevertheless, the Bankruptcy Act of 1972 nearly copied the provisions of Sections 99 and 101 of the French Bankruptcy Act of 1967 and the subsequent Sections 180 and 182 of the French Bankruptcy Act of 1985. The Bankruptcy Act of 1983 increased extension up to three (but no more) possible cases and issued additional provisions regarding other details for the consequences of the extension, such as conflicts of jurisdiction, the subsequent procedural process, legal terms, bankruptcy petitions, petitioners, lapsing of actions, Trustees in Bankruptcy for each process, separated assets of each bankruptcy proceeding, residuals, *ex nunc* consequences of the extension of bankruptcy and so on. It also made it possible to extend the bankruptcy to any individual or corporation. That is, after 1983, the subject that suffers the extension of the bankruptcy may not only be a corporation but an individual as well as set out in Section 161 of the Bankruptcy Act 1995.[41]

---

[39] This chapter will only study cases concerning the extension of the bankruptcy proceedings in respect of corporate groups in Argentina. There are many other cases referred to the extension of the bankruptcy proceedings but not concerning to corporate groups.

[40] The text of Section 168 was: "*La quiebra de la sociedad controlada importa la de la controlante, entendiéndose por ésta la que en forma directa o por intermedio de otra sociedad a su vez controlada, posee participaciones por cualquier título que importen la tenencia de más del cincuenta por ciento de los votos necesarios para formar la voluntad social.*" ["Bankruptcy of a controlled company results in bankruptcy of the controlling company, a controlling company being defined as a company that directly or through another controlled company, holds interest, for any title whatsoever, in excess of 50% of the voting stock necessary to adopt decisions."] See 29 ED 917 (1969).

[41] The text of Section 161 of the Bankruptcy Act of 1995 reads:

"*La quiebra se extiende:*
1) A toda persona que, bajo la apariencia de la actuación de la fallida, ha efectuado los actos en su interés personal y dispuesto de los bienes como si fueran propios, en fraude a sus acreedores.
2) A toda persona controlante de la sociedad fallida, cuando ha desviado indebidamente el interés social de la controlada, sometiéndola a una dirección unificada en interés de la controlante o del grupo económico del que forma parte.
A los fines de esta sección, se entiende por persona controlante: a) Aquella que en forma directa o por intermedio de una sociedad a su vez controlada, posee participación, por cualquier título, que otorgue los votos necesarios para formar la voluntad social. b) Cada una de las personas que, actuando conjuntamente, poseen participación en la proporción indicada en el párrafo a) precedente y sean responsables de la conducta descripta en el primer párrafo de este inciso.
3) A toda persona respecto de la cual existe confusión patrimonial inescindible, que impida la clara delimitación de sus activos y pasivos o de la mayor parte de ellos."

["Bankruptcy shall extend:

These rules are applicable by analogy. For some authors, like Manóvil, this extension of bankruptcy may be considered a type of "liability".[42]

Regarding the issue of *onus probandi*, the modern theory of "dynamic burdens"[43] imposes the obligation on the party that is in better condition to produce evidence. The justice can also order *ex officio* any means of proof, independently from that offered by the parties, according to Argentine Procedural Law. In Argentina, there was an intense discussion about this provision because of its rigidity and automatism.[44] It has been said that it is better to have a system of liability rather than proceedings for the extension of the bankruptcy.[45] And, *in extremis*, it is possible to obtain a bankruptcy decree with a sentence imposing the liability against the parent (or any other) corporation or individual belonging to the group.

Doubtless the impact of a significant bankruptcy case in Argentina in 1971 was an important antecedent for the Bankruptcy Act of 1972, which introduced the extension of the Bankruptcy Proceedings in a legal statute for the first time in Argentina.[46] The applicable law and jurisdiction of the court to decide on the

---

1) To any person who under the appearance of acting for the debtor has carried out actions in its personal interest and has disposed of property as if it were its own, in fraud of its creditors.
2) To any controlling person of the debtor, whenever it has unduly deviated the corporate interest of the controlled company, submitting it to a unified direction in interest of the controlling company or the economic group thereof.

For the purposes of this section, the term controlling person shall mean: a) Any person who directly or through a controlled company, holds interest, of any kind, that grants the necessary votes to adopt decisions; b) each of the persons who acting jointly hold interest in the proportion specified in a) above and are liable for the conduct described in the first paragraph of this subsection.
3) Any person as regards which property is commingled and cannot be separated so that it prevents a clear delimitation of its assets and liabilities or the majority thereof".]

This Section is complementary to Section 172 of the Bankruptcy Act of 1995 which reads: "*Cuando dos o más personas formen grupos económicos, aun manifestados por relaciones de control pero sin las características previstas en el art. 161, la quiebra de una de ellas no se extiende a las restantes.*" ["Whenever two or more persons compose an economic group, even evidenced by control relations but without the features contemplated in Article 161, the bankruptcy of one of such persons will not extend to the others".]

42 See Manóvil, *op cit* fn 32 at pp 1113, 1117. Consequently, the defendant may evade the extension of the bankruptcy by paying the debts to the plaintiff.

43 *Ibid* at p 1116.

44 *Ibid* at pp 1059, 1062 (mentioning authors). Some authors opposed to this legal provision offer reasons such as: the need for conservation of the enterprise, the complexities of a multinational bankrupt group, the uncontrolled expansion of the macroeconomic crises, the loss of income due to the judicial liquidation, the loss of the going concern value and the bankruptcy proceedings imposed on a corporation without evidence of being insolvent.

45 See Tonón, "Extensión de quiebra sin finalidad práctica", 107 ED 843 (1984); Miguens, *Extensión de la quiebra y la responsabilidad en los grupos de sociedades*, 1-6 (1998).

46 This case was *Compañía Swift de la Plata SA*, 151 LL 516 (1973) (Arg). This case began as a so-called in the Argentine Bankruptcy Law System "*concurso preventivo*",

extension of bankruptcy are those that pertain to the main bankrupt debtor. Yet the difficulties faced for a foreign jurisdiction to recognize a bankruptcy declared beyond its frontiers constitute another argument in favor of the choice to exercise liability actions rather than the extension of bankruptcy.[47] This is especially applicable to the *Swift-Deltec* case, because, as it seems, the bankruptcy decree was rejected in the United States or at least not formally accepted by a court where the American assets were located. There was no litigation on that point.

---

similar to a Reorganization in the US Bankruptcy System and specially quite similar to the "*concordato preventivo*" of the Italian Bankruptcy Law System. The judge of first instance, the Commercial Court of Appeals of Buenos Aires (Sec C) and, finally, the (Federal) Supreme Court of Argentina, applied (mainly) the piercing of the corporate veil doctrine and with this argument rejected the proposal of the debtor, declared the bankruptcy of the Argentine subsidiary, and extended the bankruptcy proceeding from the subsidiary to the whole group of companies, parents and daughters, some of them located in the United States and in the Bahamas. Also the credits of the parent corporations were rejected and not considered for election in the "*concurso preventivo*" plan, although in Argentina the subordination of credits in the bankruptcy process does not exist at all and at that time there was no conflict of interest in voting by a parent in the bankruptcy proceedings of a subsidiary, as it was later defined in the new Section 45 of the Bankruptcy Act of 1995. Undoubtedly, this case has a political meaning that must be legally analyzed in the future. See Rovira, "Responsibilities and Liabilities of Insolvent Companies in Argentina" (1988) 16 *Int'l Bus Law 500*; Dobson, "Lifting the Veil in Four Countries: The Law of Argentina, England, France and the United States" (1986) 35 *ICLQ* 839; Gordon, "Of Aspirations and Operations: The Governance of Multinational Enterprises by Third World Nations" (1984) 16 U *Miami Inter-Am L R* 301, 312; McKinnis, "The Argentine Foreign Investment Law of 1976" (1978) 17 *Colum J Transnat'l L* 357, 383-84.

On the problems of Private International Law of this case see Malbrán, *La extraterritorialidad de la quiebra en el caso Compañia Swift de La Plata SA*, 54 ED 809 [1974]. About the critical opinions of this case in the USA see Blumberg, *The Law of Corporate Groups, Bankruptcy* (vol II) pp 660-69; Gordon, "Argentine Jurisprudence: The Parke Davis and Deltec Cases" (1974) 6 *Law Am* 320; Gordon, "Argentina Jurisprudence: Deltec Update" (1979) 11 *Law Am* 43; Rosenn, "Note, Expropriation in Argentina and Brazil: Theory and Practice" (1975) 15 *Va J Int'l L* 277, 311-314; see also Evans, "Note, Judicial Decision. Jurisdiction - Forum Non Conveniens - Determination of Bankruptcy in Argentina as Presumptive Confiscatory Measure (1974) 68 *Am J Int'l L* 741 [hereinafter "Evans"]; Puno, "Note, Multinational Enterprise: Reaching the Assets of Other Members of the Corporate Group After Bankruptcy of a Subsidiary-Separate Corporate Personalities Disregarded" (1974) 15 *Harv Int'l L* J 528; Radzyminski, *Sistema de derecho internacional privado concursal argentino* 1990-A RDCO 199. Concerning the litigation in the Supreme Court of New York see *Deltec Banking Corp v Compañia Italio-Argentina de Electricidad SA*, 362 NYS2d 391(1st Dept 1974).

Some years later the Argentine Supreme Court dismissed the application of the extension of the bankruptcy proceedings against a corporation member of the group whose name was "*Ingenio La Esperanza SA*": see "Compañía Swift de La Plata SA", [1976-D] LL 314 (Arg). The main reason given in the *dictum* was that in that case there was mere control, but not a unified enterprise policy which is the second and vital element for the existence of a group of corporations. The same solution was adopted in "*Papelera Paysandú*", CNCom, sec B [1984-C] LL 219 (Arg), a corporation not pertaining to the Swift-Deltec group.

[47] *See* Manóvil, *op cit* fn 32, at p 1233.

This extension of the bankruptcy proceedings was imposed before 1972 in some judicial cases about corporate groups,[48] and also afterwards.[49] In some cases the courts denied the extension within corporate groups due to procedural reasons.[50] Such issues have been discussed in the Argentine Case Law.[51] For example, in one case the National Government put in force special regulations by

---

[48] See *"Nogoyá SA"*, CNCom, sec C [11-1971] JA 459 (Arg) (commingling of assets and debts); *"Talleres Inglemere SA"*, 1ª Inst 48 ED Buenos Aires 361 (1971) (Arg) (commingling of assets, debts and substantive and procedural consolidation).

[49] In the majority of cases the courts applied the piercing the corporate veil doctrine. See *"Tecnoforest SA"*, CNCom 7.2 1997, ED 18.12.1997 (1997), with a commentary by Games, *Sociedad controlante. Extensión de quiebra*; *"Humberto J Pontremoli SA"*, CNCom, sec C [1996-B] LL 241 with a note by Ribichini, *Extraño caso de extensión de quiebra por confusión patrimonial al propietario aparente de los bienes* ("collateral" extension: from subsidiary to another subsidiary); *"Reverdito y Cía SA"*, CNCom, sec A [1995-D] LL (Arg); *"Tucson SA"*, CNCom, sec C [1995-B] LL 400 (Arg), with a note by Nissen, *El trasvasamiento de sociedades* (emptyness of a subsidiary committed by another subsidiary); *"Exportadora Marly SA"*, CNCom, sec A [1994-E] LL 664 (Arg) with a comment by Ribichini, *Conjunto económico, control y extensión de la quiebra* (extension against an already bankrupt corporation); *"Kapelusz Revistas SA"*, 1ª Inst Buenos Aires no 9 147 ED 369 (1991) (Arg) with a note by Maffía, *Autodenuncia y extensión de la quiebra por confusión patrimonial inescindible*; *"Celcar SA"*, CNCom, sec D [1990-D] LL 242 (Arg) with a comment by Gagliardo, *Alcances concursales del control societario* (preventive bankruptcy proceedings of whole group with extension of bankruptcy proceedings afterwards); *"Cadenas Madariaga"*, CNCom, sec C 138 ED 213 (1989) (Arg); *"Carracedo"*, CApel CC, sec I (1987) (Arg) (unpublished); *"Auto Star SA"*, CNCom, sec B (1986) (Arg) (unpublished); *"Tombut SA"*, CNCom (1985) (Arg) (unpublished); *"Zárate Sulfúrico SA"*, CNCom, sec B (1985) (Arg) (unpublished); *"Oddone"*, CNCom, sec E [1984-D] LL 412 (Arg) ("downstream" extension: from the parent to the subsidiaries); *"Sasetru SA"*, CNCom, sec D [1983-B] LL 650 (Arg) (affirmation of bankruptcy agreement); *"Sasetru SA"*, CNCom, sec D [1983-C] LL 288 (Arg) (extraordinary remedy granted by Commercial Court of Appeals); *"Confecciones Galicia SA"*, CNCom, sec B, 102 ED 463 (Arg) (1982) (intragroup guaranties); *"Silos y Elevadores SA"* CNCom, sec E [1982-D] LL 295 (Arg); *"Sasetru SA"*, CNCom, sec D [1981-C] LL 181 (Arg) (extension from the parent corporation to thirty-five subsidiaries); *"Marfinco SA"*, CNCom, sec C [1980-C] LL 340 (Arg) (commingling of assets); *"Macrini SRL"*, 1a Inst sec IV, 153 ED 652 (1993) (Arg); *"Margaria"*, 1ª Inst Santa Rosa, sec I [1984-I] JA 515; *"Armadores Argentinos SA"*, 1ª Inst. Buenos Aires no 11 [1983-B] LL 561 (Arg) (centralized financing of whole group with fraudulent intragroup transactions); *"Electronec SRL"* 1ª Inst Mar del Plata IV DE 67 (1978) (Arg); *"Pazmallmann SA"*, 1ª Inst Buenos Aires no 18 [1978-B] LL 494 (Arg) (straw corporations in only one group enterprise and commingling of assets).

[50] See *"Florcam SA"*, [1996-D] LL 750 (Arg); *"Nogoyá SA"*, CNCom, sec C (1981) (Arg) (unpublished) (accounts not available in commingling of assets and debts); *"Transportes Versailles SA"*, CNCom, sec C [1979-B] LL 103 (Arg).

[51] *"Porcelanas Lozadur SA"*, CNCom, sec E, 157 ED 306 (1991) (Arg) (term of prescription); *"Costa del Sol SA"*, CNCom, sec A, 145 ED 187 (1991) (Arg) (expiration, lapsing and suspension of the term); *"Miño Pintos"*, 1ª Inst San Isidro, sec I, 160 ED 293 (1994) (Arg) (suspension of term); see also doctrines in Porcel, *Extensión de la quiebra*, [1986-D] LL 832.

two acts: number 22.229 and number 22.334 for a whole corporate group called "Greco".[52]

Since the Bankruptcy Act of 1995, it is possible to include a whole corporate group in a sort of reorganization process or preventive insolvency proceedings (called "*concurso preventivo*" in Argentina or "*suspensión de pagos*" in Spain).[53] The statute becomes operative only when the whole group submits to the bankruptcy reorganization from the very beginning, not merely a part (that is, some of all the members) of the group.[54]

The extension of bankruptcy due to a conduct originated in self-interest (Section 161.1 of the Bankruptcy Act of 1995) is not limited to the case of the "straw man" or party. It punishes a conduct with causal linkage with the insolvency, yet it is not important in whose benefit such a conduct was displayed, but that it was not in the interest of the main debtor, even if the damage or the insolvency was unintended. The element of fraud to creditors is superfluous.[55]

The extension of bankruptcy to the controlling party due to corporate interest deviation (Section 161.2 of the Bankruptcy Act) is worded with an ineffective accumulation of terms and superabundant requirements: a) all deflection of the

---

[52] "*Greco Hnos SA*", CNCom, sec B [1981-B] LL 360 (Arg). There has been a lot of criticism of this case. See Celso, *Grupo Greco: leyes 22.229, 22.334 y otras normas. ¿Cuánto poder, cuánto desorden, cuánta necesidad?*, en El Derecho Legislación Argentina, 992 (1982); Pascual, *Algunas cuestiones acerca de la ley 22.334 (quiebra de las sociedades del "grupo Greco")*, [1981-C] Sección doctrina LLA 834-37; Moreno, *Exámen crítico de la ley 22.229 de Intervención al "Grupo Greco"*, en ED, 91-279-283. The unconstitutionality of these provisions were denied by the *In re Greco Hnos SA*, CNCom, sec B [1981-B] LL 360-75 (Arg).

[53] The former case law has rejected that possibility. See "*Gafyr SA*", CNCom, sec A, 1994 RDCO 569 (Arg) (conflict of jurisdiction); "*Monómeros Vinílicos SA*", CNCom, sec D, 160 ED 620 (1993) (Arg) (conflict of jurisdiction); "*La Elvira SA Establecimientos Agropecuarios*", CNCom, sec E, 1982 ED 409 (Arg); "*Alfrombras Alpana SA*", CNCom, sec D [1981-D] LL 185 (Arg); "*Establecimientos Textiles Lobos SA*", CNCom, sec E, 95 ED 264 (1981) (Arg); "*Unzumatlán SA*", CNCom, sec B, 97 ED 689 (1981) (Arg); "*Comimar SA*", CNCom, sec A [1980-B] LL 494 (Arg); "*Fomalco SRL*", CNCom, sec D [1980-C] LL 557 (Arg) with a comment by Bergel, *Conjunto económico y concurso preventivo*; "*Producciones Argentinas de Televisión SA*", CNCom, sec B [1976-B] LL 463 (Arg); "*Promotora Internacional de Ventas SA*", 1ª Inst Buenos Aires 102 ED 557 (1982) (Arg); Gebhardt, *Insolvencia del grupo empresario*, 1985-D LL 899.

[54] See "*Leo Export SA*" CNCom, sec C, 171 ED 490 (1996) (Arg); "*Colasud SA*" CNCom, sec A, 167 ED 533 (1995) (Arg); "*Hormisur SA*" 1ª Inst Buenos Aires no 11 [1997-A] LL 268 (Arg), with a note by Vaiser, *"Un fallo ponderable sobre terreno resbaladizo"*; "*Turismo Winter SRL*" 1ª Inst no 6 de Rosario, 14.5.1996, 173 ED 572, fallo no 48.110 with a note by Odriozola, *"El concurso en caso de agrupamiento puede no incluir a todos sus integrantes"*. In my opinion this requirement is *de lege ferenda* not necessary, unfeasible and not convenient for a whole group, because usually there are only one or more members in economic crisis, not the whole group. And the present consequence for the whole group, in case of failure of approval of the payment plan is the bankruptcy liquidation of the whole group, a not desirable consequence for nobody, especially for the creditors of any "non-insolvent" member of the group.

[55] See Manóvil, *op cit* fn 32 at p 1232.

corporate interest (the rule refers to the interest *of the company*) is unlawful; b) the reference to the beneficiary of the conduct of the person to whom the rule is applied is of no material relevance; c) the means to produce the deflection, submission to unified management, is another irrelevant fact, not consistent, additionally, with the fact that the rule attaches effects to the exercise of control and not to the configuration of a group.[56]

In itself, the extension of bankruptcy proceedings is not a repressive civil penalty but a case of tort liability that requires all of its configuring elements. The most relevant of these elements is the causal link between the conduct displayed and the insolvency, both in its chronological aspect and in its quantitative and qualitative aspects. Yet its existence must be presumed: the burden of the proof must be imposed according to the dynamic principle because of the peculiarities of the circumstances.[57] The extension of bankruptcy due to commingling of assets (Section 161.3) also includes subjective commingling, and this is difficult to judge. It is more frequent that the formation of a sole estate (of assets and liabilities in a unique bankruptcy proceeding) be declared due to the commingling of assets than to find an isolated case of extension of bankruptcy for this reason. It is necessary to consider each case because in the abstract it is impossible to quantify.[58]

In the case of actions in self-interest and commingling, bankruptcy may be extended to any kind of subject. Therefore, it also extends to any type of controlling person. However it is only direct or indirect, legal (*de jure*) or factual, internal controllers and not external controllers, that can be subject of the extension of bankruptcy due to the deviation or deflection of the corporate interest.[59]

The horizontal extension of bankruptcy has no legal foundation in any Argentine Act, that is to say, the extension to one subsidiary corporation to another subsidiary of the same parent, except in case of commingling of assets.[60] In case of insolvency the extension of the bankruptcy proceedings, particularly to the controlling party, is not always the most adequate answer to the interests of the bankruptcy state. The actions of liability of Section 54.1 and 54.2 of the Companies Act of 1983 or the declaration of ineffectiveness of the legal personality of Section 54.3 of the Companies Act and even the responsibility under insolvency proceedings (Section 173 of the Bankruptcy Act) may be more effective.[61]

There are no reasons in Argentine law to hold the position that, in insolvency proceedings the intragroup credits can be subordinated, as is the case of the American law. Regarding voting rights of creditors in preventive insolvency proceedings, the exclusion of the controlling shareholder of the new Section 45 of the Argentine Bankruptcy Act of 1995 embraces all kinds of control, and this

---

56 *Ibid* at p 1232.

57 *Ibid.*

58 *Ibid.*

59 *Ibid.*

60 See Manóvil, *ibid* at p 1233.

61 *Ibid* at p 1231.

embraces all creditor corporations whose decision-making process is controlled by that controlling shareholder.[62]

In United States law, the notion of undercapitalization of the insolvent corporation is used to underpin different answers. In German law, the doctrine advocates holding partners liable due to undercapitalization. In Argentine law, section 2 of the Companies Act may be relied upon to assert that the use by individuals of a type of company with limited liability for partners presupposes the duty of those partners to create and maintain a corporate patrimony sufficient to start and develop the corporate endeavor. In certain circumstances and with due consideration, section 173 of the Bankruptcy Act and sections 54.1 and 54.2 of the Companies Act can be applied.[63]

The Companies Act System

In Argentine law, the Companies Act number 19.550, as amended in 1983, contains four provisions concerning the above. The first two provisions are section 54, paragraphs 1 and 2; the third is section 54, paragraph 3; and the fourth is section 274. These provisions are applicable both in the case of a de facto or shadow director, and in the case of *de jure* director.[64] These will now be considered in turn.

1. Section 54, Paragraphs 1 and 2 of the Companies Act Number 19.550 as Amended 1983. Sections 54.1 and 54.2 were introduced in 1983.[65] Both sections

---

62 *Ibid.*

63 *Ibid.*

64 *Ibid* at pp 671-72; see also Otaegui, *Concentración Societaria* 446 (1984) (citing section 1725 of (federal) Argentine Civil Code, sections 413 and 415 of (federal) Argentine Commercial Code, and section 127 of Argentine Company Law of 1972 as amended in 1983). Section 1725 of the Civil Code reads as follows: "*Todo socio debe responder a la sociedad de los daños y perjuicios que por su culpa se le hubiere causado, y no puede compensarlos con los beneficios que por su industria o cuidado le hubiese proporcionado en otros negocios*". ["Every member must be liable *vis-a-vis* the company for damages arising thereof on account of its negligence if such member cannot offset them against the benefits that its industry or care would bring in the business".] Sections 413 and 415 of the Commercial Code were replaced by sections 54.1 and 54.2 of the Company Act of 1972 as amended 1983. (They are very similar in content.) Section 127 of the Company Act reads: "*El contrato regulará el régimen de administración. En su defecto, administrará cualquiera de los socios indistintamente*". ["The agreement shall regulate the administration of the company. In absence of provisions thereof, any member indistinctly shall administer the company".]

65 Section 54.1 of the Companies Act reads: "*El daño ocurrido a la sociedad por dolo o culpa de socios o de quienes no siéndolo la controlen, constituye a sus autores en la obligación solidaria de indemnizar, sin que puedan alegar compensación con el lucro que su actuación haya proporcionado en otros negocios*". ["The members or those who not being members exercise control over the company shall be jointly and severally liable for any damage sustained by the company due to their willful misconduct or negligence, such members not being entitled to allege offsetting thereof against any profits they might have

are applicable to individuals and to any type of corporation.[66] The rule refers to either continuous or sporadic corporate governance, and also refers to shareholders, dominant shareholders, and non-shareholder dominant parties. Any type of control is included: *de facto* or *de jure*, internal or external, direct or indirect.[67]

The foundations of the system of group liability in Argentine law are structured in both sections of the Companies Act. The norm is not linked to the position of manager, partner, or controlling person to which it makes reference. It is not related to the concept of *de facto* manager, which offers the advantage of not requiring an extensive and permanent intrusion to constitute the *de facto* administrator. The provisions are applicable to any type of person, category of partner, and category of dominant party, even if not a partner or shareholder. Therefore, indirect control, control exercised through intermediaries, and external control are included.[68]

The requisites of the rule are: first, damage against the subsidiary caused by a shareholder or a dominant or parent corporation, including non-shareholder dominant parties. Section 54.1 embraces all kinds of damage to tangible and intangible assets that are caused by fraud or fault, by act or omission, actual business, general policies, and liability in tort, including damage to business opportunities. The second requirement is unfairness or negligence in the corporate governance. The consequence is a compensation of the losses to the subsidiary or the subsidiary's creditors, or the restitution of the resources and undue profits of the businesses. To compensate for the damages (in kind or money), the regulations of the Civil Code are applicable. Section 54.2 is complementary to the first paragraph. It includes the transfer of assets and the use of effects without any significant profit to the company. The word "effects" must be interpreted broadly: it includes intangibles assets, prestige, business opportunities, background, and the reputation or standing of the company. The duty to return the profits to the company includes all profits, not only those proportional to the share of the person who made use of such effects. In cases where evaluation is difficult, the interpretation should be that the obligation to return the profits obtained in the course of business to the controlled company is applicable when the funds or effects used were a substantial or main part of the necessary elements to carry out that business.[69]

The plaintiffs legitimated by the statute are: a) the subsidiary corporation, b) the shareholders (exercising a "corporate action," as opposed to an "individual

---

brought to the company due to their actions".] Section 54.2 of the Companies Act reads: "*El socio o controlante que aplicare los fondos o efectos de la sociedad a uso o negocio de cuenta propia o de tercero, está obligado a traer a la sociedad las ganancias resultantes, siendo las pérdidas de su cuenta exclusiva*". ["The party or controlling party who uses assets or property of the company for its own business or the business of a third party shall be liable for bringing back to the company the profits arising therefrom and shall solely bear any losses incurred".]

66 See Manóvil, *op cit* fn 32 at p 682.

67 *Ibid* at pp 683-84.

68 *Ibid* at pp 680-84.

69 *Ibid*.

action"), c) the subsidiary corporation's creditors (only in the case of the *oblique action*[70]), d) the Trustee in Bankruptcy, and e) the creditors in the bankruptcy proceedings, instead of the Trustee in Bankruptcy.[71]

The group or domination link, as a fact of objective reality, does not end in the imposition of liabilities for the settlement of the subsidiary's debts. It also casts effects over other areas of the activities of the companies involved, as a consequence of their lack of autonomy. In relation to the external contractual relationships, the category of linked legal relationships was put forward (that is, cases of intrusion in negotiation, cases in which other members of the group to which the party belongs enter or perform contracts on its behalf, and extension of effects to other legal subjects). Significant here are the "comfort letters" and the application of the doctrine of "apparent standing of created trust" and the doctrine of "own acts". Similar effects correspond to the application of the principles related to unjust enrichment in the fulfillment of certain contractual obligations and rights. For example, negative obligations (that is, to abstain from doing something) that can be applied to the other members of the group depending on the sense they might have in each specific case, and the determination of good or bad faith or the knowledge of the circumstances within the group. Included are the liabilities due to the performance of "straw" or fictitious companies, liabilities resulting from the artificial continuity of the performance of a subsidiary, and the possible liabilities of the dominant company for the damages caused by the subsidiary, its workers, or effects.[72]

2. The "Ineffectiveness of the Corporate Personality" - The Doctrine of Piercing the Corporate Veil: Section 54, Paragraph 3 of the Companies Act Number 19.550 as Amended 1983. Section 54.3 was also introduced in 1983.[73] This statute was the first of its kind in the European Civil Law system.[74] This provision embraces diverse cases of imputation: duties and rights of the company to the partner or

[70] The "*Oblique action*" is defined by section 1.196 of the Civil Code, which reads: "*Los acreedores pueden ejercer todos los derechos y acciones de su deudor, con excepción de los que sean inherentes a su persona*". ["Creditors may exercise all the rights and actions held by the debtor, except those that are exclusively personal."]

[71] See Manóvil, *op cit* fn 32, at pp 697–710.

[72] *Ibid* at pp 721-40.

[73] Section 54.3 of the Companies Act reads: "*La actuación de la sociedad que encubra la consecución de fines extrasocietarios, constituya un mero recurso para violar la ley, el orden público o la buena fe o para frustrar derechos de terceros, se imputará directamente a los socios o a los controlantes que la hicieron posible, quienes responderán solidaria e ilimitadamente por los perjuicios causados*". ["Any actions of the company that is beyond its corporate purposes, or is a mere sham to violate the law, public order or to impair the rights of third parties, shall be directly attributed to the members or controlling parties who made such action possible, they shall be jointly and severally liable for damages arising therefrom".]

[74] See Manóvil, *op cit* fn 32 at p 1009. Uruguay has similar provisions in sections 189, 190 and 191 of the Companies Act number 16.060 as amended 1989. The 1989 Uruguayan law embraced a larger scope of group situations, as it does not limit the extension or transfer of imputability to partners, shareholders and controlling parties.

controlling party and actions and duties of the controlling party or partner towards the company. Included is the "friendly"[75] disregard of the legal personality in favor of the company, the partners, or the controlling companies due to the application of analogy. Many years earlier, (since the sixties) Argentine jurisprudence accepted the doctrine of piercing the corporate veil without any duly enacted statutory provision.[76] The provision establishes the futility of certain legal effects of the corporate personality, which is limited to the concrete act or legal situation at stake and not to the effects of the type of company.[77]

With regard to the interpretation of the legal wording of the statue: a) it embraces a performance as well as an act; b) overall, what is discussed is not the existence of the company, but rather, its performance; c) the objectives outside those of the company referred to are related to the notion of the final *"causa"* of the company, and this is related to the joint entrepreneurial risk which is always appraised in connection to a specific case; d) to "conceal" does not mean to hide, for it is the same whether the penalized action is public or hidden; e) the "mere" means to which the rule refers to is not a synonym of a fictitious or "straw" company, as it does not matter if the penalized conduct is the only conduct displayed by the company; f) *"ordre public"* must be understood in its strict sense as not embracing merely imperative rules. The infringement of good faith must also embrace the hypothesis of acts against morals and moral customs frequently included in bad faith. Moreover, to apply the rule of no proof of subjective element is required to constitute the legal basis of ineffectiveness.[78]

It has also been said that the norm is applied to any kind of partner, shareholder, or controlling party, either direct of indirect, internal or external. Also, the ineffectiveness in steps or stages is possible. Third parties have legal standing to claim the ineffectiveness of the legal personality. Liability imposed by section 54.3 is independent of the declaration of ineffectiveness of the legal personality (or legal entity) in itself. Section 54.3 is not restricted to the true holders of the rights, or to those that benefit from the unlawful conduct. Further, it is not limited to only those who performed the conduct, but rather includes every

---

[75] Manóvil refers to the practice of following the German doctrine called *"freundlicher Durchgriff."* Manóvil, *op cit* fn 32 at pp 1015-17, 1229.

[76] For example, *"Fernandez Anchorena"*, CNPaz en Pleno [1969-III] JA 52 (Arg); see also *"Kellog Cia"*, CSJN [1985-B] LL 414 (Arg) (application in Argentine tax law) with a commentary by Corti, *El caso Kellogg y el restablecimiento de la doctrina "Parke Davis"*; *"Marlow"*, CNCom, sec B [1995-C] LL 280 (Arg) (application in subsequent jurisprudence).

[77] *See* Manóvil, *op* cit fn 32 at p 1018; see also *"Varrone"*, Cámara Séptima Civil y Comercial de Córdoba [1996] LL Córdoba 372 (Arg).

[78] *See* Manóvil, *op cit* fn 32 at pp 1229–30; see also, for example, *"Morrogh Bernard"*, Cámara de Apelaciones en lo Civil y Comercial de Concepción del Uruguay, 9.2.1979, [1979-D] LL 237 (Arg) with a commentary by María Josefa Mendez Costa, *Legítima y sociedades de familia*; *"Astesiano"*, CNCom, sec A [1978-B] LL 196 (Arg) (demonstrating violation of statute's mandatory provisions is one of foundations of norm) with a commentary by Zannoni, *"La desestimación de la personalidad societaria -disregard- y una aplicación en defensa de la intangibilidad de la legítima hereditaria"*.

person that, by action or omission, made it possible. All those who suffered the damage are entitled to compensation. The damages to be compensated are not only those due to the unlawful action of the corporation, but also include those that result from the declaration of ineffectiveness.[79]

The judgment declaring that the juridical personality (legal entity) is not opposable can be of detriment to third parties acting in good faith. The norm prevails over such third parties, except for third parties acting in good faith that acquired specific rights on specific assets which can be affected by the ineffectiveness. For the same reason, the bankruptcy or insolvency proceedings are not opposable to third parties that obtained the declaration of ineffectiveness of the legal personality in order to transfer the legal entitlement to assets. When the imputation of legal relationship is transferred, this happens with its assets and liabilities. The compensation of credits and debts between the third party and the person to whom the imputation is transferred to proceeds.[80]

3. The Liability of the Administrators and Directors of a Corporation: Section 274.1 of the Companies Act Number 19.550 as amended 1983. Section 274.1 of the Companies Act governs the liability of the administrators and directors of a corporation,[81] and it can be applied by analogy to the administrators or directors of the dominant or subsidiary corporation,[82] by virtue of section 59.[83] This Section is also applicable directly to the dominant corporation itself, by analogy.

Except where a domination contract has been celebrated in Germany (or when German law is applicable), in all other regulations the administrators of the subsidiary must act in the interests of the corporation that they manage. In the case of a conflict with the interests of the parent corporation, it is their duty to prefer the interests of the corporation they manage, that is, the subsidiary. When judging the due conduct of the managing board of the subsidiary in relation to the instructions

---

[79] *See* Manóvil, *op cit* fn 32 at p 1230.

[80] *Ibid.*

[81] Section 274.1 of the Companies Act reads: "*Los directores responden ilimitada y solidariamente hacia la sociedad, los accionistas y los terceros, por el mal desempeño de su cargo, según el criterio del artículo 59, así como por la violación de la ley, el estatuto o el reglamento y por cualquier otro daño producido por dolo, abuso de facultades o culpa grave*". ["Directors shall be jointly and severally liable *vis-à-vis* the company, the shareholders and third parties for any misperformance of office, under the criterion of Article 59, as well as from any violation of the law and the by-laws and for any damage arising from their willful misconduct, abuse of office or gross negligence."]

[82] *See* Manóvil, *op cit* fn 32 at pp 747-72; Bergel & Paolantonio, *op cit* fn 38 at p 235.

[83] Section 59 of the Companies Act reads: "*Los administradores y los representantes de la sociedad deben obrar con lealtad y con la diligencia de un buen hombre de negocios. Los que faltaren a sus obligaciones son responsables, ilimitada y solidariamente, por los daños y perjuicios que resultaren de su acción u omisión*". ["The managers and representatives of the company must act with loyalty and with the diligence of a good businessman. Those who fail to comply with their duties shall be unlimitedly and jointly and severally liable for any damages arising from their actions or omissions."] The officer or director must be technically prepared for each business in particular. See "*Estancias Procreo Vacunos SA*", CNCom, sec D [1996-B] LL 193 (Arg).

or directives imposed by the parent corporation, a distinction must be made according to whether or not those instructions were imparted by the formal organic channels. The common rules of liabilities for directors are applied, and where applicable, so are the rules of liability in the system of insolvency proceedings.[84]

The Civil Code System

In the Argentine Civil Code, there are three provisions applicable by analogy to liability within corporate groups. These provisions are sections 43, 1109 and 1113 of the Civil Code.[85] Section 43 of the Civil Code was partially reformed in 1968 and establishes the liability of corporations in general for any wrongdoing of their directors or administrators,[86] and the authors apply this norm by analogy to the dominant corporation when it directs a "subordinated" individual or corporation. The provision requires only a subordination relationship: an order or mandate, contractual or not contractual, permanent or temporary, remunerative or not.[87] The subsidiary or dependent person must be appointed by the dominant or parent in order to obey his instructions, which are considered mandatory. In other words, one person with the right to command and another person with the duty to obey, all in the interest of the commander.[88] Even the *subordination relationship* could be *de facto* or *de jure*, with or without a labor relationship or any other contractual relationship.[89] Section 1109 of the Civil Code[90] is applicable by analogy to

---

84 See Manóvil, *op cit* fn 32 at pp 760-76.

85 The Civil Code and the Commercial Code are rules applicable to the whole country, like the Federal Law in the United States.

86 Section 43 of the Civil Code reads: "*Las personas jurídicas responden por los daños que causen quienes las dirijan o administren, en ejercicio o con ocasión de sus funciones. Responden también por los daños que causen sus dependientes o las cosas, en las condiciones establecidas en el título: De las obligaciones que nacen de los hechos ilícitos que no son delitos*". ["Legal entities shall be liable for damages caused by their managers or administrators in the course of their duties. They shall also be liable for damages caused by their dependents or by things, under the conditions established under the heading: Obligations that arise from torts that do not qualify as crimes".] This is a very important rule and, much to the surprise of attorneys-in-law, it is not often invoked in Argentina.

87 See Manóvil, *op cit* fn 32 at p 661; case "*Acosta Héctor Raúl*", CNCiv B [1966] LL 424.

88 See de Carlucci & Parellada, *Responsabilidad Civil* at pp 336–37 (1992).

89 See the jurisprudence of the Civil Court of Appeals of Buenos Aires in "*Sievano de Díaz, María L*", CNCiv, sec E, [1977-D] LL 306; "*Máquina, Juan*", CNCiv, sec A, 30.10.1969, 140 LL 782; "*Pereyra Horacio R*", CNCom, sec A, 21.4.1970, 141 LL 710; "*Acosta, Héctor Raúl*", CNCiv, sec B, 31.3.1966, 123 LL 424; "*Barquín, Arturo R*", CNCiv, sec B, 29.2.1968, 131 LL 500; "*Mazza, Atilio*", CNCiv, sec D, 22.12.1966, 126 LL 58; "*Gómez, Raúl M*", CNCiv, sec F, 15.5.1969, 136 LL 848; "*Presmanes, Fernando A*", CNCiv, sec F, 3.7.1969, 137 LL 758 (cited in Manóvil, *op cit* fn 32 at p 663 n 311).

90 Section 1109 of the Civil Code reads: "*Todo el que ejecuta un hecho, que por su culpa o negligencia ocasiona un daño a otro, está obligado a la reparación del perjuicio. Esta obligación es regida por las mismas disposiciones relativas a los delitos del derecho civil*". ["Any person who performs an action, that due to his/her negligence or fault causes damage

corporate groups because it governs generally and implicitly wrongful or fraudulent corporate governance.[91] This section has a strong connection with section 274 of the Companies Act.

Section 1113 of the Civil Code was also reformed in 1968 and establishes the liability of any person who causes any damage, even for the action of a subordinated person.[92] But the liability of the dominant is not automatic. There must exist an unfair act against the subsidiary because the first party has intended only his personal interest and has thus caused damage to the second party. There must be an unfair prevailing interest of the dominant against the interest of the subsidiary.[93] Other requirements for liability are: a) the liability of the dependent person (because this is a case of reflexive or ancillary liability), b) damage caused to the subsidiary person, and c) a relationship between the orders and the damage.[94]

The Reform of the Argentine Law

One of the fundamental theses of this chapter is to assert that in no case is it suitable to apply the extension of the bankruptcy proceedings among the companies (or individuals, members of any juridical type) of a group, when one or some of the companies are undergoing insolvency. Moreover, it is contended that any liability system is preferable to the application of the different extension of the bankruptcy proceedings hypothesis. In the case of corporate groups, in an insolvency situation, a better solution is an alternative liability system of the director of the group, derived from his control or his unified economic policy. An essential condition for such liability is that the debts of the bankrupt company have been incurred as a result of his control. To facilitate the procedural requirements the burden of the proof should be borne by the holding or dominant company.

Such an approach is the application of the most modern comparative doctrine, legislation and case law (European and American) regarding liability within the group. In our case, it is fitting to apply them to the bankruptcy hypothesis with due analogies, by means of the argument "*a maiore ad minus*". The proposed doctrine is based, among others, on the American, English and German law. This will

---

to another person, shall be liable for redressing such damage. This obligation is governed by the same provisions as those applicable to civil torts".]

91 See Manóvil, *op cit* fn 32 at p 756; Bergel & Paolantonio, *op cit* fn 38 at p 235.

92 Section 1113 of the Civil Code reads: "*La obligación del que ha causado un daño se extiende a los daños que causaren los que están bajo su dependencia, o por las cosas de que se sirve, o que tiene a su cuidado*". ["The obligation of anyone who causes damage extends to any damage caused by those who are under his/her control or by the things used or under his/her control".]

93 See de Carlucci & Parellada, *op cit* fn 88 at p 338, noted in Manóvil, *op cit* fn 32 at p 663. But see Otaegui, *op cit* fn 64 at p 448 (disagreeing with Manóvil's position and arguing that in this case, sections 54 and 272 of the Argentine Companies Act as amended in 1983 are applicable. Sections 54 and 272 establish liability of corporate directors acting in conflict with interests of parent corporation and subsidiary).

94 Manóvil, *op cit* fn 32 at p 664.

involve disregarding the institute of the extension of the bankruptcy proceedings (contrary to the Italian, the French or the Argentine laws) and has instead other tools for the liability issues within bankruptcy procedures. The American sources are based on equity which has a special application in bankruptcy cases. The American, English and German approach is more adequate, as regards the liability of the director of the group, because they are more proportioned to the nature and way of operating of such corporations within a corporate group, especially when insolvency problems arise and must be handled with.

The dominant company must be responsible, in case of bankruptcy of a subsidiary, for the excess or negligence or fraud in the exercise of management and control, against its own social interest or against the social interest of the subsidiary. To that end, the director of the corporate group should be liable for the debts of the subsidiary in insolvency proceedings originated as a result of his control and unified economic policy. The opportunity to escape such liability should be provided if he can prove that the unified economic policy has not been practiced in a negligent or fraudulent way, and that the interest of the subsidiary has been loyally preserved during its execution.

In the continental tradition *de lege ferenda* the following provision is proposed as an appropriate reform of Argentine law:

1) *"In case of bankruptcy of the director or owner or holding or dominant company of a corporate group, under no circumstances does the extension of the bankruptcy proceedings apply to the subsidiaries. Instead, all the rights owned by the former over the latter will be disposed of, including those ones inherent to the subordination relationship and to the power of unified economic policy, in the corresponding bankruptcy stage, as part of the bankrupt's liquidation".*

2) *"In case of bankruptcy of one or some of the subsidiaries of a corporate group:*

   a) In no case is the extension of the bankruptcy proceedings possible among them or against the dominant.

   b) The dominant company or individual dominant will be responsible for all but only those bankrupt liabilities or debts, after the final distribution of the liquidated bankrupt subsidiaries, coming from one or several business decisions taken under his control or unified economic policy.

   c) The director of the corporate group can be discharged from this liability by proving that there was no professional negligence in the decisions and execution measures of the unified economic policy that gave rise to the unpaid debt of the bankrupt subsidiary. Where this cannot be proved, it will be presumed that at least such professional negligence has existed and therefore he will be responsible for such debt.

d) *The director of the group is in charge of showing that such business decisions were not taken under his control or under the unified economic policy or that they were taken autonomously by the subsidiary companies or individuals or that they have been born accidentally or due to external circumstances for which he should not be responsible as director of the group".*

3) *"In case of inseparable commingling of assets, the extension of the bankruptcy proceedings will not be declared to the whole group. Instead, the total or partial substantial consolidation of the bankruptcy proceedings and liabilities will be declared, and they will be disposed of according to the assets of the bankruptcy formed in the most convenient way, taking into account the interests of the parties involved, the possibility of the accounting reconstruction of the assets, its onerousness and the time needed for its confection".*

4) *"In case of more than one bankruptcy of corporations or individuals who are part of a corporate group, the procedural consolidation or accrual can be declared, if necessary, for the sake of procedural or material economy".*

5) *"This system is independent of liability of third parties established by the bankruptcy or corporate rulings for undue coauthorship, aggravation or prolongation of the bankrupt condition, or other damages caused to bankrupt creditors, including the board of directors taking part in corporate groups".*

Conclusion

Liability of a parent for obligations of an insolvent subsidiary strikes directly at limited liability. Equitable subordination provides a much more acceptable avenue for the application of "Enterprise Law" than the direct imposition of liability. Although in form, equitable subordination of the parent's claim is not an imposition of liability, the result in the overwhelming number of cases will be the same. The subsidiary's assets will typically be inadequate to pay all claims. As a result of subordination, assets otherwise going to the parent will be paid to the public creditors. Piercing the corporate veil jurisprudence is the traditional safety valve in "Entity Law" under which in exceptional cases liability may be imposed on a parent (or controlling shareholder) for the debts of its subsidiary.

With limited liability at stake, the courts appear firmly wedded to the traditional concepts of "Entity Law" when faced with the possible imposition of liability for the debts of a bankrupt subsidiary (or controlled corporation) upon its parent (or controlling shareholder). The jurisprudence of piercing the corporate veil is not the special concern of bankruptcy but it can provide the basis for the exception. As the United States Court of Appeals for the Second Circuit noted in another context, the "corporate veil" is not disregarded in bankruptcy "merely because it would make for an efficient and economical administration of the debtor's estate".[95]

The relief made available in the *Sea Pines* case with respect to the diversion of the subsidiary's assets for the benefit of the parent after the subsidiary has become insolvent highlights the importance of state law remedies. There is substantial state law authority providing relief in such cases of diversion of the insolvent subsidiary's assets. Such a remedy, based on the considerations underlying the fraudulent conveyance doctrine, but not subject to the statutory limitations of the Code and UFCA, may prove important to creditors and the Trustees in Bankruptcy when for some reason the protection of the statutory remedies is not available.

It is noteworthy that the Argentine Companies Act, as amended 1983 with its section 54.3, is the first one that places the overriding Anglo-Saxon jurisprudence of piercing the corporate veil involving corporate groups (especially in bankruptcy cases) in a formal statute text in one European Civil Law System. Also noteworthy is the statute concerning the extension of bankruptcy proceedings in the Argentine Bankruptcy Act, but it has been argued that the norms regarding liability are preferable, because they are more flexible and reliable, particularly in the case of multinational corporate groups in insolvency.

---

[95] *Feldman v Trs of Beck Indus, Inc* (*In re Beck Indus, Inc*), 479 F2d 410, 419 (2d Cir 1973).

PART II
CONTRACTUAL ISSUES

Chapter 6

The Enforcement of Commercial Expectations in the Law of Privity and Compound Interest

Tony Ciro and Vivien Goldwasser

Introduction

Imagine that one party induces an expectation in the mind of another, which leads to the detrimental reliance by the promisee on the promise or representation. Should the law enforce the expectation?[1] There are at least three possible responses of the law: first, the law can enforce the expectation on the basis that to do otherwise would be unfair and create an injustice to the party relying on the expectation. With this approach the law is converting the expectation into an obligation that is enforceable in equity. Second, the law can ignore the expectation and treat it as non-obligatory. This has typically been the approach of the common law in its insistence on strict legal rights. Third, the law can treat the expectation as non-obligatory but may conclude that there are important moral considerations that would make the expectation enforceable from time to time.

It is argued in this chapter that commercial expectations are playing an increasingly prominent role in recent developments in the law of privity and compound interest in Australia and the United Kingdom. These two particular although unrelated topics are selected for examination because they are both controversial and problematic: the established legal principles have been shown to be out of synchronization with commercial reality. Recent developments highlight the increasing willingness of courts, legislatures and reform bodies to overcome the gap created between commercial expectations and commercial reality on the one hand and the application of strict doctrine on the other. The bridging of the gap has been particularly evident in the two areas that have been chosen for discussion.

---

1 Spence raises a similar question when examining the role assumptions has played in the development of the law of estoppel. Spence concludes that the enforcement of assumptions have been at the forefront of the protection of reliance and the creation of a new "Australian" doctrine on estoppel. See Spence, "Australian Estoppel and the Protection of Reliance" (1997) 11 *Journal of Contract Law* 203.

The chapter will briefly explain what is meant by the term "commercial expectations" and will review a number of recent cases to show how equity is treating certain expectations as obligatory. It will be shown that in all of the cases there has been a failure in the realization of expectations and equity has intervened to address the shortcoming. The principal motivation for the intervention is to avoid an unjust result. Increasingly in the areas of privity and compound interest the court's desire to avoid under compensation has led to the law reflecting underlying commercial expectations. Giving concrete expression to such expectations is important because expectations may have significant ramifications. A failure in expectations can undermine market integrity and market efficiency because innocent parties have ostensibly relied on contractual promises and representations in the allocation of their scarce resources. To ignore these expectations would be tantamount to providing a green light for further market abuse and inefficient market practices. It is in this sense that equity can be viewed as fulfilling important public policy goals in a similar manner to other forms of regulation.[2]

The recent developments in compound interest and the inroads made into the privity doctrine are consistent with giving effect to commercial expectations.[3] The underlying drivers for the curial and statutory reforms are undeniably economic:[4] to curb market abuse, and overcome market failure through the enforcement of commercial expectations.[5]

---

2 See generally in Australia Chapter 7 of the *Corporations Act* 2001 (Cth) and the regulation of financial markets. The stated public goals of financial markets regulation is the promotion of market integrity, market efficiency and fair competition: Corporations Law Economic Reform Program, *Financial Products Service Provides and Markets Paper No 6,* (AGPS, Canberra 1997), p 50; Financial Systems Inquiry, *Financial Systems Inquiry Final Report,* (AGPS, Canberra 1997), pp 179-182; 606-616.

3 Indeed it has been suggested that curial and statutory intervention designed to stamp out abuse and overcome market failure represent restrictions on the contracting parties ability to freely contract. This ignores powerful commercial expectations underlying the contracting process. If doctrine embraces commercial expectations then one could argue that curial intervention is used positively to improve market integrity in modern day contracting. Instead of being viewed as necessarily onerous or even restrictive, curial and statutory intervention that concretises counterparty expectations can be viewed positively and consistent with normative principles of economics.

4 See Hall, "A Theory of Economic Informed Consent" (1997) 31 *Georgia Law Review* 511. Professor Hall argues that the instrumental justification for informed consent law is that individuals know better than physicians or others what best fits their personal values and therefore, following patients wishes will result in more beneficial results, *Ibid* 515-516.

5 The role of "reasonable expectations" in the development of modern day contract law was commented on by the Hon Sir Anthony Frank Mason, "Good Faith and Equitable Standards" (2000) 116 *LQR* 66 at p 72. As discussed in a later section of this chapter, the Law Commission in its review on the privity doctrine in the UK generalised its justification to abolish the doctrine on the basis that it would create an "injustice to the third party". The Commission identifies the injustice as constituted by "reasonable expectations" and where the third party has the expectations "of having the legal right to enforce the contract": See Law Commission Paper No 242, *Privity of Contract: Contracts for the Benefit of Third*

Commercial expectations have also found legal expression in recent statutory initiatives in the United Kingdom. Legislation in the form of the Contracts (Rights of Third Parties) Act 1999 (UK) has allowed third parties who are not privy to commercial contracts to sue provided that a benefit was owing to them at the time the contract was formed. Similarly, the UK Law Commission in its Consultation Paper on Compound Interest[6] stated that its preferred position was that courts should be given the power to award compound interest in all court ordered payments. The main justification for the new position is that such an award is necessary to give effect to the market expectations concerning an award of interest.

The chapter begins in Part II by outlining the importance of commercial expectations in the development of new directions for existing doctrine. We will review recent important curial and statutory developments in the law of privity in both Australia and the UK. The role commercial expectations have played in Australian case law on compound interest, and the position currently adopted by the Law Commission in its Consultation Paper will also be examined.

What are Commercial Expectations?

The fulfilment of commercial expectations as a guiding principle has both normative and positive theses. The positive thesis is that commercial expectations have found legal expression recently in the law of privity and compound interest.[7] The normative thesis is that the recent developments are justified because they reflect underlying market realities, and are consistent with the public policy goals of promoting good business practice, improving market efficiency and avoiding market failure.

The remarks of Steyn LJ in a contractual dispute involving the ad hoc representations of a bank officer and a businessman where no formal contract had been executed are of relevance. The judge recognized the importance of expectations in the development of equitable principles in *First Energy (UK) Ltd v Hungarian International Bank Ltd*:[8]

> A theme that runs through our law of contract is that the reasonable expectations of honest men must be protected. It is not a rule of principle of law. It is the objective which has been and still is the principal moulding force of our law of contract . . . if the *prima facie* solution to a problem runs counter to the reasonable expectations of honest men, this criterion sometimes requires a rigorous examination of the problem to ascertain whether the law does indeed compel demonstrable unfairness.

Parties (1996), para 3.2. See also Kincaid, "Privity and Private Justice in Contract" (1997) 12 *Journal of Contract Law* 47 at p 51.

6 Law Commission Consultation Paper No 167: Compound Interest (2002).

7 Carter and Stewart, "Commerce and Conscience: The High Court's Developing View of Contract" (1993) 23 *Western Australian Law Review* 49, 49-50.

8 [1993] 2 Lloyd's Rep 194, [1993] BCLC 1409, [1993] BCC 533.

The enforcement of expectations is pivotal to explaining the incentive not only for contracting parties, but also to third parties who may ostensibly rely on contractual undertakings to which they are not privy. This is because typically with expectations comes reliance. When an expectation has been created, whether that expectation is the third party's right to sue in the case of the privity doctrine,[9] or a promisee's right to claim compound interest for money transferred under a void contract *ab initio* and later wrongfully withheld,[10] an element of trust or reliance is invoked in the beneficiary of the promise, notwithstanding that the promise is prima facie unenforceable at law in both circumstances.

Similarly, the enforceability of promises and expectations are paramount considerations when the relationship breaks down.[11] Adam Smith, lecturing on jurisprudence suggested that the "obligation to performance which arises from contract is founded on the reasonable expectations produced by a promise, which considerably differs from a mere declaration of intention".[12] More recently other academic commentators[13] and even members of the judiciary[14] have underscored the importance of expectations in the development of equitable principles and equity doctrine.

However, it is equally worth noting that expectations on their own do not create legal obligations. As Professor Baker points out something more is required because it is "one thing to explain the binding force of promises in terms of the reasonable expectations which arise from them, and quite another to recognize a binding force in reasonable expectations in the absence of promises".[15] Baker further adds: "The disappointment of an expectation cannot by itself be a cause of action. Neither can it become a cause of action merely by the addition of the limiting adjective "reasonableness".[16] For Baker, the justification that is used to enforce reasonable expectations is that they are not only important to the parties concerned but mean more to them than the finer points of classical contractual theory.[17] Expectations are paramount to long-term business relations in much the same way honesty, fairness and trust are prominent considerations in modern day

---

9 *Trident General Insurance Co Ltd v McNiece Bros Pty Ltd* (1988) 165 CLR 107; 80 ALR 574.

10 *Westdeutsche Landesbank Girozentrale v Islington London Borough Council* [1996] AC 669 (HL). See also the decision at first instance: [1994] 4 All ER 890 and in the Court of Appeal: [1994] 4 All ER 957 (CA).

11 Eisenberg, "The Emergence of Dynamic Contract Law," (2000) 88 *California Law Review* 1743.

12 *Adam Smith Lectures on Jurisprudence* Stein (Ed) (1978) at p 92.

13 See *Salmond on Jurisprudence* (12th ed) Fitzgerald (1966), where the author states: "It is one of the leading principles of justice to guarantee to men the fulfilment of their reasonable expectations". *Ibid* at p 337.

14 See Hon Justice Mason, *op cit* fn 5.

15 Baker, "From Sanctity of Contract to Reasonable Expectation?" [1979] 32 *CLP* 17 at p 23.

16 *Ibid* p 24.

17 *Ibid* p 23.

commerce.[18] This is because parties are keen to avoiding costly litigation, and resolve any disputes "in-house" in a gentlemanly way.[19] The importance of expectations is also supported by Professor Eisenberg who posits that contract law and contract doctrine are no longer static but have become more dynamic.[20] For Eisenberg the underlying rationale for the emergence of dynamic contract law is the dynamic nature of modern day contracting. Parties do not remain static from the moment they form a contract. Instead, the parties' expectations and actions may vary because of changes in circumstances or changes in market demand.

In the case of equity relief has been described as imprecise and discretionary where jurisdiction and relief are invoked.[21] The imprecision and discretionary nature of equity is a function of circumstances relating to the dynamic nature of the parties' expectations. As expectations are initially formed at the point of dialogue actions follow and it is the actions or inactions that the law is most interested in when it comes to granting relief. Whether they arise from a contractual context or non-contractual basis equity may decide in its discretion to grant relief.

It is suggested that relief is given in equity when special circumstances are said to be present.[22] This is indeed true with the development of recent doctrines in the form of promissory estoppel, unconscionable bargains, privity and compound interest. With all of these doctrines it is argued that additional intervention is justified because there has been a failure in the institution of contract law to fulfil counterparty expectations.[23] Whether this failure is addressed fully with the award of reliance-based relief or expectation relief or even a combination of both, the point to note is this: equitable intervention and relief is fashioned according to a failure in the innocent party's expectations.

The manifestation of commercial expectations is the central hallmark of the doctrine of estoppel. The emergence of estoppel and the inroads the doctrine has made in the principles relating to consideration are reflective of the court's willingness to give effect to counterparty expectations at the time of contracting. This is the case even if the expectations form no part of the contract and cannot be used to explain the sole motive for contracting.[24]

---

[18] The work of Professor Macaulay is important here. For a small selection of references see Macaulay, "Non-Contractual Relations in Business: A Preliminary Study" (1963) 28 *Am Society Review* 55; Friedman and Macaulay, "Contract Law and Contract Teaching" (1967) *Wisconsin Law Review* 850.

[19] Allen, "The Gentleman's Agreement in Legal Theory and in Modern Practice" (2000) 29 *Anglo-American Law Review* 204. See also: Bernstein and Zekoll, "The Gentleman's Agreement in Legal Theory and in Modern Practice: United States" (1998) 46 *American Journal of Comparative Law* 87.

[20] *Ibid* at pp 1762-1764.

[21] Meagher, Gummow and Lehane, *Equity, Doctrines and Remedies,* 3rd ed (1992) at p 800.

[22] Waddams, "Unconscionability in Contracts" (1976) 39 *The Modern Law Review* 369.

[23] Carter and Stewart, *op cit* fn 6 at p 50.

[24] See the High Court's decision in *Walton's Stores (Interstate) Ltd v Maher* (1988) 164 CLR 387 where no formal contract existed because of the parties failure to counter sign and deliver leases for registration.

Similarly, the notion of good faith in Australia transgresses traditional legal wisdom to take into account broader considerations. Conventional thinking has been to rationalize good faith as an emerging doctrine to achieve fairness and morality in modern day contracting. According to Sir Anthony Mason, the emerging doctrines have been heavily influenced by traditional equitable principles of fairness and equity.[25] There can be no doubting the accuracy of his suggestion. Courts are always in search of outcomes that produce a fair and just result. Support for this can be found in *Renard Constructions (ME) Pty Ltd v Minister of Public Works*[26] where Priestly JA states:

> [P]eople generally, including judges and other lawyers, from all strands of the community, have grown used to the courts applying standards of fairness which are consistent with the existence in all contracts of a duty of good faith and fair dealing in performance. In these days anything less is contrary to prevailing community expectations.[27]

However, fairness and morality as underlying rationales do not provide a complete explanation for what motivates judicial outcomes. The courts have demonstrated a willingness to explore broader commercial considerations to assess actual outcomes.[28] This has been the case even in the absence of a legally enforceable contract. The court's enquiry in determining whether this has been the case and whether intervention on their part is justified depends on the court's consideration of the surrounding circumstances of each case.[29] When the courts do intervene they normally treat some expectations as obligatory. This is because the promisee's trust has been breached and the promisee will suffer materially detriment when they have relied on the expectation. In treating the expectation as creating an obligation, the courts carve out relief proportionate to the breach. In the case of promissory estoppel, the relief that has been provided has included expectational relief where the expectation is enforced, and reliance based relief where the promisee is compensated for reliance loss. In either case equity's aim is clear: to provide relief that is necessary "to do justice between the parties".[30]

---

[25] Mason, *op cit* fn 1 at p 83.

[26] (1992) 26 NSWLR 234.

[27] *Ibid* at p 268.

[28] McGuiness, "Law and Economics - A reply to Sir Anthony Mason CJ Aust" (1994) 1(2) *Deakin Law Review* 117. Professor McGuiness argues that the High Court has adopted a largely law and economics approach to judicial law making. This has been especially the case with the High Courts decision in *Walton Stores v Maher* (1988) 164 CLR 387 (HC): *ibid* at pp138-149.

[29] It is correct to acknowledge that commercial expectations may be displaced in favour of countervailing principles and policies. Nevertheless, the aim of protecting reasonable expectations remains constant in contract law. See also Reiter and Swan, "Contracts and the Protection of Reasonable Expectations," in *Studies in Contract Law*, Reiter and Swan (Eds) (1980) at pp 6-7.

[30] *Commonwealth v Verwayen* (1990) 170 CLR 394.

Expectations have found similar legal expression in the law of privity and compound interest. With privity, the expectation relates to a third party and their ability to sue and enforce a contractual obligation in a contract to which they are not privy. In the case of compound interest, the expectation relates to the right to seek an award of compound interest for court ordered payments where the innocent party has transferred money under a void contract, and the money has been wrongfully withheld.[31] At common law[32] and under statute,[33] an award of compound interest for judgment debts is not allowed. The ability to make the award rests in the sole jurisdiction of equity. The expectation for an award of compound interest is therefore one principally founded on the commercial realities of market rates of interest.[34] The remaining parts of the chapter will examine the role expectations have played in recent developments in both of these areas of the law.[35]

Converting Expectations into Obligations: Privity, Compound Interest and Agreements to Negotiate

Privity

The traditional rule, developed in the course of the nineteenth century in English contract law, is that only the original parties to a contract are legally bound by it or entitled to enforce it.[36] Conceptually, the doctrine of privity is coterminous with the doctrine of consideration, which stipulates that a promisor's promise must be paid for in order to be enforceable and that the payment must proceed from the

[31] *Westdeutsche Landesbank Girozentrale v Islington LBC* [1996] 1 AC 669.

[32] It was decided in *London, Chatman and Dover Railway Co v South Easter Railway Co* [1893] AC 429 (HL) that at common law there was no interest on debts unless the contract or the customs of the trade provide that there should be. At common law, late payment damages in the form of interest were only available in the case on the debt on a negotiable instrument: *De Havilland v Bowerbank* (1807) 1 Cam; 50; 170 ER 872; *Calton v Bragg* (1812) 15 East 223; 104 ER 828; *Page* v *Newman* (1829) 9 B & C 378; 109 ER 140.

[33] See Judiciary Act 1903 (Cth), s 77 MA; Federal Court of Australia Act 1976 (Cth), s 51A; Supreme Court Act 1970 (NSW), s 94; Supreme Court Act 1986 (Vic), s 60; Common Law Practice Act 1867 (Qld), s 72; Supreme Court Act 1935 (WA), s 32; Supreme Court Civil Procedure Act 1932 (Tas), s 165; Australian Capital Territory Supreme Court Act 1933 (Cth), s 53A; Supreme Court Act 1979 (NT), s 84; and in the UK: Supreme Court Act 1981 (UK), s 35A; Germany: Civil Code, art 288(1); Belgium: Civil Code, art 1153; Italy: Italian Civil Code, art 1224; Spain: Spanish Civil Code art 1108; Canada: Court Ordered Interest Act SBC 1974 (Can), c 65.

[34] Ciro, "Commercial Reality v Doctrine: Restitution and Compound Interest for Void Swaps" (2002) 30(3) *ABLR* 216.

[35] See Kincaid, *op cit* fn 5 at p 51 where the author discusses the role and significance of expectations to the law of privity.

[36] *Tweddle v Atkinson* (1861) 1 B&S 393; 121 ER 762; *Coulls v Bagot's Executor and Trustee Co Ltd* (1967) 119 CLR 460.

promisee. Accordingly, if a third party beneficiary has not provided consideration for the promise, they cannot demand that it be performed. Whether the two doctrines are treated as separate principles or two aspects of the same principle,[37] the effect of the doctrine of privity is that, at common law, even if a third party is intended to benefit under the terms of the contract, they cannot sue to obtain that benefit.

The rule that privity is required frequently causes hardship and injustice to third party beneficiaries and subverts the commercial reality of such situations, particularly where the intended beneficiary has acted in reliance on the contract, typically to their detriment.[38] There is much to be said for allowing an intended third party beneficiary to enforce the contract in these circumstances, as well as in situations where, in good conscience, the beneficiary should be entitled to enforce the contract.[39]

The Australian position There has been strong pressure in Australia to abolish the doctrine of privity. The United States abandoned the privity requirement in 1979,[40] New Zealand in 1982[41] and the United Kingdom most recently in 1999.[42] According to the provisions of the UK Contracts (Rights of Third Parties) Act 1999, a third party is entitled to enforce a contractual term if either the contract expressly provides that he may; or the term purports to confer a benefit on him.[43]

---

37 See the discussion in *Trident General Insurance Co Ltd v McNiece Bros Pty Ltd* (1988) 165 CLR 107, 114-116 (HC) per Mason CJ and Wilson JJ. In *Coulls* v *Bagot's Executor and Trustee Co Ltd*, Windeyer J said: "So long as consideration is an essential feature of English law it would seem to be immaterial whether a person is forbidden to sue on the ground that he has given no consideration or on the ground that he is a stranger to the contract. They are but two ways of saying the same thing." (1967) 119 CLR 460, 494.

38 Law Commission Report No 242, *Privity of Contract: Contracts for the Benefit of Third Parties*, Cm 3329 (1996).

39 The doctrine of estoppel may be of some assistance to third parties. In other words, the doctrine that a party may be estopped from denying to another that a contract has been made between them if the denial would be unconscionable in the circumstances, is of potential application to third parties. Although estoppel was not specifically pleaded in *Trident's* case, above, four members of the High Court recognized that it might apply (Mason CJ and Wilson JJ at 123; Brennan J at 140; Deane J at 145. Also see *Commonwealth v Verwayen* (1990) 64 ALJR 540, per Deane J at 560).

40 *Restatement 2nd, Contracts* (1979) Ch 14.

41 Contract (Privity) Act 1982 (NZ).

42 Contracts (Rights of Third Parties) Act 1999. See also Law Commission Report No 242 *op cit* fn 38.

43 Contracts (Rights of Third Parties) Act 1999, s 1(1) (a) and (b). In the case of s 1(1)(b), that is, where the term purports to confer a benefit, the third party will not be able to enforce that term if, on a proper construction of the contract, it appears that the parties did not intend the term to be enforceable by the third party: s 1(2). The Act is discussed in a later section of this chapter.

In Australia, some inroads have been made into the privity rule by virtue of statutory intervention. For example, as a result of the Insurance Contracts Act 1984 (Cth) and state legislation relating to motor vehicle insurance, the doctrine of privity as it applies to most contracts of insurance has been legislatively displaced. Moreover dissatisfaction with the privity rule led Queensland and Western Australia to pass legislation conferring rights of enforcement on third parties more generally.[44]

The High Court too seems to be moving in the direction of reform, albeit slowly. In *Olson v Dyso*, Windeyer J, after referring to the abandonment of the privity rule in the United States, expressed the view that "someday this Court too . . . will see the way clear to take the same path".[45] The High Court did not, however, avail itself of the opportunity to reconsider the privity doctrine when it arose in *Trident General Insurance Co Ltd v McNiece Bros Pty Ltd.*[46] Rather than finally determining the status of the doctrine in Australia, the case merely highlights the different attitudes of the judges to the doctrine. Mason CJ, Wilson J[47] and Toohey J[48] were prepared to relax the application of the privity rule in the context of an insurance policy where the parties clearly intended that the third party should benefit. Nevertheless the case may be seen as representing further progress because, although the High Court did not actually abolish the doctrine, it did indicate that wholesale reform of the privity rule was more appropriately to be carried out by law reform bodies and the legislature. In their joint judgment, Mason CJ and Wilson J hinted broadly that there may soon be a departure from the doctrine,[49] as did Toohey J.[50]

In the meantime, there is available to the courts a range of artificial techniques developed over the years to circumvent the harsh effects of the doctrine.[51] These techniques are not universally regarded as exceptions to the doctrine, but principles which may apply independently of the privity rule, the elements of which the third party must establish. These principles may be classified into two categories: first, means to establish that a person who is ostensibly a third party is in fact a contracting party (through the law of agency, or the notion of plurality of promisees); and secondly, means to establish that a third party, though unable to enforce the contract itself, has acquired non-contractual rights in connection with it (for example, under principles of law relating to trusts or unjust enrichment).

---

[44] Property Law Act 1969 (WA) s 11; Property Law Act 1974 (Q) s 55; Law of Property Act 2000 (NT) s 56. The relevant Western Australian provision confers a right on third parties, in certain circumstances, to sue on a contract for their benefit. The Queensland statute permits a third party to enforce a contract for their benefit in their own name.

[45] (1969) 120 CLR 365, 393.

[46] (1988) 165 CLR 107.

[47] *Ibid* at pp 123-4.

[48] *Ibid* at p 172.

[49] *Ibid* at p 123.

[50] *Ibid* at p 163. However according to Deane J, the doctrine was alive and well and still fundamental to the law of contract: (1988) 165 CLR 107, 143.

[51] It was recognized by all the judges in *Trident's* case that the privity doctrine may be capable of creating substantial injustice in many cases.

There are furthermore a number of other potential means of circumventing privity supplied by the commercial law (assignment, letters of credit, negotiable instruments, bills of lading), the law of property (covenants over land, other proprietary and possessory rights), the law of torts and estoppel.[52]

The privity rule has the potential to cause particular inconvenience and hardship in the context of the construction of exclusion clauses. By virtue of the privity of contract rule, exclusion clauses are only effective to protect the actual parties to the contract. A strict application of this rule means that a third party, for example, an employee, agent or sub-contractor who performs some of the primary party's (that is headparty's) contractual obligations, is denied the protection of the exclusion clause simply because they are not a party to the contract. Many of the cases in this area have involved the carriage of goods by sea or by road.

The UK position Induced by alleged commercial necessity, the courts devised an ingenious means, via the law of agency, of conferring protection on third parties. This possibility was first raised by Lord Reid in *Midland Silicones Ltd v Scrutton*,[53] although in that case the third party was successfully sued. Lord Reid stated that in appropriate circumstances and provided four conditions were met, a servant, agent or independent contractor could rely on an exemption or limitation of liability clause. The four requirements were subsequently adopted by the Privy Council in the *Eurymedon*,[54] and applied by the High Court in *Port Jackson Stevedoring Pty Ltd v Salmond & Spraggon (Australia) Pty Ltd.*[55] The third party must establish that the contract makes it clear that the headparty (for example, the shipowner) *intended* to protect the third party; that the headparty, by the contract, contracted for the third party's protection as well as their own; that the headparty had the authority of the third party to contract; and that there was consideration moving from the third party. The last element presents the greatest conceptual difficulties, but generally the approach has been to relax the rule that performance of an existing contractual obligation is not normally good consideration and to hold that that restriction does not apply when the performance is carried out for someone else other than the original party. In other words, the fact that a stevedore is contractually bound to unload for the shipowner does not prevent the act of unloading being good consideration as against the shipper of the goods. In *Celthene Pty Ltd v WKJ Hauliers Pty Ltd*[56] and *Life Savers (Australasia) Ltd v Frigmobile Pty Ltd*,[57] Lord Reid's four guidelines were applied and in both cases,

---

[52] The second limb of the doctrine of privity is that a person is not bound by a contract to which they were not a party. The extent to which the principles discussed above, in relation to contracts for the benefit of third parties, apply also to contracts imposing burdens on third parties is unclear.

[53] [1962] AC 446, 474.

[54] *New Zealand Shipping Co Ltd v A M Satterthwaite and Co Ltd: The Eurymedon* [1975] AC 154 (on appeal from New Zealand).

[55] (1980) 144 CLR 300.

[56] [1981] 1 NSWLR 606.

[57] [1983] 1 NSWLR 431.

the subcontractor and the carrier were protected from liability as a result of being able to rely on the terms of an exclusion clause contained in the carriage contract between the plaintiff or owner of the goods and the carrier.

The significance of *Midland Silicones,* the *Eurymedon* and *Port Jackson* does not lie in the creation of a new principle; rather that through the use (some would say manipulation) of established legal principles, a contract could be inferred so as to allow a third party to enjoy the benefit of an exclusion clause. The device used for this purpose was the fictional agency. By so doing, the courts are able to give effect to the clear commercial intentions of all the parties involved.

The Law Commission on Privity and the Contracts (Rights of Third Parties) Act 1999 (UK) The Contracts (Rights of Third Parties) Act 1999 (herein referred to as the Act) reforms a doctrine central to contract law, namely that limb of the doctrine of privity of contract under which a person can only enforce a contract if they are a party to it. The effect of the rule, as we have seen, is that even where a contract by its express terms purports to confer a direct benefit on someone who is not a party to it, that third party cannot, in its own name, take rights under the contract and cannot sue for breach.

It is important to clarify the ambit of the reform at the outset. In the first place, the reform was not intended to affect the second limb of the doctrine, which stipulates that a person is not bound by a contract to which they were not a party. In other words, the reform does not affect the rule that only parties to a contract can have burdens imposed on them by the contract. Thus the principles being discussed here in relation to contracts for the *benefit* of third parties do not also apply to contracts imposing *burdens* on third parties.[58] As Professor Burrows has pointed out, the reform was intended to be limited and moderate.[59] It does not abolish the privity doctrine as such, rather it carves out a general and wide-ranging exception to it.[60] For example, the Act does not give the third party full contractual rights, nor deem it to be a party to the contract.[61] On the other hand, the reform has implications for the doctrine of consideration because it necessarily and implicitly relaxes the importance attached to consideration.[62] Giving a third party a right to enforce the contract "can only be interpreted as also reforming the rule that consideration must move from the plaintiff".[63] Thus, the rule that consideration

[58] Law Commission Report, *op cit* fn 38.

[59] Burrows, "Reforming privity of contract: Law Commission Report No 242" [1996] *LMCLQ* 467, 486.

[60] *Ibid* at p 484. The fact that the basic doctrine of privity was not being abolished persuaded the Law Commission that a plethora of consequential amendments was unnecessary.

[61] *Ibid.*

[62] See *Williams v Roffey Bros & Nicholls (Contractors)* [1991] 1 QB 1 where performance of an existing contractual obligation was seen to constitute sufficient consideration because it provided a commercial advantage to the promisor.

[63] *Ibid* at p 483. Indeed, Professor Burrows is of the view that the doctrine of consideration should be formally reviewed by the Law Commission. *Ibid.*

must move from the promisee has been reformed to the extent necessary to avoid nullifying the reform of the doctrine of privity.[64]

Broadly speaking, the following are the salient features of the legislation. The Act sets out in section 1 the circumstances in which a third party is to have a right to enforce a term of the contract. There are two limbs to the test of enforceability.[65] The first limb applies where the contract itself expressly so provides. The second limb is satisfied where the term purports to confer a benefit on the third party, unless it appears on a true construction of the contract that the contracting parties did not intend him or her to have the right to enforce it. In order for these provisions to apply, the third party must be expressly identified in the contract by name, class or description, but need not be in existence when the contract is made.[66] This is designed to give contracting parties the ability to confer enforceable rights on an unborn child or future spouse, for example, or on a company that has yet to be registered.[67] The third party's right of enforcement is also subject to the contract's terms and conditions, so that it is possible for the contracting parties to place limits or conditions on the third party's right.[68]

In terms of remedies, the court may award the third party all the remedies which are normally available to a party bringing a claim for breach of contract.[69] The normal rules relating to causation, remoteness and mitigation apply to the third party's claim. Importantly too, the Act applies to enable a third party to take advantage of an exclusion or limitation clause in the contract, as well as to enforce "positive" rights.[70] Thus, where an exclusion or limitation of liability clause in relation to the tort of negligence expressly states that it is for the benefit of the promisee's "agents or servants or subcontractors", then these groups may enforce it although not parties to the contract.[71]

The Act then outlines the situations in which such a term may be varied or rescinded (section 2) and the defences available to the promisor when the third party seeks to enforce the term (section 3). In relation to variation and rescission, restrictions are placed on the ability of the contracting parties to subsequently vary or rescind the original contract in a way that affects the third party's rights once the

---

64 Law Commission Report, *op cit* fn 38, Section D Part XV, Summary of Recommendations, para 6.

65 Section 1(1). The Law Commission Report on which the legislation was based stipulated that this reform should not be interpreted as giving the third party full "contractual rights", nor as deeming the third party to be a party to the contract: Law Commission Report, *op cit* fn 38, para 44.

66 Section 1(3).

67 Explanatory Notes to the Contracts (Rights of Third Parties) Act 1999.

68 Section 1(4). For example, the contracting parties may stipulate that if the third party wishes to enforce the right, then they must do so by way of arbitration and not litigation: Explanatory Notes to the Act.

69 Section 1(5).

70 Section 1(6). Explanatory Notes to the Act.

71 Explanatory Notes to the Act.

third party has relied on the contractual provision or has accepted it.[72] Essentially (and provided there is no express term in the contract to the contrary) the third party must consent to such variation or rescission.[73] The court or tribunal is given power to dispense with the requirement of consent in certain circumstances, for example where the third party cannot be located or is mentally incapable of giving consent.[74] In terms of defences to a claim by the third party, the promisor is entitled to rely not only on any defence or set-off arising out of the contract which would have been available had the claim been made by the promisee, but also on any defence or set-off or any counterclaim not arising out of the contract, which is specific to the third party.[75] These provisions are subject to any express term of the contract which narrows the defences or set-offs or counterclaims available to the promisor.[76]

The Act makes it clear that section 1 does not affect the promisee's rights, or any rights that the third party may have, which are independent of the Act (sections 4 and 7(1)), thus preserving the statutory and common law exceptions to the third party rule. Protection from double liability is also provided to the promisor by ensuring that, where the promisee has recovered substantial damages representing the third party's loss, the third party will not be entitled to an award which duplicates that sum (section 5). And finally the Act is said to have no application to certain contracts, either wholly or partially (section 6).[77] For example, the Act does not undermine the existing law on who can enforce negotiable instruments.[78] And although certain contracts relating to the carriage of goods are excluded, this does not prevent a third party from taking advantage of an exclusion or limitation of liability clause.[79] In particular, this enables clauses which seek to extend the benefit of an exclusion or limitation of liability of a carrier of goods by sea to servants, agents and independent contractors engaged in the loading and unloading process, to be enforced by those servants, agents and independent contractors (so-called Himalaya clauses).[80]

The Act implements, with some amendments, the recommendations of the Law Commission in its Report No 242 on *Privity of Contract: Contracts for the Benefit*

---

72 "Acceptance" for the purposes of this provision means "an assent by words or conduct communicated by the third party to the promisor": Law Commission Report, *op cit* fn 38, Section D Part XV, Summary of Recommendations, para 14.

73 Section 2(1). It is important to note the ability of the contracting parties to expressly reserve the right to vary or cancel the third party's right of enforcement, irrespective of reliance or acceptance by the third party. Indeed the contracting parties are able to lay down a crystallisation test different from reliance or acceptance.

74 Section 2(4) and (5).

75 Section 3(2) and (4).

76 Section 3(5).

77 Explanatory Notes to the Act.

78 Section 6(1).

79 Section 6(5).

80 Explanatory Notes to the Act. There are, in addition, arbitration provisions (section 8), provisions in relation to Northern Ireland (section 9) and also in relation to the Crown.

of Third Parties (1996).[81] Whilst the Commission favoured comprehensive legislative reform over an ad hoc judicial approach, it was also of the view that the legislation should not be construed as preventing further judicial elaboration of third party rights.[82] It identified several policy considerations justifying law reform in this area, predominantly the need to give effect to the intention of the parties, the injustice caused to third parties, the difficulties created by the doctrine in commercial life and the need to harmonize English law with the legal systems of most member states of the European Union and much of the common law world which have recognized third party rights in contract.[83] It also noted the long history of criticism of the doctrine emanating from academics, law reform bodies and the judiciary both in England and in Australia.[84]

Of particular relevance to this discussion are the second and third policy categories mentioned above, which in some respects overlap, namely the injustice caused to third parties and the commercial inconvenience created by the doctrine of privity.[85] There are a number of strands to the argument, the combined effect of which was considered sufficiently weighty by the Law Commission to justify reform of the third party rule. Focusing first on the issue of injustice, the Commission acknowledged that a valid contract, albeit between two other parties, might well engender in the third party *reasonable expectations* of having the legal right to enforce the contract, especially where the third party has relied on the contract to regulate their affairs.[86] Whilst the intentions of the contracting parties would normally be consistent with the reasonable expectations of the third party, the Law Commission recognized that, in certain cases, problems might arise where the intentions of the contracting parties subsequently change. In such cases, the Law Commission attached so much significance to the third party's expectations

---

[81] *Op cit* fn 38.

[82] Law Commission Report, *ibid*, Section B Part III, Arguments for Reform, 39-52 and Section D Part XV, Summary of Recommendations, para. 3. According to Professor Burrows, the dictates of certainty required that the difficult issues raised by the reform – such as the test of enforceability, the rights of the contracting parties to vary or cancel the contract, and the defences open to a promisor – could only be decided once-and-for-all by a detailed legislative scheme: Burrows, *op cit* fn 59 at p 471.

[83] Law Commission Report, *ibid*, 1-2. Another reason relied upon was the fact that, under the doctrine of privity, the highly idiosyncratic situation was created whereby person who had suffered the loss (the third party) could not sue, whilst the person who had suffered no loss (the promisee) could sue. Furthermore, even if the promisee could obtain a satisfactory remedy for the third party, the promisee might not be able or willing to sue.

[84] *Ibid* at pp 34-35. English cases cited include *Beswick v Beswick* [1968] AC 58 per Lord Reid at 72, *The Pioneer Container* [1994] 2 AC 324 per Lord Goff at 335, *White v Jones* [1995] 2 AC 207, and in the High Court of Australia particular reference is made to the judgments in *Trident General Insurance Co Ltd v McNiece Bros Pty Ltd* (1988) 165 CLR 107.

[85] One commentator has argued that the injustice argument has never been satisfactorily explained. How can it be unjust to the third party "to deny it a right of action on a promise when the promise was not made to it and it had not paid for it?" See Kincaid, *op cit* fn 5.

[86] Law Commission Report, *op cit* fn 38 at p 39.

and the resulting injustice to that party that it recommended that these considerations should "trump" or override the intentions of the contracting parties where the injustice is sufficiently strong.[87] In other words, "the contracting parties' right to change their minds and vary the contract should be overridden once the third party has relied on, or accepted, the contractual promise".[88] As the Law Commission's Consultation Paper noted:

> Whether or not the law of contract has as its main purpose the protection of expectations reasonably created, or the protection of reliance reasonably incurred, it would not appear that the third party rule is required.[89]

The Law Commission also addressed the issue of the practical benefits of reform. The gains in terms of the commercial convenience and economic efficiency resulting from reform of the privity doctrine were considered by the Law Commission to be significant. The Commission's Report pointed to the fact that the existence of the rule, and its many statutory and common law exceptions, had given rise "to a complex body of law and to the use of elaborate and often artificial stratagems and structures in order to give third parties enforceable rights".[90] The uncertainty thereby created in order to circumvent the rule in individual cases was regarded as commercially inconvenient.[91] Reform of the rule would ensure that much of the artificiality, complexity and uncertainty could be avoided.[92] The Law Commission chose two types of contracts, construction and insurance contracts, to illustrate the real and practical difficulties caused by the rule in commercial life.[93] These contracts typify the many commercial situations in which a complex pattern or web of relationships exists from which it may be difficult to identify the traditional elements of contract formation.[94]

In the context of insurance contracts, for example, where one party takes out an insurance policy for the benefit of another, the third party rule operates to prevent the third party beneficiary (such as dependants other than spouses and children)

---

[87] Law Commission Report, *op cit* fn 38 at p 39. It has been argued however that the mere disappointment of an expectation does not, by itself, justify a cause of action: Kincaid *op cit* fn 5 at p 51; Baker *op cit* fn 15 at p 24.

[88] *Ibid* at pp 39-40. As Kincaid notes, the injustice constituted by disappointed expectations is increased where the third party had acted in reliance, although not necessarily to its detriment: Kincaid, *ibid* at p 51.

The Law Commission also discussed, under the umbrella of injustice, the perverse result of the third party rule illustrated in *Beswick v Beswick* [1968] AC 58 that the person who has suffered the loss of the intended benefit (the third party) cannot sue, whilst the person who has suffered no loss (the promisee) can sue: Law Commission Report, *op cit* fn 38 at p 40.

[89] Law Commission Consultation Paper No 121: Privity para 4.7 (c).

[90] Law Commission Report, *op cit* fn 38 at p 41.

[91] *Ibid.*

[92] *Ibid.*

[93] *Ibid* at p 43.

[94] The Consultation Paper, *op cit* fn 89 at p 72, para 4.6.

from enforcing the contract of insurance against the insurer.[95] This clearly runs counter to the commercial realities of the situation. In the context of complex construction projects, difficulties are created because the third party rule means that only the parties within each contractual relationship can sue each other. According to traditional doctrine, it is not possible in the "main" contracts, to extend to subsequent purchasers or tenants of the development or to financial institutions who might suffer loss as the result of the defective execution of the works, the benefit of the architect's and engineer's duties of care and skill, and the contractor's duty to build according to the specifications.[96] In these situations, involving a network of linked commercial contracts having a common underlying purpose, it would be contrary to the commercial realities to prevent a third party from enforcing rights under a contract executed for their benefit.[97] Reform of the privity rule was therefore seen as facilitating commercial convenience by enabling parties to simply lay down third party rights in the main contract.[98]

Overall, the juxtaposition of the doctrine of privity with its numerous "exceptions" or permutations highlights the tension that exists between the dictates of classical contract doctrine on the one hand and giving effect to the commercial realities of contracting including the expectations of the parties, on the other. The United Kingdom, Canada and New Zealand have given primacy to the latter, whereas in Australia the matter remains unresolved. It is to be hoped that the High Court of Australia or the Australian legislature does not delay much longer in rectifying the current state of uncertainty.

Compound Interest

The position in Australia The right to claim interest for judgment debts is governed by statute in both the UK and in Australia. Each Australian jurisdiction has a statute, which governs the award of interest for the payment of judgment debts.[99] Section 30c(1) and (4) of the Supreme Court Act 1935 (SA), which is similar to all other State Acts, reads in relevant part as follows:

> (1) Unless good cause is shown to the contrary, the court shall upon the application of a party in favour of whom a judgment for the payment of damages, compensation or any other pecuniary amount has been, or is to be, pronounced, include in the judgment an award of interest . . . in accordance with the provisions of this section.
>
> This section does not –

---

95 Law Commission Report, *op cit* fn 38 at p 48.

96 *Ibid* at p 44.

97 The Consultation Paper, *op cit* fn 89 at p 72, para 4.6.

98 Law Commission Report, *op cit* fn 38 at p 45.

99 See s 77 MA Judiciary Act 1903 (Cth); s 51A Federal Court of Australia Act 1976 (Cth); s 94 Supreme Court Act 1970 (NSW); s 60 Supreme Court Act 1986 (Vic); s 72 Common Law Practice Act 1867 (Qld); s 32 Supreme Court Act 1935 (WA); s 165 Supreme Court Civil Procedure Act 1932 (Tas); s 53A Australian Capital Territory Supreme Court Act 1933 (Cth); s 84 Supreme Court Act 1979 (NT).

> authorize the granting of interest on interest;
>
> . . .
>
> (e) limit the operation of any enactment or rule of law which, apart from this section, provides for the award of interest.

It is clear from subsection (4)(a) that the award of compound interest is not permitted under the Act. However this literal interpretation has been negated, to some extent, by the inclusion of subsection (4)(e). A reading of this latter provision seems to suggest some flexibility in the exercise of the court's discretion. The interaction of these two sections, in the context of the South Australian statute, was the subject of litigation in the High Court case of *Hungerfords and Others v Walker and Others.*[100]

In *Hungerfords'* case, the plaintiffs claimed that they were entitled to an award of compound interest for the overpayment of tax which had been caused by the defendant accountant's negligence in the preparation of their tax returns. At first instance, the trial judge held the accountants to be negligent but refused to make an award for compound interest on the basis of section 30c (4)(a) of the Supreme Court Act 1935 (SA), which does not, as has been shown above, allow an award of interest upon interest. On appeal by the plaintiffs, the Full Court of the Court of Appeal[101] held that the damage suffered by them, resulting from loss of use of the overpayment of moneys, was within the reasonable contemplation of the parties and should be awarded.

This is an interesting proposition when one looks at the way in which the plaintiff's claim was structured. The claim was for "loss of the use of the money" by way of damages. It did not specifically refer to an award of compound interest, but was instead couched in terms of opportunistic or expectational loss and therefore recoverable by way of damages. On appeal to the High Court, the Full Court's decision was affirmed. The majority, Mason CJ, Wilson, Brennan and Deane JJ, held that section 30c was not intended to be a comprehensive and exclusive code governing the award of interest. It was intended only to give a plaintiff some protection against the late payment of damages, by providing some interest relief in the form of simple interest rather than no interest at all.

The issue of whether one characterizes the opportunity loss as interest or damages was examined by Mason CJ and Wilson J.[102] They argued that until

[100] (1989) 171 CLR 125.

[101] *Walker v Hungerfords* (1987) 49 SASR 93.

[102] Mason CJ and Wilson J specifically view the payment of interest as compensation for the loss of opportunity. Their Honours state the following: "Judged from a commercial viewpoint, the plaintiff sustains an economic loss if his damages are not paid promptly, just as he sustains such a loss when his debt is not paid on the due date. The loss may arise in the form of the investment cost of being deprived of money which could have been invested at interest or used to reduce an existing indebtedness. Or the loss may arise in the form of the borrowing cost, that is, interest payable on borrowed money or interest foregone because an existing investment is realized or reduced . . . Opportunity cost, more so than incurred expense, is a plainly foreseeable loss because, according to common understanding, it represents the market price of obtaining money": (1989) 171 CLR 125, 143.

1952,[103] the recovery of interest stood apart from the general principles governing damages. It was only then that it was recognized that loss due to the late payment of a debt or damages might be recoverable in accordance with *Hadley v Baxendale.*[104] The rule in *Hadley v Baxendale* allows the recovery of "expectational" damages and compensation for loss of the use of money (that is, an equivalent to compound interest). This would appear to be an ingenious argument to circumvent the apparent ban on the award of compound interest. If one views the opportunity loss as damages instead of compound interest, one escapes the provisions of the statute and falls within the principles of *Hadley v Baxendale.*

The authors of *Restitution Law in Australia*[105] suggest that a right to compound interest for restitution claims should be made available independently of statute. The authors suggest that the basis for this right would be unjust enrichment.[106] The unjust factor would be to allow the defendant to pocket the commercial benefits from the use of the plaintiff's money and similarly, for the plaintiff to suffer an opportunity loss equal to the defendant's wrongful gain. Equity would be justified in its intervention to reverse the unjust enrichment and award compound interest in favour of the plaintiff.[107]

Support for this proposition can be found in the Federal Court decision of Wilcox J in *State Bank of New South Wales v Federal Commissioner of Taxation.*[108] The facts of the case can be briefly summarized. In February 1992 the Federal Commissioner of Taxation (FCT) was ordered to repay two sums, $420,161.86 and $143,959.08, to the State Bank of New South Wales. The FCT repaid the two instalments but refused to pay interest for the period during which the Commissioner had wrongfully withheld the monies. The State bank commenced proceedings for recovery of interest.

Wilcox J allowed the claim and awarded the State Bank of New South Wales simple interest at the rate of 10% per annum on the two sums. What makes the case significant is that interest was awarded not as damages or under statute but under the restitutionary principle of unjust enrichment. Wilcox J concluded that

---

[103] See *Trans Trust SPRL v Dasubian Trading Co Ltd* [1952] 2 QB 297 (CA). The Court of Appeal recognized that a failure to pay money under the contract would give rise to damages, provided the loss suffered as a consequence of non-payment was foreseeable at the time of the contract.

[104] (1854) 9 Ex 341; 156 ER 145.

[105] Mason and Carter, *Restitution Law in Australia,* (1995), ch 28.

[106] *Ibid* at p 951.

[107] The notion of "unjust enrichment" as the underlying principle in the law of restitution is reflected in a passage in the judgment of Deane J in *Pavey & Matthews Pty Ltd v Paul* (1987) 162 CLR 221 at pp 256-7 in which he said the concept of unjust enrichment: "constitutes a unifying legal concept which explains why the law recognizes, in a variety of distinct categories of case, an obligation on the part of a defendant to make fair and just restitution for a benefit derived at the expense of a plaintiff and which assists in the determination, by the ordinary processes of legal reasoning, of the question whether the law should, in justice, recognize such an obligation in a new or developing category or case". See also Davenport and Harris, *Unjust Enrichment* (1997) ch 6.

[108] (1995) 132 ALR 653.

the Commissioner of Taxation had derived a benefit and had been unjustly enriched at the bank's expense:

> As the law of restitution is based on the concept of unjust enrichment, it is important to take into account the fact that any benefit gained by the Commonwealth by the presence of the bank's (and the applicants) money in the Trust Fund was a benefit gained by it pursuant to an arrangement that was suggested by the bank and that conferred substantial advantages on the bank . . . It seems to me that the retention of these sums during those periods represented an unjust enrichment of the Commonwealth at the expense of the applicant. [109]

Although the quantum of interest awarded was simple and not compound, the basis of the Federal Court's decision is significant because it allows a claimant to claim compound interest where he/she can show such a rate is necessary to avoid unjust enrichment. This is particularly important if money has been paid to the defendant and no contract exists because the agreement has been declared null and void. A plaintiff confronted with these circumstances would be given the opportunity to claim compound interest if the defendant was unjustly enriched at the plaintiff's expense.

An alternative to an independent restitutionary action would be to amend the legislation governing the award of interest for judgment debts.[110] Amending the provisions of statutory interest to expressly allow an award of compound interest would achieve the dual objectives of fairness and certainty. An award of compound interest would reverse the defendant's unjust enrichment, and would compensate the plaintiff for the lost opportunity with the use of their money.[111]

There remain a number of shortcomings with this approach. Statutory interest is not applicable where the plaintiff's substantive claim is settled before judgment.[112] Nor is the statute applicable where the claim for interest arises independent of the plaintiff's substantive claim. Further, the process would be time consuming because it would require each State and Territory and the Commonwealth to agree to amend their respective statutes to allow for the award of compound interest.

---

[109] *Ibid* at pp 66-667.

[110] For a comprehensive and uniform approach this would mean amending each statute in Australia's nine jurisdictions. See fn 99 above.

[111] By providing comprehensive reform specific exceptions would no longer apply. A point that was noted by the Law Commission in its Consultation Paper on Compound Interest *op cit* fn 6 at para 4.8:

> It was clear in the judgment in *Westdeutsche Landesbank* that the House of Lords considered that the justice of the case required compound interest and that they were only restrained from awarding it by the express provisions of section 35A of the Supreme Court Act 1981. They also expressed the clear hope that this area of the law would be reformed by the legislature.

[112] *Mathew v TM Sutton Ltd* [1994] 1 WLR 1455. Compare *In re the Australian Metal Co Ltd* (1923) 33 CLR 329 at p 346.

For these reasons it is argued that an independent restitution action allowing an award of compound interest would be desirable. Allowing such a claim would have the advantage of achieving certainty and justice and would also be practical because there would be no need to enact cumbersome uniform State and Commonwealth legislation. An independent resitutionary action also has the added advantage of flexibility because it does not suffer the same restrictions that apply under statute.

Statutory interest in the UK A related issue that has come before the UK courts, but not directly in Australia, is whether there exists equitable jurisdiction to award compound interest to a counterparty who is expecting payment under a void derivatives agreement. Applying the decision of the House of Lords in *Westdeutsche Landesbank Girozentrale v Islington LBC,*[113] the answer is that compound interest would not be awarded. Briefly, the facts in *Westdeutsche* concerned the right to claim compound interest for payments made under a void agreement. The appellant bank had entered into a number of swap agreements with the local authority. Following the House of Lords decision in *Hazell v Hammersmith & Fulham LBC,*[114] the swap agreements were held to be void for ultra vires. Counsel for the German bank, Westdeutsche, claimed compound interest on payments they had made to Fulham, pursuant to the now, void swap agreements. Unlike the majority judgment, the two dissenting Law Lords in *Westdeutsche*, Lord Goff and Lord Woolf, favoured making the award of compound interest having regard to the commercial realities of the case. Lord Goff stated his support for this approach in the following terms:

> The council has had the use of the bank's money over a period of years. It is plain on the evidence that, if it had not had the use of the bank's money, it would have borrowed the money elsewhere at compound interest. It has to that extent profited from the use of the bank's money. Moreover, if the bank had not advanced the money to the council, it would itself have employed the money on similar terms in its business. Full restitution requires that, on the facts of the present case, compound interest should be awarded, having regard to the commercial realities of the case. As the judge said there is no reason why the bank should be denied a complete remedy.[115]

---

[113] [1996] 2 All ER 961.

[114] [1992] 2 AC 1. Following the House of Lord's decision in *Hazell*, a number of cases were brought before the courts in the UK. For a small selection of these cases see: *Morgan Guaranty Trust Co v Lothian Regional Council* [1995] SLT 299; *Kleinwort Benson Ltd v Lincoln County County Council* [1998] 3 WLR 1095 (HL); *Guinness Mahon & Co Ltd v Kensington and Chelsea Royal London Borough Council* [1998] 3 WLR 3 (CA); *Morgan Grenfell v Welwyn Hatfield DC* [1995] 1 ALL ER 1; *Kleinwort Benson Ltd v Lincoln CC* [1998] WLR 1095 (HL); *Kleinwort Benson* v *South Tyneside MBC* [1994] 4 All ER 972.

[115] [1996] 2 All ER 961, 975. Lord Goff was here applying the reasoning of Hobhouse J at first instance. In the view of the trial judge, "Anyone who lends or borrows money on a commercial basis receives or pays interest periodically and if that interest is not paid it is compounded . . . I see no reason why I should deny the plaintiff a complete remedy or allow the defendant arbitrarily to retain part of the enrichment which it has unjustly enjoyed": [1994] 4 All ER 890 at 955.

Put simply, Lord Goff attempted to provide the bank with a complete remedy. Since the local authority was at fault in not paying the lump sum back to the bank, the true cost to the bank was the loss of compound interest they could have earned on the funds had the funds been under their control. According to Lord Goff, to "do justice" or afford "full justice", an award involving compound interest was required.[116] Since the local authority had been given the use of the bank's money, the council would have had to pay compound interest if it had borrowed the money from some other financial institution.[117] Justice was effectively equated with commercial reality. The award of compound interest was "just" because commercial reality demanded it. To do otherwise would allow the local authority to have profited from the bank's money. Similarly, Lord Woolf commented on the potential gulf between commercial realism and doctrine. In His Lordship's view, a decision not to award compound interest would deny the claimant their rightful claim to full restitution.[118]

The majority of the House of Lords refused to endorse the approach of Lords Goff and Woolf. Instead, the majority held that the plaintiff bank was entitled to an award of simple interest under common law and statute. The majority held the Court had no jurisdiction to award compound interest, except against a trustee or other persons owing fiduciary duties. The local authority was simply a recipient of money under a contract subsequently found to be void for ultra vires. The Court rejected the bank's submission concerning an equitable proprietary claim. Instead, the Court held that money received under an *ultra vires* contract was a personal action based on a total failure of consideration.[119] The majority considered that an award of simple interest was appropriate given that the legislature had considered the issue twice, both in section 3(1) of the Law Reform (Miscellaneous Provisions) Act 1934 and its successor section 35A of the 1981 Act. In both instances the award of compound interest was not authorized.

The award of simple interest, however, fails to take into account the commercial realities of financial markets and banking practice. Simple interest does not represent the price or value of money in the marketplace. The award of compound interest is a more accurate and realistic measure of interest rate payments, and hence the price of money, within financial markets. This point was recognized by Hobhouse J in earlier proceedings where he stated:

> Simple interest does not reflect the actual value of money [in a commercial case]. Anyone who lends or borrows money on a commercial basis receives or pays interest periodically and if that interest is not paid it is compounded.[120]

---

[116] [1996] 2 All ER 961, 979.

[117] *Ibid* at p 981.

[118] [1996] 2 All ER 961, 1002.

[119] The judge held that there were two pre-conditions for an award of compound interest: first, that the plaintiff have an equitable proprietary interest in the money paid to the defendant and second, that the proprietary interest still exists against the defendant's assets. See also: Birks, *Private Law* in Birks and Rose (Eds), *Lessons of the Swaps Litigation* (2000).

[120] [1994] 4 All ER 890, 955.

The decision in *Westdeutsche* illustrates the point that at times the legal framework fails to keep pace with underlying commercial reality. One suggestion for an improvement to this area of the law would be to amend the Supreme Court Act (1981) UK and allow the award of compound interest at common law. According to Burrows this would then remove the need to rely on equitable principles for an adequate remedy.[121]

An alternative to statutory modification would be to redress the gulf between commercial reality and doctrine by re-examining the basis of doctrinal law. If law is to do justice, then the law must acknowledge and give effect to commercial expectations. In the absence of fraud, deceit, servitude or unconscientious dealing there is no basis to reject the full-blooded outcome of compound interest. To do so would be a dogmatic assertion of doctrine with the implicit endorsement of an unjust result.

The High Court of Australia decision in *Hungerfords v Walker,* discussed above, demonstrates the flexibility of equity to oil the wheels of doctrinal law, with the aim of making the law more responsive to commercial expectations. However the decision in *Hungerfords* does not address completely whether full restitution can be achieved under a void agreement as was the case in *Westdeutche.* There the contract was held to be void *ab initio.* With no contract, there can be no breach. The plaintiff must initiate an action for restitution for the return of payments under the void agreement, including any claims made for interest.

If restitution is the pre-requisite to successfully argue for return of funds, can the doctrine also be used to claim compound interest? Mason CJ and Wilson J suggested that it could, provided there were special circumstances. They stated that:

> Equity has adopted a broad approach to the award of interest. It has long been accepted that the equitable right to interest exists independently of statute: *Wallersteiner* v *Moir* [No 2].[122] Equity courts have regularly awarded interest, including not only simple interest but also compound interest, when justice so demanded, for example, money obtained and retained by fraud and money withheld or misapplied by a trustee or fiduciary: *La Pintanda.*[123]

The High Court decision in *Hungerfords v Walker* is clearly to be preferred to the House of Lords decision in *Westdeutsche.* The decision in *Hungerfords'* case, and the views of the minority expressed in *Westdeutsche,* are more in tune with commercial reality. The price of borrowing money in the marketplace is fully reflected in compound interest. To allow an award of compound interest to a rightful claimant was not only reflective of commercial reality and commercial expectations but was necessary to avoid unjust enrichment. The High Court in *Hungerfords'* case recognized this fundamental principle.

---

[121] Burrows, "Swaps and the Friction between Common Law and Equity" [1995] *RLR* 15, 28.

[122] [1975] QB 373.

[123] [1985] AC 104, 117.

An equitable doctrine founded upon commercial reality, free of fraud, deceit and unconscientious dealing can not only be reconciled with the desire to afford full and complete justice, but also improves market efficiency by overcoming the potential for abuse.[124] The lesson of *Hungerfords'* case is that, in exercising their equitable jurisdiction, the Courts of equity have the capacity to be flexible in order to achieve justice, and avoid the problem of under or overcompensation when it comes to determining the appropriate award of interest. This is because they are guided by considerations of commercial expectations in the exercise of their discretion.

It is submitted that Lord Goff and Lord Woolf in *Westdeutche* were correct in suggesting that an award of compound interest would be necessary to achieve complete restitution. There are of course strong economic arguments that can be made in support of an award of compound interest. Interest reflects the "time value"[125] of money. Compound interest reflects the cost and function of interest and represents the price one pays for the use of money in a commercial environment. The award of simple or statutory interest runs contrary to the current pricing of interest in the commercial market place, and fails to compensate the plaintiff for the loss that is sustained when money is wrongfully withheld.[126]

Recent developments: The Law Commission's Consultation Paper on Compound Interest The UK Law Commission issued its Consultation Paper on Compound Interest for public comment.[127] The Law Commission provisionally concludes: "the power to award compound interest should not be limited to, or excluded in relation to, any particular category of claim".[128] The Commission recommends that, "section 35A [of the Supreme Court Act 1981] be amended to state that any interest awarded shall be compound unless there are good reasons to the contrary".[129] Moreover, the Commission recommends there should be a standard prescribed rate enacted under section 35A, and that "the section should provide that this rate shall be used unless there is good reason to the contrary".[130]

In arriving at its provisional conclusions, reform of the law of statutory interest was of paramount importance to the Law Commission.[131] The Commission's central criticism on the current state of the law is that it fails to reflects economic reality and underlying commercial expectations:[132]

---

[124] Ciro, *op cit* fn 34.

[125] The term is used by Goff J in *BP Exploration Co (Libya) Ltd v Hunt (No2)* [1979] 1 WLR 783, at 799 and 804.

[126] *Westdeutsche v Islington LBC* [1996] 2 All ER 961, 955 per Lord Goff.

[127] The Law Commission Consultation Paper Compound Interest, Consultation Paper No 167 (2002).

[128] *Ibid* at para 4.27.

[129] *Ibid* at para 4.36.

[130] *Ibid* at para 4.44.

[131] *Ibid* at Part II.

[132] *Ibid* at para 4.1.

> If a claimant should have had money earlier, and in fact had it later, he or she has either missed an opportunity to invest it, or had to borrow to cover, in either case at compound interest. It follows that simple interest can never be relied upon to produce a just indemnity for the claimant for the loss occasioned by the delay in payment.[133]

Moreover, the Commission justifies an award of compound interest on the basis that such an award would provide the economically correct scale of compensation.[134] The problem of under compensation is most serious with long-running disputes or disputes involving large sums of money.[135] This is because with the current award under statute limited to only simple interest for judgment debts, and under common law no award is made, the problem of under compensation remains highly relevant for long running disputes. The most notable recent examples of the problem involved the swaps litigation where average lengths of trial ran for a number of years and the disputes involved large sums.

The Law Commission's provisional conclusions are not only entirely consistent with commercial expectations and economic reality they are also supported by other law reform bodies. The Law Reform Body of British Columbia published a report[136] on the Court Order Interest Act SBC 1974 c 65 and recommended that interest should be compounded, and determined by reference to the prime-lending rate of the Canadian Imperial Bank of Commerce. Similar recommendations were made in other Canadian provinces.[137] The same conclusion was reached by the New Zealand Law Commission.[138] The NZ Law Commission recommended that there should be mandatory compound interest on all judgments for money claims, at rates fixed by reference to the yield on Government stocks.

Agreements to Negotiate

It is, however, worth noting somewhat briefly at this point that the trend towards converting expectations into obligations has not been monolithic. In particular, in the area of the enforceability of agreements to negotiate, where the parties defer agreement on certain matters and enter into a legally binding commitment to continue negotiations at some future time, the courts have largely resisted giving effect to such agreements, and the expectations to which they give rise. The traditional response of the law has been not to recognize such agreements, which are felt to be either inherently vague, in terms of the language used, or incomplete, in the sense of there being lack of agreement in respect of significant aspects of the

---

[133] *Ibid.*

[134] *Ibid* at para 4.18.

[135] *Ibid* at para 4.19.

[136] Law Reform Commission of British Columbia, *Report on Court Order Interest Act*, (1987) LRC 90.

[137] Law Reform Commissions of Manitoba: *Report on Pre-judgment Compensation on Money Awards* (1982) and Ontario: *Report on Compensation for Personal Injuries and Death* (1987).

[138] NZ Law Commission Report: *Aspects of Damages: The Award of Interest on Money Claims*, Report No 28.

transaction.[139] In particular cases, there might be elements of both uncertainty and incompleteness.[140]

The courts have largely given effect to the policy that they will not craft an agreement for the parties where they themselves have failed to do so. The English courts in particular have steadfastly refused to enforce agreements to negotiate. The traditional approach to the issue is reflected in the House of Lords decision in *Walford v Miles.*[141] The case involved negotiations for the sale of a photographic processing business, in which two buyers were interested. The plaintiff buyer alleged that the defendant seller undertook not to deal with any third party and furthermore, that there was an implied term that the defendant would continue to negotiate in good faith with the plaintiff. The defendant sold the business to a third party, whereupon the plaintiff claimed damages. On the issue of whether the alleged agreement constituted a lock-in, in other words an agreement in which one party was committed to negotiate with another, the House of Lords unanimously rejected the idea of enforcing such an agreement. An agreement to negotiate in good faith went far beyond a "best endeavours" clause, which the law is prepared to recognize, and required the court to apply a subjective test as to the intention of the party who resiled from the negotiations. The court could not police such an agreement. It could not make an assessment as to whether a party was justified in withdrawing from negotiations, judged subjectively. Indeed each party involved in negotiations must be able to use the threat of withdrawal as a bargaining lever. An agreement to negotiate in good faith was therefore inherently inconsistent with the adversarial position of the parties when involved in negotiations.[142] Provided no misrepresentations were made, each party was entitled to pursue their own self-interest in negotiations.[143]

The difficulty with such an approach is that it fails to accommodate the dynamic and complex nature of much of commercial contracting today. Empirical studies have shown that businesspeople in significant on-going commercial relationships place a high premium on flexibility and trust, frequently conclude their agreements informally, use language with little legal precision, leaving many matters to be decided as and when circumstances arise and with reference to trade custom and norms.[144] The courts are then faced with the dilemma of whether to uphold the reasonable expectations of parties who believed they had a binding contract, but who have not met the formal legal requirements of contract formation.

As Carter and Harland point out, there has been a tendency in recent years for the courts in this country to be more astute than previously in finding ways in

---

[139] Seddon and Ellinghaus, *Cheshire and Fifoot's Law of Contract,* 7th ed (1997) at p 222.

[140] Carter & Harland, *Cases and Materials on Contract Law in Australia,* 3rd ed (1998) at p 82.

[141] [1992] 2 AC 128.

[142] *Ibid* at p 138.

[143] *Ibid.*

[144] Macaulay, *op cit* fn 18 at p 55; Beale and Dugdale, "Contracts between Businessmen: Planning and the Use of Contractual Remedies" (1975) 2 *British Journal of Law and Society* 45.

which to uphold seemingly uncertain or incomplete agreements, especially commercial arrangements.[145] Unlike their English counterparts, Australian courts are beginning to follow the lead shown by courts in the United States in this respect, although the approach is still one of caution. The underlying policy considerations were articulated by Kirby P in *Coal Cliff Collieries Pty Ltd v Sijehama Pty Ltd,*[146] which involved the execution of a "heads of agreement" document which allegedly imposed an obligation on the parties to negotiate a joint venture agreement in good faith. After noting how disproportionately significant failure of negotiation cases have been in the US in comparison with England or Australia, and how the US courts have been prepared to employ estoppel and restitution principles "to supplement the sometimes meagre assistance available from the law of contract",[147] the judge commented as follows:

> Behind the decisions and articles lie the general issues of legal policy which a case such as this presents. Should the law wash its hands of "agreements" where the parties have failed to specify essential terms? By doing so, does the law withhold support for the legitimate expectations of the parties, in certain circumstances, that obligations will be enforced? Where the parties have failed to spell out essential terms of their agreement are the courts well equipped to fill in the blanks with what they determine to be reasonable on their interpretation of the evidence? Do the obligations which courts quite regularly assume to predict future events extend to predicting the course of negotiation between business people legitimately motivated by the pursuit of their own interests and profit?[148]

Although on the facts of the case Kirby P (with whom Waddell A-JA concurred) was unable to find a legally enforceable contract, His Honour made it clear that he did not share the view of the English Court of Appeal that no promise to negotiate in good faith would ever be enforced by a court: "I reject the notion that such a contract is unknown to the law, whatever its term. I agree with Lord Wright's speech in *Hillas* that, provided there was consideration for the promise, in some circumstance a promise to negotiate in good faith will be enforceable, depending upon its precise terms . . . "[149] On the other hand, Handley JA, who agreed that the promise in the instant case was uncertain and therefore binding in honour only, felt that the question should be decided on the basis of well established English and Australian authority and that it was unnecessary to consider the US material and academic writing on the subject.[150]

In the decision of the Federal Court in *Ravinder Rohini Pty Ltd and amor v Krizaic,*[151] the issue was whether the parties had formed the intention of making a concluded bargain, despite many unresolved matters including the appropriate

[145] Carter and Harland, *op cit* fn 140 at p 82.
[146] (1991) 24 NSWLR 1.
[147] *Ibid* at p 23.
[148] *Ibid.*
[149] *Ibid* at p 26.
[150] *Ibid* at p 43.
[151] (1991) 105 ALR 593.

legal vehicle for the venture, or whether the agreement was simply "an agreement to agree". The case involved discussions between K and S about the redevelopment of a hotel site owned by Ravinder Rohini, a company controlled by S. K and S made arrangements whereby each was to contribute to the redevelopment in different ways. K and S each took some action pursuant to those arrangements and approval for the redevelopment was obtained. S then decided not to proceed and Ravinder Rohini sold the hotel site. According to Wilcox and Miles JJ, although a future partnership was contemplated if the project proved viable, the parties had not actually entered into a currently operative partnership to develop the hotel site. Nevertheless a contract had been created with respect to its redevelopment. The parties had agreed not only to collaborate in the redevelopment but also to share the profits of such redevelopment. The agreement was breached by S when he withdrew from the agreement and arranged to sell the site. Wilcox J argued that there was no conceptual difficulty about a contract in the form thus described. He continued:

> It is true that such a contract would leave unresolved many of the detailed matters which would inevitably arise in connection with a project of this nature and size. Moreover, there could be no guarantee that the project would proceed at all; NCDC approval might be denied, the project might prove infeasible or otherwise be frustrated. If so, it would be no breach of contract for a party to refuse to proceed further. But I do not think that these considerations mean that the agreement between Mr Sharma and Mr Krizaic was no more than "an agreement to agree". This is not a case like *Courtney & Fairbairn Ltd v Tolaini Brothers (Hotels) Ltd* [1975] 1 WLR 297 . . . where there was an agreement by a building owner to employ a builder at a price to be negotiated. This is a case where the steps to be taken by each party, antecedent to the establishment of the partnership, were agreed between them.[152]

Furthermore, according to Davies and Wilcox JJ (Miles J dissenting), the circumstances were also such as to give rise to a fiduciary relationship between K and S. S was in breach of his fiduciary duty to K by appropriating to Ravinder Rohini the benefit of the increase in value of the hotel site flowing from the development approval. Since Ravinder Rohini took that benefit with knowledge of the breach of duty, it was accordingly accountable to S for the benefit.

As noted earlier, in *Coal Cliff Collieries,* the court was unable to find a legally enforceable contract on the facts. Consequently the observations made by Kirby P in that case, *obiter dicta,* represent a small, but nevertheless significant, break through in judicial thinking on the subject of agreements to agree. The outcome in *Ravinder Rohini* on the other hand highlights the somewhat extraordinary lengths to which the court was prepared to go in upholding the reasonable expectations of the innocent party, where previously contract law provided no relief.

The Federal Court of Australia in *Ravinder Rohini* demonstrated the court's innovation in essentially enforcing an agreement to negotiate by stealth. The court was not prepared to find that an agreement to negotiate existed on the facts. This had more to do with the issue of precedential compliance with the earlier House of

---

[152] *Ibid* at p 603.

Lords decision in *Walford v Miles* and the NSW Court of Appeal's decision in *Coal Cliff Collieries* where both courts refused to enforce agreements to agree on the facts of their respective cases. In *Ravinder Rohini*, the court was not willing to disturb the previous two decisions, but nevertheless was prepared to find a binding legal contract or as an alternative, to rely on trust principles to enforce the expectations of the innocent party. Hence, the court in *Ravinder* upheld an agreement to agree in substance, if not in form.

Conclusion

This chapter has argued that the manifestation of commercial expectations has been at the forefront of recent developments in the law of privity and compound interest. There has been an increasing willingness by the courts and Parliament to accommodate commercial expectations, and to overcome the rigidity and inefficiency posed by archaic law. The commercial emphasis of litigation, the large sums involved and the sophisticated nature of business transactions and litigants necessarily entail the consideration of commercial expectations.

The breakdown of the parties' relationship because commercial expectations remain unfilled provides the context for judicial and legislative intervention. Unfulfilled expectations are costly, not only to the individuals concerned but society as a whole. The driver of many of the common law and statutory initiatives that have emerged in recent decades has not simply been policies underpinned by consumer-welfarism. These interventions are driven too by the imperatives of commercial reality and may be seen as examples of a larger agenda involving the court's desire to enforce commercial expectations through active judicial intervention.

Chapter 7

E-Commerce: Recognizing the Context

Elizabeth Macdonald and David Poyton

Introduction

E-commerce and, in particular, contracting by e-mail or via a website, which will be referred to here as "electronic contracting", has become a commonplace phenomenon and it is easy for familiarity to diminish the perception of the distinctive features of anything we are dealing with. It is the purpose of this chapter to argue for appropriate recognition of the e-commerce context from three perspectives: when considering the applicability of traditional rules, when drafting legislation which will impact upon the e-commerce area, and even, when considering a generally applicable rule, the impact which the e-commerce context may have on it. Each of these perspectives will be considered in turn.

E-Commerce Context and History

Signature

The first situation to be considered when looking at the application of an historically adopted rule and the recognition of the significance of the e-commerce context is that in relation to rules dealing with the incorporation of terms by signature. In English Law if a contractual document[1] is signed then, in the absence of fraud, misrepresentation, or a plea of *non est factum*, the signatory will be bound by its terms and it is irrelevant whether that party has read them or has any knowledge of them.[2] This plainly makes a signature of great significance and it creates a great deal of certainty. Without the other party's signature, a party with standard terms, for example, will have to rely upon supplying "reasonably sufficient notice" of those standard terms to incorporate them.[3] So, the question will arise as to what is to be regarded as sufficient to have this significant effect of a "signature" in the electronic context. In particular, the question to be addressed

---

1 *Grogan v Meredith Plant Hire* (1996) 15 Tr LR 371.

2 *L'Estrange v F Graucob Ltd* [1934] KB 394, *Parker v South Eastern Ry Co* (1877) CPD 416, 421.

3 *Parker v South Eastern Ry Co* (1877) CPD 416.

here is whether "clicking on a website button" should be regarded as a signature for this purpose.

The initial point should be made that there are a whole variety of electronic "actions" which could be described as signature. This is illustrated by the broad approach taken by the Law Commission to what they considered could satisfy statutory requirements for signature. In that context, the Law Commission take the view that: "Digital signatures, scanned manuscript signatures, typing ones name (or initials) and clicking on a website button are, in our view all methods of signature which are generally capable of satisfying a statutory signature requirement".[4]

The production of most of these types of "signature" is self evident but some brief explanation of "digital signature" can be given. A "digital signature", unlike a scanned manuscript signature or even a typed version of a person's name, will not look like anything normally conceived of as a signature, rather it is generated cryptographically. Perhaps the best known is that using two "keys":

> One way of providing electronic signatures is to make use of what is known as *public key*, or *asymmetric, cryptography*. Public key cryptography uses two keys, also known as a *key pair*. (These keys are both large numbers with special mathematical properties.) When this technique is used for signatures, the *private key* (which as the term suggests is known only to its owner) is used to transform a data file, by scrambling the information contained in it. The transformed data is the electronic signature and can be checked against the original file using the *public key* of the person who signed it. Anyone with access to the public key (which might, for example, be available on a website) can check the signature, so verifying that it could only have been used by someone with access to the private key. If the only one with access to the *private key* is its owner, then the owner must have signed the message . . . If a third party had altered the message, the fact they had done so would be easily detectable.[5]

However, it is not such "digital signatures" which are the concern here. What will be questioned here is whether "clicking on a web-site button", should be regarded as sufficient to have the effect that, in the absence of fraud, misrepresentation, or a plea of *non est factum*, the "clicking party" will be bound by the standard terms on the website, with it being irrelevant whether that party has read them or has any knowledge of them or has even been given "reasonably sufficient notice" of them.

What must first be considered are the reasons behind the Law Commission's approach in the formality context and their relevance here. In considering what could amount to signature in relation to formality requirements, the Law Commission approached its consideration of the electronic context, by looking at the functional approach taken by UNCITRAL in formulating its Model Law. On that basis if an action in the electronic context, could be seen as sufficiently fulfilling the functions of the formality requirement in the paper-based context, then it would be seen as equivalent to any such requirement. They took the view

---

4 *Electronic Commerce: Formal Requirements in Commercial Transactions* Advice from the Law Commission (Dec 2001), para 3.39.

5 *Building Confidence in Electronic Commerce – A Consultation Document.*

that: "The principal function of a signature is to demonstrate that the signatory had an authenticating intention. What is required therefore is something which is not purely oral and which evidences that authenticating intention".[6]

They applied this in the "click-button" context, concluding:

> We do not believe that there is any doubt that clicking on a website button to confirm an order demonstrates the intent to enter into that contract. That will satisfy the principal function of a signature: namely demonstrating an authenticating intention. We suggest that the click can reasonably be regarded as the technological equivalent of a manuscript "X" signature. In our view, clicking is therefore capable of satisfying a statutory signature requirement (in those rare cases in which such a requirement is imposed in the contract formation context).[7]

Although the Law Commission's focus was formalities, this reasoning would seem equally to provide an argument here. However, accepting the analogy with the "manuscript 'X' signature" and, more broadly, accepting the "click-button" as a signature to incorporate terms should be questioned.

The first point to be made is as to the alerting function of a signature. An analogy can be made with formality requirements in that they can, *inter alia,* be used to encourage full consideration of the legal obligations being undertaken.[8] The Law Commission acknowledged this in relation to contracts of guarantee.[9] They noted that the "long-standing" requirements of writing and signature "have the effect of bringing home to the guarantor the seriousness of the commitment they are entering into".[10] Further, they took the line that there "may be a risk that if a guarantee is entered into through web-site trading, or by e-mail, the seriousness would not be as apparent to the guarantor, and they might not therefore be protected from hasty or ill considered conduct". They therefore suggest that some further form requirement might be seen as required for contracts of guarantee in the electronic context, such as requiring not merely a "signature", but a "digital signature", taking the line that "digital signatures are likely to become associated in the public mind with undertaking of significant or important transactions".[11]

However, it can be suggested that signature itself, in its everyday sense of a manuscript signature, has an alerting function in the type of context in which the "click-button" approach is likely to most significantly impact: the consumer context. When consumers are asked to put pen to paper to sign their names, they are alerted that what they are undertaking has some legal significance. Indeed it is a commonplace, albeit one seldom acted upon, that "you should read a contract before signing it". Businesses may be used to the typed name, or rubber stamp,

---

6 *Ibid* at para 3.28.

7 *Ibid* at para 3.37.

8 For example, Fuller (1941) 41 *Col LR* 799, Law Com Rep No 164 (1987).

9 *Electronic Commerce: Formal Requirements in Commercial Transactions* Advice from the Law Commission (Dec 2001), para 3.46.

10 *Ibid.*

11 *Ibid.*

taking legal effect as a signature,[12] but it is suggested that the consumer is not, that consumers would not regard the "click-button" as a signature, and the need to perform such an action is unlikely to alert them as to the significance of the obligations undertaken. Further, it is suggested that it will be most commonly consumers who will be found to be contracting through such a device. Certainly contracts between businesses would seem more likely to be made using a less "mechanised" procedure. It is suggested that the "click-button" signature does not have the type of alerting function identified here. Furthermore, a box at the end of the contract, or other document, in which the relevant person is asked to insert their name would not seem to create any great barrier to electronic transactions, and it is at least closer to the consumer's ordinary idea of a signature.

The second point to be made here relates to the evolution of the rules dealing with signature in making a contract. As has been indicated, a signature has a very significant impact in this context. If a contractual document[13] is signed then, in the absence of fraud, misrepresentation, or a plea of *non est factum*, the signatory will be bound by its terms and it is irrelevant whether that party has read them or has any knowledge of them.[14] Plainly, even when it is emphasized that the terms of the contract are determined objectively, this approach to signature can be seen as a very artificial means of determining contractual agreement. That artificiality has been acknowledged,[15] and elsewhere has been reduced.[16] In England and Wales, there have been attempts to introduce the "red hand rule" into the context of incorporation of terms by signature from that of incorporation from unsigned documents. As has been indicated, in the latter context incorporation occurs through the provision of reasonably sufficient notice of the terms. However, where unreasonable or unusual terms are included, the "red hand rule"[17] requires additional efforts to be made to draw attention to them, if there is to be reasonably sufficient notice to incorporate them.[18] In recent years the argument has been made

---

12 See for example *Goodman v J Eban Ltd* [1954] 1 QB 550.

13 *Grogan v Meredith Plant Hire* (1996) 15 Tr LR 371.

14 *L'Estrange v F Graucob Ltd* [1934] KB 394, Parker *v South Eastern Ry Co* (1877) CPD 416, 421.

15 *McCutcheon v David McBrayne* [1964] 1 WLR 125, 133; *Jones v Northampton BC* (1990) *The Times* 21 May; *Levison v Patent Seam Cleaning Co* [1978] QB 69, 78; *Bridge v Campbell Discount* [1962] 1 All ER 385, 399.

16 In the Canadian case of *Tilden Rent-A-Car v Clendenning* (1978) 83 DLR (3d) 400 unusual and onerous printed clauses were not incorporated. The line was taken that signature could only be relied upon as showing assent to a document when it was reasonable for the person relying on the signed document to believe that the signatory assented to its contents.

17 The nomenclature stems from a *dictum* of Denning LJ in *J Spurling v Bradshaw Ltd* [1956] 1 WLR 461, 466 – "the more unreasonable a clause is, the greater the notice which must be given of it. Some clauses which I have seen would need to be printed in red ink on the face of the document with a red hand pointing to [them] before the notice could be held to be sufficient".

18 *Thornton v Shoe Lane Parking* [1971] 2 QB 163; *Interfoto v Stilleto Visual Programmes Ltd* [1988] 1 All ER 348.

that such a requirement should also apply to unreasonable or unusual terms in the context of incorporation by signature.[19] At present it is not prevailing, probably because of the statutory means which have been provided for the policing of exemption clauses in the Unfair Contract Terms Act 1977 and of unfair terms more generally, in the consumer context, under the Unfair Terms in Consumer Context Regulations 1999. Nevertheless, the possibility has been raised of extending the red hand rule into the context of incorporation by signature. Encompassing the "click-button" action within the meaning of signature in this context might tip the balance in favour of extending the rule and reducing the efficacy of signature. That would have an unfortunate effect on certainty. Atiyah has made the point that: "A signature is, and is widely recognised by the general public as, a formal device, and its value would be greatly reduced if it could not be treated as a conclusive ground of contractual liability at least in all ordinary circumstances".[20] If it is thought inappropriate to treat the action of "clicking the button" as a signature to incorporate terms, then a distinction could be made on the basis that the action does not produce anything visible to constitute a "signature".[21] Further, the "manuscript 'X' signature" analogy can be challenged. The point can be made that the law does evolve to meet changing circumstances. It may expand definitions to take account of technological or other developments, but equally it can dispense with a rule which is seen as a product of circumstances which no longer appertain. In *Mannai Investment v Eagle Star*[22] the House of Lords applied "commercial construction" to decide the effectiveness of a notice purporting to exercise the tenant's contractual right to determine a lease, but which gave the wrong date. They dismissed the historically applied approach that precluded evidence of background to determine the meaning of the notice. Against the background of the lease, the meaning of the notice was clear to the reasonable landlord and effective. The previous rule, which had applied "for at least 200 years" was "highly artificial and capable of producing results which offend[ed] against common sense".[23] It has been seen as explicable against the background of circumstances which were no longer relevant by the time the House of Lords had to decide *Mannai*. The point has been made that the line previously taken was laid down:

> in the 18th and 19th centuries in conditions of trial very different from those which now exist
> (a) The taking of evidence before a jury was separated from legal argument before the court in banc.

---

19 *Ocean Chemical Transport Inc v Exnor Craggs Ltd* [2000] 1 All ER 519; *Mongomerey Litho Ltd v Maxwell* 2000 SC 56; *Yoldings v Swann* 12 Oct 2000; *Jonathan Wren & Co Ltd v Microdec plc* 65 Con LR 157; *Bankway Properties v Penfold-Dunsford* [2001] 1 WLR 1369, [15]; *HIH Casualty and General Ins v New Hampshire Co* [2001] 1 Lloyd's Rep 161, [209].

20 "Form and Substance in Contract Law" in *Essays in Contract* (1986) at p 109.

21 A point which is recognised by the Law Commission, para 3.38.

22 [1997] 3 All ER 352.

23 Lord Hoffmann at p 378.

(b) The strict rules of pleading tended to produce narrow issues of fact.
General demurrers were deployed to raise issues of law without resort to any evidence.
(c) The restrictions imposed by the rules regarding admissibility and the competency of witnesses.
(d) The primitive means of taking and recording evidence.[24]

Similarly here, a device developed to deal with historical levels of illiteracy, need not be influential in determining the meaning given to signature in a very different social and technological context. Changing circumstances and the lack of visible manifestation provide a basis for not making the "X" analogy and not allowing a "click-button action" to be seen as a signature to incorporate terms (or indeed in relation to formalities[25]).

The Postal Rule

The second area to be considered in this section, addressing the recognition of the significance of the e-commerce context in relation to an historically adopted rule, is probably one of the most often considered questions in relation to electronic contracting. It is the question of which rule should be applied to determine when an acceptance will be effective.[26] The normal rule is that an acceptance is effective upon receipt,[27] but there is a significant exception where an acceptance is posted.

---

[24] Baker, "Reconstructing the Rules of Construction" (1998) 114 *LQR* 55 at pp 59-60.

[25] The argument about the lack of alerting function in the "click button" action is as applicable in the formality context as in that addressed here. In addition, whilst the second argument about undermining certainty specifically addresses the evolutionary pressures on the rule about incorporation of terms by signature, if there is sufficient reason not to regard the "click button" as a signature in that context, the impetus to uniformity would tend to its non-acceptance in the formality context.

[26] For example, Gardener, "The Postal Rule in Contract Law and the Electronic Marvels" (1994) 2 *CCL* 49; Davies, "The Internet and the Elephant" (1996) *International Business Lawyer* 151; Fasciano, "Internet Electronic Mail: A Last Bastion for the Mailbox Rule" (1997) 25 *Hofstra* LR 971; Hill, "Flogging a Dead Horse - The Postal Acceptance Rule and E-mail" (2001) 17 *JCL* 151; Gardener, "Trashing with Trollope: A Deconstruction of the Postal Rules in Contract" (1992) 12 *Ox Jo LS* 170; Murray, "Entering into Contracts Electronically: the Real W.W.W" in Edwards & C Waelde (Eds), *Law and the Internet: A Framework for Electronic Commerce* (2000); Davies, "Contract Formation on the Internet: Shattering a Few Myths" in Edwards & Waelde (Eds), *Law and the Internet: regulating cyberspace* (1997).

[27] For example *McIver v Richardson* (1813) 1 M&S 557; *Mozley v Tinkler* (1835) 1 CM&R 692; *Carlill v Carbolic Smokeball Co* [1893] 1 QB 256, 262, 269; *Household Fire and Carriage Accident Ins Co Ltd v Grant* (1874) 4 Ex D 216 at 221; *Entores v Miles Far East Corp* [1955] 2 QB 327, 336. The reference to "receipt", rather than communication as such, is merely a recognition that what is in question is an objective approach and written communications are not always read at the time when they arrive (or even at all). So for example, it has been said that a telexed acceptance is effective when it arrives on the offeror's machine during office hours, without any need for it to be read by the offeror – *Brinkibon Ltd v Stahag Stahl unde Stahlwarenhandelgesellscaft mbH* [1982] 1 All ER 293.

A posted acceptance is effective on posting.[28] This latter, "postal" rule, was extended to telegrams,[29] but not to telexes[30] and, despite attempts to justify it, it has been seen as "in truth an arbitrary rule",[31] and a "rule of convenience, and a somewhat arbitrary one".[32] Yet, as has been indicated, there has been considerable discussion of, and even support for, the idea that it be extended into the electronic context. Here it is being contended that any such extension is inappropriate. The distinction which has grown from the case law on whether or not the rule should be used in the context of telexes will be considered and the contention will be made that the modern electronic context should be seen as providing an opportunity to break from prior analysis and adopt a more appropriate approach.

Instantaneous communication

When what is at issue is whether the postal rule should be applied in a new context, the cases on whether or not it applied to telexes[33] are seen as giving rise to a distinction based on whether or not the method of communication is seen as "instantaneous", with the postal rule being inapplicable where the method is seen as "instantaneous." This has, for example, led to the contention by Murray that the rule be reformulated to take account of new technologies as: "where an offer contemplates acceptance by non-immediate forms of communication, that acceptance is effective from the time it leaves the acceptor's control".[34]

Plainly, the postal rule puts the risk of the acceptance being delayed or lost on the offeror, and this formulation has the benefit of expressing a limit often stated to exist at common law, that the offer should contemplate acceptance by a form of communication to which the rule would apply.[35] However, the lynch pin of the reformulation is whether or not the method of communication is "non-immediate". The change of language, from "instantaneous", is an attempt to produce something less artificial. In treating a telex as "instantaneous" and so not subject to the postal rule, the artificiality of the classification was acknowledged by the Lord Fraser in *Brinkibon Ltd v Stahag Stahl unde Stahlwarenhandelgesellscaft mbH:*

> The question is whether acceptance by telex falls within the general rule that it requires to be notified to the offeror in order to be binding, or within the exception of the postal rule whereby it becomes binding when (and where) it is handed over to the Post Office.

---

[28] *Adams v Lindsell* (1818) 1 B& Ald 681, *Dunlop v Higgins* (1848) 1 HLC 381.
[29] *Stevenson, Jacques & Co v McClean* (1880) 5 QBD 346, *Cowan v O'Connor* (1888) 20 QBD 640,642.
[30] *Brinkibon Ltd v Stahag Stahl unde Stahlwarenhandelgesellscaft mbH* [1982] 1 All ER 293; *Entores v Miles Far East Corp* [1955] 2 QB 327.
[31] Treitel, *The Law of Contract* 11th ed (2003), 25.
[32] *The Law of Contract*, Furmston (Ed) 2nd ed (2003) 2.244.
[33] *Brinkibon Ltd v Stahag Stahl unde Stahlwarenhandelgesellscaft mbH* [1982] 1 All ER 293; *Entores v Miles Far East Corp* [1955] 2 QB 327. See below.
[34] Murray, "Entering into Contracts Electronically: the Real W.W.W" in Edwards & Waelde (Eds), *Law and the Internet: A Framework for Electronic Commerce* (2000) 26.
[35] See for example *Entores v Miles Far East Corp* [1955] 2 QB 327, Parker LJ, at p 336.

> The postal rule . . . has been extended to apply to telegrams sent through the Post Office, and in strict logic there is much to be said for applying it also to telex messages sent by one business firm directly to another. There is very little, if any, difference in the mechanics of transmission between a private telex from one business to another and a telegram sent through the Post Office, especially one sent from one large city to another. Even the element of delay will not be greatly different where the operator of the recipient's telex is a clerk with no authority to conclude contracts, who has to hand it to his principal. In such a case a telex message is not in fact received instantaneously by the responsible principal. I assume that the present case is a case of that sort.
>
> Nevertheless, I have reached the opinion that, on balance, an acceptance sent by telex directly from the acceptor's office should be treated as if it were an instantaneous communication between the principals, like a telephone conversation.[36]

This acknowledges the artificiality of the "instantaneous communication" distinction, but, nevertheless Lord Fraser was of the view that the telex "should be treated as if it were an instantaneous communication". The difficulty then lies in relying on a distinction which is not a reflection of reality and the change to "immediate" does not seem to help with this. The problem can be emphasized by considering contrasting approaches to whether e-mail communication should be regarded as "instantaneous". Thus Murray takes the view that "e-mail is not an instantaneous form of communication like the telephone, telex or fax" and so, in his view the postal rule should be applied.[37] However, Hill takes the line that:

> it is unlikely in an age when I can communicate a question to a colleague in London over late afternoon tea and have a response before I leave for the day, that e-mail will be deemed anything other than instantaneous. Delays on intra-country e-mail can be measured in seconds, not hours . . . Any delay in the electronic relaying of an e-mail message is now infinitesimal.[38]

Reference to whether the communication is such as to be "treated as instantaneous" or even "immediate", does not produce a helpful distinction. Its origins can be considered and it can be contended that it should be dispensed with.

As has been indicated, consideration of whether or not a communication is "instantaneous" when looking at the applicability of the postal rule stems from the judgments in *Entores Ltd v Miles Far Eastern Corp*[39] and those should now be considered. In *Entores*, Denning LJ considered different forms of communication – face to face, telephonic and telex – and situations in which the acceptance should, or should not, be effective. As has been indicated, the normal rule that communication of acceptance must be received, and the postal rule, both allocate the risk of the acceptance not being received or being delayed. The ordinary rule allocates that risk to the offeree. The postal rule allocates it to the offeror.

---

[36] [1982] 1 All ER 293.

[37] Murray, "Entering into Contracts Electronically: the Real W.W.W" in Edwards & Waelde (Eds), *Law and the Internet: A Framework for Electronic Commerce* (2000) 25.

[38] Hill, "Flogging a Dead Horse - The Postal Acceptance Rule and E-mail" (2001) 17 JCL 151, 158-159.

[39] [1955] 2 QB 326.

However, those rules deal with the non-fault situation. In his brief survey of the problem Denning LJ primarily dealt with situations in which one party should have known that a message had not arrived. Under those circumstances, the answer as to whether or not there has been an effective acceptance is self-evident – the risk should lie with the party who is, in some sense, at fault. What is really of concern is the situation in which the delay or non-arrival of the communication of acceptance has not been shown to involve the fault of either party. In effect, in that situation, Denning LJ simply stated that the ordinary rule should apply and not the postal rule. He concluded his examples of situations involving fault and then said:

> But if there should be a case where the offeror without any fault on his part does not receive the message of acceptance – yet the sender of it reasonably believes it has got home when it has not – then I think there is no contract. My conclusion is, that the rule about instantaneous communications between the parties is different from the rule about the post. The contract is only complete when the acceptance is received by the offeror.[40]

There is here a reference to "instantaneous communications", but his reasoning had not provided any basis for the distinction as the determinative basis of the application of the postal rule and he had himself earlier recognised its artificiality in referring to communications by telephone and telex as "virtually instantaneous",[41] but again as a label rather than to point out any justification for the difference in approach. Similarly, Birkett LJ provided no reasoning to justify his conclusion that the postal rule should not apply to telexes, beyond stating that telex communications "do not differ in principle from the cases where the parties negotiating a contract were actually in the presence of each other" and emphasising that he was applying the "ordinary rule" rather than an exception.[42] Parker LJ did attempt to explain the need to justify the postal rule and provide a distinction on that basis. He said:

> Since, however, the requirement as to actual notification of the acceptance is for the benefit of the offeror, he may waive it and agree to the substitution for that requirement of some other conduct by the acceptor. He . . . may do so impliedly by indicating a contemplated method of acceptance, for example, by post or telegram. In such a case he does not expressly dispense with actual notification, but he is held to have done so impliedly on grounds of expediency. Thus, in *Adams v Lindsell*, [(1818) 1 B&Ald 681, 683] the court pointed out that unless this were so no contract could ever be completed by the post. For if the defendants were not bound by their offer when accepted by the plaintiffs till the answer was received, then the plaintiffs ought not to be bound till after they had received the notification that the defendants had received their answer and assented to it and so it might go on ad infinitum . . . Where, however, the parties are in each other's presence or, though separated in space, communication between them is, in effect, instantaneous, there is no need for any such rule of convenience. To hold otherwise would leave no room for the operation of the general rule that notification of the acceptance must be received. An acceptor could say: "I spoke the words of

40 [1955] 2 QB 326, at pp 333-4.
41 At p 332.
42 At p 335.

> acceptance in your presence, albeit softly, and it matters not that you did not hear me"; or, "I telephoned to you and accepted and it matters not that the telephone went dead and you did not get my message". Though in both these cases the acceptor was using the contemplated or, indeed, the expressly indicated mode of communication, there is no room for any implication that the offeror waived actual notification of the acceptance.[43]

The chain of communication "*ad infinitum*" argument does not provide a basis for the postal rule – all the postal rule does is allocate risk at the point favouring the offeree. The "potential chain" could equally be broken at a point favouring the offeror. The "potential chain" argument cannot provide a meaningful basis for the postal rule, or for distinguishing it. Further, although there is much to be said for Parker LJ's wish to preserve the scope of the "general rule", the examples he provides involve fault and thus do not provide helpful guidance for the situation needing to be addressed – the acceptance which is lost or delayed without fault.

The judgements in *Entores* provide little reasoning to underpin the conclusion reached; that the postal rule should not extend to telexes. It is contended, however, that they reached the correct conclusion and that what they were in effect doing has much to commend it and is being advocated more broadly here. It should be emphasized that what is really at issue is where the risk of delay or loss of the acceptance should lie when there is no fault. It is helpful to put this question in a slightly expanded form, that is, the question is whether the offeror should be assigned the risk of being contractually bound without their knowledge, or a reasonable opportunity of becoming aware of it, or whether the offeree, should, without their knowledge, or a reasonable opportunity of becoming aware of it, find themselves not in a contractual relationship when they thought they were. It is contended that, once put in this expanded form, the answer to where the risk should lie is plain. It is, in general, better that someone be at risk of not being in a contract when they thought they were, than that someone should be at risk of being subject to obligations they are unaware of. That is the way in which the ordinary rule allocates the risk of acceptance being lost or delayed. It should not be departed from by use of the postal rule in any further situations than those to which that rule already applies. The most obvious characteristic of telex communication, as distinct from postal communication, is its speed. It is contended that that was simply being emphasized in *Entores* to provide an apparent justification for not following the postal rule. The court's reasoning does not provide any effective analysis of why it should make that distinction. Of course, the point can be made that the closer to instantaneous a form of communication is, there would seem to be less chance of it being lost or delayed without at least one party being aware of it, and thus at fault in not attempting to clarify the situation. Nevertheless, what is in question is the allocation of risk of loss or delay where there is no fault and that allocation must be made whatever the speed of the communication. It is contended that what was happening in *Entores* was that an historically adopted rule which is "arbitrary" and which, as a risk allocation rule, can be seen as misconceived, was not being extended. The court was seizing on the most obvious characteristic of

[43] At pp 336-337.

the, then, new technology not to extend it, but they were not providing a meaningful test for its future application. Rather they should be seen as indicating that it simply should not be extended to different forms of communication. The modern electronic context provides an opportunity to take what underlies *Entores* further, to declare the inappropriateness of the distinction between "instantaneous" and "non-instantaneous" methods of communication, and to deny the further extension of the application of the postal rule.

Drafting Legislation

In this section consideration will be given to the need to give sufficient recognition to the e-commerce context in new legislation which will impinge upon it. Some of the difficulties in doing so, in particular because of the shift in concepts which may be required, to take account of the new environment, will be examined. The specific piece of legislation which will be looked at is the Council Regulation (EC) No 44/2001 of 22 December 2000, on "jurisdiction and the recognition and enforcement of judgments in civil and commercial matters"[44] ("the Regulation") as it was introduced to update the 1968 convention on "jurisdiction and the enforcement of judgments in civil and commercial matters", (the "Brussels Convention"), in particular taking account of e-commerce. It was intended to introduce uniform modern standards for jurisdiction in civil and commercial matters "taking into account new forms of commerce which did not exist when the Brussels Convention was introduced".[45] There were clear references throughout the development of the Regulation to the concerns of companies engaging in electronic commerce and which were unsure of their position in jurisdictional disputes under the provisions of the Brussels Convention.[46] This was seen as a disincentive to the development of electronic commerce and it was hoped that clarification, in the form of the new Regulation, would remove uncertainty.[47] The key amendments to the Brussels Convention include:

- the introduction of a common concept of the domicile of legal persons;[48]
- the clarification of the special jurisdiction rules in contract law;
- new provisions to cover all consumer contracts.

Consideration will be given to these in turn, to highlight some of the difficulties which remain for the application of the provisions in the electronic context. The

[44] OJ L 12/1 (16.1.2001).

[45] See press release, "Commission adopts draft Regulation on Jurisdiction, Recognition and Enforcement of Judgements in Civil and Commercial Matters" 14 July 1999, IP/99/510 at p 2.

[46] *Ibid.*

[47] *Ibid.* See also the Opinion of the Economic and Social Committee on the "Proposal for a Council matters" OJ C 117/6, (26.4.2000), para 2.1.2.1.

[48] *Ibid.*

shift in concepts which may be seen as required in such legislation, in particular, is away from too great a reference to physical location.

Domicile of Legal Persons

The core principle of the Brussels Convention was that, as a general rule, action should be taken in the courts of the state within which the defendant was domiciled. This "home-state" principle applied to individuals and corporations or other associations. It was seen as providing for the efficient administration of justice and affording the defendant a fair and just opportunity to respond to the claim in a familiar legal environment. Obviously it made domicile a key concept. In determining domicile the court seized would apply the "internal law" of the relevant state. The Regulation retains this core "home state" principle but introduces a "common concept of domicile of legal persons" to harmonise the divergent approaches to the domicile of legal persons in the Member States. Article 60 defines the domicile of companies and other legal persons as "the place where they have their statutory seat, central administration, or principal place of business".[49] In the e-commerce context, use of "domicile" can be questioned as a criterion traditionally linked to a physical presence in a state. It could be argued that in an era in which technology has begun to remove the need for physical location or the creation of a physical presence in a state to be an effective commercial actor there, the emphasis on domicile can be seen as inappropriate. It should be asked whether the definition avoids this difficulty.

It may be significant that the criteria in the article are listed as alternatives, rather than a progressive list. It would appear that a corporation or other association may be treated as domiciled in the place where it has *any* of the listed criteria. Of course, with a traditional business the three elements described in the article will often be found in the same place, for example Harrods' Registered office (hence statutory seat) is the same address as its central administration and principal place of business. However, with the advent of the Internet it is quite possible that all three will be in different jurisdictions. For example, a company may be created and registered in a particular state because of a favourable regulatory or taxation environment. The parties controlling and managing the business, the directors, owners or parent company, may reside in a variety of other states exercising their control by communicating electronically. The company's business transactions may be entered into via websites stored on servers situated in a number of other states dictated by their Internet Service Provider or matters of convenience. The main business of the company may be conducted electronically with parties in one or a number of other states with no other connection with the company. In such a case the statutory seat of the company and the location of its central administration, if it can be established at all, bear no relationship to the business activities of the company. This may be completely fortuitous or it may be a deliberate attempt to evade the jurisdiction of the courts of a particular state

---

49 Article 60(1) (a, b & c).

whilst exploiting the market in the same way that a company registered and physically located there would. It might be contended, however, that the "principal place of business" criteria provides the court with an opportunity to consider the reality of the company's activities in relation to a particular state. It could be contended that if a company conducts all or the majority of its business with customers in the UK via an interactive website, its principal place of business is in the UK. However, with no guidance in the Regulation itself, older case law on what constitutes a "principal place of business" may be relied upon[50] and the older authorities define principal place of business as essentially linked to its central administration. A new approach to "principal place of business" will be required if it is to provide a suitable basis for jurisdiction in the e-commerce context.

The Special Jurisdiction Rules in Contract

Article 5 of the Brussels Convention contains a number of exceptions to the home-state principle where the subject matter of the dispute has a "close connection" with a state other than that in which the defendant is domiciled. The Regulation retains this provision and introduces specific amendments intended to clarify uncertainty relating to the special jurisdiction rules in contract law. The basic exception found in Article 5(1) of both instruments, states that a party domiciled in a contracting state may be sued in the courts of another contracting state "in matters relating to a contract, in the courts for the place of performance of the obligation in question".[51]

With an electronic contract the performance of the obligations may be seen as taking place in numerous jurisdictions. For example, a contract with an ISP for storage, e-mail and web-hosting may be provided in a number of jurisdictions depending on the technology in use. If the basis of the dispute is the obligation to provide these services, then the question of "place of performance" becomes somewhat problematic. If the physical "place of performance" can be ascertained, such as the relevant server, this may have little or no connection with the parties themselves or the contract.

The Regulation seeks to provide some assistance in relation to difficulties occasioned by the phrase "place of performance of the obligation in question" but nevertheless retains this terminology. Article 5(1) of the Regulation reads:

> A person domiciled in a Member State may, in another Member State, be sued:
> (a) in matters relating to a contract, in the courts for the place of performance of the obligation in question;
> (b) for the purpose of this provision and unless otherwise agreed, the place of performance of the obligation in question shall be:

[50] As occurred in *King v Crown Energy Trading AG* [2003] EWHC 163; [2003] ILPr 28; Times, 14 March 2003. Chambers J relying heavily on *Owners of Cargo Lately Laden on Board the Rewia v Caribbean Liners (Caribtainer) Ltd (The Rewia)* [1991] 2 Lloyd's Rep 325.

[51] Article 5(1).

in the case of the sale of goods, the place in a Member State where, under the contract, the goods were delivered or should have been delivered,
in the case of the provision of services, the place in a Member State where, under the contract, the services were provided or should have been provided,
(c) if subparagraph (b) does not apply then subparagraph (a) applies.

The addition of Article 5(1)(b) clarifies the place of performance in contracts for the sale of goods or provision of services. However, in the context of e-commerce, the additional provisions are not necessarily helpful. Certainly, contracts for intangible items or "data products" which form a large proportion of the growing electronic commerce market may well not be categorised as either involving a sale of goods or provision of services, and even if they are, problems remain in identifying the relevant locations. The Article does envisage the situation where contracts do not fall within these categories (paragraph 1(c)) but simply refers back to the "place of performance of the obligation in question" qualification without further direction.

With the stated objective of clarification it is unfortunate that the Commission adopted an approach which, in the context of electronic commerce, does very little to provide clear assistance in relation to electronic services such as web-hosting or in relation to the provision of the intangible items which form a common subject-matter of electronic contracts. The "place of performance of the obligation in question" remains an area of uncertainty.

Consumer Contracts

In contracts between consumers and businesses, "consumers" are usually the economically weaker parties. As such, within the UK and EU, the consumer is afforded greater protection in relation to substantive and procedural matters associated with contracts. In particular here, articles 13-15 of the Brussels Convention departed from the home-state principle, in specific circumstances, in favour of the consumer. They provided the consumer with the option of initiating proceedings in the courts of the State of his, or her, own domicile, or in the courts of the State in which the other party is domiciled. Conversely, the consumer could only be sued in the courts of the state of his, or her, domicile.[52] To benefit from this provision the relevant party had not only to fall within the definition of consumer but had also to have entered a contract falling within one of a number of listed categories. The definition of consumer employed is common to many European instruments[53] and was not the subject of review in the Regulation. What constitutes a "consumer contract" was however amended in the Regulations in the light of the e-commerce context. The original requirements and their amendment must be considered.

Under the Convention the contract had to be:

---

[52] Article 14 para 3. The provisions do not affect the right of either party to bring a counter-claim to the court in question.
[53] For example, the Unfair Terms in Consumer Contracts Directive.

- a contract for the sale of goods on instalment credit terms; or,
- a contract for a loan repayable by instalments, or for any other form of credit, made to finance the sale of goods; or
- any other contract for the supply of goods or a contract for the supply of services, and
  - (a) in the State of the consumer's domicile the conclusion of the contract was preceded by a specific invitation addressed to him or by advertising; and
  - (b) the consumer took in that State the steps necessary for the conclusion of the contract.[54]

To satisfy paragraphs 1 and 2 the contract had to relate to the sale of goods or supply of services. As has been indicated, in the e-commerce context, much of what may be supplied is not easily fitted into the traditional goods or services categorisation – computer software, music, video and other multimedia downloaded directly from the supplier's site to the customer's computer provide obvious examples. However, the third paragraph of Article 13 also raised other significant issues for the e-commerce context. The contract must have been "preceded by a specific invitation addressed to him or by advertising" in the State of the consumer's domicile. The "or by advertising" criteria, in particular, raised important issues as to how widely it should be construed in the e-commerce context. Did it for example, encompass any advertising website which was accessible from the consumer's domicile? Whilst the wording of the Article in itself was capable of encompassing a very broad range of activities, including such accessible website advertising, the predominant interpretation of the article required the supplier to have taken specific steps to market his product in the consumer's State, or in some way directed his advertising to that State.[55]

---

[54] Article 13 (1-3).

[55] Susman, "International Electronic Trading: Some Legal Issues" [2000] Feb/Mar *Computers and Law*. Susman argues that the trader must in some way solicit or target consumers in a particular state:

> ". . . the trader must have directed the advertising to that state: he is not subject to its jurisdiction merely because a publication in which he advertises finds its way into that state if he is not targeting consumers in that state; and the same is thought to apply in respect of an advertisement on a Web site accessible in a state which is not directed to consumers in that state." Available at: http://www.scl.org/Services/default.asp?p=156&c=-999&ctID=12&cID=1140000216&pm=1.

This approach is supported by the interpretation suggested in the background documentation to the Convention. In his Report on the Accession Convention, Professor Schlosser refers us to the report by Professors Giuliano and Lagarde, and their consideration of identical terminology found in the Rome Convention:

> "The first indent relates to situations where the trader has taken steps to market his goods or services in the country where the consumer resides. It is intended to cover *inter alia* mail order and door-step selling. Thus the trader must have done certain acts such as advertising in the press, or on radio or television, or in the cinema or by

Recognising some of the difficulties created for the electronic environment by the consumer provisions of the Brussels Convention, some amendments have been made in the relevant provisions which now form Articles 15 to 17 of the Regulation. The third possibility is no longer confined to the goods and services context. Further the phrase "preceded by a specific invitation . . . or by advertising" is replaced with a requirement that the supplier "pursues commercial or professional activities in the Member State of the consumer's domicile or, by any means, directs such activities to that Member State or to several States including that Member State".[56] However, whilst the new Article removes some of the uncertainty attributed to its predecessor, the terminology adopted raises its own questions, in particular, the issue arises as to what qualifies as "pursuing" commercial or professional activities or "directing" such activities to a Member State or group of States, particularly in the e-commerce context.[57] Again the question arises as to whether the mere accessibility of a trading web site is sufficient and in an earlier proposed version of the Regulations the Commission had, in fact, included clarification in a recital which stated:

> . . . Account must be taken of the growing development of the new communication technologies, particularly in relation to consumers; whereas in particular, electronic commerce in goods and services by a means accessible in another Member State constitutes an activity directed to that State. Where that State is the State of the consumer's domicile, the consumer must be able to enjoy the protection available to him when he enters into a consumer contract by electronic means from his domicile.[58]

This recital which the Commission had proposed to include in the Regulations would have made it plain that mere accessibility of a website was sufficient to constitute "an activity directed to that State". It did not, however, survive into the final version of the Regulations. The point was made that "the prospect of being brought before foreign courts could deter small and medium-sized enterprises from using the internet to promote their services".[59] What remains is uncertainty.

---

catalogues aimed specifically at that country, or he may have made business proposals individually, through a middle man or by canvassing."

The narrow approach would also seem to have been re-enforced by recent case law, for example, *Andrew Rayner v Richard Davies* [2002] EWCA Civ 1880; [2002] WL 31676420 (CA).

56 Article 15(1)(c).

57 St Oren, "Jurisdiction over Consumer Contracts in e-Europe" (2003) 52 *ICLQ* 665.

58 Amended proposal for a Council Regulation on jurisdiction and the recognition and enforcement of judgments in civil and commercial matters. COM (2000)689 final Ex - Recital 13. This recital did nevertheless retain a reference to "goods and services", potentially excluding intangible items which are arguably not "goods" or "services".

59 Opinion of the Economic and Social Committee on the "Proposal for a Council Regulation (EC) on Jurisdiction and enforcement of judgments in civil and commercial matters" at para 4.2.2.

The Electronic Context for Legislation

Drafting legislation for the e-commerce context may be made difficult by factors which impinge upon the drafting of any legislation. It may not be possible to clarify an ambiguity because doing so will require a movement in a contested direction. It may mean, for example, greater consumer protection, and a greater burden for business. The ambiguity may remain because the tensions cannot be resolved. However, the relative novelty of the electronic context provides an additional hurdle to clear drafting. It may require a reconsideration of the use of some concepts which we are long conditioned to use but the overuse of which can be inappropriate in the electronic environment, such as some links which are dependent upon physical location.[60]

Recognising the E-Commerce Context in More General Contexts

The final section here is concerned with the potential for the e-commerce context to influence the approach taken in the broader application of a more general measure. The Unfair Terms in Consumer Contracts Directive[61] will be specifically considered. However, the possibility has already been raised of the approach taken to signature in the e-commerce context impacting upon the certainty provided by the current rules as to incorporation of terms by signature generally, so as to influence the evolution of the general rule.[62]

The Unfair Terms in Consumer Contracts Directive is partly a consumer confidence measure, to promote cross border contracts through providing consumers with the assurance of policing of unfair terms throughout the Member States.[63] It is not specifically concerned with e-commerce but plainly, it is a general measure which should be directly relevant in the e-commerce and less plainly, it could be seen as indirectly so. In relation to the important "country of origin principle" approach to regulation under the e-commerce Directive[64] the point has been made that: "the country of origin principle is only possible because of the large degree of harmonization which has already taken place in fields such as consumer protection . . ."[65]

However, the extent of the helpfulness of the Unfair Terms Directive in the e-commerce context must be questioned in the light of the approach of the ECJ to the relationship between itself and national courts in relation to the Directive's operation. That relationship was considered in the recent case of *Freiburger*

---

[60] Obviously individuals will have a physical location even when contracting electronically.

[61] EC Directive 93/13.

[62] See text at fn 13 above.

[63] Recitals 6 and 7.

[64] EC Directive on Certain Legal Aspects of Electronic Commerce in the Internal Market (2000/31/EC). For implementation in the UK see The Electronic Communications (EC Directive) Regulations 2002 and the Electronic Communications Act 2000.

[65] Reed and Slatter, "E-Commerce" in Reed and Angel, *Computer Law* (2003).

Kommunalbauten GMBH Baugesellschaft & Co KG v Hofstetter[66] and that must be considered here.

Freiburger was concerned with a reference by the German Budesgerichtshof (Federal Supreme Court) to the ECJ under Article 234 on the application of the Unfair Terms in Consumer Contracts Directive. The question was:

> Is a term, contained in a seller's standard business conditions, which provides that the purchaser of a building which is to be constructed is to pay the total price for the building, irrespective of whether there has been any progress in the construction, provided that the seller has previously provided him with a guarantee from a credit institution securing any monetary claims the purchaser may have in respect of defective performance or non-performance of the contract, to be regarded as unfair within the meaning of Art 3(1) of the Council Directive 93/13 of April 5, 1993 on Unfair Terms in consumer Contracts?

The "building" in question in *Freiburger* was a parking space in a multi-storey car park that Freiburger contracted to sell to Mr and Mrs Hofstetter before the car park was built. The contract provided for payment of the contract price by the Hofstetters as soon as Freiburger provided a guarantee in relation to defective or non-performance. In the event of late payment the purchasers were liable to pay default interest. The guarantee was delivered on 20 May. The Hofstetters did not pay the contract price until 21 December, after they had accepted the parking place, free of defects. The ECJ declined to provide an answer as to the fairness of the particular term, ruling that it was for the national court to decide that issue. The view was taken that the role of the ECJ is to "interpret general criteria used by the community legislature in order to define the concept of unfair terms" but that it "should not rule on the application of these general criteria to the specific term".[67] Nevertheless, in a previous decision, a particular term had been ruled unfair by the ECJ. In *Oceano Grupo Editorial SA v Murciano Qunitero*[68] the term in question had conferred jurisdiction in respect of all disputes arising under the contract on the court in the territorial jurisdiction of which the seller had his principal place of business. The court in *Freiburger* took the view that the ECJ's assessment in that case:

> . . . was reached in relation to a term which was solely to the benefit of the seller and contained no benefit in return for the consumer. Whatever the nature of the contract, it thereby undermined the effectiveness of the legal protection of the rights which the Directive affords to the consumer. It was thus possible to hold that the term was unfair without having to consider all the circumstances in which the contract was concluded and without having to assess the advantages and disadvantages that that term would have under the national law applicable to the contract.

---

66 Case C-237/02.

67 At p 22.

68 C 240-244/98) [2000] ECR I-4941.

It would seem that there will be terms which will be seen as unfair under any possible appropriate application of the fairness test and on those the ECJ will rule. Otherwise they will merely interpret the general criteria used to state the fairness test in the Directive.

There may be much to be said for the approach of the ECJ when, as in *Freiburger*, the case is one which basically arises within the boundaries of a particular Member State. A contract terms is unfair under the Directive if "contrary to the requirement of good faith, it causes a significant imbalance in the parties' rights and obligations arising under the contract, to the detriment of the consumer"[69] and the point has been made that:

> an interpretation of good faith which is oriented to the peculiarities, opportunities, risks and dangers of a specific production regime would indeed result in widely divergent rules in different countries, even in contradictory decisions in apparently equal cases. These cleavages cannot and should not be papered over by European zeal for harmonization . . . European efforts at harmonization have not yet seriously taken into account the 'varieties of capitalism', the difference in production regimes.[70]

Against this background the approach of the ECJ is one which allows the fairness test under the Unfair Terms Directive to encompass relevant diversity.

Nevertheless, the approach of the ECJ obviously allows for the same facts to give rise to different conclusions as to fairness in different Member States. Plainly, more uniformity would be more directly, and indirectly, helpful in the e-commerce context. At the moment, although e-commerce may have increased the number of consumer transactions that cross boundaries between Member States, undoubtedly such transactions are still only a small proportion of the transactions to which the Directive is relevant. There may, however, come a point when the e-commerce context is a more significant part of the general context of the application of such a general measure, when that occurs, the type of approach taken in *Freiburger* may come into question, with greater pressure to give more significance to the e-commerce context.

Conclusion

Appropriate recognition of the e-commerce context provides a broad range of legal challenges and opportunities. Some of them have been identified here. It may provide sufficient perspective to allow for the curtailment, or even disposal, of historically adopted rules which have had (or largely had) their day. It may provide legislative drafting challenges of the kind provided by legislation generally, but it also conjures up unique ones, in terms of the development of concepts suitable to the distinctive environment. More broadly, it may also

---

69 Art 3(1).

70 Teubner, "Legal Irritants: Good Faith in British Law or How Unifying Law Ends Up in New Divergences" (1998) 61 *MLR* 11 at p 31.

provide challenges for the general law, producing a new set of evolutionary pressures on laws which impact on the general as well as the electronic environment.

PART III
INTERNATIONAL REGULATION

Chapter 8

The Evaluation of International Money Laundering Regulation

Anu Arora

Within a decade, a global legislative and regulatory framework has been established to fight one of the most serious crimes of modern times: money laundering. A multitude of "hard" and "soft" laws have introduced measures, which have created new crimes; introduced new policing measures; and imposed responsibilities on private parties to assist the authorities to counter the threats of money laundering.

Money laundering requires the disguise of the criminal and illegal nature of that property. Simply hiding the unlawful funds without disguising their criminal origin is not money laundering, so that if criminal money, for example, is moved to a jurisdiction where the use of the money is not illegal, it is difficult to see that laundering has occurred. Instead what has happened is that the money has been hidden from the enforcement agencies of the country where the criminal offence took place.[1] Its criminal origin is still there and the money has not been cleansed or legitimized. It is only when the criminal origin of the money has been concealed, disguised or obscured and the appearance of legitimacy acquired in a place where sanctions against its criminal origins would be imposed that money laundering is deemed to have taken place. Thus, where funds acquired as a result of criminal activity are mixed with the proceeds of a legitimate business activity and the whole declared to be the profits of the business money laundering will have occurred.

The distinction between simply hiding unlawfully acquired wealth and laundering is recognized by the Vienna Convention 1988[2] which requires state parties to criminalize the conversion or transfer of property, knowing that such property is derived from drug-related offences for the purpose of "concealing or disguising the illicit origin" of the property. Article 3(1)(b)(ii) also requires the criminalization of "the concealment or disguise of the true nature, source, location, disposition, movement of rights or with respect to, or ownership of property knowing that such property is derived from drug-related offences". The concealment or disguise of the criminal origin of property, therefore, is the essence

---

[1] UN Office for Drug Control and Crime Prevention, *Financial Haven, Banking Secrecy and Money Laundering* (1988) UN Sales No E 99 IV2, at 1-4.

[2] Article 3(1)(b)(i).

of money laundering. Although the focus of the Vienna Convention was to criminalize the laundering of the proceeds of drug related crime both governments and law enforcement agencies have recognized the need to fight all forms of money laundering, particularly proceeds of organized. The Second EU Directive on Money Laundering and the Proceeds of Crime Act 2002 criminalize money laundering on an "all crime basis".

The Challenges Posed by Money Laundering

Criminal activity, particularly organized crime, produces significant rewards and the traditional deterrents including imprisonment are not necessarily a sufficient deterrent. The proceeds of organized crime, if laundered successfully, will not be recognized as the fruits of criminal activity and will therefore not be confiscated. The profits associated with criminal activity may therefore more than warrant the risk of criminal activity and the dangers associated with the laundering process. However, one must not overlook the involvement of the idealist or fantasist who may have a total disregard to the profit but whose objective is to cause human distress and/or headline news for his cause. Although, financial gain may therefore not be a priority such groups will require funds to advance their causes. The proceeds of money laundering are a huge incentive to those willing to take the risks of involvement with criminal activity. Apart from the damage money laundering causes to the economy, the financial institutions, and society, wealth unlawfully accumulated but successfully laundered allows organized crime to acquire a foothold, and sometimes undermine, legitimate business activity.

Organized crime will not only become involved in legitimate business activity but is likely to seek to dominate the market, engage in predatory pricing, extortion, and corrupt employees and officials.[3] Money Laundering is also likely to have other negative financial and economic impact. An efficient allocation of resources will only exist in the economy where there is a free play of market forces and risk adjustments made in the free economy as a result of supply and demand. The costs of money laundering, both economic and human, will distort that market, for example, the costs of drug trafficking are obvious. Money launderers are only concerned with cleansing the proceeds of criminal activity to ensure that the proceeds of crime appear to have a legitimate source. In a world of money laundering, therefore, genuine capital investment is therefore reduced.[4] The inflow of large amounts of funds from laundering could also significantly impact exchange rates and interest rates or create artificial demand and affect pricing in the area, for example, housing market and land. This type of situation could result in incorrect economic policies being implemented to the detriment of the economy.

[3] Sherman, "International Efforts to Combat Money Laundering: The Role of the Financial Action Task Force". Hume Papers on Public Policy, Vol 1, No 2 on *Money Laundering*, McQueen (Ed).

[4] Tanzi, "Money Laundering and the International Financial System" 6-7, IMF Working Paper, Fiscal Affairs Department, WP/96/55 (1966).

It should be noted that transfers of funds for laundering purposes tend to be temporary and financial institutions involved in these transfers are likely to develop unstable asset structures affecting the stability of the institution or even, more fundamentally, the monetary stability of the country. Such national financial problems can easily turn national problems into problems with an international dimension due to the global financial markets. Loss of confidence in the financial markets resulting from either knowingly or unwittingly becoming involved in laundering will have damaging effects on the institutions perceived to be associated with criminal activity. This may deter the public from undertaking perfectly legal transactions with the institutions concerned and create instability in the market.

Money laundering damages the social and economic basis of society. There is increasing motivation for individuals to be tempted by criminal activity and laundering, so the financing of crime takes on a more organized basis, and damage will inevitably result to the integrity and stability of the financial and economic fabric of society. A number of high profile cases over a number of years have emphasized the extent of laundering in the UK for example, BCCI; other London banks have been found to have laundered $1.3 billion on behalf of General Abacha of Nigeria; and the passing of tainted funds have resulted in the arrests of employees of the Bank of New York, in London.[5] The National Criminal Intelligence Service (NCIS) 2003 annual report[6] states that the "overall size of criminal proceeds in the UK is not known, nor is the amount that is laundered. However, HM Customs and Excise recently estimated that annual proceeds from crime in the UK at anywhere between £19 billion and £48 billion, with £25 billion possibly being a realistic figure for the amount actually laundered".

The Laundering Process

The laundering process can be epitomised as a three stage process: placement; layering; and integration.[7]

- The placement stage corresponds to the moment where the cash derived from criminal activity is first introduced into the financial system or is used

---

[5] *Butterworths International Guide to Money Laundering Law and Practice*, 2nd ed, Graham (Ed).

[6] http://ncis.co.uk/ukta/2003/default.asp.para.6.5.

[7] This tripartite structure is used in most academic works. See Parlour, *Butterworths International Guide to Money Laundering Law and Practice* (2003)(1). The Financial Action Task Force Report of 6.2.1990 refers to the following key stages for the detection of money laundering operations: where cash enters into the domestic financial system, either formally or informally; where it is sent abroad to be integrated into the financial systems of regulatory havens; and where it is repatriated in the form of transfers of legitimate appearance. See also: Peter Lilley, *Dirty Dealing: The Untold Truth About Global Money Laundering* (2000).

to purchase an asset. Whilst this first stage is essential to the legitimization process it is also essential that no suspicion arises in this early stage when the proceeds of crime are introduced into the legitimate banking system. The placement stage may involve single or multiple transactions often using one or more bank accounts or the purchase of easily negotiable investments. Although this stage generally involves conventional banking institutions money launderers also use a range of other non-traditional financial institutions, for example, insurance companies and bureaux de change for the purpose of introducing the cash proceeds of criminal activity into to the system.[8] Indeed, as criminals have become more adept in handling this early stage of the laundering process they have, for example, diversified the range of activity which may be used in the placement stage and cash intensive businesses have frequently been targeted, for example, casinos, bars, restaurants, retail outlets. The placement stage of the process, therefore, involves the physical disposal of the bulk cash proceeds of criminal activity. This is a risky stage since cash may have to be presented to a financial or other institution and it is at this stage that there exists a direct connection between the profits and the crime.

- The layering stage is the first attempt at concealment, disguising or obscuring the source of the ownership of the funds. This is also known as the agitation or commingling stage and unless this stage is completed, the money although having been placed in the banking system can still be identified as a single block. The essential element at this stage is to move money around either in the same or other institutions or across national boundaries, into different currencies and/or other types of investments. This is achieved by the creation of one or more layers of financial transactions designed to interrupt any audit trail and may involve the creation of a false paper trail, for example, the production of false documents to disguise the true source, ownership or location of the funds; or the conversion of cash into monetary instruments, such as traveller's cheques, money orders, bonds or stocks, or the purchase of tangible assets. The layering stage of the rehabilitation of the proceeds of criminal activity is likely to involve cross-border transactions where the enforcement authorities of the country where the predicate crime has been committed will have difficulties in carrying forward the investigation. Whilst cooperation from the overseas law enforcement agencies may be forthcoming there may be delays, or the results of such cooperation may not be admissible in the court of the requesting country.[9] There are various techniques that may be used in the layering stage for example, the purchase of negotiable instruments or electronic systems of funds transfers such as

---

8 Savla, *Money Laundering and Financial Intermediaries* (2001) at p 7.

9 The Report on Money Laundering Typologies of the FAFT (1999) states that "virtually every member represented reported having experienced problems in pursuing anti-money laundering investigations with links to off-shore financial centres".

the Society for Worldwide Inter-bank Financial Telecommunications (SWIFT) to transfer funds overseas instantaneously.

- Having successfully concealed the criminal origins of the funds in the layering stage the next step is to integrate the proceeds into legitimate activity so as to give the proceeds the appearance of money originating from legitimate transactions and/or business activity. Assets are assimilated into the legitimated business or financial sectors and criminals are therefore likely to transfer funds back to themselves for further use, legitimate or otherwise. The most effective method therefore is to copy a normal on-going business relationship. Hence, the need for organized crime to move in legitimate business.

Whether the three stages in the laundering process are clearly discernible will depend upon the complexity of the money laundering process. Some aspects of the process will undoubtedly overlap.

Evolution of Money Laundering Controls

The Council of Europe took the first systematic steps to focus on the international problem of money laundering. The late 1970s prompted the Council of Europe to establish a Select Committee of Experts to examine the problems related to money laundering. The first stage of its work compelled the Committee to focus "on the serious problems raised in many countries by the illicit transfer of funds of criminal origin frequently used for the perpetration of further crime". This process of deliberation and review culminated in the adoption of a formal recommendation entitled *Measures Against the Transfer and Safekeeping of Funds of Criminal Origin.*[10] The Recommendation emphasized the importance of combating money laundering through prevention, and control of the role played by banks in this respect. It stated that all private and public banks should "as a minimum" undertake identity checks on customers whenever securities deposits are opened, safe deposits rented; cash transactions of a certain magnitude are entered bearing in mind the possibility that transactions may be in several parts. Although the Council of Europe Recommendation was not widely adopted its influence cannot be discounted. It articulated the proposition that countering money laundering required the support and cooperation of the financial sector and highlights the significance of the "know your customer" procedures and cooperation with the investigating authorities.

In 1986, the European Ministers of Justice requested the European Committee on Crime Problems to develop international norms and standards to guarantee effective cooperation between judicial authorities in respect of detection, freezing

[10] Measures against the Transfer and Safekeeping of Funds of Criminal Origin: Recommendation and Explanatory Memorandum; Committee of Council of Europe, Rec No R (80) 10 (27 June 1980) cited in Gilmore at 135, 175.

and forfeiture of proceeds of illicit drug trafficking.[11] In turn, the Committee on Crime Problems established a Select Committee to investigate the practice of national and international money laundering, particularly in relation to banking operations that is, in relation to non-drugs related money laundering. The work of the Committee led to the adoption of the 1990 Council of Europe Convention on *Laundering Search, Seizure and Confiscation of the Proceeds from Crime* which set out to provide a complete set of rules in respect of investigation, proceedings and enforcement of a confiscation decision in foreign jurisdictions. Further, one of its main objectives was to maintain the standards introduced by the 1988 UN Convention against *Illicit Traffic in Narcotic and Psychotropic Substance* (Vienna Convention). Article 6 of the Council of Europe Convention goes beyond the 1988 UN Convention by imposing obligations (although limited) on participating states to criminalize money laundering on an "all crimes" basis regardless of whether or not the predicate offence was subject to the criminal jurisdiction of the Party.[12] This separation of money laundering from drugs related crime has been followed by several jurisdictions and, significantly, by the Financial Action Task Force (FATF). The widening of the offence is accompanied by the extension of the definition of proceeds to include "any economic advantage from offences",[13] and by the criminalisation of certain acts, including negligent laundering.[14]

International efforts to counter the effect of drug trafficking reflect the concerns of the governments to control the effects of this illegal activity. Even in the early 1980s the United Nations voicing the concerns of member states passed General Assembly Resolution 35/195 of 15 December 1980 whose third Preamble paragraph refers to the growing threat caused by the spread of drug abuse, its serious impact on human health, its adverse effect on social development (social disintegration, increasing criminality), economic advancement and national security in a number of countries. Again the General Assembly Resolution 36/168 of 16 December 1981 refers to the "scourge of drug abuse" having reached epidemic proportions in some countries and urged further national and international action. The further Resolution 37/168 of 17 and 18 December 1982 called for international action; and Resolution 38/93 of 1983 called for measures to improve co-ordination and co-operation in the international struggle against illegal production of drugs, illicit drug trafficking and drug abuse.

The increasing recognition of the dangers of drug abuse and trafficking have stimulated the creation of an anti-money laundering regime based on the premise that denying launderers the opportunity to enjoy the illegally obtained proceeds of criminal activity was the best strategy to discourage large, multinational criminal organizations. The battle against laundering the proceeds of drugs crime, in particular, was recognized as an essential strategy to counter the problems caused by modern international drug trafficking. The United Nations has therefore taken a

---

[11] Council of Europe, *Convention on Laundering, Search, Seizure and Confiscation of the Proceeds from Crime and Explanatory Report* (1995) at p 5.

[12] Article 6(2)(a).

[13] Article 1(a).

[14] Article (6)(3).

lead in establishing a comprehensive strategy linked to the prevention, reduction and rehabilitation of offenders. Thus the Preamble to the 1988 United Nations Convention against Illicit Traffic in narcotic Drugs and Psychotropic Substances[15] highlights the link between drug offences, organized crime and money laundering. Article 3 requires the international community to criminalize money laundering and imposed on participating countries an obligation to enable the confiscation of the proceeds derived from, and the substances, materials, equipment and other instruments used in drug trafficking. Article 5 obliges the parties to the Convention to empower their courts or other competent authorities to order that bank, financial or commercial records to be made available or seized. These confiscation measures aim to "incapacitate, by depriving a person of the physical or financial ability, power, or opportunity to continue to engage in proscribed conduct, to prevent offenders from unjustly enriching themselves, by eliminating the advantages and benefits which the offender has gained through his or her illegality . . ." The article also provides that parties shall not decline "to render mutual assistance . . . on the ground of bank secrecy". The Vienna Convention unequivocally calls for know your customer procedures,[16] mandatory reporting of suspicious transactions, and the principle that domestic bank secrecy provisions should not impede or hinder anti money laundering legislation and practices.

The objectives established by the UN Convention in respect of confiscation were reinforced by the work of the Basle Committee. Again in 1988 the Basle Committee on Banking Regulation and Supervisory Practices adopted a Statement of Principles on the *Prevention of Criminal Use of the Banking System for the Purpose of Money Laundering.* The Statement marks the ethical standards of conduct to which banks should adhere and aims to encourage vigilance against the criminal use of the payments system. The committee adopted the view that whilst bank supervisors cannot be held primarily responsible for ensuring that every bank transaction is legitimate they cannot be indifferent to the exploitation of the banking system through money laundering. It highlighted bank mangers as the first and most important safeguard against ensuring that their institutions are not used by criminals as a channel for money laundering.[17] The Committee therefore instructed banks to establish systems and procedures to determine the true identity of all customers requesting the institution's services and identify ownership of the accounts. It exhorts banks to institute effective procedures for obtaining the requisite identification from new customers, and to refuse to deal with existing customers who are unable to provide proof of identification. Indeed, the principles state that it should be explicit policy that significant transactions will not be undertaken if customer identity is not established. The Committee also recommended that "banks cooperate fully with the national law enforcement authorities to the extent permitted by local regulations relating to confidentiality." The Statement advised that where banks become aware that deposits are the proceeds of crime or that transactions are criminally motivated, they take

---

[15] UN DocE/CONF 82/15,28; Vienna Convention.

[16] As they became subsequently known.

[17] Basle Statement at Preamble Para 6.

appropriate steps, for example, denying assistance, severing links with the customer, and closing or freezing accounts.[18] The Committee encourages measures putting these principles into effect including "implementation of specific procedures for customer identification and for retaining internal records of transactions" and for effective training of staff for internal audits. The Basle Statement has no binding effect on the G10 countries but does serve as an influential form of soft law by reinforcing the notion that financial institutions are the centrepiece of effective money laundering monitoring and detection. The Statement also emphasizes the importance of countries adopting the "know your customer" procedures. This concept has become integral to national anti-money laundering programmes.

The European Directive on Money Laundering[19] was adopted in response to fears amongst EU leaders that removal of internal barriers and the creation of an integrated European financial system may enable drug traffickers and money launderers to flourish. The Directive was accompanied by a lengthy Preamble that provided a lengthy justification for the measure. The Preamble raised concern that lack of Community action "could lead Member States, for the purpose of protecting their financial systems, to adopt measures which could be inconsistent with completion of the Single Market".[20] Following the Basle Declaration, the Preamble also acknowledged "when credit and financial institutions are used to launder proceeds from criminal activities, the soundness and stability of the institution concerned and confidence in the financial system as a whole could be seriously jeopardised, thereby losing the trust of the public". Both individual institutions and the financial sector are seen as under threat, as indeed is, European integration. The Preamble then states: "Launderers could try to take advantage of the freedom of capital movement to supply financial services which the integrated financial area involves, if certain co-ordinating measures are not adopted at community level". Coupled with market considerations the Directive also acknowledged the influence of money laundering on the increase of drug trafficking and organized crime.

The measures introduced by the Directive reflect both criminal and market considerations. The Directive contained a prohibition on money laundering[21] and contained penal measures to support the criminalisation of money laundering. It also established duties on credit and financial institutions in the fight against money laundering. The Directive prohibited:[22]

- The conversion or transfer of property, knowing that such property is derived from criminal activity or from participating in such activity, for the purpose of concealing or disguising the illicit origin of the property or

[18] Basle Statement at s IV.
[19] Council Directive of 10 June 1991 on the Prevention of the Use of the Financial System for the purpose of Money Laundering, 91/308/EEC; OJ 166, 28 6 1991 at p 77.
[20] Recital 2.
[21] Article 2.
[22] Article 1, third indent.

assisting any person who is involved in the commission of such activity to evade the legal consequences of this action;

- The concealment or disguise of the true nature, source, location, disposition, movement, rights to ownership or property, knowing that such property is derived from criminal activity or from participation in such activity;
- The acquisition, possession or use of property, knowing at the time of receipt that the property was derived from criminal activity or from participation in such activity.

The Directive therefore reiterated the money laundering definition adopted by the Vienna Convention. Again in accordance with the Convention the Directive prohibited intentional money laundering but not negligent money laundering. Moreover, following the Vienna Convention the Directive broadened the scope of property and provided that property means "assets of every kind, whether corporeal or incorporeal, movable or immovable, tangible or intangible, and legal documents or instruments evidencing title to or interests in such assets".

The Directive adopted a minimum standard approach to the definition of money laundering. It confined money laundering to at least to the proceeds from drug offences as specified in the Vienna Convention with Member States being given the discretion to broaden the scope of the legislation by adding further predicate offences. This approach led to inconsistency in Member States with some states opting for long, exhaustive lists of predicate offences (for example, Greece) whilst others have chosen to criminalize the proceeds on an all crimes basis (for example, France). With hindsight perhaps the aspect of the Directive that should have been better thought-out was the requirement that customer identification was only required when the institution entered into transactions with a customer of more than ECU 15,000.

The 2001 Second Money Laundering Directive[23] had to be implemented by Member States by mid-2003. As amended the Directive required Member States to criminalize money laundering. The predicated crime covers a broad range of criminal activities not merely drug related crimes and these crimes can be committed in either the Member State or a third country. The Directive imposes certain duties on credit institutions including the duty to identify customers, to verify beneficial ownership, to keep identification and transactional records for five years, to exercise due diligence, to report any suspicion of money laundering and to establish a programme against money laundering including training employees to assist in the detection of laundering operations. The amended Directive extends the scope of the anti-money laundering legislation to include accountancy and legal firms, estate agents, and dealers in precious materials. The reason for this extension is that such firms and people hold monies and other

---

[23] Council Directive 2001/97/EC amended the Money Laundering Directive of 1991 (Council Directive 1991/308/EC). The Directive was given effect in the UK by the Criminal Justice Act 1993 and Money Laundering Regulations 2003 implemented the 2001 Directive.

valuables for their clients, and therefore perform a similar role to the financial sector. However, they are not covered by the strict record-keeping requirements and monitoring procedures. The Proceeds of Crime Act 2002 and the 2003 Regulations consolidated the Criminal Justice Act 1993 and the associated Regulations give effect to the Second Money laundering Directive. The Draft Third EC Money Laundering Directive[24] is intended to repeal the amended 1991 Directive and give effect to the June 2003 FATF Recommendations. However, until the draft 2004 Directive is implemented the Law is as implemented in the Proceeds of Crime Act 2003 and the 2003 Regulations.

The principles first introduced in the Council of Europe Recommendation and later reinforced by the Basle Statement, and later still by the first Money Laundering Directive were refined through the work of the Financial Action Task Force (FATF). The leaders of the Group of Seven Nations (G7) established FATF, in 1989, and is the only international body devoted solely to fighting money laundering. The G7 leaders mandated FATF to "assess the results of co-operation already undertaken in order to prevent the utilisation of the banking system and financial institutions for the purpose of money laundering, and to consider additional preventative measures in this field".[25] One of the major contributions of FATF has been the 1990 Report of the so-called Forty Recommendations which were designed to provide a blueprint for action against money laundering covering the criminal justice system and law enforcement; the financial system and its regulation; and international co-operation. In 1996 these Recommendations were first revised and after the 2001 terrorist attack in the US, FATF expanded its mandate to include the financing of terrorism, in addition to money laundering.

The 2003 revision contains the Forty Recommendations plus eight special recommendations on the financing of terrorism. The 1996 Forty Recommendations have been endorsed by more than 130 countries and are the international anti-money laundering standard. The eight special recommendations on terrorist financing contain a set of measures aimed at combating the funding of terrorist acts and terrorist organizations and a key element in the fight against money laundering and the financing of terrorism is the need for countries to cooperate with investigators and policing agencies. The Recommendations allow for considerable flexibility and are intended to establish minimal general principles for combating money laundering. The cornerstone of the FATF initiative seeks to enhance the role of the financial institutions and calls on them to comply with a series of measures:

- Repressive measures. FATF recommends that countries criminalize money laundering in accordance with the Vienna Convention although the predicate crime is not limited to drug-related crimes and extends to all serious offences, which includes certain designated crimes.[26] It also suggests that countries provide measures enabling the identification and

---

24 CMARKT/MLCC/02/04/2004.

25 G7 Economic Declaration of July 1989, point 53.

26 Recommendation 1.

tracing, freezing, seizing, and preventing the transfer or disposal, and confiscation of proceeds.[27]

- Customer identification and record keeping. The FATF Recommendations are intended to help financial institutions detect potential money laundering and relate to due diligence, record-keeping, and suspicious transaction reporting and compliance. The reason for early stage diligence, as emphasized in the first FATF report, is that money laundering is most likely to be detected at the point where the proceeds first enter the legitimate system.[28] Customer due diligence and record-keeping duty apply to both financial and non-financial businesses and professions, for example, casinos, estate agents, dealers in precious metals and stones, lawyers, notaries, members of the legal and accountancy professions[29] in certain circumstances. Financial institutions are required to pay special attention to complex or unusual transactions whose background and purpose must be examined. Similarly, all designated non-financial businesses and professions are required to report suspicious transactions and implement compliance programmes.[30] FATF also calls for supervisory or regulatory agencies to ensure that supervised institutions implement FATF Recommendations[31] and establish guidelines and provide feedback to assist institutions in applying national measures to counter money laundering and terrorist financing.[32]
- Institutional and other measures. FATF recommends establishing the Financial Intelligence Unit (FIU) for receiving, requesting, and analysing and disseminating suspicious transaction reports and other information on potential money laundering.[33] It suggests that countries authorise law enforcement agencies to compel production of financial records held by financial intuitions, to conduct search and seizure of evidence.[34] It also calls on countries to equip supervising authorities with power to monitor and ensure compliance with the requirements to combat money laundering and terrorist financing, and with power to impose administrative penalties for non-compliance.[35] Moreover, statistical data should be maintained to monitor the effectiveness of their systems. This may include statistics on suspicious transaction reports, on investigations, prosecutions and convictions of money laundering and terrorist financing, assets seized or confiscated property, and on international cooperation.[36]

---

27 Recommendation 3.
28 First Report on Money Laundering, FATF (1990) at p 9.
29 Recommendation 12.
30 Recommendation 24.
31 Recommendation 23.
32 Recommendation 25.
33 Recommendation 26.
34 Recommendation 28.
35 Recommendation 26.
36 Recommendation 32.

- International Cooperation. The last group of FATF Recommendations calls for countries to sign up to the relevant international instruments, for example, the Vienna Convention; the UN International Convention for the suppression of the Financing of Terrorism 1999. FATF envisages the widest possible range of mutual legal assistance in investigation, prosecution and related proceedings in respect of money laundering and terrorist financing. Any request for assistance should not be refused on the grounds that the laws of confidentiality protect the information. FATF also calls on countries to provide expeditious and effective confiscation cooperation, extradition and other forms of cooperation.[37]

Although, the FATF Recommendations are without the force of international law the influence of FATF in helping to draw up a blueprint for a programme of action against international money laundering cannot be underestimated. Indeed the European Community through the directive mechanism and other countries through other initiatives have transformed many of these Recommendations into law.

Preventative Measure

In general legal measures, which are focused on the prevention of money laundering, are those, which impose on financial institutions those measures that discourage laundering operations. These obligations, while initially limited to banks have been extended to non-bank institutions, for example, bureau de change, and even non-financial businesses and certain professions including casinos, dealers in precious metals and stones, lawyers and accountants.[38] The main justification for their extension is that launderers have turned more and more to non-banking institutions to non-financial businesses and professions to launder the proceeds of crime. Financial institutions are therefore required to enable suspicious transactions to be recognized and reported; and to ensure that the institution has a sufficient audit trial should a customer/or client come under scrutiny. The Money Laundering Regulations 2003 cover internal controls and communications; identification procedures; recognition of suspicious transactions and reporting procedures; training of employees; and record keeping. The Joint Money Laundering Steering Group (JMLSG) issued guidance notes for the UK financial sector on compliance with the 2003 Regulations. A court may take these guidance notes into consideration when determining whether supervisory, trade or other professional association guidelines have been breached. These guidelines give effect to the FATF Recommendations.[39] The regulations make it a criminal offence not to keep proper records of customer and transaction information. The regulations/consequent guidelines impose the following obligations.

---

[37] Recommendations 35-40.

[38] See FATF Forty Recommendations 2003; Money Laundering Regulations (2003).

[39] 2003.

Customer Identification

Financial Institutions have had to tighten up their procedures both in respect of customer identification and customer record keeping. Customer identification procedures have two broad elements: obtaining documentary proof of the customer's identity; and obtaining sufficient understanding of the customer's status, source of income and funds and the likely use of the account. Most criminals would prefer not to reveal their true identity, particularly at the placement stage where the proceeds of crime are introduced into the legitimate financial system and where there is the greatest chance of detection. Thus, requiring proof of identity[40] and an indication of the usage of the account may help reduce the risk of the account being used for money laundering purposes.

Following these FATF recommendations certain exemptions are given from the general requirement to verify customer identity, for example, where the relationship is to consist solely of a one off transaction a prescribed limit (15,000 Euros) or a series of linked transactions below the limit or where a larger transaction is proposed but the applicant is introduced by another regulated entity from a country with EU equivalent anti-money laundering legislation; or where the applicant itself is a UK or EU institution; or the transaction relates to certain low risk products (personal investments);or for an existing customer for the institution. The FATF recommendations suggest that institutions use reliable, independent source documents in customer identification. The UK JMLSG recommends sound processes and systems are adopted for customer verification with appropriately qualified staff responsible for the identification and documentation gathering processing. Obviously, it is preferable for the institutional staff to meet the customer direct but where the customer is not available for a meeting then an enhanced due diligence check should be performed.[41]

Due Diligence

This obligation imposes on financial institutions a requirement that they undertake a proper examination of transactions to ensure they are not intended to further money laundering. The focus of due diligence is on the nature of the transaction and not on the identity of the customer although in reality the obligations cannot be isolated. The obligation of institutions to exercise due diligence is particularly when the suspicion based reporting obligations become effective. Whilst financial institutions must have in place systems for customer identification this alone is not enough in respect of suspicious transactions. Generally, suspected money laundering transactions will only be detected if, and when, financial institutions match transactional information obtained through the due diligence obligation with

[40] For example, in the case of individual customers through sight of original passport; identity cards; driving licenses or other similar documents; and in the case of corporate entities proof of identification may relate to proof of incorporation or other proof of legal status, names and addresses of trustees or directors and proof of authority to bind the entity.

[41] Guidance Notes para 4.90-4.100 (December 2001).

data from the customer and his operation of the account. FATF has taken the view that the due diligence obligation should not be applied in respect of all transactions but those types of transactions likely to be related to money laundering.[42] FATF also recommends that the due diligence obligations should only be applied when transactions are complex, unusually large, or they come from countries which do not, or insufficiently, apply its recommendations or make written records of the background and purpose of the transactions.[43] Institutions should exercise due diligence in respect of such transactions even if they have not yet become suspicious about money laundering.

A high risk based approach and enhanced due diligence should be exercised where a business deals with so-called "high net worth individuals" (HNWIs). The risk-based approach is appropriate where the size of the transactions and (frequently) their international nature mean that there may be a serious risk of money laundering so that a thorough understanding of the business is essential.

Record Keeping Obligation

The purpose of this duty is to produce a paper trial for use as evidence in a subsequent criminal investigation. Although UK law does not require records to be kept in any specific form they must be maintained in an admissible form and must contain sufficient information to enable law enforcement authorities to reconstitute individual transactions for the purpose of investigation and prosecution.[44] The records that need to be kept must relate to the identity of the customer; all transactions carried out by the customer; records of internal and external reports; and records of money laundering training, compliance monitoring and other records kept by the regulator. Compliance with recommendation 10 of FATF requires that such records must be kept for a minimum of five years.[45]

The UK Law on Money Laundering

Historically, the UK law on money laundering has grown on a piecemeal basis and because of this the criminal offences relating to money laundering could be found in various statutes. Moreover, because of this piecemeal development of the legislation there were inconsistencies in the offences recognized. However, in the aftermath of the Abacha scandal, and following a report by the UK Performance and Innovation Unit, the Treasury decided that new legislation was required to effectively counter the growing threat of money laundering. The major problem was seen as the failure to report and hence too few prosecutions. The Financial Services Authority committed itself to supporting this process by enforcing the 1993 Regulations to the letter and banks were consequently required to provide

42 Recommendation 5.
43 Recommendations 11 and 21.
44 Recommendation 10.
45 SI 1993/1933, regs 12 and 13.

documentary evidence to show they complied with the regulatory requirements. The events of 11 September 2001 suddenly established a clear link between the atrocity in the USA, the use to which terrorist monies may be put and the need to prevent money laundering.

The implementation of the Proceeds of Crime Act 2002 (PCA)[46] creates a single set of money laundering offences applicable to the proceeds of all crimes thereby abolishing the distinction between drugs and non-drugs related crimes. The provisions of the PCA 2002 follow the provisions of the Vienna Convention 1988 and the first EU Money Laundering Directive of 1991, although the 2002 Act goes further than the Convention and the Criminal Justice Act 1988 (CJA). Further, the Act introduces a new offence intended to apply to the financial services: that of negligent failure to report suspicions relating to any crime (not simply drugs and terrorism). The 2002 Act recognizes a number of repressive measures offences that apply in England and Wales and outlaws money laundering in terms of concealing, disguising, converting, transferring or removing from the United Kingdom, criminal property.[47]

There are two elements to the definition of criminal property[48] namely:

- The property constitutes a person's benefit from criminal conduct. The Act does not preserve the distinction between the proceeds of indictable and summary offences contained in the previous legislation. Although, the Act expressly provides that it is immaterial when the criminal conduct took place the legislation cannot be intended to have retrospective effect. Instead, it is intended to apply to laundering activity, which takes place after the PCA 2002 comes into effect in relation to criminal property derived from crimes committed before the Act. The definition of criminal property also expressly provides that it is immaterial who carried out the criminal conduct. Thus, the section applies to property in the hands of the predicate offender or other third party.
- The further element of the definition is that the offender must know or suspect that the property in question constitutes or represents a benefit from criminal conduct. A feature of s 327 is the broad scope of activity covered. The section in effect replaces and combines two offences from the earlier legislation; namely those offences of concealing or disguising criminal proceeds and converting or removing from the jurisdiction criminal proceeds for the purposes of avoiding a prosecution for a money laundering offence or in order to avoid an enforcement order, and either concealing, disguising, converting or transferring criminal proceeds with the knowledge or reasonable suspicion that the funds were criminally derived.[49] Under the 2002 Act, Parliament has made some crucial changes to the offence, specifically that neither the objective *mens rea* (that is, the

[46] Implemented on 24 February 2003.
[47] Section 327 Proceeds of Crime Act 2002.
[48] Section 340 (2).
[49] Both these offences were inserted into the CJA 1988 by s 31 CJA 1993.

reasonable grounds for knowledge or suspicion of money laundering) nor the purposive element survive. Hence the offence of concealing, disguising, converting, transferring or removing criminally derived property from the UK is now solely committed through the commission of such acts, provided the person accused cannot rely on one of the statutory defences. There is a necessary element of *mens rea* however, as in order for the property to be criminal, not only must the property in fact be criminal,[50] but the accused must know or suspect that the property is criminal. The other crucial addition to this section is the insertion of statutory defences.

- Although such defences were available under the previous legislation, the defences are available presumably because of the view taken in Parliament that the offence could not be committed unwittingly due to the purposive element of the first offence, and the objective element of *mens rea* required for the second.[51]

The breadth of the s 327 offence and the absence of any purposive or mental element do justify the insertion of statutory defences. These defences are as follows: where disclosure is authorised;[52] where the person intended to make such a disclosure but has a reasonable excuse for failing to;[53] where the act is done in fulfilment of a function he has relating to any legislative provision concerning criminal conduct or benefit there from.[54] The defence under s 327 (2)(b) applies specifically where the person concerned intended to make disclosure but failed to so. Such a person will not be guilty under s 327 provided he has a reasonable excuse for his failure to report. The defence in itself is not unique, being available as a defence to certain offences connected with money laundering under the earlier legislation. The defence has always been subject to severe criticism.[55] It will be interesting to see how the courts give effect to this legal, even if somewhat impractical, defence.

Entering into, or becoming concerned with an arrangement which facilities the acquisition, retention, use or control of criminal property[56] This offence may be committed by anyone who enters into, or becomes concerned with an arrangement, which he knows or may suspect assists in the acquisition, retention, use or control of criminal property by or on behalf of another. The provision is a reworking of the previous offence of entering into arrangements, which facilitate the laundering

---

50 Under s 340 (3)(a).

51 Hansard, HL Vol 540, col 1492 (3 Dec 1992) in relation to the relevant provision of the Drug Trafficking Bill.

52 Section 327 (2)(a).

53 Section 327 (2)(b).

54 Section 327 (2)(c).

55 See Morrison, Money Laundering Legislation in the UK (1995) 14(1) IBFL 3.

56 Section 328.

process.[57] As with other provisions of the PCA 2002 this section is widely drafted. Section 328 is intended to apply to persons who do not have a direct link with either the predicate crime or with the money laundering activity. As with s 93A of the CJA 1988, s 328 of the PCA 2002 is intended to catch those with a remoter link to the laundering activity. As Bosworth-Davies observed in relation to s 93A of the CJA 1988 "the forms of facilitation envisaged by the Parliamentary draughtsmen are limitless".

Acquiring, using or having possession of criminal property This offence is a reworking of the earlier offence established in s 93(B) of the CJA 1988 and deals with the acquisition, possession or use of the proceeds of criminal conduct. The only required *mens rea* is that in relation to the criminal property. The section also provides that a person acquires, uses or possesses the criminal property for inadequate consideration where the value of the consideration is significantly less than the value of the acquisition, use or possession.[58]

Failing to disclose knowledge or suspicion of money laundering, which came to his attention through the course of a business in the regulated sector[59] This section is significant to those professionals who have dealings with the regulated sector. The section provides that a person commits an offence where, through the course of his business in the regulated sector, he knows or suspects that another person is engaged in money laundering, and he fails to make the required as soon as reasonably practicable. The failure to report their suspicions or knowledge of money laundering is punishable[60] on indictment. Section 330 creates an "all crime" Duty Working Group on Confiscation[61] to report suspicion or knowledge of money laundering previously limited to proceeds of drug monies or proceeds of terrorist crimes. The offence under s 330 is structured on tripartite basis and all three elements must be satisfied in order to secure a conviction as follows:

1. The person must know or suspect, or have reasonable grounds for knowing or suspecting that another person is engaged in money laundering;
2. The information on which his knowledge is based, or which gives him reasonable grounds for such knowledge or suspicion, must have come to him through the course of a business in the regulated sector; and
3. He must fail to make the necessary disclosure as soon as reasonably practicable after the information has come to his attention.

The first condition appears to be no more than a reinstatement of the earlier reporting obligations requiring disclosure based on knowledge or suspicion of money laundering. This requirement caused both grave academic and other

---

57 See s 50 of the Drug Trafficking Act 1994 and s 93A of the Criminal Justice Act 1988.
58 Section 329 (3)(a) and (b).
59 Section 330.
60 Section 334 (2)(a).
61 See Third Report, *Criminal* Assets. November 1998.

concern[62] particularly as the disclosure requirement became effective once a professional person had doubts in respect of the validity of the client, such suspicion was sufficient to necessitate the reporting requirement. However, the negligence-based requirement under s 330 (2)(b) is a major addition to the new offences as the earlier legislation failed to impose liability for mere negligence non-disclosure.

The negligence based liability is intended to prevent professional people falling within the scope of s 330 (2)(b) from claiming ignorance of any suspicion or knowledge regarding a money laundering transaction as a defence in circumstances where a reasonably competent professional person would be alerted by the transaction in question. There was considerable discussion of the imposition negligence based liability on professionals during the discussion stages of the Proceeds of Crime Bill[63] where such liability was seen as a "desire to instil terror into those who handle money" for the purposes of or in connection with money laundering. In reality the imposition of negligence based liability is the result of the mixed reception to the 1993 Regulations which imposed training and reporting procedures, with many firms failing to report suspicious transactions because of a lack of appropriate training of employees. In its 2000-01 Service Plan the NCIS reported that only 126 of approximately 500 deposit-taking institutions have reported suspicious transactions with approximately 78% of the reports being filed by only 10 banks. The lack of reporting compliance was reinforced by the FSA following the Abacha scandal[64] when it was discovered that 23 banks had held accounts for the President of Nigeria, all of which had shortcomings in their money laundering procedures.

The second part of the tripartite requirement under s 330 is that the information, which causes the professional person to know or suspect money laundering, must come to his attention through the course of a business in the "regulated sector". Paragraph 3 of Schedule 9 defines the scope of business carried on through the regulated sector in "negative terms" by providing that a business is not in the regulated sector to the extent that it engages in certain types of activities, for example, activities carried out by the Bank of England; or any activity of which an exemption order under s 38 of the Financial services and Markets Act 2000 has effect if it is carried on or falls within a class or persons specified. Given the width of what constitutes a business in the regulated sector and that the scope of the disclosure requirements has been extended by the 2003 Regulations,[65] professional persons required to make disclosure include auditors; external accountants and tax advisors; real estate agents; notaries and other legal professionals acting on behalf of clients in the buying and selling of real property or business entities; managing client money; opening or managing bank or savings or securities accounts; dealers in high value goods, for example, precious stones or metals, or works of arts;

62 See Radmore, "Money Laundering Prevention: Effect of the New Law on Solicitors" (1995) 16(5) *Comp Law* 155; Hansard, HC cols 981-982, 17 January 2002.

63 See Hansard, HC col 1089, 9, 22 January 2002.

64 FSA Press Release, 8 March 2001.

65 Which implements the Second EC Money Laundering Directive.

organizing of contributions necessary for the creation, operation or management of companies; and creation, management of trusts, companies or similar structures.

The final requirement the non-compliance of which will impose liability under s 330 is that the person fails to make the "required disclosure" as soon as reasonably practicable after the information comes to his attention. The term "required disclosure" is defined under s 330 (5), which requires that disclosure must be "made up the line," that is, to a nominated officer[66] or to any person authorised to receiver such disclosures by the Director general of the NCIS. In respect of the requirement that disclosure must be made as soon as reasonably practicable there is no threshold which underlines when disclosure must be made but it is unlikely that a court will look favourably on any professional person who failed to make disclosure of suspicion or knowledge of money laundering for any significant period of time. It must be remembered that on a strict interpretation of the section the mere suspicion of money laundering requires disclosure.

Again the failure to make disclosure may be justified if the person concerned can bring himself within a series of statutory defences. The second of these defences is specifically to members of the legal profession and the information, which causes suspicion of money laundering, came to his knowledge in the course of a privileged communication.[67] However, the defence under s 330 (10) is restricted by sub-section (11) which provides that where the information or other matter is communicated or given with the intention of furthering a criminal purpose, the legal privilege defence is unavailable. In *Ex p* Francis[68] the court interpreting s 10 of the Police and Criminal Evidence Act 1984 concluded that the term "criminal purpose" refers to the criminal purpose of the client, and that of the solicitor.

The final issue to note in respect of the defence under s 330 is the guidance issued by the supervisory or other appropriate body. The court must consider such guidance in determining whether the person has committed an offence under s 330. This is particularly important in respect of liability for negligent non-disclosure. In determining whether a person is guilty of negligent non-disclosure the court must consider the standards adopted by the industry as to whether a reasonably prudent professional would have been altered as to the suspicious nature of the funds in question. It is against the reasonable standards and practices of the industry against which the professional person will be judged.

Failure to disclose knowledge or suspicion of money laundering, which came to his attention by virtue of his position as the nominated officers in the regulated sector. This provision is essentially a reworking of the s 330 offence but with specific reference to nominated officers in the regulated sector. This provision therefore applies specifically to those whose responsibility it is to receive internal reports regarding suspicious transactions and whose function it is to decide whether there are sufficient grounds to warrant a disclosure to the NCIS. Again,

---

[66] Under s 330 (9) the person appointed to receive and handle money laundering disclosures in the disclosure's company.

[67] Section 330 (10).

[68] [1989] AC 346.

the offence may be committed negligently under s.331(2)(b) although it may be less contentious to impose liability on such persons since they would be expected to show due diligence and care in the fulfilment of their functions.

The disclosure of information prejudicial to an investigation This offence is committed where a professional person makes "a disclosure which is likely to prejudice money laundering investigation being undertaken by the law enforcement agencies". However, where a person does not know or suspect that the disclosure is likely to be prejudicial to an investigation the offence is not committed. Similarly, an offence will not be committed where the disclosure is a law enforcement officer discharging his official duty, nor where legal privilege may be invoked by the disclosure.[69] As with the its predecessor, the tipping off offences under s 53 of the Drug Trafficking Act 1994 and s 93 (D) of the Criminal Justice Act 1988 is punishable, in accordance with s 334 (2) by summary trial or on indictment.

The repressive measures under the Proceeds of Crime Act 2002 are directed against all serious crimes, particularly those crimes that generate large amount of profit and not merely drug related or terrorism offences. A number of reasons have accounted for this trend namely the increasing recognition that criminal organizations engage in a range of criminal activity such as fraud, extortion and corruption and not just drug trafficking. Further proceeds from other types of laundering, not merely drug trafficking, undermine the integrity of the financial institutions and the stability of the financial system.

To restrict prosecution of proceeds of money laundering merely to the proceeds of drug trafficking is to encourage other types of criminal activity and restrict the work of the law enforcement agencies. Another repressive measure is the confiscation of the proceeds of money laundering crime. Most members of FATF have only in recent years allowed this type of confiscation. The scope of UK confiscation regime under the Proceeds of Crime Act 2002 is outside the scope of this chapter.

The Future of Money Laundering Regulation

In March 2004, the European Commission issued a working paper on the draft Third Directive on Money Laundering and Terrorist Financing.[70] The draft Third Money Laundering Directive is intended to repeal the first directive on money laundering.[71] Two broad tendencies are identified (at this stage) in the draft text as follows: first, preference for a relatively basic implementation of FATF's 40 Recommendations, leaving the detail to domestic implementation; second, a more ambitious harmonizing approach, seeking to add greater detail to the FATF

[69] Section 334.
[70] MARKT/MLCC/02/04/2004.
[71] 91/308/EEC as amended by Directive 2001/97/EC.

standards. The informal consultation on the Third EC Money Laundering Directive[72] indicates that the UK favours the former approach.

The draft Third Money Laundering Directive will affect the regulated sector to whom its provisions will apply consisting of credit institutions; financial institutions, auditors, external accountants and tax advisors; notaries and other independent legal professionals; trust and company service providers; life/investment insurance intermediaries; estate agents; money service businesses, including Bureau de Change; dealers and auctioneers in high value goods, whenever payment is made in cash and for an amount in excess of 15,000 euros; and casinos.

This list is similar to the list of the scope of the Money Laundering Regulations issued in 2003. Public sector bodies engaged in regulation of any of these institutions and law enforcement bodies working in the area of money laundering will be affected by the Directive. The latter include the Financial Services Authority; HM Revenue Agencies; the Gaming Board of Great Britain; the National Criminal Intelligence Service; and Police Forces. Although not directly applicable (as currently drafted) self regulating organizations such as the Law Society and Institute of Chartered Accountants may also wish to place consideration on the scope of these directives.

Those sectors already subject to the Second Money Laundering Directive will be covered by the proposed Third Directive. However, Article 3 proposes that anti-money laundering controls be extended to include Life/investment insurance intermediaries and trust and company service providers. In reality these sectors are already covered under the FATF's 40 Recommendations and by the UK's Money Laundering Regulations 2003. These provisions of the proposed Directive are therefore likely to have a limited impact in the UK. However, the proposed Directive[73] provides that trust and company service providers should be registered or licensed which would require the UK to establish a licensing and supervision system for such entities. Trust and service providers are defined in Article 1(1) and mirrors the FAFT definition.

The proposed Directive makes some general changes to the existing money laundering legislation. The previous EC directives have only been extended to suspicious, risks and controls against money laundering but the draft third Directive includes terrorist financing and each of the money laundering provisions will therefore apply to the proceeds of terrorist activity. The definition of terrorist financing is an amalgamation from existing EU and UN measures. This aspect of the Directive will involve minimal change in the UK as there are already strict controls of terrorist financing through the Terrorism Act 2000.

The draft third Directive extends the definition of "criminal activity" to include all offences involving a sentence of at least six months to a year imprisonment. However, the UK already considers all crimes to be predicates for money laundering offences and therefore this provision will have no impact in the UK. Furthermore the draft Directive overhauls the previous provisions on customer due

---

72 HM Treasury, May 2004.

73 Article 23 (1) and (2).

diligence and largely mirrors the FATF's recommendations. Article 5 of the draft Directive makes clear that all of the regulated sector will be required to carry out certain customer due diligence provisions whenever they establish a business relationship; carry out occasional transactions amounting to 15,000 euros or more (whether a single operation or linked operation); or there is a suspicion of money laundering/terrorist financing; or doubts about the veracity or adequacy of previously obtained customer identification data. The customer due diligence requirements are set out in Article 5(3). Sub paragraph (b) refers to identifying the beneficial owner and taking reasonable measures on the basis of a risk-based approach to verify the identity of the beneficial owner. Sub paragraph (b) also refers to a risk-based approach when conducting ongoing due diligence and the business relationship and scrutiny of transactions undertaken throughout the course of that relationship. Although the UK has strongly promoted a risk-based approach, there is no general application of such an approach to the whole of Article 5(3). The FATF approach has a more general rider stating that all of the customer due diligence provisions should be applied but the institution concerned "may determine the extent of such measures on a risk sensitive basis depending on the type of customer, business relationship or transaction". The current position in the UK is found in Regulation 4(3) of the 2003 Money Laundering Regulations and to an extent, the proposals in the third Directive appear simply to set out what is widely practised in the UK and set out in guidance notes.

The Commission's definition of beneficial ownership can be seen in draft Article 1(8) and covers trusts and well as companies and other legal persons. The UK's current regulations already state that where an applicant for business "acts or appears to act for another person, reasonable measures should be taken for the purpose of establishing the identity of that person". This standard has been developed in the guidance notes for the financial sector of the joint Money Laundering Steering Group and the notes stress the importance of looking behind the corporate identity to identify those who have ultimate control.

The draft Directive proposes that member states allow the regulated sector to reduce the due diligence requirements (subject to conditions) in certain low-risk situations. Article 8 contains a non-exhaustive indicative list of situation where this may be appropriate. The UK's current risk-based approach allows not only for reduced or simplified due diligence but follows the second EC Money Laundering Directive in permitting no due diligence at all in very specific low-risk situations. It is not clear whether the draft Article 8 of the proposed Directive permits for there to be no due diligence beyond checking whether or not an individual case, product or category is low-risk. If this is permitted and given that the list is not exhaustive, the impact of this provision in the UK is not likely to be significant.

The draft Directive in Article 9 proposes that the regulated sector apply a higher level of due diligence in certain high risk situations. The 2003 Money Laundering Regulations already require the regulated sector to "take into account the greater potential for money laundering which arises when [the applicant for business] is not physically present when being identified". It is not therefore clear whether Article 9(a) will add anything to the current UK arrangements. Cross-border correspondent banking and relations with politically exposed persons are already covered in UK guidance although not in the Regulations. It is therefore unlikely that the draft Article 9 will do anything more than put into legislation what is already industry practice.

Other provisions in the draft Directive relating to anonymous accounts; extending the scope of the money laundering legislation will have very little effect on the UK as provisions in respect of these issues have already been implemented by the 2003 Regulations.

Conclusion

The focal point in controlling money laundering is the identification of the proceeds of crime as the investigatory lead to uncover the crime. This is a new way of investigating crime since investigators have traditionally placed less emphasis on the proceeds of the crime. However, with the increase in crimes which result in significant monetary gains, and where the victims may be not be directly identifiable traditional means of investigation have had to be reviewed. Criminal investigation now needs to focus on the identification of the proceeds of crime and on being identified the proceeds both being confiscated and used as the investigatory lead to uncovering the crime and the perpetrator. This approach to criminal investigation is effective in the fight against profit-driven crime and organized crime. The enormous profit from such crime is the incentive to commit such crimes further. Confiscation of the proceeds of crime therefore removes the incentive to the commission of such acts and provides the necessary deterrent.

A significant amount of profit driven crime is business related and committed by those with expertise in the business. Often such white-collar crime is difficult to prove. The laundering offences are therefore a potentially effective means of controlling such crimes. The Proceeds of Crime Act 2002 and the emphasis of a suspicion based regulatory framework, therefore, impose significant responsibility on the professional operating within the financial sector. Indeed, the suspicion based reporting regime is the cornerstone of the new regulatory regime with the overriding requirement that that those who are likely to come across money laundering are under a legal duty to report such suspicions or knowledge of such activity.

The regulatory framework is based on the professional guarding the integrity of financial services with appropriate record keeping, due diligence, and training obligations imposed. The reporting system has clearly been successful in the UK, as the constant increase in the quantity of data to the NCIS demonstrates. However, these obligations have clearly eroded the confidentiality aspects of the relationship between the professional/client. Even so, suspicion-based reporting forms the cornerstone of the PCA 2002 but the term defies precise definition. Whilst the objective of the Government was to simplify the system of money laundering reporting and investigation, in practice, the requirement of reporting based on suspicion (as opposed to suspicion based on reasonable grounds) will pose its own challenges to those under an obligation to report as well as the courts.

Chapter 9

Fighting Corruption in International Trade: Towards Improving Strategy

Indira Carr

Introduction

Corrupt practice in international business transactions, be it in the form of kickbacks,[1] bribes[2] is not a new phenomenon. Globalization arguably has contributed to the increase in the incidence of corruption. The recent communications revolution in the form of the Internet means that suspicions, allegations and incidents of corrupt activity are circulated freely and widely, thus bringing wider recognition of the problem. The cost of corruption to the world economy has been periodically reviewed by international organizations. Well known are the publications of Transparency International (hereinafter TI)[3] and the World Bank Institute (hereinafter WBI). In a recent news item from the WBI published in April 2004[4] the cost of corruption in both rich and developing countries is estimated at $1,000 billion ($1 trillion)[5] a year. According to Daniel Kaufmann, the Institute's director of governance this figure is an estimate of actual bribes paid. The news item also goes on to state that with better governance and anti-corruption measures a country with a per capita income of $2,000 a year would see this, in the long run, increase to $8,000 per year.

Despite popular belief, corrupt practices are not a developing country's problem. It is global and affects both the developed and the developing, as the reviews indicate.[6] Corrupt practices, as indicated by the WBI, economically harm

---

1 Part of an income paid to a person having influence over the size or payment of the income – especially by some illegal arrangement.

2 To promise, offer or give something often illegally to procure services or gain influence.

3 The TI periodically publish Corruption Perception Index based on their surveys which are perception based, that is on information provided by country experts. Organizations such as the WBI also carry out surveys that are based on experiences. The TI reports are available at http://www.ti.org.

4 Available at http://www.worldbank.org.

5 All references to $ in this paper are to US Dollars.

6 According to the Association of Certified Fraud Examiners (http://www.cfnet.com) corruption and fraud claim more than $700 million a year in the US. The US introduced anti-corruption legislation (in respect of corruption of foreign officials) with Foreign Corrupt Practices Act in 1977. The 1977 Act was a result of investigations by SEC

a nation's wealth and the prosperity of its citizens. Effects of corruption may not be that obvious or felt that immediately in developed countries that have achieved and continue to have a minimum standard of living, and provide the necessary infrastructure for healthcare, education and employment. However, the effects of corruption are stark and patently obvious in the developing world affecting billions of people across the continents. A majority of the global population live on the poverty line or below the poverty line and it is these that should be the primary focus of politicians, policymakers and legislators. As the UK White Paper on International Development highlights: "It is poor people who suffer most from corruption. Essential medicines are diverted; unofficial payments are commonly required for water and electricity connections, as well as education and healthcare . . ."[7] Political speeches, regardless of political ideologies and affiliations abound with rhetoric about the betterment in the condition of the masses, of inroads into prosperity and a crime and corruption free environment.

It must however be noted that corruption is not restricted to practices at the petty level of obtaining public services such as electricity and telephone connections but exists at a higher level,[8] in the form of bribes to public officials and politicians for obtaining lucrative contracts, licences for manufacture of goods and other favours such as tax concessions thus distorting the decision making process and resulting in an overall undermining of the policy objectives of the state. The very participants (the government, investors in industry, foreign and domestic) who promise prosperity to the masses break their promises to satisfy their financial greed.

Given the economic harm not just to a nation's wealth but the erosion of a fair and competitive international business environment, be it foreign investment, sales of goods and services,[9] corrupt practices caught the attention of policymakers and

---

(Securities and Exchange Commission) in the 1970s. It found that more than 400 US based companies had made illegal payments of well over $300 million to foreign government officials and political parties to ensure the facilitation of trade. Legislation was introduced to stop this prevalent practice on the part of US firms. The text of this legislation is available at http://www.ta.doc.gov/legal.

7 *Eliminating World Poverty: Making Globalization Work for the Poor* Cmnd 5006 (2000) at p 25. Also available at http://www.globalization.gov.uk. See also Lovei and McKechnie, *The Costs of Corruption for the Poor* (2000).

8 The UK White Paper draws a distinction between "petty corruption" and "grand corruption". The same distinction is also drawn by the WBI (see http://www.worldbank.org).

9 See Bardhan, "Corruption and Development: A Review of Issues" 1997 (35) *Journal of Economic Relation* 1320; Elliott (Ed), *Corruption and the Global Economy* (1997); Ward (Ed), *Corruption, Development and Inequality, Soft Touch or Hard Graft?* (1989); Leiken, "Controlling the Global Corruption Epidemic" 1996 (105) *Foreign Policy* 55; Shady, *The Whistleblowers: Exposing Corruption in Government and Industry* (1989); Ross, *Shady Business: Confronting Corporate Crime* (1992); George *et al*, "On the Threshold of the Adoption of Global Antibribery Legislation: A Critical Analysis of Current Domestic and International Efforts Toward the Reduction of Business Corruption" 1999 (32) *Vanderbilt Journal of Transnational Law* 1. See also Hunt, "Trust and Bribery: The Role of the Quid

legislators in the early 1990s. The mid 1990s saw a flurry of activity on the international front with a number of organizations issuing declarations and setting up committees to address the problem through international instruments. The United Nations, for instance, issued a non-binding Declaration in 1996 against Corruption and Bribery in International Commercial Transactions[10] which called upon UN member states to criminalize bribery of public officials, and promoted greater co-operation between member states to combat corruption and bribery in international commercial transactions. The OECD[11] in 1994 issued the Recommendation on Bribery in International Business Transactions. It called for criminalization of bribery, modification of tax laws so as to end tax deductibility of bribes in the form of expenses, transparency in accounting and auditing practices, and international co-operation in the form of sharing of information. In Europe, in 1997 the Heads of Government of the Member States of the Council of Europe adopted a document entitled "20 Guiding Principles for the Fight Against Corruption"[12] which also called for the criminalization of corruption, nationally and internationally, and co-operation amongst member states. The EU also adopted a comprehensive policy on corruption inside the EU.[13]

The many efforts worldwide have seen the emergence of a number of international and regional instruments. To name a few:

Inter-American Convention Against Corruption adopted by the Organization of American States in 1996.[14]
Convention on Combating Bribery of Foreign Public Official in International Business Transactions adopted by the OECD in 1997.[15]
Criminal Law and Civil Law Conventions on Corruption adopted by the Council of Europe in 1999.[16]
ICC Rules of Conduct on Extortion and Bribery in International Business Transactions.[17]
ICC Manual of Best Corporate Practices to provide guidance for compliance with the OECD Bribery Convention.[18]

Pro Quo and the Link with Crime" 2004 NBER Working Paper No 10510 available at http://www.nber.org for an interesting account on the relationship of implicit *quid pro quo* and the reduction of corruption.

[10] UN Doc GA A/Res/51/191/ Available at http://www.un.org.

[11] Organization for Economic Co-operation and Development. Website address: http://www.oecd.org.

[12] Available at http://www.coe.int .

[13] See COM (2003) 317 final available at http://europa.eu.int.

[14] For text see (1996) 35 ILM 724.

[15] Text available at http://www.oecd.org.

[16] ETS 173 and ETS 174 available at http://www.coe.int.

[17] Adopted 1996; revision of 1977 Rules of Conduct. The 1977 Rules prohibited extortion and bribery in connection with obtaining or retaining business. New rules prohibit extortion or bribery for any purpose. Further information available at http://www.iccwbo.org.

[18] Vincke, Heimann and Katz (Eds), *Fighting Bribery: A Corporate Practices Manual* (2000).

A most recent addition to this list of instruments is the United Nations Convention on Corruption adopted in December 2003.[19]

The aim of this chapter is twofold: to critically comment on the current schemes adopted toward combating corruption in the international business environment and to propose improvements in the penultimate section that could effectively reduce the incidence of corruption. Beside the obvious choice of controlling corruption through multilateral treaties and sanctions, anti-corruption strategies include, for instance, the involvement of the media and civil society,[20] including Non-Governmental Organizations (NGOs). This chapter will therefore consider other anti-corruption mechanisms besides regulation with a view to assessing their usefulness in the global fight against corruption. While the emphasis of this chapter is legal, it inevitably draws upon research on corruption in other disciplines such as economics, development studies, politics and philosophy in proposing improvements to the current regime for a number of reasons. First, there is a vast body of literature on corruption and much of it is written in the context of development studies, politics or economics.[21] Second, corruption in the business environment has both a social and economic dimension. As such a better understanding is gained if viewed in this wider context. Before moving on, a few words on the causes of corruption follow since knowledge of its causes may well prove useful in formulating devices for its eradication.

Causes of Corruption

There is a corpus of literature that addresses causes of corruption and largely uses the annual indices of perceived corruption produced by TI. Corruption has been linked variously to economic development of a state, centralisation, structure of government institutions and political process,[22] colonial connections,[23] legal culture,[24] gender and religion. For instance, according to some, a significant link

---

19 Considered further under Scheme I – The Regulatory Approach below. Text of Convention available at http://www.un.org.

20 A wide term which includes citizens, NGOs and other associations (such as professional associations, chambers of commerce) that promote causes in order to influence policies.

21 Klitgaard, *Controlling Corruption* (1988); Rose-Ackerman, *Corruption: A Study of Political Economy* (1978); Rose-Ackerman, "The Economics of Corruption" (1975) 4 *Journal of Public Economics* 187; Lamsdorff, "How Corruption Affects Public Welfare" (2001) Discussion Paper 9, Center for Globalization and Europeanisation, University of Goettingen; Dudley, "The Rotten Mango: The Effect of Corruption on International Development Projects" available http://www.user.gwdg.de.

22 See Schleifer & Vishny, "Corruption" [1993] *The Quarterly Journal of Economics* 599.

23 See Treisman, "The Causes of Corruption: a Cross-National Study" (2000) 20 *Journal of Public Economics* 399.

24 *Ibid.*

exists between empowerment of women and lower levels of perceived corruption,[25] while others see a link between Protestant adherents and lower perceived corruption.[26] Successful economic development is also cited as a noticeable factor in lowering corruption,[27] so also a strong tradition of procedural justice since judges are perceived in these settings "as a useful check on corrupt politicians and bureaucrats".[28] Interestingly, openness to international trade is seen as a contributor to higher levels of corruption especially where there are trade barriers in the form of import duties and complex bureaucratic structures for customs clearance.[29] Wage structures in the public sector also influence corruption. Lower wages result in higher levels of corruption, particularly at the petty level, since bribes are seen as a means of supplementing meagre incomes. There is no doubt that these studies and the connections they highlight on the basis of available surveys provide an important insight into the phenomenon of corruption. It would however be premature to reach any solid conclusions from them. The studies draw from a variety of sources relating to different countries with varying economic, political and cultural backgrounds and it is questionable whether the derived generalisations are defensible. Gathered data are prone to differing interpretations as the following illustration indicates. For instance, economists who have examined the relationship of decentralization and corruption on data gathered by international organizations reach different conclusions. According to a study conducted by Fisman and Gatti[30] decentralization lowers corruption whereas Huther and Shah[31] reach an opposite conclusion. As the OECD itself indicates in relation to decentralization and corruption "[t]he links between corruption and decentralization and the potential for decentralization to reduce corruption are not at all straightforward, many examples can be cited where decentralization . . . has . . . in the short run decentralised corruption. On the other hand, there are specific examples . . . where corruption in local and city government is being reduced".[32] Regardless of these shortcomings what these various perceived causal connections indicate is that corruption is a complex multi-faceted phenomenon and might

---

[25] Dollar, Fisman and Gatti, "Are Women Really the 'Fairer' Sex? Corruption and Women in Government" *Policy Research Report on Gender and Development* (1999) Working Paper Series No 4, Washington; World Bank Research Group.

[26] See Tanzi, "Corruption Around the World: Causes, Consequences, Scope and Cures" (1998) 45 *IMF Staff Papers* 559.

[27] See Andig & Fledstad, *Corruption: A Review of Contemporary Research* (2001).

[28] See Treisman, *op cit* fn 23 at 425.

[29] See Hors, *Fighting Corruption on Customs Administration: What can we Learn from Recent Experiences* Technical Paper 175, 2001 Paris: OECD Development Centre. See also Krugman, "Growing World Trade: Causes and Consequences" (1995) Brookings Papers on Economic Activity.

[30] *Decentralization and Corruption: Evidence Across Countries* (2000).

[31] *Applying a Simple Measure of Good Governance to the Debate on Fiscal Decentralization* (1998) World Bank Policy Research Papers 1984.

[32] See OECD Doc DCD/DAC/GOVNET(2003)1 "Synthesis of Lessons Learned of Donor Practices in Fighting Corruption" available at http://www.oecd.org at para 74.

require a variety (and perhaps a combination) of means for combating it, ranging from the legal, cultural, political and the administrative to the economic.

The Current Regime

It would be convenient for the purposes of this chapter to categorise the current regime for combating corruption into four schemes. Scheme I is regulatory in character and dependent on legislative instruments. Scheme II adopted by international aid and donor agencies links the giving of aid/loans with certain conditions to be met by the recipient state. Scheme III advocates the use of the media while Scheme IV sees people centred participation in the form of NGOs, and community based associations as a means controlling corruption. It must be added that the current regime consists of the use of all four schemes to varying degrees depending on the conditions in a state.

Scheme I – The Regulatory Approach

When the large scale debilitating effects (in economic and social terms) of corruption hit the international scene, regulation was seen as the obvious choice to counter the problem and multilateral treaties were seen as the best option for its eradication since they would introduce not only harmonization at the substantive level but a degree of unification in accounting/auditing practices alongside making way for mutual legal assistance. Prominent amongst the conventions in force that has received a healthy number of ratifications is the Convention on Combating Bribery of Foreign Public Official in International Business Transactions adopted by the OECD in 1997 (hereinafter "OECD Convention"). An official Commentary accompanies the OECD Convention which provides useful information for the purposes of interpretation. The OECD Convention has been implemented by both developing[33] and developed nations.[34] The United Kingdom ratified it in December 1998 and legislation covering aspects addressed by the OECD Convention formed part of the Anti-Terrorism Crime and Security Act passed in 2001.

According to the OECD Convention it is a criminal offence for any person intentionally to offer, promise or give any undue pecuniary or other advantage to a foreign public official in order to obtain or retain business or other improper advantage (such as licences, permits) in the conduct of international business.[35] The inducement may be direct or made through an intermediary such as a local broker for the offence to be committed. Under this provision the very act of uttering, even in the absence of current or subsequent performance (for example, the physical act of handing over the agreed advantage), is sufficient for the offence

[33] For example Mexico, Brazil, Turkey. For a complete list of ratifications see http://www.oecd.org.

[34] For example Australia, Canada, the US.

[35] See Article 1(1).

to be committed. A foreign public official, defined in its Article 1(4), is sufficiently wide to include civil servants, members of parliament, the judiciary and those working in public undertakings be it at a national or a local level. The structure of public undertakings varies from country to country and even amongst public undertakings within the same country. While most public undertakings receive subsidies and other privileges from the government and are subject to dominant influence from the government there are public undertakings that operate at a commercial level and there is nothing much to distinguish them from a private enterprise. The promise or offer of pecuniary advantages to officials in such enterprises presumably would not be considered an offence since the official would not be deemed to perform a public function – explained in the Commentaries as "activity in the public interest, delegated by a foreign country, such as the performance of a task delegated by it in connection with public procurement". This highlights one of the major drawbacks of the OECD Convention: its restriction to bribery in the public sector when it is common knowledge that bribery is practised equally in the private sector. Another peculiarity of this convention is its focus on the offence committed by the person who promises or gives the bribe (often called "active bribery" or "active corruption"), not the one who takes it (often termed "passive bribery").[36] Presumably, this restrictive focus was to avoid potential problems of jurisdiction over a foreign public official. Another reason could be to avoid potential clash with the law of the State to which the public official belongs and is subject to. It could also be explained in terms of tactics – reduction of active bribery would see an overall reduction of corruption itself.

The OECD Convention includes provisions on sanctions and liability of legal persons. Sanctions are expected to be effective, persuasive and dissuasive criminal penalties which could include deprivation of liberty. However, where under a Contracting Party's legal system criminal responsibility is not applicable to a legal person then sanctions could be of a monetary kind that are effective, persuasive and proportionate. There are further provisions regarding accounting practices – on the maintenance of books and records and their disclosure, and financial statement disclosures. These are included with the intention of prohibiting off-the-books account and recording of non-existent expenditure and the incorrect identification of objects. These provisions reflect one of the pillars of World Bank's multi-pronged approach to fighting corruption – improving financial management through better accounting and auditing practices. Mutual legal assistance in the form of providing information and documents facilitating investigations is another feature of the OECD Convention. Interestingly, the OECD Convention does not define international business transactions. This presumably is to be gathered from prevalent practices. International business transactions are likely to include, besides international sales of goods and services other forms of business such as foreign investment and sales of know-how.

---

[36] Passive bribery refers to the request by a person (such as a public official or employee of a firm) of an undue advantage in the doing of an act or refraining from acting in the exercise of his function.

Before moving on to the Council of Europe legislation, we shall briefly consider the UK law[37] relating to corruption. At the time the OECD Convention was adopted, the UK had anticorruption law spread across a number of sources – common law and a number of statutes – Public Bodies Corrupt Act 1889, the Prevention of Corruption Act 1906 and the Prevention of Corruption Act 1916. The UK law covered both active and passive bribery (Public Bodies Corrupt Act 1889), and applied to both private and public sector bribery (Prevention of Corruption Act 1906). The definition of public body in the 1889 Act was widened by the Prevention of Corruption Act 1916 so that local and public authorities of all descriptions could be included. In light of the existing offence of bribery it was felt that all that was required to implement the OECD Convention were a few amendments to existing statutes and common law such that the offences of bribery could be extended to include foreign bribery. Accordingly, s 108 of the Anti-Terrorism, Crime and Security Act 2001 (hereinafter "Anti-Terrorism Act") introduced the foreign element into the common law offence of bribery and, amended s 1 of the Prevention of Corruption Act 1906, s 4(2) of the Prevention of Corruption Act 1916, and s 7 of the Public Bodies Corrupt Act 1889. Interestingly no separate definition of "foreign public official" was provided and was left to be interpreted by reference to terms such as "public body", "public office" found in the statutes. This lack of definition of "foreign public official" met with some disapproval from the Working Group in the OECD.[38] The UK authorities strongly felt that a definition was unnecessary due to the ambit of the common law offence of bribery; it covers "any person whatsoever in a public office".[39] Doubts in respect of whether the UK legislation brought foreign judges into its fold were equally allayed by the Law Commission's reference to decided cases – albeit from the late nineteenth and early twentieth century.[40]

The issue of jurisdiction is addressed by s 109 of the Anti-Terrorism Act. By virtue of this section courts in the UK have jurisdiction over offences committed outside the territory of the UK by UK nationals or bodies incorporated under UK law. Exchange of information between prosecuting authorities is enabled by s 19 of the Anti-Terrorism Act.

Under UK law corruption prosecutions are subject to consent from the Attorney General. This again has been criticized. For instance, GRECO (Group of States Against Corruption),[41] in an evaluation report, is of the view that a review by a Law Officer such as the Attorney General could be seen as a form of political

---

[37] Applies to England, Wales and Northern Ireland.

[38] See *Review of Implementation of the Convention and 1997 Recommendation Phase I Bis Report* available http://www.oecd.org.

[39] Common law defines bribery as the receiving or offering of any undue reward by or to any person whatsoever, in a public office, in order to influence his behaviour in office, and to incline him to act contrary to the known rules of honesty and integrity. See *Russell on Crime* (1964) London: Stevens.

[40] See Law Commission Report No 248, *Legislating the Criminal Code: Corruption* (1998).

[41] Formed by the Council of Europe in 1998 – Resolution 98(7) of 4 May 1998. The UK is an active member of GRECO.

control. The OECD has suggested that this be reconsidered even though they were assured by the UK that the Law Officer acts as "impartial guardian of the public interest".

In March 2003, as a result of dissatisfaction expressed by the Law Commission with the complex and obscure state of corruption law, the Home Office published a draft Corruption Bill (hereinafter "Bill").[42] The Government intends to introduce the Bill when parliamentary time permits.[43] The aim of the Bill is to provide a comprehensive statute on corruption. It repeals the common law offence of bribery, the Public Bodies Corrupt Act 1889 and parts of the Prevention of Corruption Act 1906, and s 4(2) of the Prevention of Corruption Act 1916. It also addresses acts of corruption committed outside the UK. It provides a definition of "what acting corruptly actually means"[44] and bases its analysis on a conception of corruption as a lack of loyalty between principal and agent. For instance clause 3 states that "a person commits an offence if he performs his functions as an agent corruptly" and the meaning of agent is provided in clause 11. The Bill creates in its first three clauses three offences – corruptly conferring an advantage, corruptly obtaining an advantage, and performing functions corruptly. The issue of what acting corruptly means is to be gathered from clauses 5, 6 and 7 which delineate the circumstances in which it could occur. Of course, the drawback of such an approach is that the circumstances listed may prove inexhaustive. Clauses 5, 6 and 7 are complexly worded and it is difficult to derive a clear definition of corruption from them. Reliance on the OECD Convention or for that matter the Council of Europe instruments may well have resulted in a better description of corruption. The Bill makes no change in respect of consent from the Attorney General in respect of prosecution. There is however a proposal that the Director of Public Prosecutions with power to delegate to a named specific deputy would be a better alternative.[45]

The Council of Europe followed the OECD with two conventions related to corruption – Criminal Law Convention on Corruption 1999[46] (hereinafter "COE Convention") and the Civil Law Convention on Corruption 1999.[47] The COE Convention is a vast improvement on the OECD Convention both in relation to substantive and procedural matters. At the substantive level, it includes both the private and public sector and covers both active and passive bribery of domestic public officials and foreign public officials.[48] Public official[49] is defined in a manner that does not raise doubts about whether a judge, a mayor or magistrate

---

[42] Cmnd 5777 (2003). Text available at http://www.hmso.gov.uk.

[43] Personal Communication from Home Office, August 2004.

[44] Foreword, Draft Corruption Bill, Cmnd 5777.

[45] See Hansard Debates (HL) 16 July 2004, Col 1554. Available at http://www.parliament.the-stationery-office.co.uk .

[46] Came into force on 1 July 2002.

[47] The text of these conventions are available at http://www.coe.int. The Civil Convention came into force on 1 November 2003.

[48] Articles 2, 3, 5, 7 & 8.

[49] Article 1.

does or does not fall within its scope. It also has specific provisions on the bribery of members of domestic public assemblies,[50] members of foreign public assemblies,[51] officials of international organizations,[52] international parliamentary assemblies,[53] and judges and officials of international courts.[54] It also creates an offence of trading in influence in Article 12. Accordingly, the intentional promising, giving, or offering, directly or indirectly, of any undue advantage to anyone who asserts or confirms that he or she is able to exert an improper influence over the decision making of a public official, or a judge regardless of whether the supposed influence leads to the intended result is an offence. This offence brings within its fold activities of brokers or touts who offer their services for easing of bureaucratic nightmare and influencing decisions. Since tightening of accounting procedures is an important factor in the eradication of corrupt practices, it is addressed in Article 14. Improper accounting practices such as omission of recording a payment, or recording false information where this is done with the intention of concealing or disguising the offences referred to in its Articles 2 to 12 – namely, bribery of public officals, bribery of judges etc is an offence. In respect of sanctions the COE Convention leaves it to the contracting parties to provide effective, proportionate and dissuasive sanctions including penalties and loss of liberty.[55]

As for procedural matters the COE Convention is comprehensive and provides for co-operation with and between national authorities[56] and general principles and measures for international co-operation[57] and mutual assistance.[58] Also measures need to be put in place for facilitating the gathering of evidence and the confiscation of proceeds. The Civil Law Convention on Corruption enables civil remedies – such as compensation – at a national level to those have suffered damage as a result of corruption.[59] Where the damage is a result of the behaviour of a public official then the State has the responsibility for compensating the claimant.

The COE corruption conventions are comprehensive and clear. Unlike the Corruption Bill, the COE Convention gives a clear understanding of bribery. For instance, according to Article 2 the promising, offering or giving by any person, directly or indirectly, of any advantage to a public official, for himself or anyone else, for him to act or refrain from acting in the exercise of his functions constitutes the offence of bribery. The Civil Law Convention on Corruption also provides a definition of corruption in its Article 2 according to which it is "requesting,

[50] Article 4.
[51] Article 6.
[52] Article 9.
[53] Article 10.
[54] Article 11.
[55] Article 19.
[56] Article 21.
[57] Article 25.
[58] Article 26.
[59] Article 1.

offering, giving, or accepting directly or indirectly, a bribery or any other undue advantage or prospect thereof, which distorts the proper performance of any duty or behaviour required of the recipent of the bribe, the undue advantage or the prospect thereof'. Both these definitions have some similarities with the OECD Convention offence of bribery. It is a pity that the Corruption Bill did not use this as a model for drafting its definitions.

As stated earlier, the latest addition to the international instruments on corruption is the UN Convention against Corruption (hereinafter "UN Convention"). There is a great deal of similarity between the COE Convention and the UN Convention in respect of the offences. The offence of bribery is couched in similar terms. For instance, according to Article 15(a) of the UN Convention the offence of bribery of a public official is "the promise, offering or giving, to a public official, directly or indirectly, of an undue advantage, for the official himself or herself, or another person or entity, in order that the official act or refrain from acting in the exercise of his or her official duties" when it is committed intentionally. The UN Convention recognizes both active and passive bribery, and also covers bribery of foreign public official, and of public international organizations.[60] Like the COE Convention, trading in influence is covered by Article 18. Bribery in the private sector is another aspect covered by the UN Convention. A special provision addresses embezzlement, misappropriation or other diversion of property by a public official.[61] As with the COE Convention enforcement is facilitated through various provisions on co-operation between national authorities for obtaining relevant information for investigation purposes,[62] international co-operation,[63] extradition[64] and mutual legal assistance.[65] It also makes room for bilateral/multilateral treaties between contracting states for transfer of sentenced persons.[66] What is unique about the UN Convention is Part II entitled Preventive Measures. This reflects many of the multi-pronged measures the World Bank[67] expects donee states to adopt in its fight against corruption. The UN Convention expects contracting states to take a number of measures – promotion of civil society, proper management of public affairs and public property and putting in place transparent and accountable management systems.[68] States are also required to establish bodies that are reponsible for implementing anti-corruption policies and wide dissemination of knowledge about prevention of corruption.[69] There are also provisions in respect of the public sector's recruitment, retention and promotion of civil servants. The UN Convention expects contracting states to

[60] Article 16.
[61] Article 17.
[62] Article 38.
[63] Article 43.
[64] Article 44.
[65] Article 46.
[66] Article 45.
[67] See Scheme II – Aid Subject to Conditions below.
[68] Article 5.
[69] Article 6.

provide adequate training to individuals in public positions considered vulnerable to corruption, and periodic rotation of these postholders. As stated earlier, one of the causes of corruption, atleast at the petty level, is low wage structure in the civil service.[70] The UN Convention therefore requires that contracting states provide adequate renumeration and adopt equitable pay scales in accordance with the economic development of the Contracting State.[71] Funding of political parties also makes its appearance in the UN Convention and contracting states are expected to take measures to enhance transparency. They are also expected to adopt a code of conduct for public officials that promotes integrity, honesty and responsibility amongst its public officials.[72] Since public procurement contracts are susceptible to corruption, Article 9 deals with various aspects that affect public procurement such as transparency of procedure, disemmination of award criteria, tendering rules and an effective system of appeal. Equally, states are expected to take measures to prevent corruption amongst members of the judiciary.[73] It would not be an exaggeration to say that the UN Convention is an ambitious piece of legislation and if widely adopted[74] will tackle corruption from a number of angles – from introduction of transparent measures and promoting integrity within the public sector, and creation of a comprehensive range of offences to facilitating exchange of information for investigation and enforcement purposes. It is still early days to say whether this instrument will be effective in achieving global or near global harmonization of anti-corruption legislation. Its comprehensivesness may prove to be its downfall since many might see it as too meddlesome a convention to ratify.

The international instruments referred to above cast their net wide and adopt a multi-faceted approach to corruption, from the creation of offences through to exchange of information for the purposes of enforcement. While there is no doubt that widespread regulation of this sort has the potential to play an important role in deterring criminal acts, its effectiveness is debatable at the enforcement stage. The task of enforcement is especially problematic where the crime is a hidden one. The link between enforcement deficit and hidden crimes is amply illustrated by the case of computer crime legislation. With the cheap availability of personal computers and the emergence of the Internet it became obvious that computer technology was going to play a key role in global commerce. It also became obvious in the late 1980s/early 1990s that computer networks were vulnerable to external threats such as computer hacking, computer fraud, which had the potential to cause huge economic losses. The result was the passing of computer misuse legislation worldwide.[75] Regardless of widespread legislation and international co-operation amongst enforcement authorities huge economic losses caused as a result

70 See Causes of Corruption above.

71 Article 7.

72 Article 8. It recommends the International Code of Conduct for Public Official (GA Resolution 51/59, 12 December 1996) as a possible model.

73 Article 11.

74 It requires 30 ratifications to come into force (Article 68).

75 The most recent legislation is an international one – Council of Europe Convention on Cyber-Crime 2001 available at http://www.coe.int.

of computer misuse, such as hacking and theft of computer held information continue. Newspapers continue to report on a frequent, if not on a daily basis about breach of computer systems and resulting losses. Regardless of widespread incidents of computer misuse there are hardly any prosecutions. For instance, in the UK since the passing of computer misuse legislation in 1990 at most there have been only 30-35 prosecutions![76] Part of the problem, in the dearth of computer misuse prosecutions, is related to enforcement – shortage of resources in the form of personnel, and difficulties countered in investigating a crime where electronic trails may not be always that easy to follow.

Corruption is a hidden crime like much of computer crime and investigation can prove a costly exercise. Bribe givers and bribe takers are unlikely to publicise their activities and good information gathering and investigative techniques are essential components of exposing corrupt practices. It requires sophisticated skills and a motivated investigative team that has substantial resources allocated to them. An informal survey of enforcement authorities carried out by this author suggested that the level of resources devoted to investigation of alleged corruption was rather limited with the result that some of the enforcement authorities had a backlog of cases going back some twenty years. This is equally true of cyber crime investigations. In developing countries, it is not unknown for politicians to allege corruption on the part of members of the government for political advantage. Often, in these circumstances valuable skills and resources in short supply are diverted to allay political unease.

Another factor to bear in mind is not all bribes are of a monetary kind that can be caught by money laundering legislation,[77] the removal of bank secrecy and the involvement of banks in reporting large movements of funds across borders. Bribes of a non-monetary kind could involve, for instance, healthcare subsidies and jobs for the family and friends of the bribe taker. Evidence for bribes of this kind may be difficult to obtain, and the accuracy of anecdotal evidence is highly questionable. It is possible that with greater control on monetary movement those involved in the giving and taking of bribes may use non-monetary forms that are not that easily traceable.

Even where sufficient evidence is available for prosecution a corrupt judiciary could easily alter the balance in favour of corrupt practices. Regulation as a tool assumes that judicial and enforcement authorities are objective and not vulnerable to corruption. It is only in this context that regulation has a chance of success.

---

[76] See Carr & Williams, "Crime, Risk and Computers" [2002] *Electronic Communications Law Review* 23.

[77] Apart from tracing illicit funds from illegal trade such as drug trafficking, money laundering legislation was also introduced to address illicit proceeds from corruption. For further on money laundering see Lacey and George, "Crackdown on Money Laundering: A Comparative Analysis of the Feasibility and Effectiveness of Domestic and Multilateral Policy Reforms" [2003] *North Western Journal of International Law and Business* 263.

Scheme II – Aid Subject to Conditions

This scheme envisages international donor agencies such as the World Bank and state agencies such as USAID to play a prominent role in influencing policies within a recipient state to take adequate steps to counter corruption. While institutions such as the World Bank raised corruption concerns when funding projects with donees regularly, it was only in 1996 that it strongly announced its commitment to "fighting the cancer of corruption".[78] For the World Bank corruption is a product of bad governance and the weaknesses inherent in public sector institutions. Reducing these shortcomings in donor countries is seen as a means of reducing corruption. It does this in a number of ways: by strengthening management controls over investment lending;[79] by taking factors such as financial management, auditing and accounting practices, supervision and corruption risks in assessing funding applications; by proactively helping donees to move towards good governance, better public sector management, judicial and legal reform, administrative and civil services reform; and, through seminars and workshops for disseminating various anti-corruption strategies.[80] From the World Bank[81] reports it is obvious that the scheme they have adopted is proving successful,[82] though they realise that "fighting corruption is a long-term problem" and that they have to be realistic in their expectations. A special feature of the World Bank anti-corruption strategy is sanctioning.[83] Where there is evidence of fraud and corruption in bank

---

78 This point was made again in 1999 by Mr Wolfensohn of the World Bank at the Ninth International Anti-Corruption Conference when he said:

> So far as our institution is concerned, there is nothing more important than the issue of corruption . . . At the core of the incidence of poverty is the issue of equity, and at the core of the issue of equity is the issue of corruption. Corruption has to be dealt with by a combination of forces within the country . . . as an institution the best could do was to try and assist in the building of the coalitions and in the forging of that interest in the issue of corruption and inequity, and get it out there.

(Address available at http://www.worldbank.org.)

79 The Bank works with the borrowers from the initial stages of the project through to its completion to ensure that there are adequate management, procurement and financial systems in place. See Annex II *Helping Countries Combat Corruption Progress at the World Bank since 1997* (2000).

80 The World Bank describes its approach as multi-pronged strategy that uses economic policy reform, administrative and civil service reform, improvement of legal and judicial systems, improvement of public expenditure and financial management, and strengthening public oversight and other external accountability mechanisms. See Chapter 3 *Helping Countries Combat Corruption Progress at the World Bank since 1997* (2000).

81 Note that the International Monetary Fund (IMF) also has anti-corruption policies in place. See http://www.imf.org for further information.

82 For instance, they have helped Albania, Guatemala and Morocco with judicial reform; Chad, Zimbabwe with good governance and public sector reform. See Annex III *Helping Countries Combat Corruption Progress at the World Bank since 1997* (2000) for a full list.

83 The Sanctions Committee of the World Bank was set up in 1998 and it has now considered well over 100 cases. Further details are to be found at

financed projects the Bank can declare the ineligibility of the firm involved from taking part in future projects financed by the Bank. As part of this "zero tolerance" approach adopted towards corruption the names of firms found ineligible are widely publicised. The sanctioning is not limited to firms but includes individuals. There are reports of civil actions against Bank employees and outside contractors for fraud and conspiracy.[84]

State donor agencies such as USAID[85] also adopt a view similar to that of the World Bank and have encouraged governments and other bodies such as trade associations in donee countries to adopt better governance and introduce legal reform. For instance, USAID's bureau in Africa worked with the Confederation of Mozambique's Business Associations in its efforts to reduce red tape. Similarly it worked with Ukrainian Oblast Co-ordinating Committee to introduce administrative reforms for streamlining licensing procedures that would reduce the incidence of corruption.[86]

This two pronged approach of imposing conditions on donee States in respect of governance improvement and reform of legal framework along with the blacklisting of companies from taking part in future bids for funded projects is useful towards reducing corruption at both ends – in the giving and in the taking. There are some shortcomings nonetheless. Introducing anti-corruption measures through aid/loan programmes is not near universal since it affects only developing countries and least developed nations who are the recipients of such aid/loans for development projects. However the practice of blacklisting firms involved in World Bank funded projects is likely to have wider impact since it will affect firms from developed nations as well. Regardless, it is debatable whether it will prove effective in real terms since it is always possible for a blacklisted firm to trade under another name. There is nothing to stop them from doing so. Blacklisting of individuals arguably could prove much more effective.

Scheme III – Controlling Corruption through the Media

This scheme perceives various forms of media such as newspapers, television, the radio and the Internet as playing an influential role in not only publicising the ill effects of corruption to the community at large but also in exposing corruption amongst various sectors of society from the public sector to the private sector. There is no denying that the media, has over the years, come to play an important role in the lives of citizens, and can affect various aspects of social activity,

---

http://www.worldbank.org. The sanctions committee consists of both internal and external members.

84 Further details available on http://www.worldbank.org.

85 US Agency for International Development. For more information see http://www.info.usaid.gov.

86 *Promoting Transparency and Accountability: US AID's Anticorruption Experience* (2000) Center for Democracy and Governance, USAID.

including voter turn out.[87] Use of media as a tool to stop corruption makes a number of assumptions in respect of its characteristics and the environment within which it operates. First, it assumes there is an effective media in the given country, that is, the media has an audience that has access to one of the forms of media – such as radio, television, or the Internet. Where the media involves the written word the level of literacy becomes an important issue. While audiences in developed countries may meet the criteria – for example purchasing power, literacy, and computer skills to access the Internet – this is not true of all developing countries. Many developing countries are still in the process of providing basic amenities such as clean water and sufficient food for the majority of their population. Second, it assumes that the press enjoys freedom of information and freedom of expression, and that these freedoms are protected by the State; that the media will have the freedom to investigate, obtain information and publish not only what is inoffensive but also that which shocks, offends or disturbs. Assumptions are also made about journalists and the political ideology of the State, that journalists are honest,[88] operate in a democratic society, and the media is not subject to State control even where it operates in a democratic society, and that there is an adequate legal framework within which journalists can operate securely – for instance, protection of confidential sources, insulation from liability, criminal or otherwise, for publishing sensitive documents if they are in the public interest. Many countries – developing and developed – still have a poor record of human rights and do not believe in freedom of information[89] that are vital if the media is to make any inroads into curbing corruption. While it cannot be denied that the media in ideal (or near ideal) conditions is a powerful tool, seen from a global perspective it perhaps has a limited role to play.

Scheme IV – Non-Governmental Organizations (NGOs), The People's Voice

The recent past has seen an unprecedented growth in the number of NGOs[90] worldwide[91] and their widening influence not only on the citizens but on the conscience of governments and international organizations is noticeable. Their influence on trade and environment policies in recent World Trade Organization's negotiations provides an instance of their emerging role on the global arena.[92] The

---

[87] See Larcinese, "Information Acquisition, Ideology, and Turnout: Theory and Evidence from Britain" (2002) London School of Economics Working Papers; see also Larcinese, "The Instrumental Voter Goes to the News-Agent: Demand for Information, Election Closeness and the Media" (2003) available at http://pareto.uab.es.

[88] For further on professional codes of conduct see http://www.uta.fu/ethicnet.

[89] Interestingly, the UK passed the Freedom of Information Act as recently as 2000. It comes into force in 2005. The text of this Act is available on http://www.hmso.gov.uk

[90] NGOs are normally private, non-profit making organizations. They usually promote causes such as the plight of the poor, the underprivileged, community development, environmental protection, and human rights.

[91] According to recent estimates there are more than 2 million NGOs around the world.

[92] See Bhagwati, *In Defense of Globalization* (2004). For more information on WTO see http://www.wto.org.

NGOs are also emerging as an important tool in publicising corruption and mobilising public opinion against corrupt public officials. Recent successes in some of the Asian countries highlight the importance of NGOs as a useful anti-corruption strategy. For instance, a network of NGOs in Thailand was instrumental in exposing irregularities in public procurement of medical supplies and for successfully canvassing for the removal of certain key public officials.[93] Similarly there are reports from countries such as Korea[94] and the Philippines[95] where NGOs played an influential role in exposing corrupt practices resulting in convictions.[96]

Alongside these activities, the NGOs are also involved in raising public awareness of corruption and gathering public concerns that will contribute to shaping policies. While all these efforts are commendable it must be pointed out that all these activities are possible only where certain freedoms and recognitions are allowed, such as freedom to establish a NGO, freedom to canvass opinion, freedom of information and freedom of expression. That is, the success of NGO activity is subject to the political, government and legal constraints of a state. From a cynical perspective it is questionable whether all NGOs are purely motivated by concerns for the public at large. It is likely that many are motivated by their moral and political agenda, and particular ideologies. Since they are not subject to regulation and lack transparency the credentials of many are open to doubt and scepticism. As Bhagwati writes "[I]f transparency is not routinely practiced by NGOs, it would be nothing short of a miracle if NGOs did not produce their own counterparts of the occasional corruption of some multinationals such as Enron".[97] Regardless of these lurking dangers the NGOs (where it is possible for them to carry on their activity) have a useful role in highlighting the ill effects of corruption and alerting the population to ways and means of combating it, and is a useful adjunct to anti-corruption legislation.

Towards Improving the Current Regime

It is noteworthy that the above schemes have not sought to seriously engage the business sector in the anticorruption drive. After all, their participation would

---

93 See Treerat, "Controlling Corruption in Thailand: Transforming the Problems and Paradoxes" in Bhargava and Bologaita, *Challenging Corruption in Asia* (2004).

94 See Park, "State Capture and Good Governance: The Challenge of the Republic of Korea's Experience" in Bhargava and Bologaita, *Challenging Corruption in Asia* (2004).

95 See Gonzalez and Mendoza, "Anticorruption Initiative in the Philippines" in Bhargava and Bologaita, *Challenging Corruption in Asia* (2004). See also *Public Sector Corruption: An International Survey of Prevention Measures* (1999).

96 Interestingly, the UN Convention in Article 13 requires contracting states to take appropriate measures to promote the active participation of individuals and groups (such as community based organizations and NGOs) outside the public sector in the prevention of corruption. Article 13 also requires an undertaking from contracting states to promote non-tolerance of corruption in public education programmes, including university curricula.

97 *In Defense of Globalization* at p 44.

result in a massive reduction in corruption levels globally. How can they be brought within the equation? What can a business do to curb corrupt practices not only on its part but also on the part of its competitors? Before putting forward suggestions mention needs to be made of the UN Convention. In its Article 12, contracting states are required to prevent corruption in the private sector and suggests, amongst others,[98] development of standards in the private sector as a means of achieving this. However sufficient guidelines are not provided on how this could be achieved. Even if they were, it is debatable whether these would have achieved the intended objective since it would require the willing participation of the private sector. Indeed greater strides could be made towards achieving the goal of lessening corruption were the private sector to regulate their behaviour, since overarching regulation that includes mandatory codes of conduct within its purview has the danger of introducing cumbersome bureaucracy which can prove time consuming and expensive.

With the intention of finding out whether actors in the private sector would be willing to take anti-corruption measures through self-regulation, an informal semi-structured[99] survey of a small number of private firms (conducted by this author) revealed unanimous preference for self-regulation through codes of conduct (business codes). Codes of conduct can be drawn up in a number of ways. A company can draft its own code of conduct which it intends to follow. Another possibility is a collective code of conduct – that is, where a trade association drafts a code of conduct for use by its members. Codes of conduct can vary in content from a simple mission statement to well articulated standards and enforcement mechanisms.[100]

Participants in the survey acknowledged the serious economic detriment caused by national and international corruption, and the pivotal role of the business sector in curbing it. They preferred collective codes of conduct to introduction of codes of conduct through regulation of the kind suggested by the UN Convention since state intervention was seen as meddlesome. It was also justified in terms of receptiveness. Codes of conduct drafted by trade associations were likely to be seen as reflecting the specificities of a particular industry and hence likely to be taken seriously with a high level of commitment, essential for its credibility.

Collective codes of conduct were preferred to individual codes for a number of reasons including the desire for uniform practices across the industry. It was also strongly felt that the adoption of an industry/business standard drafted by their trade/business association would protect the reputation of those participating within the scheme and would therefore boost the integrity of the members of the association alongside boosting the confidence not only of organizations dealing with the members but also of the public at large. In many cases, boosting the confidence of the greater public was seen as an essential aspect due to their

---

98 These include accounting practices, auditing control, and restrictions on employment of retired public officials in the private sector.

99 The survey was semi-structured in order reach as much data as possible.

100 For further on code of conduct see http://www.onlinethics.org, http://www.codesofconduct.org. See also Mannheim, *Corporate Conduct Unbecoming* (2000).

recognition of the greater role of public participation in influencing consumer trends. Boost in consumer demand of "environmentally friendly" products even in developing countries such as India was cited as an instance.

There is however a major problem with codes of conduct. A code of conduct to be effective requires both intra-industry trust and extra-industry trust – that is trust amongst members of the association that each will follow the adopted code and trust on the part of the wider public, the state and other organisations that the members of the association can be trusted to follow their code of conduct. Trust[101] is a complex notion and plays an integral part in many aspects of human life – from familial relationships, social relationships, and within communities to the rebuilding of broken communities as a result of incidents such as civil strife and wars.[102] Without trust, relationships, at best, if possible, are tenuous. So what minimal conditions need to be satisfied? At a minimalist level, Hardin's analysis of trust as encapsulated interest provides the answer. According to this analysis, trust involves the encapsulation of the interests of the truster by the trusted. Converting this to the practical how does this apply to the business sector, a sector that makes no secret about its profit motivation. Why should a firm "X" agree to follow a particular code of conduct that might well affect its competitive edge and eventually its level of profits? Why should X play by the agreed rules? Why should X wish to be seen as following the codes in respect of curbing corrupt practices by other firms? Equally, why should X concern itself with the interests of the public at large? What is the incentive? The answer lies within the very motives that guide businesses – profit. It would be profitable for X to assure other firms that it is taking their interests – access to a level playing field - into account and that it itself is not engaging in corrupt practices. In so doing, X tries to ensure that none of its competitors gain a competitive advantage by engaging in corrupt activities. The trust relationship that is created between the firms is one of utility. As for taking the interests (economic well-being) of the public at large, the incentive is yet again of an economic nature. To do so, would enhance X's reputation and in a world where consumer trends are driven by global ethical concerns firms that follow a code of conduct that involve ethical standards (such as specific anti-corruption strategies in the form of greater transparency, detailed accounting practices, protection of whistleblowers) are likely to see a higher turnover of their goods which in the longer term will yield better profits. Such an analysis can be charged with being cynical about the business sector; however to say that a business is not motivated by profit concerns is unthinkable in a

---

[101] Trust is closely related to notions such as friendship, compassion and integrity – aspects that have been analysed in philosophical literature of both ancient and modern times, and in both Eastern and Western traditions. The most well known analysis of the notion of friendship is that of Aristotle in *Nicomachean Ethics*. According to Aristotle friendship based on utility is not friendship.

[102] See Lenard, "Rebuilding Broken Societies: Which Model of Trust should we Use?" available at http://www.cda-cdai.ca. See also Ullman-Margalit, "Trust, Distrust, and In Between" in Hardin (Ed) *Distrust* (2002).

capitalistic context. After all they have to take into account the interests of shareholders and others who have advanced capital.

While codes of conduct have the potential of achieving the desired result in curbing corrupt practices that the business sector engage in, nevertheless there are some that will inevitably break the agreed code. Further, a mere statement by the trade association and its members will be ineffective in assuring the public and the state authorities that the codes of conduct are being adhered to. So a system of checks needs to be introduced. A system that could prove useful is an independent body consisting of representatives from the business sector, professional bodies (such as accountancy, law, engineering) and civil society (NGOs, community associations, and lay members) with authority to carry out surveys/audit of firms randomly and periodically. Where there is evidence of corrupt practices the matter could be referred to state authorities. And where there are shortcomings in some of the measures taken the trade association could take on a more active role in ensuring that the member makes the required rectifications to its practices. The advantage of adopting a model along these lines for monitoring purposes is that it boosts the confidence of the public at large in the business sector (which if anything can only prove profitable for the business sector), and also assures that business that it has the freedom to develop and flourish in a regulation free environment and interference from the state.

Of course, many businesses across the world are not part of trade associations[103] for the simple reason there are no associations pertaining to that particular trade, or they do not have the necessary knowledge and funds to form trade associations. This is especially true of developing countries. This is an area where international organizations such as the World Bank, IMF and donor agencies can provide help in various ways: expertise, education and funds.

Conclusion

This chapter, after due consideration of the current regime suggests that willing participation of the business sector (who play a prominent role in contributing to the incidence of corruption world wide) through self-regulation is essential for the fight against corruption. Self-regulation in the form of codes of conduct that are subject to regular monitoring by an independent body is aimed at setting minimum standards of behaviour on the part of the business sector and to ensure that these standards are adhered to. Participation of the business sector in this way is by no means intended to replace the current regime consisting of legislation, use of the media and NGOs for spreading the anti-corruption message, and detecting/ publicising instances of corruption, and the involvement of aid agencies in setting up minimum anti-corruption measures. Instead it should be actively included and promoted as another important anti-corruption strategy in the current fight against corruption. To succeed, corruption must be fought at all levels and on all fronts.

[103] See http://www.marketingsource.com for information on forming a trade association.

Chapter 10

Particularly Sensitive Sea Areas and International Navigation Rights: Trends, Controversies and Emerging Issues

Aldo Chircop*

Introduction

Since the adoption of the International Convention for the Prevention of Pollution from Ships in 1973 (as amended in1978; MARPOL 73/78)[1] and the United Nations Convention on the Law of the Sea in 1982 (LOS Convention),[2] there have emerged two particular regulatory ocean zoning practices aimed at the protection of the marine environment from operational vessel-source pollution and sanctioned through the International Maritime Organization (IMO). The first was commenced in 1973 and concerns the designation of entire marine regions, in the form of regional seas, as "special areas" which call for a higher level of protection from specific types of vessel-source pollution than the norm. The second was initiated in 1991 and concerns a new type of ocean zoning, practised by individual or groups of states, and aimed at protecting particularly sensitive coastal and marine environmental areas. This is the so-called particularly sensitive sea area (PSSA), and is the focus of this chapter.

---

* The author is grateful to Jean-Claude Sainlos, Director of the Marine Environment Division at the International Maritime Organization, John Liljedahl, lecturer at the World Maritime University and Cecilia Denne, librarian at the World Maritime University, for assistance with specific queries.

1 *International Convention for the Prevention of Pollution from Ships, 1973, as modified by the Protocol of 1978 relating thereto*, London, 17 February 1978, 1340 UNTS 62-265 (1983). The convention was further amended by the *Protocol of 1997 to amend the International Convention for the Prevention of Pollution from Ships, 1973, as modified by the Protocol of 1978 relating thereto*, London, 26 September 1997, which added Annex VI. The latter is not yet in force. There have been numerous amendments to the annexes. For a consolidated version of MARPOL 73/78 and annexes, see IMO, *MARPOL 73/78 Consolidated Edition, 2002* (IMO, 2002).

2 Adopted in Montego Bay, 10 December 1982, in *The Law of the Sea: Official Text of the United Nations Convention on the Law of the Sea* (United Nations, 1983).

Between 1990-2000, only Australia and Cuba submitted proposals for PSSA designation and which, after technical consideration, were designated by the IMO and are now operational.[3] Since 2002, there has been a significant surge of new PSSA proposals to the IMO, and it is now clear that this new zoning practice is spreading to many more marine regions. This surge seems to have been triggered in part by widely-publicised oil pollution casualties and perceptions of the safety, environmental, social and economic threats posed by single-hull tankers, ageing or substandard shipping, and generally commercial navigation in coastal waters and the exclusive economic zone (EEZ) and vulnerable ecosystems within them. Submissions of proposals for new PSSAs since 2003, in particular for Western European waters and the Baltic Sea, have sparked a contentious debate on the future directions of PSSA designation. The concerns expressed go beyond the technical concerns of combating vessel-source pollution, which in itself is still a much smaller marine pollution source than land-based activities. At issue is the meaningfulness of PSSA designation and concerns with consistency with pertinent provisions in the LOS Convention. The outcome of the debate and the manner through which IMO member states settle their differences could have far-reaching implications on marine environmental protection measures and international navigation rights in zones of national jurisdiction.

Over the last three decades, the protection of the marine environment from vessel-source pollution has evolved into a regime with four distinct levels of protection. At a global level there is first a general global (and regional) obligation for coastal and maritime (that is, flag) states to protect the marine environment from vessel-source pollution, which notionally can be considered as "Level 1" protection. Because of particular considerations that justify a higher protection level for certain large marine regions from vessel-source pollution, there is the possibility of "Level 2" protection, which in this chapter is proposed as the regime for special areas under MARPOL 73/78 and the IMO's Special Area Guidelines. Where there is concern that the existing legal and management regime is insufficient to meet the protection needs of very sensitive marine areas from international shipping, there is the possibility of "Level 3" under LOS Convention Article 211(6) and the IMO's PSSA Guidelines. Although not the subject of this paper, it should be borne in mind that in exceptional and *ad hoc* situations, there is the possibility of "Level 4" protection where coastal states, motivated by serious concerns for self-protection, are empowered to intervene in relation to shipping casualties "to prevent, mitigate or eliminate grave and imminent danger to their coastline or related interests from pollution" or the threat thereof under the *International Convention relating to Intervention on the High Seas in Cases of Oil Pollution Casualties*, 1969,[4] and the LOS Convention.[5]

---

[3] Identification of the Great Barrier Reef Region as a Particularly Sensitive Area, IMO/MEPC.44(30), 16 November 1990, which was extended to include the Torres Strait; Report of the Marine Environment Protection Committee on its Forty-Ninth Session, IMO/MEPC 49/22, 8 August 2003; Identification of the Archipelago of Sabana-Camaguey as a Particularly Sensitive Sea Area, IMO/MEPC.74(40), 25 September 1997.

[4] 970 UNTS 211-283 (1975), art 1.

In some regions there is additional protection initiated in regional, rather than global fora, which should be mentioned, although not discussed in this chapter. Regional protection efforts do not, and cannot, supplant global initiatives. Rather, regional initiatives may cut across the first three protection levels, thus serving to regionalize global obligations, reinforce special regional sea protection and occasionally focus on particular areas in those seas. There are also marine protected areas (MPAs), which may be national or transboundary, but which are not considered here, except to the extent that they relate to international regulatory efforts on vessel-source pollution. National MPA protection measures may also draw on all three levels of protection.

Thus, this chapter will address the first three protection levels, concentrating on PSSA matters, and will identify and analyse trends, controversies and issues in the protection of the marine environment from the risk of vessel-source pollution.

Level 1: Duty to Protect the Marine Environment from Vessel-Source Pollution

LOS Convention parties have a fundamental legal obligation to protect and preserve the marine environment.[6] This includes a duty to harmonize their policies and to take individual or collective measures to prevent, reduce and control pollution.[7] Specifically in relation to vessel-source pollution, this duty translates into a further duty to take measures to minimize both operational and accidental pollution.[8] The taking of such measures must not unjustifiably interfere with the exercise of legitimate rights by other state parties.[9] Such measures "include those necessary to protect and preserve rare or fragile ecosystems as well as the habitat of depleted, threatened or endangered species and other forms of marine life".[10] Thus, the basic principle is that while coastal states are empowered, and indeed have the duty to take protective measures against vessel-source pollution, they must do so in a manner that does not interfere unjustifiably with international navigation rights. In general, if there is to be interference, it must be in accordance

---

5 LOS Convention, *loc cit* fn 2, art 221.

6 LOS Convention, *ibid*, art 192. The performance of this obligation is further developed through a multilateral obligation to "co-operate on a global basis and, as appropriate, on a regional basis, directly or through competent international organizations, in formulating and elaborating international rules, standards and recommended practices and procedures". *Ibid* art 197.

7 *Ibid* art 194(1).

8 Specifically, "pollution from vessels, in particular measures for preventing accidents and dealing with emergencies, ensuring the safety of operations at sea, preventing intentional and unintentional discharges, and regulating the design, construction, equipment, operation and manning of vessels". *Ibid*, art 194(3)(b).

9 *Ibid* art 194(4).

10 *Ibid* art 194(5).

with international rules and standards. This applies to the territorial sea,[11] international straits[12] and EEZ.[13] In fact, the protective action to be taken must be in accordance with international rules and standards adopted through the IMO and may include routeing schemes to minimize threats to local interests.[14] Moreover, the process of adoption of a measure that interferes with international navigation requires not only justification of the measure, but also approval through the IMO. Because of wide global membership in the IMO, the international community is able to screen such measures. In providing the framework for protective action, the LOS Convention managed to craft a delicate balance between coastal state interests and international navigation rights. Although MARPOL 73/78 was adopted prior to the LOS Convention, and amended several times since then, that balance has been maintained. Thus at Level 1, whereas the LOS Convention provides the general framework, MARPOL 73/78 provides the substance and regulatory teeth for the prevention of pollution from ships through a standard-setting approach and a compliance system.

Level 2: Protection Through Marpol 73/78 Special Areas

Special areas under MARPOL 73/78 precede the arrival of PSSAs. The precursor of MARPOL 73/78, the *International Convention for the Prevention of Pollution of the Sea by Oil*, 1954 (OILPOL), introduced no-discharge zones for oily wastes.[15] As part of the general rules in the annexes, MARPOL 73/78 continued and further strengthened the restrictions on discharges within 50 nautical miles of the coast as Level 2 protection. Special areas employ those and additional restrictions over a larger area. Like PSSAs, they are special regulatory zones adopted under the

---

[11] "Coastal States may, in the exercise of their sovereignty within their territorial sea, adopt laws and regulations for the prevention, reduction and control of marine pollution from foreign vessels, including vessels exercising the right of innocent passage. Such laws and regulations shall, in accordance with Part 11, section 3, not hamper innocent passage of foreign vessels." *Ibid* art 211(4); in relation to this provision see also art 24. Art 21 concerns, *inter alia*, the coastal state's legislative jurisdiction for safety of navigation and marine environment protection in the territorial sea. Art 221(2) provides that "[Such] laws and regulations shall not apply to the design, construction, manning or equipment of foreign ships unless they are giving effect to generally accepted international rules and standards". See also art 22 in which the coastal state may designate or prescribe sealanes and traffic separation schemes for ships exercising innocent passage in the territorial sea. In doing so, it is required to take into account IMO recommendations.

[12] *Ibid* arts 41 and 42.

[13] *Ibid* art 211(5). See also art 56(1)(b)(iii) concerning the allocation of marine environmental jurisdiction to the coastal state and art 58 on the rights and duties of other states in the EEZ.

[14] *Ibid* art 211(1).

[15] *International Convention for the Prevention of Pollution of the Sea by Oil*, 12 May 1954, 327 UNTS 3. This instrument was amended in 1962, 1969 and 1971, and is largely superseded by MARPOL 73/78.

auspices of the IMO and aimed at addressing vessel-source pollution concerns in certain marine regions. A special area is:

> . . . a sea area where for recognized technical reasons in relation to its oceanographical and ecological conditions and to the particular character of its traffic, the adoption of special mandatory methods for the prevention of sea pollution by oil, noxious liquid substances, or garbage, as applicable, is required.[16]

MARPOL 73/78 provides a procedure for the designation of certain marine areas susceptible to particular kinds of vessel-source pollution as special areas under the convention's annexes. To facilitate this process of designation, the IMO has developed the Special Area Guidelines for submissions of special area proposals under MARPOL 73/78.[17] While designed to assist, the intention is to avoid a proliferation of such areas.[18] By the time the guidelines were adopted, most of the special areas were already designated; the Guidelines have thus been applied only to Antarctic (Annexes I, II and V), North-West European Waters (Annex I) and Wider Caribbean (Annex V) areas.

There is no specific limit to the size of a special area, but the designations to date relate to marine regions, that is, entire seas and/or EEZs because of their oceanographic, ecological and vessel traffic conditions. These criteria have to be satisfied. On oceanographic matters, proponent states have to show that the physical conditions are such that they "may cause the concentration of harmful substances in the waters or sediments of the area".[19] These could include, for example, restricted hydrology or extreme ice conditions. In the case of the Baltic, it takes 30 years to re-cycle the waters in that region. Ecological criteria include threats to marine species, protection of high biological productivity areas, nurseries and habitats, migratory routes for marine avifauna and mammals, and protection of rare or fragile coastal and marine ecosystems.[20] As for vessel traffic characteristics:

> The sea area is used by ships to an extent that the discharge of harmful substances by ships when operating in accordance with the requirements of MARPOL 73/78 for areas other than special areas would be unacceptable in the light of the existing oceanographic and ecological conditions in the area.[21]

---

[16] Guidelines for the Designation of Special Areas under MARPOL 73/78 and Guidelines for the Identification and Designation of Particularly Sensitive Sea Areas, IMO Doc A 22/Res 927, 15 January 2002. The guidelines for special areas and PSSAs are separate annexes (I and II respectively) adopted in the same IMO Assembly Resolution A 927(22), 29 November 2001. Hereafter, the short reference is to the Special Area Guidelines and PSSA Guidelines. The Special Area Guidelines were formulated for Annexes I, II and V, and do not concern emission control areas in VI.

[17] Special Area Guidelines, *ibid.*

[18] IMO/MEPC 30/19/1, 17 August 1990, 24.

[19] Special Area Guidelines, *loc cit* fn 16, para 2.4.

[20] *Ibid* para 2.5.

[21] *Ibid* para 2.6.

In addition to these three criteria, additional arguments that may strengthen a special area proposal are threats to amenities (for example, coastal values), threats by other sources of marine pollution and existing management regime.[22] These arguments are important because consideration would be given to cumulative impact; at the same time, other measures planned or taken to combat these other pollution sources would strengthen a proposal. Further, a special area proposal may need to be coordinated with other regional management initiatives (such as a UNEP Regional Seas Programme applicable in the area) and national integrated coastal and ocean management initiatives. The proposal requirements are detailed and rigorous, and in addition to placing the burden of proof as to why a marine area should be designated a special area on the proponent(s), there is the further onus to provide information on the availability of reception facilities.[23] As will be seen below, this is a critical requirement.

Differently from the designation of a PSSA, the designation of a special area actually entails an amendment of the parent convention. To date, the seas or marine areas that have been so designated in the relevant MARPOL 73/78 annexes are listed in Table 10.1.

Table 10.1: MARPOL 73/78 Special Areas and Atmospheric Emission Control Area

Annex I: Oil pollution	**Annex II : Noxious liquid substances**	**Annex V: Garbage**	**Annex VI: Atmospheric emission control area (SOx)**
- Mediterranean Sea - Baltic Sea - Black Sea - Red Sea - Gulfs area - Gulf of Aden - Antarctic area (south of 60 degrees latitude) (Antarctic Treaty Area) - North-West European Waters (comprising the North Sea, Irish Sea, Celtic Sea, English Channel and part of the North-East Atlantic west of Ireland)	- Baltic Sea - Black Sea - Antarctic area (Antarctic Treaty Area)	- Mediterranean Sea - Baltic Sea - Black Sea - Red Sea - Gulfs area - Antarctic area (Antarctic Treaty Area) - North Sea (including the Skagerrak and English Channel) - Wider Caribbean	- Baltic Sea - North-West European Waters

22 *Ibid* paras 2.7, 2.8 and 2.10.

23 *Ibid* Part 3.

Special areas are designated in response to specific types of operational vessel-source pollution. While operating at sea ships may generate different types of waste, the discharge of which is mostly banned. When and where a controlled discharge is permitted, the discharge tends to be at a regulated low level. With very few exceptions,[24] in special areas the discharge level is at or close to zero release. The designation occurs under a specific annex, which in turn focuses on a particular type of discharge. To date, special areas proper have been designated under Annex I, which deals with oily discharges, Annex II concerning noxious liquid substances, and Annex V on garbage. Although no special areas have been designated under Annex IV on sewage, the term "from the nearest land" for discharge purposes was re-defined in the case of the coast of north-eastern Australia, in relation to the Great Barrier Reef, to enable authorized releases further out at sea than would otherwise be the case.[25] Identical terms are also to be found in Annexes I, IV and V.[26] In the case of Annex VI concerning atmospheric emissions, SOx emission control areas, which technically are not special areas, have been designated.

There are a number of difficulties that have been faced with special areas and which bear on their effectiveness. Annexes III-V are optional.[27] MARPOL 73/78 annexes did not enter into force for a long period after adoption. Thus, despite the adoption of Annexes I-V in 1973 (and re-incorporation into the 1978 Protocol), Annex I came into force in 1983, Annex II in 1987, Annex III in 1992, Annex IV in 2003 and Annex V in 1988. Annex VI, which was introduced into MARPOL 73/78 as a result of an amendment in 1997, is not yet in force.[28] Another major concern is the extent to which the conditions for special area designation in the regions concerned are being abided by all affected states. Coastal states geographically located in special areas have an obligation to provide adequate reception facilities for oily residues and mixtures,[29] noxious liquid substances,[30] sewage[31] and garbage[32] and to inform the IMO accordingly. Although today there

[24] MARPOL 73/78, *loc cit* fn 1, Annex 1, reg 11, concerning discharges in cases of *force majeure*, as a result of damage to ship or equipment and where there is approval of a national maritime administration to combat a pollution incident.

[25] MARPOL 73/78, *ibid* Annex IV: Regulations for the Prevention of Pollution by Sewage, reg 1(5).

[26] The adjusted definition of "nearest land" in the case of Australia had been introduced earlier in an amendment to OILPOL, *loc cit* fn 15, art 1, by IMCO (now IMO) Assembly Resolution A 232 (VII), 12 October 1971.

[27] MARPOL 73/78 (convention text), *loc cit* fn 1, art 14.

[28] For Annex VI to come into force, the 1997 Protocol needs to come into force. This will occur 12 months after 15 or more MARPOL 73/78 state parties representing 50% of the world gross tonnage become parties to the protocol. 1997 Protocol, *loc cit* fn 1, art 6. The anticipated date of entry into force is 19 May 2005.

[29] MARPOL 73/78, Annex I, *loc cit* fn 1, regs 10(7)(8) and 12.

[30] MARPOL 73/78, *ibid* Annex II, reg 7.

[31] MARPOL 73/78, *ibid* Annex IV, reg 10. It is appropriate to note that despite the late entry into force of this annex, many state parties had already implemented its provisions into national law (for example, Denmark and Canada).

are 128 state parties to MARPOL 73/78,[33] by 2003 only 57 of these had actually communicated information on reception facilities for oily residues and mixtures to the IMO, and many of the submitted reports did not demonstrate a capability to accept all the expected oil wastes.[34] This is important because special areas under the annexes come into force after the necessary reception facilities are established and this information is communicated to the IMO; it appears that not all designated special areas are actually in force.[35] The special area practice to date appears to be mixed and its effectiveness remains to be assessed.

Level 3: LOS Convention Article 211(6) and PSSAs

Level 3 protection is perhaps the most complex for two major reasons. First, there are significant differences in the international maritime community on what LOS Convention Article 211(6) permits. Second, the relationship between Article 211(6) and the IMO's PSSA Guidelines is not sufficiently clear.

LOS Convention Article 211(6): special mandatory measures

Article 211(6) of the LOS Convention provides the following:

> (a) Where the international rules and standards referred to in paragraph 1 are inadequate to meet special circumstances and coastal States have reasonable grounds for believing

---

32 MARPOL 73/78, *ibid* Annex V, reg 5(4), (5).

33 IMO, Summary of Status of Conventions (31 July 2004), online: http://www.imo.org/Conventions/mainframe.asp?topic_id=247 (date accessed: 3 September 2004).

34 The wastes at issue are dirty ballast water, tank-washing slops, oily mixtures containing chemicals, scale and sludge from tank cleaning, oily bilge water and sludge from fuel oil purifier. See Facilities in Ports for the Reception of Oily Wastes from Ships, IMO/MEPC 3/Circ 4, 18 November 2003. At its 12th Session in March 2004, the IMO Sub-Committee on Flag State Implementation has embarked on an initiative to address the problem of low level reporting by disseminating a questionnaire. See IMO/MEPC/Circ 417, 7 July 2004. See also IMO, *Comprehensive Manual on Port Reception Facilities*, 2nd ed (1999).

35 For example in relation to Annex I, see reg 10(7)(a)(i) and (iii). Also, "The requirements of a special area designation can only become effective when adequate reception facilities are provided for ships in accordance with the provisions of MARPOL 73/78". Special Area Guidelines, *loc cit* fn 16, para 2.7. As of 2002, the following special areas entered into force: Annex I – Mediterranean, Baltic and Black Sea areas on 2 October 1983, Antarctic on 17 March 1992 and North-West European Waters on 1 August 1999; Annex II - Baltic on 6 April 1987 and Antarctic on 1 July 1994; Annex V – Baltic on 1 October 1989, North Sea on 18 February 1991, Antarctic on 17 March 1992 and Wider Caribbean on 4 April 1993. IMO, *MARPOL 73/78 Consolidated Edition*, *loc cit* fn 1, 455-457; and Status of Multilateral Conventions and Instruments in respect of Which the IMO or its Secretary-General Performs Depositary or other Functions, as at 31 December 2002, IMO/J/8387 (hereafter Status of Multilateral Conventions). Thus, the following special areas are not in effect: Annex 1 – Red Sea, "Gulfs" and Gulf of Aden; Annex II – Black Sea; Annex V – Mediterranean, Black Sea, Red Sea, "Gulfs" and Wider Caribbean.

that a particular, clearly defined area of their respective exclusive economic zones is an area where the adoption of special mandatory measures for the prevention of pollution from vessels is required for recognized technical reasons in relation to its oceanographical and ecological conditions, as well as its utilization or the protection of its resources and the particular character of its traffic, the coastal States, after appropriate consultations through the competent international organization with any other States concerned, may, for that area, direct a communication to that organization, submitting scientific and technical evidence in support and information on necessary reception facilities. Within 12 months after receiving such a communication, the organization shall determine whether the conditions in that area correspond to the requirements set out above. If the organization so determines, the coastal States may, for that area, adopt laws and regulations for the prevention, reduction and control of pollution from vessels implementing such international rules and standards or navigational practices as are made applicable, through the organization, for special areas. These laws and regulations shall not become applicable to foreign vessels until 15 months after the submission of the communication to the organization.

(b) The coastal States shall publish the limits of any such particular, clearly defined area.

(c) If the coastal States intend to adopt additional laws and regulations for the same area for the prevention, reduction and control of pollution from vessels, they shall, when submitting the aforesaid communication, at the same time notify the organization thereof. Such additional laws and regulations may relate to discharges or navigational practices but shall not require foreign vessels to observe design, construction, manning or equipment standards other than generally accepted international rules and standards; they shall become applicable to foreign vessels 15 months after the submission of the communication to the organization, provided that the organization agrees within 12 months after the submission of the communication.

The first observation to be made is that this provision does not provide for the designation of special areas or PSSAs *per se*, but rather the adoption of special mandatory measures in special circumstances. Second, the reference to "special area" in this provision is distinct from MARPOL 73/78 special areas.[36] It has been suggested that Article 211(6) was modelled on the MARPOL 73/78 special area provisions in the Annexes, although this view also holds that the LOS provision provides for a much wider application than the MARPOL 73/78 equivalents.[37]

The idea for special protection, that is, referring to particular marine areas that deserve a higher level of protection from shipping activities, precedes both the LOS Convention and MARPOL 73/78. OILPOL no-discharge zones have already been referred to. At least one submission in 1972 to the Seabed Committee preparing the agenda for the Third United Nations Conference on the Law of the Sea (UNCLOS III) set to start in 1973, referred to the principle of "special authority of the coastal state in areas adjacent to its territorial waters" and,

---

36 Nordquist, (Ed), *United Nations Convention on the Law of the Sea 1982: A Commentary*, Vol 4 (Rosenne and Yankov, Vol Eds) (1991) (hereafter Rosenne and Yankov), 181; Molenaar, *Coastal State Jurisdiction over Vessel-Source Pollution* (1998), 403.

37 Molenaar, *ibid* at p 403.

significantly, "a specific and limited exercise of residual authority by the coastal state to ensure compliance with internationally agreed standards or with special local standards".[38] This was a Canadian contribution and was probably influenced by the unilateral initiative for special protection of the Arctic through the revolutionary (at the time) *Arctic Waters Pollution Prevention Act* in 1970.[39] Some of these ideas made it into the International Conference on Marine Pollution that produced the original MARPOL convention in 1973.

The diplomatic history of UNCLOS III sheds useful light on the origins and intentions of this provision, for which many proposals were submitted over several conference sessions. In 1974, Kenya advanced a proposal for "appropriate standards for special situations".[40] Again that year, in the same conference, a proposal by ten states referred to special circumstances for which coastal states could adopt laws and regulations in additional to or more stringent than international rules and standards, including stricter standards justified by exceptional hazards and special environmental vulnerability.[41] A "softer" text and one that encapsulated some of the key concepts to eventually appear in this provision (that is, special area, recognized technical justification, special mandatory measures, application to the IMO) was advanced in 1975 by nine states.[42] In 1975 the Informal Single Negotiating Text captured most of these ideas, but placed as a premise the inexistence or inadequacy of international rules and standards to deal with special circumstances, as well as the coastal state's reasonable beliefs concerning needed measures. The zone would be "a particular area" of the EEZ.[43] By and large, and with adjusted text, the same ideas were reproduced in the Revised Single Negotiating Text in 1976. In this text, the terms "special" and "particular" appear more than once in the same provision. This would also carry through the Informal Composite Negotiating Text (ICNT) in 1977, which further developed and refined the text, and clearly setting out that the determination of special areas belonged to the IMO, not to the proponent state, and only after such a determination could the coastal state proceed with domestic action.[44] This was necessary if coastal state measures were to be legislated, as well as enforced against international navigation. In effect, the coastal state would be enforcing international rules and standards, as implemented. As a result of the "Amoco Cadiz" disaster in 1978, France introduce more proposals to emphasize

[38] Rosenne and Yankov, *op cit* fn 36 at pp 183-184.

[39] RS 1985, c A-12. This initiative eventually influenced the adoption of LOS Convention art 234 on the protection of ice-covered areas. On the Canadian view of the relationship of this provision to MARPOL 73/78, and reactions from the United States and several European states, see Status of Multilateral Conventions, *loc cit* fn 35, 79.

[40] Rosenne and Yankov, *op cit* fn 36 at p 186.

[41] Canada, Fiji, Ghana, Guyana, Iceland, India, Iran, New Zealand, Philippines and Spain. *Ibid* at pp 186-187.

[42] Belgium, Bulgaria, Denmark, German Democratic Republic, Federal Republic of Germany, Greece, Netherlands, Poland and the United Kingdom. *Ibid* at p 187.

[43] *Ibid* at p 189.

[44] *Ibid* at pp 192-193.

preventive measures, such as routeing systems and notification of coastal states.[45] Following much debate, a compromise proposal was submitted by Tanzania and included in the second revision of the ICNT, and eventually in the LOS Convention.[46]

It was clear from the negotiations of Article 211(6) that what was being sought was the possibility of stricter measures than the norm, and with reference to "a particular, clearly defined area" of the EEZ. Special mandatory measures meant that international standards for special areas would be raised or made more stringent. There does not appear to be anything that suggests the inclusion of an entire EEZ, hence the distinction that was maintained with special areas in MARPOL 73/78, which evidently could include entire EEZs in semi-enclosed seas. It must be re-called that the intention of the LOS Convention negotiators at UNCLOS III was to "replace a plethora of conflicting claims by coastal states with agreed limits" for the maritime zones, and that the freedom of navigation was facilitated, *inter alia*, by the compromise reached on the status of the EEZ.[47] That a PSSA (including the connotation of further restrictions on international navigation) could encompass an entire EEZ does not appear to be consistent with the delicate balance that UNCLOS III negotiators attempted to reach, and produced.

It is against this backdrop that the conditions in Article 211(6) should be interpreted. The conditions justifying special mandatory measures under this article are:

(1) The normally applicable international rules and standards are inadequate to meet *special circumstances* (at a minimum, this means that Level 1 protection is not sufficient, but arguably "applicable" may also refer to Level 2 protection); *and*

(2) The coastal state has reasonable grounds for believing that a particular, *clearly defined area of its EEZ is an area* where the adoption of *special mandatory measures* for the prevention of pollution from vessels is required for:
   - (a) recognized technical reasons in relation to the area's oceanographical and ecological conditions; *and*
   - (b) the utilization or the protection of the area's resources; *and*
   - (c) the particular character of the area's traffic.

The burden of proof rests with the coastal state requesting a special designation and the procedure applicable is as follows:

(1) The coastal state is required to conduct appropriate consultations with other concerned states through the IMO. "Concerned states" may well be more than states that actually express a concern, and could include any IMO member state that expresses an interest. Basically, this is a duty to consult.

---

45 *Ibid* at pp 193-194.

46 *Ibid* at pp 196-199.

47 "A Constitution for the Oceans, "Remarks by Tommy T B Koh, of Singapore, President of the Third United Nations Conference on the Law of the Sea, in *Law of the Sea*, *op* cit fn 2 at p xxxiii.

(2) After such consultations, the coastal state *may* (suggesting discretion) submit supporting scientific and technical evidence and information on reception facilities for the area concerned. The coastal state has to formally submit a well-founded proposal.

If a coastal state makes such a submission, the IMO has a 12-month period within which to deliberate on whether the area concerned does indeed satisfy the above conditions. The coastal state has to persuade other IMO member states of its proposal. Should the IMO (in effect the IMO member states, presumably participating in the deliberations of the Marine Environment Protection Committee [MEPC]) decide that this is the case, the coastal state may proceed to legislate international rules and standards that the IMO has made applicable for such areas. Note the restrictions on the content of that legislation in Article 211(6)(c). The coastal state's legislation becomes applicable to international navigation, at the earliest, 15 months after the formal submission to the IMO.

Although the IMO has not developed Article 211(6)-specific guidelines to date, there is a practical relationship between, on the one hand, the provisions of this article and, on the other, PSSA designation and adoption of associated protective measures in accordance with the PSSA Guidelines. In addition to other LOS provisions, Article 211(6) has become part of the "test" to which PSSA proposals to the MEPC are put, and the onus that the proposal does not breach those provisions lies with the proponent state(s). It has been suggested that IMO should develop procedures for Article 211(6).[48] Should the IMO decide to pursue this suggestion, the possibility of integrating such procedures into the existing PSSA Guidelines should be considered in the interest of harmonization. Article 211(6) could provide an even higher level of protection in PSSAs (Level 3b-type) because it authorizes *special mandatory measures*, whereas associated protective measures adopted under the current PSSA Guidelines may include *non-mandatory* measures.

Particularly Sensitive Sea Areas

In 1978 the IMO was called upon to commence studies to produce an inventory of sea areas in special need of protection from vessel-source pollution and dumping.[49] The call requested an assessment of the extent of the need for such areas and the appropriate action. Action in this regard commenced at the MEPC's 23rd session in 1986. The early discussions did not command acceptance of any one term to

---

[48] The United States has recently proposed this. See Proposed Amendments to Assembly Resolution A 927(22) to Strengthen and Clarify the Guidelines for the Identification and Designation of Particularly Sensitive Sea Areas, Submitted by the United States, IMO/MEPC 52/8, 9 July 2004 (US Amendments), 3 and 11, fn 12.

[49] In the International Conference on Tanker Safety and Pollution Prevention, Resolution 9, February 1978. For an overview of the early history, see: Gjerde and Freestone, "Particularly Sensitive Sea Areas – An Important Environmental Concept at a Turning Point" (1994) 9 *Int J Mar & Coastal Law* 431-468; Peet, "Particularly Sensitive Sea Areas – A Documentary History" (1994) 9 *Int J Mar & Coastal Law* 469-506.

capture the nature of the proposed protective zone, raising some questions on the relationship between MARPOL 73/78 special areas, ice-covered areas (then a provision being negotiated at UNCLOS III) and generally the special area reference in Article 211(6) of the LOS Convention. In addition to "PSSA" as a term of art, other terms were employed to capture the same idea, including "special area," "particularly sensitive area" (which is the Great Barrier Reef's official designation), and "ecologically sensitive area". Already at the 23rd session it was recognized that the focus should be on a concept for the protection of sea areas (distinct from the MARPOL 73/78 special area concept) that were considered to be *particularly* sensitive to vessel-source pollution. The Great Barrier Reef was often used as an example, and at the same time it was recognized that there were a number of international conventions that also called for special protection for specific types of areas.[50] There was concern over the possibility of standard-setting for vessel-source pollution occurring outside the global framework provided by the IMO. If stricter standards were to be adopted, it was thought that there should first be consideration as to whether such higher standards should be adopted on a global basis; if the need was for something less than a global approach, then, it was thought that MARPOL 73/78 provided an opportunity for the designation of stricter standards for large sea areas.[51] If additional protection was needed for even smaller areas, it was conceivable to simply limit navigation in such areas and use buffer zones, and the *International Convention for the Safety of Life At Sea*, 1974 (SOLAS), already provided for routeing, designation of areas to be avoided and other measures for safe navigation.[52] Thus, the IMO could entertain requests for additional protection requested by member states, on a case-by-case basis, and prescribe measures from within its arsenal as may be proposed by those states. These ideas were further developed between 1986 and 1990 and led to the adoption of the first PSSA Guidelines in 1991; they were amended in 1999 and 2001.[53] All along the distinction between special areas and PSSAs was maintained. Whereas special areas are direct creatures of a multilateral convention, PSSAs are not, but their designation must be consistent with the provisions of the LOS Convention,

---

[50] For example, Convention on Wetlands of International Importance Especially as Waterfowl Habitat, Ramsar, 2 February 1971, online: http://www.ramsar.org/key_conv_e.htm; Convention for the Protection of the World Cultural and Natural Heritage, Paris, 23 November 1972, online: http://whc.unesco.org/world_he.htm; Convention on the Conservation of Migratory Species of Wild Animals, Bonn, 23 June 1979, online: http://fletcher.tufts.edu/multi/texts/BH752.txt; and several regional conventions. Also, at the time, Unesco's Man and Biosphere Programme called for the designation of biosphere reserves. IMO/MEPC 30/19/1, 17 August 1990, 14-18.

[51] *Ibid* at p 20.

[52] *International Convention for the Safety of Life at Sea, 1974*, (1974), 1184 UNTS 2, in particular Chapter V (Navigation). As an example, see General Provisions on Ships' Routeing, IMO Assembly Resolution A 572(14), 20 November 1985.

[53] IMO Assembly Resolution A 720(17), 6 November 1991, as amended by A 885(21), 25 November 1999. In addition to the 2001 amendments, the MEPC also approved a Guidance Document for Submission of PSSA Proposals to IMO, IMO/MEPC 48/7/1, 30 April 2002 (hereafter PSSA Guidance Document).

and in particular Article 211(6). It has been stated that a "PSSA has no legal significance in and of itself" and it is the associated measures that carry legal significance.[54] At the same time, the PSSA Guidelines "derive from the provisions" of LOS Convention Article 211(6), but are also "far more detailed and 'liberal' in their approach".[55] As a result, the process of adoption of a PSSA does not require amendment of any instrument, but simply requires a direct submission to the IMO.[56]

A PSSA is a marine area "that needs special protection through action by IMO because of its significance for recognized ecological, socio-economic, or scientific reasons and because it may be vulnerable to damage by international shipping activities".[57] It has been described as a "comprehensive management tool," but in reality the management measures to be adopted are selective tools and specifically in relation to international shipping activities.[58] As noted earlier, since the adoption of the PSSA Guidelines in 1991 and until 2002, there were only two proposals that led to PSSA designations. Since 2002, however, there have been several new proposals submitted to the IMO and these have also led to PSSA designations (see Table 10.2), together with the adopted appropriate measures.

Occasionally, the MEPC required re-submission of a proposal before further consideration and approval. Colombia's first proposal to designate Malpelo Island as a PSSA was not designated before additional information was requested and provided.[59] Others, both by individual and groups of states, have been considered and approved by the IMO, but only in principle, pending consideration of proposals for appropriate protective measures submitted within the required time frame (see Table 10.3). More proposals to the IMO can be expected in due course as a result of initiatives by international non-governmental organizations and concerned governments, such as for an area in the Northwest Atlantic off Canada, Barents Sea, Sulu-Sulawesi Sea, Andaman and Nicobar Islands in the Indian Ocean, and the Saba Reef in the Caribbean.

---

[54] US Amendments, *op cit* fn 48 at p 3.

[55] Comments made by the Division for Ocean Affairs and the Law of the Sea of the United Nations (DOALOS) in connection with Issues Raised in Document LEG 87/16/1, IMO LEG 87/WP 3, 13 October 2003 (hereafter DOALOS Comments).

[56] The IMO's general authority in this regard stems from its own constitutive instrument. *Convention on the International Maritime Organization*, 3 September 1976, 1143 UNTS 105, Art 1(a). According to DOALOS, the PSSA "Guidelines conform to the requirements of article 237 [of the LOS Convention], as a subsequent agreement adopted by IMO Assembly in furtherance of the general principles set forth in the Convention, in particular, those in part XII *loc cit* fn 55.

[57] PSSA Guidelines, *loc cit* fn 16 at para 1.2.

[58] PSSA Guidance Document, *loc cit* fn 16 at para 1.2.

[59] This occurred during consideration at the MEPC's 44th session, 6-13 March 2000. The Colombian proposal, although based on the 1991 PSSA Guidelines, lacked information required by the 1999 amendments. See Additional Information for the Designation of Malpelo Island as a "Particularly Sensitive Sea Area," IMO/MEPC 46/6/3, 16 February 2001.

Table 10.2: PSSAs designated to date

PSSA	Year adopted	Proponent states	Appropriate protective measures adopted
Great Barrier Reef	1990	Australia	Compulsory pilotage IMO-recommended pilotage Mandatory reporting
Sabana-Camaguey Archipelago	1997	Cuba	Traffic separation schemes Area to be avoided Prohibited discharges
Wadden Sea	2002	Denmark, Germany, Netherlands	No new additional measures; only existing measures invoked (compulsory reporting and traffic surveillance, routeing systems)
Florida Keys	2002	United States	Areas to be avoided (new and amendment of existing) No anchoring area
Malpelo Island	2002	Colombia	Area to be avoided
Paracas National Reserve	2003	Peru	Tanker traffic restrictions Prohibited discharges Traffic separation schemes

The key criteria to be satisfied both for PSSA designation and the adoption of related measures are in three steps: (1) the area's environmental conditions, (2) its vulnerability to international navigation and (3) availability of measures within the IMO's competence.[60] It should be emphasized that the PSSA designation is a problem-oriented mechanism to enable the adoption of measures to protect against damage to such areas from international navigation, and not from other ocean uses. Other threats to the same areas (for example, dumping) are covered by other regimes.

Step 1 criteria share some substantive similarities with those for MARPOL 73/78 and Article 211(6) special areas, and include clusters of (1) ecological, (2) social, cultural and economic, and (3) scientific and educational criteria, as listed in Table 10.4. Only one of these criteria within each of the clusters need be satisfied before proceeding with consideration of the Step 2 criterion.[61] This "minimalist" requirement is cause for significant concern because virtually any area of the oceans subject to international navigation could qualify, and as a result the effect of providing special protection for very special places (that is, particularly sensitive) may be undermined.

---

[60] PSSA Guidelines, *loc cit* fn 16 at para 1.5.

[61] *Ibid* para 4.4.

Table 10.3: PSSAs approved in principle

PSSA	Year designated	Proponent states	Proposed appropriate measures
Great Barrier Reef: Torres Strait Region extension	2003	Australia and Papua New Guinea	Two-way shipping route Extension of GBR compulsory pilotage
Western European area	2003	Belgium, France, Ireland, Portugal, Spain and UK	Mandatory ship-reporting system
Canary Islands	2004	Spain	Restricted navigation areas Routeing systems for ships transiting through the PSSA Notification of entry in/departure from PSSA
Galapagos Archipelago	2004	Ecuador	Discharge restrictions Area to be avoided (as a buffer zone) Incident reporting (includes planes) Will include international routeing chart in the future
Baltic Sea (less Russian waters)	2004	Denmark, Estonia, Finland, Germany, Latvia, Lithuania, Poland and Sweden	No new measures were proposed at the submission stage. Various measures are already in place in some areas (for example, compulsory reporting and traffic surveillance, routeing systems, compulsory pilotage, special area under MARPOL 73/78 annexes I, II, V, and annex VI (SOx Emission Control Area)

Since the designation of the Great Barrier Reef and the Sabana-Camaguey Archipelago as PSSAs, much of the practice has been related to demonstrably sensitive coastal and marine ecosystems, that probably satisfied more than one criterion. They have tended to be very special places. Malpelo Island's waters are biologically very productive, biogeographically significant and are home to a unique Pacific coral reef community. The waters had already been designated as a national marine protected area.[62] Also sensitive to commercial and recreational shipping activities, the Florida Keys have a different but equally fragile barrier coral reef system (third largest in the world) and which is also a national marine

[62] MEPC 46/6/3, *loc cit* fn 59.

sanctuary.[63] The Paracas National Reserve was designated a Ramsar Convention site because of its great biodiversity and a regional reserve for migratory birds, thus making it unique, exceptional and highly sensitive.[64] Peru was able to argue that there was a trend in increased shipping through or in the vicinity of the reserve, as well as accidents and operational pollution in the area. The Wadden Sea, on the other hand, has a very different sensitive coastal ecosystem in the form of a highly dynamic tidal ecosystem shared by three countries, and deserving of special protection.[65] Similar situations and considerations were weighed in the case of the Canary Islands and Galapagos PSSA proposals.[66] All of these PSSAs are considered of global and/or regional importance. They are also actively under national protection, and therefore provide a persuasive argument for further protection from international navigation activities that they could not otherwise receive through domestic regulation alone.

Table 10.4: PSSA Criteria

Ecological cluster	**Social, cultural and economic cluster**	**Scientific and educational cluster**
(1) Uniqueness or rarity (2) Critical habitat (3) Dependency (4) Representativeness (5) Diversity (6) Productivity (7) Spawning or breeding grounds (8) Naturalness (9) Integrity (10) Vulnerability (11) Bio-geographical importance	(12) Economic benefit (13) Recreation (14) Human dependency	(15) Research (16) Baseline and monitoring studies (17) Education

If any of the 17 criteria is satisfied, a Step 2 assessment requires that "the area should be at risk from international shipping activities".[67] This entails consideration of vessel traffic characteristics (operation factors, vessel types, traffic characteristics, harmful substances) and natural factors (hydrographical,

63 Designation of the Marine Area around the Florida Keys as a Particularly Sensitive Sea Area, Submitted by the United States, IMO/MEPC 46/6/2, 19 January 2001 (hereafter Florida Keys Submission).

64 Designation of the Marine Area of the Paracas National Reserve as a "Particularly Sensitive Sea Area" Submitted by Peru, IMO/MEPC 48/7, 18 April 2002.

65 Designation of the Wadden Sea as a Particularly Sensitive Sea Area, Submitted by Denmark, Germany and The Netherlands, IMO/MEPC 48/7/2, 28 June 2002.

66 Designation of the Waters of the Canary Islands as a Particularly Sensitive Sea Area, Proposal Submitted by Spain, IMO/MEPC 51/8, 24 October 2003; Designation of the Galapagos Archipelago as a Particularly Sensitive Sea Area, Submitted by Ecuador, IMO/MEPC 51/8/2, 24 December 2003 (hereafter Galapagos Submission).

67 PSSA Guidelines, *loc cit* fn 16 at para 5.1.

meteorological, oceanographical).[68] Additional information such as on impact of shipping activities, past casualties, foreseeable incidents, other environmental stresses and existing measures (and their impact) facilitates risk assessment and the determination of appropriate protective measures.[69] For example, in the case of Malpelo Island the threats posed included illegal fishing, diving activities from cruise ships and major international commercial traffic in the vicinity of the island.[70] The threats to the Florida Keys included, among others, high risk from one of the most heavily trafficked sea lanes in the world and physical damage of the coral reef area from ship groundings and anchoring.[71]

There does not appear to be a limit on size, and an area may include a buffer zone.[72] On size, a number of states have taken the view that a PSSA should be a local area within the territorial sea and/or an EEZ, and therefore should not encompass an entire EEZ, or EEZs, or whole seas. Size should also be related to ecosystem(s) that need additional protection. The MEPC would have to determine whether "the size of the area is commensurate with that necessary to address the identified need",[73] and that need is necessarily the sensitivity of the area with reference to the threat posed by international navigation. The PSSAs designated to date have not raised concerns on size, including the very large Great Barrier Reef. In relation to the latter it was never in dispute that it required additional protection as a whole. However, size is a major issue with the current Baltic[74] and Western European[75] PSSAs-in-principle. Both of these proposals appear different in geographical and ecosystemic scope from earlier PSSA designations, which tended to focus on "local" sensitivities.

A strong argument has been made for the Baltic as a unique ecosystem. However, it is not clear from the submission that the various MARPOL 73/78 special area designations are insufficient to protect the Baltic, and if this is the case why is it so, and whether strengthened implementation of MARPOL 73/78 annexes would be sufficient, and if not that Level 3 protection is needed. In opposition, the Russian Federation argues that the proposal does not provide added value to the Level 2 MARPOL 73/78 special and emission control areas protection, and

---

68 *Ibid* Part 5 and para 7.4.1.

69 *Ibid* Part 5 and para 7.4.1.

70 MEPC 46/6/3, *loc cit* fn 59.

71 Florida Keys Submission, *loc cit* fn 63 at pp 9-10.

72 For example, the Galapagos submission proposed an area to be avoided that would function as "a separation zone or contiguous zone for the proposed PSSA", justified on the basis of currents, logistical concerns in tackling spills and correspondence of buffer area to the existing national marine protected area. Galapagos Submission, *loc cit* fn 66 at pp 20-21.

73 *Ibid* para 8.3.3.

74 Designation of the Baltic Sea Area as a Particularly Sensitive Sea Area, Submitted by Denmark, Estonia, Finland, Germany, Latvia, Lithuania, Poland and Sweden, IMO/MEPC 51/8/1, 19 December 2003.

75 Designation of a Western European Particularly Sensitive Sea Area, Submitted by Belgium, France, Ireland, Portugal, Spain and the United Kingdom, IMO/MEPC 49/8/1, 11 April 2003.

Helsinki Commission efforts in the region.[76] Moreover, the elimination of Russian Federation waters from the Baltic Sea proposal raises a fundamental question as to the viability of a PSSA that is supposed to protect the entire sea. An important related matter to this proposal is the position of equally interested regional and other maritime states, but which happen to disagree with the initiative, in this case Liberia, Panama and the Russian Federation. If the argument that PSSAs have no legal significance holds, then it is not opposable to objecting states, in which case the purpose and effectiveness of the PSSA may be greatly reduced in the face of opposition. In this scenario, the value of protective measures could also be reduced either because they are watered-down (for example, the withdrawal of the single-hull ban in the Western European Waters PSSA proposal) or because persistent objection might turn into non-cooperation.

The Western European PSSA-in-principle (which is approximately of a comparable size to the Great Barrier Reef) is home not to one, but to several ecosystems that are captured within the 200 nautical mile EEZs proposed for the PSSA. Strong concerns have been expressed in relation to consistency with the LOS Convention.[77] A more justifiable approach would have been to designate a system of PSSAs (including buffer zones) that are more local ecosystem-specific. The proposed size would have pushed more shipping into the open ocean and its accompanying risks and for neighbouring states (for example, Norway) the risk would be brought closer to their maritime zones. As a result, the northern limit of the proposed PSSA had to be adjusted to respond to this particular concern. Further, the concern was raised that if more shipping is pushed out to the high seas, there could be an issue concerning the feasibility of search and rescue, as well as provision of places of refuge.[78]

As for Step 3, PSSA proposals may propose associated protective measures in the submission itself, but this is not absolutely necessary at the time of submission, although there should be an indication of types of measures contemplated.[79] However, where the MEPC designates a PSSA in principle it also provides a two-year period within which at least one appropriate measure has to be proposed and adopted through the IMO.[80] Failing such submission, the designation lapses. The proponent has to propose to the MEPC measures and indicate how "they provide the needed protection from the threats of damage posed by international maritime activities occurring in and around the area."[81] Such measures may be actual

---

[76] Report of the Marine Environment Protection Committee on its Fifty-First Session, IMO MEPC 51/22, 22 April 2004 (hereafter MEPC 51 Report), 34-35 and Annex 8.

[77] Designation of a Western European Particularly Sensitive Sea Area, Submitted by Liberia, Panama, the Russian Federation, BIMCO, ICS, INTERCARGO, INTERTANKO and IPTA, IMO/LEG 87/16/1.

[78] Report of the Marine Environment Protection Committee on its Forth-Ninth Session, IMO/MEPC 49/22, 8 August 2003, 47. A similar concern raised by Brazil also in relation to the Baltic and Canary Islands' proposals. MEPC 51 Report, *loc cit* fn 76.

[79] PSSA Guidance Document, *loc cit* fn 53 at Part 3.5.

[80] PSSA Guidelines, *loc cit* fn 16 at para 7.1.

[81] *Ibid* para 7.4.2.1.

measures adopted by the IMO or within its competence, if not yet adopted.[82] Also, such measures may be by virtue of LOS Convention Article 211(6).[83] By referring to the latter, the PSSA Guidelines in effect maintain a distinction with the Article 211(6) special mandatory measures, while at the same time establishing a link to it. In general, the IMO favours least restrictive options in the interests of commerce.[84] For instance a no-anchoring area may be more appropriate than an area to be avoided, if the principal threat is from anchoring and not from navigation activity.[85] The measures may apply to particular categories of ships and their assessment will include impact on navigation safety and efficiency.[86] Should there be non-compliance with the measures, as may be adopted by the IMO, the coastal state concerned would be in a position to undertake actions to ensure compliance, and in doing so must act consistently with the LOS Convention. Such national compliance-control action also needs to be communicated to the MEPC with the proposal for associated protective measures.[87]

There are various types of navigation measures that the IMO is competent to endorse, including routeing measures,[88] reporting systems[89] and other forms of navigation assistance.[90] In implementing those measures, the coastal state must not require new design, construction, manning or equipment standards, unless they are IMO-adopted standards and have been endorsed as appropriate measures for the area concerned, otherwise there would be a risk of violating international navigation rights.

---

[82] Several potential new measures in the MEPC, including: "designated anchorage areas and methods; no anchorage zones; closure of routes to certain types of vessels or cargoes; speed restrictions; compulsory pilotage or tug escort to ensure safe navigation in or near PSSAs; prohibitions/restrictions on cargo transfer; required submission of pre-filed passage plans and adherence to time schedules; special under-keel clearance restrictions; regulation of offshore bunkering; prohibition of intentional discharges, including ballast waters; seasonal closures to protect migrating marine mammals;" among still others. Additional Protection for Particularly Sensitive Sea Areas (PSSAs), IMO/MEPC 46/6/1, 19 January 2001 (hereafter PSSA Additional Protection, para 2.4.10. See also Draft Guidance Document on Associated Protective Measures for Particularly Sensitive Sea Areas, Submitted by WWF, IMO/MEPC 49/8/2, 8 May 2003. One interesting idea advanced in the latter document is air pollution emission limitations, which could require utilization only of high quality low sulphur fuels in or near PSSAs.

[83] PSSA Guidelines, *loc cit* fn 16 at para 7.4.2.1.(a)(iii).

[84] PSSA Additional Protection, *loc cit* fn 82 at para 2.1.3.

[85] This was the case in the Florida Keys. See Florida Keys Submission, *loc cit* fn 63, and US Amendments, *loc cit* fn 48 at p 2.

[86] PSSA Guidelines, *loc cit* fn 16 at para 7.4.2.2 and .4.

[87] *Ibid* para 7.7. See also PSSA Guidance Document *loc cit* fn 53 at para 3.5.3.

[88] For example: areas to be avoided, traffic separation schemes, inshore traffic zones, deep water routes, precautionary areas, recommended routes and vessel traffic service systems.

[89] For example: radar surveillance and interactive ship/shore reporting.

[90] For example: pilotage and towage.

The Baltic PSSA-in-principle has not had measures proposed at the time of writing.[91] Some Baltic states hope that compulsory pilotage, among other measures, could be considered, but it is already evident that there will be objection to such a measure. The original Western European PSSA submission proposed an associated protective measure that would have banned single-hull traffic in the area and a mandatory 48-hour notice requirement for all laden double-hulls entering or exiting the reporting area.[92] The ban appeared to be inconsistent with Article 211(6)(c) because it addressed design and construction standards when it could not. A contentious debate in the MEPC, not surprisingly, forced a withdrawal of the single-hull ban, but retained the 48-hour notice area in accordance with SOLAS (Chapter V/11).[93] Outside the PSSA discourse, there was already agreement between the EU and IMO to accelerate the phase-out of single hulls from 2015 to 2010;[94] the proposed PSSA protective measure seemed to suggest another acceleration.

Alternatively, where IMO measures already exist in the area, the proposal does not need to propose new measures. It may be questioned as to what is the purpose of a PSSA proposal for an area that is already protected by existing measures. One answer to this is that PSSAs and their associated protective measures are designated on navigation charts in accordance with International Hydrographic Organization (IHO) symbols,[95] thus ensuring that they are brought to the attention of seafarers navigating in or in the vicinity of a PSSA. Also, flag states have a responsibility to ensure compliance by their ships with the protective measures.[96]

Towards Amendment of the PSSA Guidelines

During the debates on the Western European and Baltic PSSAs Liberia, Panama and the Russian Federation, supported by the industry organizations, suggested that a moratorium on new PSSA designation should be introduced and maintained until

---

91 Designation of the Baltic Sea Area as a Particularly Sensitive Sea Area, Submitted by Denmark, Estonia, Finland, Germany, Latvia, Lithuania, Poland and Sweden, IMO/MEPC 51/8/1, 19 December 2003. However, the proposal indicated that there a number of protective measures already in place, namely compulsory reporting in some areas and traffic surveillance, routeing systems in certain areas for big draught ships, local pilotage and the MARPOL 73/78 special area and emission control area. Also, the proposal indicates that new measures that will be considered include: common monitoring system based on compulsory reporting and traffic surveillance, routeing systems, escort and escorting tugs, pilotage and areas to be avoided. *Ibid.* See also HELCOM Expert Working Groups, Submitted by Denmark, Germany and Sweden, IMO/NAV 50/INF.5, 29 April 2004.

92 *Loc cit* fn 75.

93 Mandatory Ship Reporting System for the Western European Particularly Sensitive Sea Area, Submitted by Belgium, France, Ireland, Portugal, Spain and the United Kingdom, IMO/NAV 50/3/6, 2 April 2004.

94 See "IMO Saves Face and EU Claims Victory" *Fairplay*, 11 December 2003, 4.

95 *Ibid* para 9.1.

96 *Ibid* para 9.3.

the PSSA Guidelines are reviewed and amended. There was division between those states that felt revisions were needed and those that thought otherwise.[97] The moratorium was objected to so that consideration of the PSSAs-in-principle could continue, it was agreed that the PSSA Guidelines should be reviewed,[98] and several proposals for amendment, and comments on those proposals, have been submitted for consideration at the MEPC's 52nd session in October 2004.[99] The principal amending suggestions have been submitted by the United States and concern four major areas, namely the criteria for PSSA designation, establishment of link between vulnerability and a proposed measure, legal basis for protective measures and procedural matters.[100] In order to avoid PSSA proliferation,[101] the Russian Federation has suggested amendments that emphasize the exceptional nature of a PSSA as Level 3 protection, in comparison to Level 2 protection under MARPOL 73/78 special areas or some other regional regime.[102]

PSSA Criteria

It has been noted above that only one criterion need be satisfied to justify a PSSA. The Russian federation would like to see a prioritization of criteria, with the highest emphasis to be given to ecological criteria.[103] In addition, like several other delegations, the US is of the view that "the criteria are not as clear and meaningful as they should or could be, thus making it difficult to conduct a meaningful review of proposed PSSAs".[104] A major concern that the World Wildlife Fund (WWF) has raised is that the precautionary character of the PSSA criteria should be

---

[97] Report of the Marine Environment Protection Committee on its Fifty-First Session, IMO/MEPC 51/22, 22 April 2004 (hereafter MEPC 51 Report), 29-32.

[98] It was felt by Norway, and the MEPC agreed, that the institution of a moratorium was outside the MEPC mandate and would have to be proposed to the Assembly. *Ibid* at p 32.

[99] In particular: US Amendments, *op cit* fn 48; Proposed Amendments to Guidelines for the Identification and Designation of Particularly Sensitive Sea Areas (Annex 2 of IMO Assembly Resolution A 927(22)), Submitted by the Russian Federation, IMO/MEPC 52/8/1, 6 August 2004 (hereafter Russian Federation Amendments); Proposed Amendments to Resolution A 927(22) on the Identification and Designation of Particularly Sensitive Sea Areas (PSSA), Submitted by the International Chamber of Shipping (ICS) and INTERTANKO, IMO/MEPC 52/8/2, 6 August 2004; Proposed Amendments to Resolution A 927(22) on the Identification and Designation of Particularly Sensitive Sea Areas (PSSA) – PSSA Proposal Review Form, Submitted by ICS and INTERTANKO, IMO/MEPC 52/8/3, 6 August 2004; and Proposed Amendments to Assembly resolution A 927(22) to Strengthen and Clarify the Guidelines for the Identification and Designation of Particularly Sensitive Sea Areas (PSSAs) – Comments on MEPC 52/8, Submitted by WWF, IMO/MEPC 52/8/4, 18 August 2004 (hereafter WWF Comments).

[100] US Amendments, *op cit* fn 48.

[101] Proliferation is a concern expressed by the Russian federal, Panama, Liberia and several industry bodies. See " 'Politically Sensitive Sea Areas' Agreed in principle" *Fairplay*, 8 April 2004, 6.

[102] Russian Federation Amendments, *op cit* fn 99 at p 2.

[103] *Ibid.*

[104] US Amendments, *op cit* fn 48 at p 2.

maintained.[105] A tightening of the criteria in the US proposal to emphasize "scientifically-recognized" as an element in the criteria could conflict with the needs of precaution. This point is further carried into the strengthening of the link between vulnerability and proposed measure, which should also be guided by the precautionary approach, and the concern over the US suggestion to eliminate designations in principle.[106]

Prompted by the Baltic PSSA-in-principle controversial decision, the Russian Federation is proposing an additional criterion with reference to the interests of other states in the PSSA area, with the consequence that in the case of enclosed or semi-enclosed seas the designation should be made on the basis of consensus.[107] The emphasis should be on "local" ecosystems, which might perhaps justify national MPA protection in the first place.[108] Consistently, with reference to the need for compliance with LOS Convention Article 211(6), the US proposal emphasizes the legality test for special mandatory measures with reference to the "particular, localized circumstances of the proposed area".[109]

Measure-Vulnerability Link

It has been felt that PSSA proponent states to date have not always sufficiently demonstrated the nexus between identified vulnerabilities of the area and the associated protective measures proposed, so that area size (spatial dimension) and propriety and sufficiency of the proposed measure can be ascertained, and the least restrictive measure approved. The US proposed amendments attempt to place greater emphasis on the purpose of the proposed measure in addressing identified vulnerabilities, in particular to relate the international shipping threat more directly to the vulnerabilities of the area, the degree of actual and/or potential harm and reasonable forseeability.[110] This is an argument for greater added value for Level 3 protection from vessel-source pollution.

Legality of Proposed Measures

It has not always been immediately apparent what is the legal basis of a proposed measure, thus raising concerns on legitimacy. The proposal for associated protective measures could in effect lead to restrictions on international navigation rights. For such restrictions to be legitimate, and thus not be tantamount to mere encroachments on the right of international navigation, it is necessary to have appropriate legal justification, as well as be submitted through a proper process. The US suggests that the proposed measure "meets the requirements of the

---

[105] WWF Comments, *op cit* fn 99 at p 2.
[106] *Ibid* 3 and 4.
[107] Russian Federation Amendments, *op cit* fn 99 at p 2. Also suggested by ICS and INTERTANKO, *op cit* fn 99.
[108] *Ibid.*
[109] US Amendments, *op cit* fn 48 at p 11.
[110] US Amendments, *op cit* fn 48 at Annex, 7-8.

appropriate legal instrument establishing such measure, must have been approved or adopted by IMO to prevent, reduce or eliminate the identified vulnerability."[111] The advantage of this suggestion is that the proposed measure is readily identified and understood. Although the US proposal has already been criticised for its emphasis on measures that have been or will be approved or adopted by the IMO, rather than simply generic ideas for measures that fall within the competence of the organization, [112] in reality it allows development of other measures "provided they have an identified legal basis," for example, the LOS Convention.[113] One measure that can be expected to raise concerns on legality is compulsory pilotage. Both the US and Russian Federation[114] propose that this be struck out of the PSSA Guidelines, whereas WWF suggests that it be maintained.[115] Although compulsory pilotage as a protective measure is already in place in the Great Barrier Reef and eventually in the Torres Strait extension, its potential application in parts of semi-enclosed seas (for example, Baltic) can be expected to be divisive.

Structure and Process

The US has proposed that the designation or approval in principle pending submission of appropriate measures be discontinued.[116] An advantage of this current practice is that it is consistent with the precautionary approach in responding in a temporary manner to a recognized risk or threat and until more substantive action may be taken.[117] At the same time, it is important for the review process to have the full picture presented, that is, the need for a PSSA because of certain vulnerabilities and the precise measures needed to address those vulnerabilities without having to wait for two years (the current time frame for proposing measures after obtaining MEPC approval in principle). This change would also entail that the legality of the proposed measures would need to be established at the time the PSSA proposal is submitted.[118]

Also, it is being suggested that the MEPC should establish a specialised "technical working group, comprising representatives with appropriate environmental, scientific, maritime, and legal expertise, to assess the elements of the proposal" and proposed measures.[119] This proposal would effectively create a multidisciplinary and integrated peer review process whereby all aspects of the proposal are screened in an expert manner. The onus will be fully on the

---

[111] *Ibid* Annex, 2.
[112] WWF Comments, *op cit* fn 99 at p 3.
[113] US Amendments, *op* cit fn 48 at Annex, 8. "If the measures are not already available under an IMO instrument, the proposal should set forth the steps that the proposing Member Government or Governments has taken or will take to establish the legal basis for a generally applicable measure through IMO." *Ibid* Annex, 9 and 11.
[114] Russian Federation Amendments, *op cit* fn 99.
[115] WWF Comments *op cit* fn 99 at p 3.
[116] US Amendments, *op cit* fn 48 at p 3.
[117] WWF Comments, *op cit* fn 99 at p 4.
[118] *Ibid.*
[119] *Ibid* Annex, 13.

proponent state. There have been instances where insufficiency of information required the MEPC to request further information, giving the impression that the onus was reversed.

Conclusion

Clearly, one major argument in support of PSSAs is the higher levels of protection that may be achieved at the national level, where the responsibility for the implementation of global standards for vessel-source pollution ultimately lie. There is a presumption that proponent states have the political and management will to act, and hopefully to strengthen special area implementation. At the same time, however, proponent states should endeavour to better implement existing Level 1 and 2 responsibilities to justify additional encroachments on international navigations rights through Level 3 action. There is relatively little practice to indicate how effective PSSAs really are, partly because the majority of PSSAs have been designated or approved in principle in the last two years. Effectiveness will depend on the nature of associated protective measures and how they are implemented by the coastal state(s) concerned. Thus, recently, Australia reported that since compulsory pilotage was introduced in 1991 the rate of accidents with in the Great Barrier Reef was reduced by more than 50%. This is a significant achievement, even though accidents continue to happen.[120] The value of such a measure is even more evident when it is considered that despite the recommended pilotage for the Torres Strait (prior to the PSSA-extension approval in principle and in accordance with an earlier IMO resolution), Australia reported declining compliance.[121] There is thus what appears to be a clear cause-effect relationship to justify a PSSA and associated protective measures for the area concerned, and which may need to be updated to respond to evolving problems. A potential difficulty here is the proposed extension of compulsory pilotage in the Torres Strait outside the territorial sea and into the EEZ;[122] the argument would need to be made that this qualifies as a special mandatory measure under Article 211(6).[123]

The need to avoid a proliferation of MARPOL 73/78 special areas was addressed successfully, at least judging by the fewer number of special area proposals submitted after the adoption of the Special Area Guidelines. There is now a risk of proliferation of PSSAs instead, and not necessarily as well argued or

---

[120] Torres Strait PSSA Associated Protective Measure – Compulsory Pilotage, Submitted by Australia and Papua New Guinea, IMO/MEPC/NAV 50/3, 22 March 2004 (hereafter NAV 50/3). See also Results of a Safety of Navigation Assessment Conducted for the Torres Strait, Submitted by Australia, IMO/NAV 50/INF 2, 2 April 2004.

[121] NAV 50/3, *ibid.*

[122] See the concern expressed in Torres Strait PSSA Associated Protective Measure – Compulsory Pilotage, Submitted by the International Chamber of Shipping (ICS), IMO/NAV 50/3/12, 14 May 2004.

[123] In fact this is the position taken by Australia and Papua New Guinea in NAV 50/3 *op cit* fn 120.

justified as the first six PSSAs designated. Like earlier versions, the current PSSA Guidelines are not sufficient to ensure rigorous screening of eligible areas so as to clearly distinguish why the proposed areas require Level 3 protection, rather than Level 1 or 2, and also why the utilization of specific SOLAS (Chapter V) measures is not sufficient. The Guidelines should require satisfaction of multiple criteria that are sufficiently rigorous as to survive proper scientific, technical, legal and management peer review. The international maritime and environmental communities cannot possibly be well served by the designation of areas that are stronger on optics than on effective management responses to particularly sensitive areas. As industry has cautioned, there is a danger of watering-down the special character and value of PSSAs.

The PSSA discourse in the IMO is likely to remain contentious and, given the perceived stakes by those states that represent minority but significant views, it may well be that majority decision-making could have unhappy consequences. Unfortunately, majority decision-making substituted consensus, despite the sharp differences over the Western European and Baltic PSSA applications. The concern here is particularly accentuated when differences are not necessarily purely political or economic, but may also involve important issues of principle, such as whether the international law of the sea permits the restriction of international navigation rights in an entire EEZ (or series of connected EEZs) or a semi-enclosed sea. The ecological imperative may well lean in the direction of PSSA proliferation; however, in the interests of truly global standard-setting, it is essential that there be consensus on key principles to guide this special ocean zoning process. The rush to have PSSAs designated on the basis of the weak PSSA Guidelines before they are amended is unfortunate in this respect. A consequential danger is that the PSSA designation and associated protective measures may not be recognized by objecting states, and in turn this could raise difficulties with compliance.[124]

The IMO has played a critical role in ensuring that international standards are adopted on the basis of principles agreed upon in instruments adopted at international diplomatic conferences. Should there be need for a change of basic principles and norms, such as the full extent of international navigation rights in zones of national jurisdiction, and the counterpart full extent of coastal state jurisdiction over international navigation, it ought to occur in the appropriate diplomatic forum, and in turn this would guide deliberations in the IMO as a global forum. If it were otherwise, there could be a danger that important balances achieved through the lengthy multilateral diplomacy of UNCLOS III could be undermined. It would be difficult to justify, and secure global support, for further restrictions on international navigation rights in national maritime zones.

---

[124] The Russian Federation has already provided such notice; "The Russian Federation does not agree with this decision to grant PSSA status to the whole Baltic Sea, does not associate itself with this decision and, should the Organization approve any other recommendations, regulations or action for adoption on the basis of the Baltic Sea's designation as a PSSA, reserves its right not to give effect to any such decision." MEPC 51 Report, *op cit* fn 76, Annex 8.

On a concluding note, the PSSA discourse with its animated arguments by all sides on how best to protect the marine environment within national jurisdiction without imposing unnecessary encroachments on international navigation rights may well serve to enhance procedures for coastal state transparency in this regard. Those states that wish to exercise greater marine environmental authority have to demonstrate that they are fulfilling their basic responsibilities in the first place.[125]

[125] Following submission of this chapter, the MRPC's 52nd session was convened between 11-15 October 2004. It was decided that the review of the PSSA Guidelines would be continued by a correspondence group, to report by 2005.

Index

For Product Safety Concerns and Information please contact our EU representative GPSR@taylorandfrancis.com
Taylor & Francis Verlag GmbH, Kaufingerstraße 24, 80331 München, Germany

www.ingramcontent.com/pod-product-compliance
Ingram Content Group UK Ltd.
Pitfield, Milton Keynes, MK11 3LW, UK
UKHW022223190926
475702UK00003B/477
9780815389880